Redefining Russian Society and Polity

Redefining Russian Society and Polity

Mary Buckley

University of Edinburgh

WESTVIEW PRESS

Boulder • San Francisco • Oxford

Copyright © 1993 by Westview Press, Inc.

Published in 1993 in the United States of America by Westview Press, Inc., 5500 Central Avenue, Boulder, Colorado 80301-2877, and in the United Kingdom by Westview Press, 36 Lonsdale Road, Summertown, Oxford OX2 7EW

Library of Congress Cataloging-in-Publication Data
Buckley, Mary [date]
   Redefining Russian society and polity / Mary Buckley.
      p.   cm.
   Includes bibliographical references and index.
   ISBN 0-8133-1580-8 — ISBN 0-8133-1579-4 (pbk.)
   1. Russia (Federation)—Social conditions.   2. Russia
(Federation)—Politics and government.   3. Soviet Union—Social
conditions—1970–1991.   4. Soviet Union—Politics and
government—1985–1991.   5. Glasnost.   6. Perestroïka.   7. Social
change—Russia (Federation)   I. Title.
   HN530.2.A8B81   1993
   306'.0947—dc20
                                                                93-15755
                                                                CIP

Printed and bound in the United States of America

The paper used in this publication meets the requirements
of the American National Standard for Permanence of Paper
for Printed Library Materials Z39.48-1984.

10   9   8   7   6   5   4   3   2

To Mariia, Nikolai, and Leonid

Contents

Tables

Acknowledgments

A one-year research fellowship from the Nuffield Foundation enabled me to indulge full time in this project by freeing me from teaching responsibilities at the University of Edinburgh. This was a most welcome opportunity and privilege, for which I am immensely grateful, at a time when the Soviet system was in one of its most exciting, albeit confusing, periods in history and nearing its end.

Support from the British Academy and the Soviet Academy of Sciences made possible essential on-the-spot research in September 1989 and again in September 1990. As well as giving me the chance to interview specialists and political actors, this research brought the additional pleasure of enjoying the rumors, stories, and myths that were circulating in Moscow and Leningrad, later St. Petersburg, and helped me begin to grasp some of the reactions, fears, and hopes expressed by different social and political groups about economic, political, and social reform.

I am particularly grateful to the Institute of State and Law in Moscow for hosting me so warmly in 1990 and to its scholars for being generous with their time. Special thanks are due to Valentin Patiulin, Iurii Baturin, Vladimir Lysenko, Villiam Smirnov, Anatolii Kovler, and Vladimir Guliev for sharing their views with me. They will not, however, necessarily agree with the arguments of this book.

I should also like to record my thanks to Professor Paul Dukes for setting up an exchange between Scottish Universities and the Institute of History in Moscow and to the British Council for partially funding it. I benefited from this link in the spring of 1991, which led me to Iurii Zhukov, member of the institute and people's deputy in Krasnopresnenskii *raion*. For his introductions to other deputies, indispensable to this book, I am indebted. Discussions with him in the spring and autumn of 1991 and again in the spring of 1992 kept me abreast of changing developments in the soviets.

Valentina Konstantinova of the Center for Gender Studies, part of the Institute of Socio-economic Problems of the Population, kindly helped arrange interviews in the Russian parliament and in the Moscow City Soviet. Liudmila Sherova most efficiently persuaded deputies of the Moscow City Soviet and Moscow oblast soviet to meet me at very short notice. Particular gratitude for talking to me on repeat occasions is due to Aleksandr Krasnov, A. V. Kurochkin, and Kirill Lisenkov of the soviet in Krasnopresnenskii *raion;* Aleksandr Kalinin of the Mossovet; and Ekaterina Lakhova of the Russian parliament and subsequently of the Kremlin.

Earlier one-month visits in 1985 and 1987 to Moscow University, arranged by the British Council, gave me insight into the early Gorbachev years. A brief trip to Vil'nius with my students in March 1989 made me appreciate more fully the goals and dilemmas of Lithuanian nationalism. Small grants from the Travel and Research Committee of Edinburgh University and the Hayter Fund contributed toward a further two weeks in Moscow in August 1991, followed by a brief "post-failed-coup" visit in September. The Carnegie Trust for the Universities of Scotland and the Travel and Research Committee of Edinburgh University enabled me to return to Moscow in March 1992. Appreciation must also be expressed to the Rockefeller Foundation for a residency in the spring of 1990 at the Villa Serbelloni in Bellagio, where I devoted time to some of the social issues discussed here.

I owe particular thanks to Russian friends who enlarged my collection of new newspapers, on which much of this book is based, and to Christine Thomas of the British Library in London. The State Public Historical Library of the RSFSR also gave access to the new informal press. For more conventional references, I relied upon the Lenin and INION libraries in Moscow, the newspaper library at Colindale, and the library of the School of Slavonic and East European Studies at the University of London, where I was a visitor during the 1990–1991 academic year. The press group of the school drew my attention to articles I might otherwise have missed, as did the Russian research group of Edinburgh University during the following year.

In the recent past, colleagues have been busy swapping a vast number of relevant references that no one working on his or her own could have possibly found or digested. For pointing me to particular articles and journals I am grateful to Archie Brown, Terry Cox, Lisa Dominguez, Jim Riordan, Judith Shapiro, Anne White, and Mariia Zezina. Indispensable for accurate translations of colloquial Russian, Gerry Smith advised me how best to interpret Russian words not found in dictionaries. Cathy Porter also readily discussed the nuances of translation.

Three of the chapters that follow draw on material published elsewhere: "Social policies and new social issues," in Stephen White, Alex Pravda, and Zvi Gitelman, eds., *Developments in Soviet Politics* (London, Macmillan, 1990), pp. 185–206; "Glasnost' and the woman question," in Linda Edmondson, ed., *Women and Society in Russia and the Soviet Union* (Cambridge, Cambridge University Press, 1992), pp. 202–226; and "Political groups and crisis," *Journal of Communist Studies*, vol. 9, no. 1, March 1993, pp. 173–191. I must thank the editors for permission to reproduce statistics and tiny extracts.

This book has benefited from the advice of friends and colleagues. Linda Edmondson cast her meticulous eye over the entire second draft and made astute suggestions. Laura Swartz examined the manuscript with painstaking care and offered helpful criticisms. Gratitude is also due to Barbara Heldt for her reflections. In Edinburgh, Roger Jeffery scrutinized the first draft and produced useful comments. And Malcolm Anderson and John Gooding deserve thanks for their general thoughts.

Jennie Somerville and Nigel Bowles commented on selected chapters. John Anderson, Lisa Dominguez, and Peter Duncan checked particular sections. I am indebted to them all for their encouragement. None, of course, bears responsibility for my errors and misinterpretations.

Feedback from anonymous readers chosen by Westview Press was especially helpful as I formulated the final draft, providing me with perceptive and challenging remarks. And special gratitude is due to Susan L. McEachern for her refreshing enthusiasm and excellent editorial skills.

Russian and Ukrainian colleagues and friends have, over the past fifteen years, enriched my understanding of life in the USSR and CIS, teaching me a great deal that I might not have fathomed without them. Hitherto, I have always hesitated to name them, and now it gives me great pleasure to acknowledge the accumulated debt. My deepest gratitude is owed to Mariia Zezina of Moscow University for her advice and efficient direction when she was my supervisor in 1985 and 1987 and for our numerous subsequent conversations about politics, society, and change. For her friendship and her wonderful recitations of Russian verse, I am grateful. To her family, too, I owe fond thanks for sharing their lives with me. My earlier supervisor in 1978, Galina Dmitrieva of Kiev University, did much to induct me into the practices and values of the Soviet education system. Zhenia Kozlova, in a very different way, since the late 1970s has instructed me in the techniques for getting one's way under Soviet socialism, often through her unending *skandaly,* many of which I would have happily missed at the time but have come to appreciate for their idiosyncratic specificity to the bureaucratic and corrupt system in which they were taking place.

Other friends and acquaintances, too numerous to name, have helped draw me into the rich variety and complexity of the Russian, Soviet, and post-Soviet social fabrics. To Misha Rachkov, in particular, I am grateful for deepening my knowledge of traditional Russian culture and for relentlessly contesting most of my ideas and assumptions.

Mary Buckley

Glossary

apparat	Communist Party administrative apparatus
CPSU	Communist Party of the Soviet Union
dacha	house in the country
dachniki	owners of dachas
defederalizatsiia	defederalization
demokratiia	democracy
demokratizatsiia	democratization
denationalizatsiia	denationalization
departizatsiia	departization (banning of party cells in the workplace)
desovetizatsiia	desovietization
DPR	Democratic Party of Russia
glasnost	openness or publicity
Gosplan	State Planning Committee
goszakaz	state order
grazhdanskoe obshchestvo	civil society
ispolkom	soviet executive committee
khozraschet	cost accounting
Komsomol	Communist Youth League
kooperatory	owners of private cooperative businesses
krai	territory
Lensovet	Leningrad City Soviet
Mossovet	Moscow City Soviet
nomenklatura	nomenclature (posts on *nomenklatura* lists whose holders were always handpicked in advance by the party)
obkom	oblast-level party committee
oblast	region
partokratiia	partocracy
partomafia	party mafia
perestroika	restructuring
pliuralizm	pluralism
podmena	substitution (usurping of functions)
pravovoe gosudarstvo	legal state

raiispolkom	executive committee of district soviet
raikom	district party committee
raion	district
raisovet	district soviet
RKP	Russian Communist Party
samizdat	self-published (previously illegal) material
samogon	bootleg vodka
samogonchiki	distillers of *samogon*
uskorenie	acceleration
zhensovety	women's councils

This book uses the Library of Congress transliteration system with the exception of names and words whose more customary English forms are now widely adopted. Thus Gor'kii, El'tsin, Iakovlev, Afanas'ev, and Migranian become Gorky, Yeltsin, Yakovlev, Afanasyev, and Migranyan. Some soft signs at the ends of words have also been dropped. So glasnost', oblast', Kazan', Pamiat', and tsar' are simply glasnost, oblast, Kazan, Pamiat, and czar.

Introduction: Ideas in Historical Context

WHAT NEW IMAGES of society and polity did the Soviet press and academic journals present to citizens from 1985 to 1991? How did political actors and journalists redefine and reassess key political concepts? What were the characteristics and consequences of changing public discourse? And what are their implications for Russia in the 1990s?

These guiding questions prompt others. How and why did the timing of the scrutiny of different issues vary? Which new categories, terms, and notions became popular? Where did the emphases of inquiry fall? What were the central questions, and how did they alter over time? What was ignored or evaded? Why did some issues, once raised, provoke stormy and extensive debate, while others were pursued with circumspection? In sum, what was asked when, how soon, where, by whom, and how? And what strategies for change were put forward?

This book grew out of a compulsion to examine changing historical context and the place in it of new ways of defining social and political reality. The central focus here is on the changing categories and concerns that framed discussion, debate, and conflict in an authoritarian state socialist system during processes of reform, transition, breakdown, and disintegration. Emphasis falls on perceptions of reality, labels, and the presentation of information.

I argue that the "opening" of social issues long taboo, such as crime, drugs, and prostitution, paved the way for more critical assessments of political life. Discourse about polity did not automatically follow from debates about society and could not have taken place without particular changes in leadership policies. But new interpretations of society prepared citizens for reevaluations of the political system and contributed to pressures for them.

Redefining society and polity in conceptual terms, but initially within proscribed limits, was made possible by reform. Fresh definitions and interpretations in turn challenged previously dominant assessments of society and polity, prompted further redefinition, and thereby fueled debate beyond politically acceptable boundaries, which were forced ultimately to broaden. The discourse resulting from reform was one factor, among others, that pushed it further.

The redefining of society and polity was a process that both shaped and reflected the politicization of society. It affected how citizens came to reassess reality and their role in it and also contributed to the formulation of demands made on the state. Many of the images, ideas, and interpretations that blossomed led to social and political visions that were incongruent with the prevailing system and could not be met by it. As they grew in strength in an increasingly divided society, they played a part in transforming transition into breakdown and disintegration.

Redefining Russian Society and Polity sets out to chart the nature of discourse integral to social and political change, to account for its characteristics, and to consider its implications. This is important since part of the struggle between conflicting political groups concerned definition and assessment of the conditions of society and polity. Mikhail Gorbachev's interpretations were not overwhelmingly accepted. Different political actors, social groups, and political movements were at odds with them at different times and in different ways.

In staying close to the vocabulary of those who redefined reality, I intend to recreate the atmosphere of change. It is vital to capture different perceptions, arguments, and emotions when a system is in a state of rapid political change. If we cannot grasp what is being said by journalists, political figures in dispute, social movements, and citizens on the street, we not only lack a feel for the period but also miss the impact of processes of change on assessments of social and political life and overlook the ways in which actors in the social and cultural environment react to new policies.

To understand the dynamics and predicaments of political change, we must grasp the complexities of the social fabric. Appraisals of social problems affect the formulation of policies and solutions. And the social structure of society, its traditions, and its cultural patterns influence how groups respond to initiatives from leaders. Changes in polity have an impact on society and vice versa. In crucial ways, the two are locked in interaction, notwithstanding pockets of autonomy. And in the period studied here the boundaries between state and society shifted. After 1989, an emergent civil society was expanding in size and in political significance, faster in some republics than in others and at greater speed in urban areas than in rural ones. The fates of society and polity were organically interlinked.

Glasnost as Prerequisite

Glasnost played a crucial role in the early stages of redefining society and polity, which would have been impossible without it. How glasnost developed therefore had a crucial impact on how problems and concepts were approached.

Western literature on glasnost has concentrated on the frankness that resulted from it and on the reporting of "bad news," in particular the explosion at Chernobyl, train crashes, and ethnic unrest.[1] Attention has also been paid to the term's use before the 1980s, noting that the concept was not a new one, even though it came to be closely associated with Gorbachev.[2] Subsequent discussions considered the responsiveness and diversity that stemmed from glasnost and looked at central debates about history, religion, justice, economy, nationality, and foreign policy.[3]

My purpose here is not to dwell on glasnost's etymology in Russian history; it is to go beyond the question "What was new because of glasnost?" I attempt to produce a more systematic, wide-ranging, and detailed account that traces the opening of selected social issues and the adoption of key concepts, examining how they were treated on new and evolving agendas. This book shows how glasnost's limits shifted over time, varied across issues, and ultimately betrayed the confines of perestroika by outstripping its mandate. A protracted process of revelation and deeper discussion, hesitant and halting at first, frequently painful, spanned seven increasingly turbulent years.

Underpinning the chapters that follow is the conviction that, although glasnost *tout court* did not lead to a legitimacy crisis for the USSR or result in processes of disintegration and revolution, it was nonetheless essential to them. In a context of democratization, glasnost fueled criticisms of society and polity and fed into politicization of the people. Although glasnost had been granted "from above" to facilitate perestroika, once in the hands of critical journalists, reformers, and a growing array of political activists, it was ultimately used against the state as well as for the purposes defined by Gorbachev. Without glasnost and democratization combined, the legitimate authority of the Communist Party of the Soviet Union (CPSU) would not have been questioned, and constellations of power would not have radically changed. Glasnost was integral to rethinking, indeed to thinking at all, and led to exposure and then to open recognition of a range of previously taboo social and political problems and to reconsideration of them. Glasnost was an enabling factor behind revelation, critique, debate, and the formulation of alternative political ideas and strategies.

Detailed treatment of the "opening" in public of fresh issues and concepts shows that this, like democratization, was a complex process. The way in which glasnost was applied was not smooth, unilinear, homogeneous across topics, nor was glasnost without boundaries. Scrutiny of selected issues illustrates variety in the timing of their "discovery," changing emphases in successive phases of interpretation, and differences in the breadth of debate, notwithstanding similarities.

Social issues received more extensive treatment earlier since they were politically "safer." Drug abuse and prostitution, although indicators of the imperfections of socialism, could be discussed more easily in 1986 than pluralism or democratization because the former topics did not automatically result in calls for an overhaul of the political system. Social issues also came onto agendas first because Gorbachev's commitment in 1986 to economic reform and to consideration of the "human factor" preceded his serious push in 1988 for political reform. This meant that many political issues could not legitimately be discussed in public until 1989 since official approval was wanting.

By locating the uses of glasnost, and then the more unfettered discussions once glasnost had become part of reality, in broader historical, political, and economic contexts, this book aims to provide a modest contribution to an understanding of the processes that criticized and undermined Soviet state socialism and generated its collapse. This book is concerned mainly with ideas, arguments, discourse, and reactions—and also with emotions, myths, analogies, and jokes—rather than with events, laws, leaders, parties, and movements. The latter are relevant insofar as they may provide opportunities; trigger expectations, possibilities, and processes; then respond to them; and thereby prompt further reactions from society. But they are not the central focus here. Several solid accounts are already in print that explore the chronology of Gorbachev's leadership, his policies, and their results.[4] My aim here is not to duplicate these analyses.

This text covers years in which Soviet citizens experienced a plethora of emotions—hope, hesitancy, exhilaration, disappointment, fear, anger, aggression, cynicism, weariness, uncertainty, despair, renewed elation, and disorientation. These emotions are relevant to a study of discourse since glasnost gave them license to be expressed publicly (although they would have circulated in society anyway) and was, in its own applications, charged by them. Moreover, social moods fluctuated and with them myths came and went. The opinions, assessments, and rumors of February 1986 were very different from those of January 1987, September 1990, April 1991, August 1991, or July 1992. They can be linked back to historical context, cues from leaders, economic problems, political developments, key events, and shifting debates. For instance, late 1985 and early 1986 brought a window of hope for intellectuals wanting freedom of expression since roundtable debates and more investigative reporting were encouraged in the run-up to the Twenty-seventh Party Congress. Their hopes were raised again in January 1987 when at the Central Committee plenum Gorbachev made a bolder commitment to glasnost and to change. But lack of success in economic reform had dampened spirits by December 1987, as had resistance to glasnost from its opponents.

Violent reactions from the center to nationalist demands that had developed as a part of democratization fanned more heated emotions. In April 1989, the use of lethal chemical weapons in Tbilisi, capital of Georgia, provoked outrage and impatience for independence. Likewise, in January 1991, the use of troops in the Baltic states hardened convictions of the need to break away from Moscow. In a context of democratization and glasnost, policies from the center perceived as repressive in the republics ensured an escalation in pressures on the Union for fundamental change. The nature of the relationship between rulers and ruled, the use of force by the state, or the threat of its use vitally affected processes of fragmentation and the waning of legitimacy.

Emotions and Methodology

Social scientists rarely indulge in their own emotions about the systems that they research. They are supposed to be dispassionate, objective, and distanced. But in truth, scholars are driven by an attraction, an involvement, and a sense of purpose. Something, often undefined, bewitches them about the field they study, holds them to it despite their own better attempts to escape it. Whether in the Soviet case it was once the thrill of penetrating an oppressive "enemy" system, the pleasant lure of the simple generosities of Russian collectivism, or well-wishing for more humanitarian values (disastrously unfulfilled), or all three and much more, is in the narrow "professional" sense irrelevant. One's research proposals should be theoretically inspired and methodologically as sharp as possible, blended with intuition and a sound familiarity with history and system. But in a more personal way, which undoubtedly feeds one's sense of what "professional" is, feelings about one's material do matter, as do the reactions to what one is doing of those whom one studies.

Russians are always quick to point out that they have lived through a history that strangers cannot feel in the same way, however many months or years we spend in their lands, however many hours we enjoy there talking to friends and acquaintances, or however many times we hear painful stories of what it was like to fear the knock at the door under Stalin, to be related to an "enemy of the people," or to speak out during the Khrushchev years, despite limited de-Stalinization. The same applies to recent tales of emotional trauma by those who left the CPSU in 1990 or to defensive stories of those who claimed that they wanted to leave the party but did not do so then for reasons of professional comfort, pension benefits, and apprehension about the future. We can be gripped by accounts of the political chaos in the Moscow City Soviet (Mossovet) and Leningrad City Soviet (Lensovet) in 1990 and 1991 and be spellbound by descriptions of encounters with the *pervyi otdel* (first department—the KGB) in the workplace and of arrests in the Gorbachev era.[5] We can be moved by the fortitude, stoicism, and joviality of many democrats during the tense days of 19 and 20 August 1991, when the fate of democratization was briefly threatened. But this is not our world, however much it has become a part of us, relentlessly pulling us back as soon as we have flown away from it. It may have a powerful intellectual and emotional hold over us, but parts of it are ever distinct, out of our grip, suddenly baffling, strangely and unpredictably remote, notwithstanding the depth of our familiarity with the society and system.

Westerners can drink vodka with Russians until 3 A.M., hearing all the favorite folk and spiritual songs; spend weekends at country dachas enjoying long chats while gathering mushrooms among the silver birch trees; conduct interviews in research institutes, universities, factories, and offices—but however much we have seen, felt, shared, and endured, we have not been confronted daily since birth by frustrating bureaucratic procedures or been socialized into "Soviet" norms and values grafted onto complex cultural patterns. We can smile when friends take the windshield wipers off their cars every time they park, feel angry at waiting in line forty minutes for good roast chicken on Kirov Street when everyone else calmly accepts this fate, or become exasperated at queueing over an hour for gas when, irrationally, only one pump out of eight has been switched on. But these are Western reactions. However many hours we spent watching Soviet television and reading Soviet books, journals, and magazines, we did not think or respond like a member of this society, notwithstanding the great variety across citizens.[6] The more time we spend in Russia, the more this seems graphically so, even though it may be a conclusion that in earlier, more idealistic days we hesitated to embrace. The familiarity of queues, bureaucratic inertia, rude service, poor food in many public places, crowded buses, and daily wear and tear, all of which persist after Gorbachev, were the mere backdrop to much deeper behavior patterns, rich discourses, sudden and surprising rumors, strange collective myths, and wild individualism unlocked only in the intimate and protective circles of close friends and family and generally aided by the downing of a bottle or three of vodka *do kontsa* (to the end).[7]

These reflections are, of course, methodological truisms. The Soviet system was not the British one, and Russians, Kazakhs, Georgians, and Estonians are not Italians, Swedes, Canadians, or Scots. This does not, and should not, stop us from studying the former USSR or the newly independent states. At best, we can be aware of the limits to *verstehen* and recognize that we need to visit as often as possible to keep as informed as possible.[8] The field of comparative politics has, since the 1960s, dwelt on methodological issues of similarity, difference, equivalence, and disparity.[9] The practical upshot of these contemplations is that we do the best we can from a distance, all the time sensitive to the immensity of what we are missing, aware that problems of inadequate sources remain, and conscious of the serious risks of imposing inappropriate Western expectations, responses and categories on our data.

The pace of change has further complicated the difficulties of understanding. In 1992, bewildered Russians regularly remarked that events were moving by the day, even by the hour, leaving them emotionally battered, dazed about the future, and unsure of what now constituted "normal" reference points. Foreigners not constantly on the spot therefore missed much of what was relevant. Scholars began lamenting that the historical record would not capture many nuances of change; ephemeral newspapers would be lost, records would be incomplete or lost, diaries would not be kept, and interviews would not be conducted. These worries had been expressed before 1992, too, but the speed of change and further social instability heightened their salience.

The charge that understanding and explanation are rendered hazardous by rapid change is serious. The inability to get close to many complexities and subtleties of speedy change is a problem—one often played down by comparativists. My conviction is that sound comparative research can result only from a prior specialist knowledge. The two are mutually beneficial, not mutually exclusive. But to take the charge to its logical extreme would mean that the sane academic should scrutinize only stability and pattern maintenance. That would not enhance our general understanding of the grand themes of change and continuity. Nor would it contribute to our knowledge about the formation and disintegration of states and the changing relations between state and society. More specifically, it would preclude study of breakdown, turbulence, legitimacy crisis, and revolution. Since, moreover, politics in most systems is unstable, excessive preoccupation with the minority of relatively stable liberal democracies, still characteristic of British and North American political science, creates rather distorted pictures for students of forms of "the political." Grasping the significance of various aspects of fast social and political change is indeed difficult and requires careful selection of relevant factors and a notion of their interrelatedness. The task is essential, even if vexing, frequently elusive, and plagued by problems of access to sufficient and reliable sources.

Makers of History and Objects of Research

As they lived through the Gorbachev years and into the Commonwealth of Independent States (CIS), many citizens were conscious of being both the makers of history and the objects of Western research. In their animated public debates and conversations of 1989 on the Arbat in Moscow and on Kazan Square in Leningrad, people in intense huddles drew parallels and contrasts with different months of 1917. Clustering in small groups, strangers and friends had heated discussions about the course of events. Sometimes these talks were acrimonious, sometimes lighthearted and amusing. The freedom to speak out briefly turned public places into charged debating arenas, until the thrill wore off and the traders moved in to sell paintings, wooden dolls, and other souvenirs to tourists, preferably Americans and Germans, at prices exorbitant for Russians and offensive to them. By 1991, before the coup, more gloomy historical lessons were being cited in daily conversations. Russia had always endured reaction and crackdown after liberalization. Would history repeat itself?[10] Would intervention by the army or civil war be among the consequences? The poets of the Arbat increasingly warned of crackdowns and delivered trenchant personal attacks on current leaders and on Raisa Gorbacheva.[11]

During these years of rapid change, Russians in particular reiterated before Westerners the differences they perceived between our worlds, even if they had never visited North America or Western Europe, and emphasized what these differences meant for reform. Here myths and misunderstandings abounded; yet simultaneously there was a definite sense of distance and isolation from the West and of being looked at. Numerous jokes, for instance, told in 1991 by the popular comedian Genadii Khazanov (to packed stadiums at a time when theaters were less than half full) involved stories about how Japanese, Australian, or other foreign visitors reacted to various situations in the USSR. Focus fell on what surprised foreigners, on what they found odd, disturbing, unbelievable, or inefficient. Each amusing scene was a biting indictment of Soviet life. One joke ran as follows:

> An Australian visits a collective farm. One day he notices two men digging. One digs a hole and the other covers it in. All day they work in this way. They dig one row, then another, then another. "What are you doing?" asks the puzzled Australian. "I always dig a hole," says the first. "And I always fill it in," said the second. "We do this every day. Although usually there is a third person who plants a tree. But he is ill today."[12]

One subtext of this and many other jokes was that deeply ingrained norms and values were bewildering to the rest of the world, not "normal," not yet "civilized," and highly resistant to transformation in ways not easily grasped by outsiders.

Perestroika and glasnost were ridiculed, too, as failed policies and as absurd or empty slogans. At a time of food shortages, Khazanov gave hilarious descriptions of appropriate recipes. He also mimicked Gorbachev, to the audience's delight, making fun of frequently used phrases, expressions, and promises. Gorbachev's tendency to put the wrong stress patterns on certain verbs was already the target of jokes among intellectuals.[13]

That Khazanov could tell these jokes in public was one of glasnost's successes, but it was no longer enough for his audiences. By 1991, many citizens had become impervious to the victories of glasnost, wishing instead for lower prices and a predictable supply of food without *talony* (ration coupons). Glasnost was no longer of novelty value and at any rate could not transform vital aspects of daily life. People wanted a higher standard of living and dignity rather than a vacuous openness, unfulfilled political promises, empty shelves in state shops, and unwelcome food parcels from the West.[14] One of the reactions to rationing, shortages, and price increases was desperate laughter and ridicule. Telling jokes was a cathartic mechanism for coping and for defusing anger, as it always had been in state socialist systems and in earlier autocratic ones.

Sensitive to immense differences between East and West, often overstating them or being preoccupied with ones that visitors found the least important, Russians who knew Westerners relatively well often admitted to experiencing in their company a blend of envy, lack of dignity in financial matters, spiritual superiority, and cynicism. Some confessed to despising Western materialism while at the same time wanting it and to feeling impecunious and dependent, frequently calculating how to extract economic advantage in both professional and personal life but simultaneously believing themselves to be emotionally richer in mystical terms—often hard for observers to grasp. Many Russians also ridiculed political promises that could not be met while simultaneously wanting desperately to believe in fairy-tale solutions. And claims to emotional depth frequently seemed to be little more than defenses of retrograde inequalities and sexual stereotypes[15] coupled with a belief in absurd superstitions.[16] But alongside calculating behavior patterns, which were encouraged by perceived relative poverty, coexisted the bursting generosity and openheartedness characteristic of a collective-spirited culture. Cultural patterns are complex, rich, and often apparently contradictory. Their subtleties and meanings cannot be grasped immediately, and our own cultural prisms often impede the process of understanding.

But we should not talk of "them" and "us," although I have just done so here for simple shorthand to highlight cultural differences, divides, and perceptions. A variety of responses to perestroika, glasnost, and democratization existed among Russians and far more among erstwhile Soviet citizens. Nevertheless, cultural patterns, with all their elusive characteristics, were relevant to reactions to reform and also to our understanding of those reactions. And the complications of our relationships to and with Russians feed into and affect our research. I refer frequently here to Russians and not to other nationalities since most of my written sources concerned Russia, apart from a few pertaining to Azerbaidzhan and the Baltic states. My sources were also limited to the Russian language. And most of my interviews and conversations were with Russians, apart from a tiny number of interviews with Lithuanians and Ukrainians.

As I researched for this book, I developed a growing preoccupation with anthropological questions of sense and meaning. As I ventured deeper into Russian society after 1989, a society not new to me, these questions became haunting. Although a sensitivity to cultural differences underpins this book, it does not directly affect my approach to the material discussed, save to reinforce a long-held conviction that the ideas, arguments, and conclusions of different political actors and social groups must be discussed only after they have been presented in the terms used by these actors, citing their concepts, phrases, and reflections. Only then can we begin to capture the ideas and reactions to events and policies between 1985 and 1991 and gain a sense, albeit inadequate, of the social and political atmosphere and of the discourse thrown up by it and shaping it.

Sources and Approach

Official documents, newspapers, magazines, journals, pamphlets, television programs, radio broadcasts, rumors, jokes, plays, and films were my main sources. Interviews with people's deputies, academics, and a range of citizens from different social groups, social movements, and political parties provided vital supplementary information about Russian responses and interpretations. Frequent visits to the USSR enhanced my appreciation of changes in social mood, expectations, and myths.

The questions posed earlier cannot be answered definitively with neat measures or absolute certainty. But by drawing on a wide range of primary sources, I can provide an interpretive analysis of the way in which key issues and central concepts were defined and portrayed. This interpretive approach straddles political science, sociology, history, and anthropology and is eclectic out of necessity. A starting assumption is that we cannot begin to grasp the changes of 1985 to 1991 without looking at the ideas that blossomed about both society and polity since they affected and fed off each other. Their neat separation may be analytically convenient but does not help our understanding of the processes of change. Those who find comfort in disciplinary boundaries or in institutional frameworks will probably find the scope of this book too broad and its answers imprecise.

Organization

Chapter 1 summarizes what perestroika, democratization, and glasnost entailed; introduces their consequences; and surveys reactions to them. It sets the context for more detailed discussions of glasnost, society, and polity.

Chapter 2 explores more closely the relationship between glasnost and perestroika, as initially conceived by Gorbachev; traces how glasnost grew in strength after 1987; and notes the various ways in which it was applied. By 1989, different political actors had very different conceptions about glasnost's desirability and significance. Centrists interpreted glasnost as Leninist and positive, more radical reformers believed it should go beyond Leninism and lead to more open and unbridled inquiry, and traditional Leninists condemned it for being disorienting and destabilizing.

Since social problems were redefined before political ones, Chapter 3 examines changing coverage in the press and journals of crime, drugs, prostitution, acquired immune deficiency syndrome (AIDS), rape, child abuse, and suicide. These topics all became live issues in the late 1980s, some sooner than others. At first, more open reporting was received with thirst and enthusiasm, even when it was sensational and rather crude. Its revelations soon led, in 1987 and 1988, to anxiety about personal safety. And by 1990, persistent coverage of social ills in a context of failed economic reform and nationalist separatism was fueling concerns about instability and disintegration. Discussions of crime in particular contributed to the growing sense of social collapse and insecurity.

Thus, glasnost exposed and contributed to social problems; it also triggered shame at the failures of social policy. Chapter 4 shows how journalists and academics approached housing, contraception, abortion, and infant mortality rates. These topics, too, were all more vigorously analyzed after 1987. Again, treatment was often sensational and upsetting. But it fed less into the growing sense of disintegration; rather, it emphasized the inadequacies and weaknesses of past social policies. Embarrassment and shame at the failures of the "socialist" construction resulted.

Investigative reporting of social problems affected politics. Discussions of crime, drug abuse, and prostitution fed into arguments about the need for tougher law and order and for firm direction from above. It became fashionable among opponents of reform (and among advocates, but for different reasons) to stress the need for executive clout that would ensure stability (an old argument revamped). Opponents railed against hazy democratic dreams that were utopian and unrealizable and constituted recipes for more immorality, disorder, and instability. Nationalist ferment in the republics, topped with violent clashes between Armenians and Azerbaidzhanis, Georgians and Ossetians, Uzbeks and Meskhetians, charged their case. But at the same time, the failures of social policy were cited by democrats as conclusive evidence that rule for more than seventy years by a corrupt party-apparat had produced intolerably low living standards for the majority of the population. A tiny elite had benefited at the expense of the people whose interests it was supposedly in power to defend. The abundant mistakes of the CPSU, and the crimes perpetuated by it, demanded redress. Totalitarian rule, many reformers believed, had to be replaced by democracy.

Sharply conflicting interpretations of society and polity meant that discussions of "pluralism" were laced with other subtexts. Chapter 5 looks at fresh views of what the concept meant. For years, it had been dismissed as bourgeois and ideologically unsound. Then, in 1987, Gorbachev referred positively to "socialist pluralism," thus giving it political legitimacy. Thereafter, more radical views clashed with conservative ones about its scope and significance. Pluralism was seen as essential to reform by proponents of a multiparty system. Critics, however, believed that it undermined their values and was ultimately destabilizing; pluralism brought the disorder of competing opinions, incoherence in policy making, and the danger of moving in a nonsocialist direction. Pluralism ushered in uncertainty and instability instead of firm direction based on clear socialist convictions, as had been fostered by democratic centralism and a united CPSU.

Those who defended pluralism in thought and action generally supported radical political change. These unwavering adherents of democratization, as Chapters 6 and 7 show, became impatient with the slowness of political reform, with the limits imposed on what the newly elected soviets could do, and with the lack of clarity concerning the responsibilities of soviets at different administrative levels. Stricter Leninists, however, on the right of the CPSU wished to slow democratization down, even halt it.[17] In their view, political reforms heralded immorality, demagogy, and disintegration, whereas Leninism guaranteed purity, equality, and a defense of workers' rights.

Chapter 6 examines central arguments about democracy and civil society. Both concepts were essential to reflections of the reform process, although much greater attention was paid to the former. How they were defined and assessed affected the political significance accorded them. And what "democracy" and "democratization" meant to political actors and analysts changed as events rapidly unfolded. After 1989, the relationship between democratization and the growth of civil society became central to the discourse of a minority of intellectuals. Although many failed to link the two, advocates of parliamentary democracy increasingly argued that without civil society democratization would not be successful.

Chapter 7 focuses on discourse about the practical problems of democratizing the political system. In a historical context of freer elections and greater candidate choice, this topic preoccupied politicians, journalists, and academics in the aftermath of elections in 1989 and 1990. The revitalized soviets came under intense scrutiny for their democratic credentials and for their ability to take on new political roles. The chapter draws heavily on interviews with people's deputies to stay close to their concepts, perceptions, and appraisals.

If "democracy" was a buzzword in 1988 and 1989, its counterpart in 1990 was "crisis." Again, historical context determined the concept that gripped commentators and that dominated their thoughts. It was often linked with "collapse," "disintegration," "chaos," and "despair." By 1990, real crises were occurring, not only economic and fiscal ones but also crises of state power. The democratizing soviets operated chaotically, as Chapter 7 describes; relationships between political institutions were rapidly shifting as Supreme Soviets in the republics and even local soviets assumed powers for which they had not been granted authority by the level above; and the center increasingly suffered a crisis of legitimacy. Both political order and the state were disintegrating.

Chapter 8 explores different interpretations of crisis as viewed by political actors, selected social movements, and political groups across the spectrum. Chapter 9 looks at alternative perceptions of crisis emanating from much less powerful groups, including Pamiat, monarchists, greens, feminists, and anarchists. Both chapters underscore the immense variety of views, assessments, remedies, and strategies coming from a divided society.

Like pluralism and democracy, crisis was a concept defined in a huge number of ways, often tied to broader reflections on economic, political, and social reform. Interpretations of all three terms fed into political conflicts and were of immense practical significance for alternative conceptions of the running of polity, economy, and society. This was graphically illustrated by the coup of August 1991, an attempt by members of the CPSU, KGB, and military-industrial complex to find a way out of the crisis as they understood it. Competing democratic conceptions of crisis drove a sufficient number of citizens and politicians to mobilize against it in a way that they would not have dared six or even three years earlier.

Reflections about social and political issues followed rather different timetables. Chapter 10 comments on these and briefly considers key characteristics of the redefining of society and polity after January 1992, suggesting similarities and differences with the discourses of the previous seven years.

A key assumption underpinning all chapters is that we must examine social and political thought from 1985 to 1991, as well as the historical, economic, political, and social context within which it was set, for an adequate understanding of these initial years of transition, and also for the ones that follow, since images, categories, arguments, and debates are not merely reactions to prevailing situations but are also factors affecting political reality. And although August 1991 is a neat historical divide for demarcating a new phase of change, like October 1917 it is in some respects a false break since many views of problems and perceived obstacles to solving them persist. The following chapters do not pretend to be exhaustive in their coverage of interpretations of social and political issues. Rather, they are meant to contribute to our appreciation of social and political discourse during the momentous Gorbachev era and a little beyond.

NOTES

1. Nick Lampert, "The dilemma of glasnost," *Journal of Communist Studies*, vol. 4, no. 4, December 1988, pp. 48–63. Lampert focused on criticisms of officialdom, on plurality in the world of publishing, and on bad news.

2. Natalie Gross, "Glasnost': Roots and practice," *Problems of Communism*, November-December 1987, pp. 69–80.

3. Alec Nove, *Glasnost' in Action: Cultural Renaissance in Russia* (Boston, Unwin Hyman, 1989); R. W. Davies, *Soviet History in the Gorbachev Revolution* (London, Macmillan, 1989); Andrei Melville and Gail W. Lapidus, eds., *The Glasnost Papers: Voices on Reform from Moscow* (Boulder, Westview, 1990); Stephen F. Cohen and Katrina Vanden Heuvel, *Voices of Glasnost* (New York, Norton, 1989). For a more general historical overview, see Ben Eklof, *Soviet Briefing: Gorbachev and the Reform Process* (Boulder, Westview, 1989).

For criticism of the view that glasnost was a cosmetic exercise in public relations or a deliberate attempt to deceive the West, refer to David Wedgwood Benn, *From Glasnost to Freedom of Speech* (London, Pinter, 1992). Although glasnost and new thinking were not synonymous, glasnost facilitated the latter. For redefinitions of polity, economy, the national question, foreign policy, and world communism, see Archie Brown, ed., *New Thinking in Soviet Politics* (London, Macmillan, 1992). For the argument that glasnost not only was an instrument of policy but also implied a new form of politics, see Ronald J. Hill, "Glasnost' and Soviet politics," *Coexistence*, no. 26, 1989, pp. 317–331.

4. These texts include Anders Aslund, *Gorbachev's Struggle for Economic Reform*, 2d ed. (London, Pinter, 1991); Richard Sakwa, *Gorbachev and His Reforms, 1985–1990* (London, Philip Allen, 1990); Stephen White, *Gorbachev and After* (Cambridge, Cambridge University Press, 1991); Catherine Merridale and Chris Ward, eds., *Perestroika: The Historical Perspective* (Dunton Green, Edward Arnold, 1991).

5. The KGB department in workplaces was generally referred to as the "first department." In 1992, the secret service persisted in some places of work. It was not systematically abolished, although its functions were frequently much tamer than before.

6. For relevant political satires, see Alexander Zinoviev, *Homo Sovieticus* (London, Victor Gollancz, 1985); Alexander Zinoviev, *Yawning Heights* (Harmondsworth, Penguin, 1981); and Alexander Zinoviev, *Perestroika in Partygrad* (London, Peter Owen, 1992).

7. Russian tradition does not allow an opened bottle of alcohol to go unfinished. The social pressures on men by men to consume large amounts of spirits to demonstrate their manhood are oppressively strong.

8. For Max Weber's discussion of *verstehen*, see his "The interpretive understanding of social action," in May Brodbeck, ed., *Readings in the Philosophy of the Social Sciences* (London, Macmillan, 1968), pp. 19–33.

9. Classic texts advocating and debating comparative approaches include Robert T. Holt and John E. Turner, *The Methodology of Comparative Research* (New York, Free Press, 1970); Adam Przeworski and Henry Teune, *The Logic of Comparative*

Social Inquiry (New York, Wiley Interscience, 1970); Lawrence C. Meyer, *Comparative Political Inquiry* (Homewood, Ill., Dorsey Press, 1972); James A. Bill and Robert L. Hardgrave, Jr., *Comparative Politics: The Quest for Theory* (Columbus, Ohio, Charles E. Merrill, 1973).

10. For examination of the arguments voiced by Soviet historians about the likely repetition of past cycles, refer to Robert C. Tucker, "What time is it in Russia's history?" in Merridale and Ward, eds., *Perestroika*, pp. 34–45.

11. After 1985, Raisa Gorbacheva was highly unpopular in the USSR. Russian women, in particular, despised her frequent appearance next to her husband on the front page of newspapers and her varied wardrobe. They envied her clothes and felt that it was inappropriate of her to show them off when the bulk of Soviet women could not enjoy such luxuries. Many citizens also found it odd that she was always by Gorbachev's side. This implied interference in his work. As one of my acquaintances explained, "We got rid of the czarina in the revolution. We do not want another one."

Many jokes also circulated about Raisa and her high self-opinion. One ran as follows: Gorbachev and Raisa are in bed. "Misha, Misha," cries Raisa, "who would have thought ten years ago that today you would be in bed with the wife of the president of the USSR?"

12. On 29 April 1991, thousands packed the modern Izmailov cultural center in Moscow to hear Genadii Khazanov, where he told this joke. It was especially amusing since Khazanov was wonderfully on target in imitating foreign pronunciations of Russian. He also made fun of typical grammatical errors made by foreigners.

13. Among the jokes circulating in Soviet society in 1991 were the following:

Gorbachev meets Reagan. "What's the English for *nachat'*?" asks Gorbachev. Reagan thinks and answers, "*Begin*." This joke is getting at what many Russians perceive as Gorbachev's poor pronunciation. The stress on the Russian verb nach*at'* (which means to begin) falls on the second syllable. Gorbachev, however, revealing his background in Stavropol, incorrectly places the stress on the first syllable. Reagan imitates this by stressing the first syllable of *be*gin.

After Gorbachev opened up the border, he woke up the following day and found Raisa Maksimovna missing. He went out into the street, and not a soul was there. In the Kremlin—no one! Emptiness. Suddenly the telephone rang.

"Mikhail Sergeevich? How are you? It's Ligachev here."

"Egor Kuz'mich, what has happened?"

"I told you, Mikhail Sergeevich. I advised you not to open the border! And now everyone is leaving … the whole Union."

"Yes. That means that just you and I are left?"

"Why me? I am phoning from Sweden!"

IN SCHOOL: What is socialism? It's the longest path to capitalism.

Ascending to the Peak of Communism, the mountain climbers discovered full communism: There was not even snow there.

14. In 1990 and 1991, many proud citizens disapproved of food aid and criticized Gorbachev for courting Western help in such a manner. Similar regrets were heard under Yeltsin. As one woman put it to me in April 1992, shortly after more aid parcels had arrived from Western Europe and the United States, "I remember aid parcels coming from the Americans during the war. I did not like it then, and I don't like it now."

15. Linda Edmondson made the point that arguments about "emotional depth" and "spirituality" frequently feed off myths about "essential" womanhood and manhood. See her "Women's emancipation and concepts of sexual difference" (Paper delivered at the conference Women in the History of the Russian Empire, University of Akron and Kent State University, 11–14 August 1988).

16. When Gorbachev and Yeltsin were interviewed on U.S. television after the failed coup, one question put to them was whether they were religious. Gorbachev announced that he was an atheist, and Yeltsin replied that he had been to church a few times, adding that he was superstitious. The significance of this remark probably passed by most viewers. Numerous superstitions and folk beliefs persist in Russia not only in the deeply superstitious countryside but also in urban homes. For example, professional Muscovites among my acquaintances will not have dried flowers in the home because they believe these bring bad luck. They hesitate to return home for something they have forgotten because to go back is a bad omen. To bring good financial fortune during the coming year, they put a herring bone in their wallet on New Year's Eve. To wish someone a full life, in particular to bear children, they fill their wine glass or teacup to the brim.

17. The terms *right* and *left* have in recent years come to be applied in the opposite way from their use in the 1920s. Thus, in the 1980s, those on the right of the CPSU were Leninists who opposed reform. Those on the left were democrats who supported reforms in the direction of a market economy and parliamentary system of government.

1

Reactions to Perestroika

ON 25 DECEMBER 1991, Mikhail Gorbachev was constrained by historical circumstances to resign from the presidency of the USSR.[1] Almost seven years earlier, in March 1985, he had been chosen by his colleagues on the Politburo to become general secretary of the CPSU. None of them could have anticipated that his policies would initiate processes of change that would result, in 1990, in the demise of the Politburo as the top decision-making body and, in 1991, in the end of the Union of Soviet Socialist Republics. Had they foreseen in 1985 that under Gorbachev, "communist" would become a pejorative term for many, that popular fronts would challenge the legitimacy of decisions made by the leadership of the CPSU in Moscow, and that communist leaderships would be toppled throughout Eastern Europe, they would have had second thoughts about their choice. The consequences of Gorbachev's leadership were far-reaching for his own people, for East Europeans, and for the world.

Gorbachev set out, not to overthrow the existing system, but to reform economy, polity, and society within its bounds. His discourse of redefining reality was "socialist" and "Leninist." But as a result of democratization, new social movements and political parties formed. Their discourse was critical of the status quo, which led them to make fresh demands on the state. Nationalism, in particular, challenged the raison d'être of the political system. Gorbachev was forced to confront issues that he had never intended to put on formal political agendas, such as independence for the republics and modification of Article 6 of the Soviet constitution, which had enshrined the "leading and guiding role of the CPSU." Alteration of the latter in 1990 meant that the constitution was adjusted to fit changing political reality.[2] The final symbol of domination by one party was thereby removed, stimulating further political diversity and also giving it legitimacy.

But a discourse loyal to CPSU hegemony, Union, stability, and socialism found new political parties, disintegration, disorder, and transition to a market economy intolerable. Critical reaction by hard-liners to the results of perestroika made Gorbachev the victim, in August 1991, of a coup, which soon failed. Thereafter political change accelerated at a previously unimaginable pace amid persisting chaos. Radical changes that in 1985 would have been unthinkable were now demanded by opponents of the state of emergency.

What Was Perestroika?

In 1986, at the Twenty-seventh Party Congress and after, Gorbachev outlined the importance of "economic acceleration," democratization, and activation of the human factor. He described perestroika as a revolutionary process of interrelated changes in economy, polity, and society that would occur within the boundaries of Leninism and socialism. Gorbachev had dreamed of a more efficient economy benefiting from improved technology, *khozraschet* (cost accounting), *samofinansirovanie* (self-financing), a committed work force, and far fewer administrative orders sent down from bureaucrats to factory directors. But he did not wish to embrace capitalism. That was ideologically undesirable and, in any case, politically impossible in 1986.[3]

The shortcomings of the command-administrative system of central planning, however, had to be exposed and openly discussed before they could be tackled. Falling growth rates, bottlenecks in supply, the stifling role of ministries, and widespread corruption had to be examined. Reform had to be seen as necessary, and support from the people had to be won. Gorbachev advocated glasnost as the necessary means to the end of perestroika. Glasnost would uncover the deficiencies and problems of system and society, thereby promoting the necessary awareness for successful reform. Glasnost would thus serve perestroika.[4]

Gorbachev realized that, to be effective, changes in the economy demanded changes in society and polity. Citizens needed to be less passive in the workplace, where they had become accustomed to waiting for orders from above. They had been socialized into hesitating to take responsibility and into fearing the consequences if they did. Instead, in Gorbachev's view, workers needed to develop a "new psychology" and a "new thinking."[5] That way, they would more readily take initiative. And glasnost would help them do this. Citizens, however, often baffled about what exactly was being asked of them, could not easily change how they behaved and anyway were anxious about the reprisals that might result if policy changed course. Deeply ingrained psychological reflexes, constructed by decades of repressive authoritarian rule and reinforced by the lurking presence, sometimes more apparent than real, of the KGB, had programmed them not to speak out and not to act.[6]

Not all citizens, of course, fitted this image of passivity. Initiative in tackling problems of daily life was certainly not absent, and much creativity had routinely been applied to the second economy. Neither did all Russians match the stereotype of a lazy Oblomov.[7] But hesitation to step out of line at work and in politics afflicted many.

Economic reforms were initially halting, contradictory, painful, and limited. As they visibly failed, Gorbachev came to believe that widespread resistance to them, which was embedded in the structures, logic, and practices of the system itself, could best be tackled by political changes that made ministers accountable to democratically elected politicians. He advocated a radical overhaul of the electoral system, a choice of candidates, revitalized and more powerful soviets, reform of the CPSU itself, and the growth of groups independent of the CPSU.[8] These changes gave political space to societal pressures and demands that transformed the system still further and in directions unwelcome to Gorbachev.

By 1990, sufficient changes had occurred in society and polity to ensure in some social groups the breakdown of past norms and values. In particular, glasnost and democratization combined had exposed citizens to the lies and injustices of the past; had empowered them to speak out, even if at first haltingly and anxiously; and had enabled them to mobilize politically. In this context, and initially with Gorbachev's encouragement, in 1987, 1988, and 1989, myriad new social clubs and political groups formed, then larger movements and weak political parties.[9] Gorbachev's hope was for new movements to show support for perestroika and thereby help strengthen his political position in struggles with opponents of reform. So individuals who were politically active outside the CPSU were no longer automatically labeled "dissident," although intimidation and harassment by the KGB persisted. In 1990, passage of the Law on Public Associations provided the necessary legality for the formation of a multi-party system.[10]

Citizens also became active voters, being given the opportunity in 1989 to vote for the Congress of People's Deputies and in 1989 and 1990 for local soviets and republican Supreme Soviets. Although in 1989 not all constituencies offered a choice of candidate, and 750 out of the 2,250 seats on the Congress of People's Deputies were reserved for "social organizations" (with 100 seats saved for the CPSU alone), significant democratic developments were taking place.[11] Likewise, the powers and possibilities of the new-style soviets may have been vague, often decidedly ad hoc, and frequently limited by the apparat or by a different administrative level, but a new electoral system was nonetheless replacing the much derided no-choice system of the past, which had offered only one candidate. Although the soviets were beset with numerous difficulties, their very existence represented, for some commentators, a significant step on the very long path to an embryonic civil society. Developments could at any time be reversed since the instruments of rule able to turn back the clock were still in place. But with every fresh change that further modified the old system, reformers gained confidence and pushed for more. Optimists among them came to believe that changes were irreversible because society had sufficiently altered and a significant number of citizens, even if a minority, were committed to more change.

Reactions to the Failures of Economic Reform

Whereas citizens in various occupations were wondering in 1985, 1986, and 1987, "What *is* perestroika?" and frequently admitted their confusion by posing this question in the press, by 1990 many of them were repeatedly asking, "Why do we *need* perestroika?"[12] The failure of economic reforms brought rationing in 1989 of selected items in short supply, such as sugar.[13] In 1990 came the rationing of cigarettes. Regional variations meant that some areas were more heavily rationed than others. For example, some items that were rationed in Leningrad were not in Moscow. Availability, too, varied. In some districts of the capital, Muscovites complained that they rarely saw eggs at all, whereas in others eggs were generally on sale most days.[14] But when bread, the symbol of successful agriculture, totally disappeared from Moscow's shops for three days in September 1990, for many that was the definitive proof of perestroika's failure. The simultaneous closing down for repair of two bread factories was one reason given.[15] A similar excuse was made in Soviet Abkhazia in the summer of 1990 when milk was suddenly not to be found.[16] There was a confusing gap between the visible results of perestroika and the rhetoric that had promised economic acceleration, efficiency, intensive growth, and higher-quality goods. Instead, citizens witnessed worsening shortages and rationing, followed in 1990 by inflation and budget deficits and in April 1991 by threefold price increases and unemployment. Inflation and unemployment in particular were supposed to be the evils of capitalism, not state socialism.

The emotional results among citizens were weariness and shame. Newspapers captured their mood: "Rationing—the misfortune of our time" and "Rationing—the guilt of our society."[17] A loss of dignity accompanied the use of ration coupons and *visitki*—cards showing proof of residence in a particular city for the purpose of purchasing goods in that city, thereby, in theory, preventing outsiders from buying products there.[18]

In the autumn of 1990, there was little fresh fruit in state shops; it could best be procured in private markets at high prices, such as three rubles for two pears. For low-paid workers, this price represented 3 percent of their monthly wage. Even apples were scarce. Only lucky *dachniki* (owners of dachas) and their friends could be assured of a regular supply.

By August 1991, sugar had become extremely hard to find in shops. One result was that disappointed *dachniki* complained bitterly that they would be unable to make next year's prized supply of jam from fresh fruit in their gardens. Those fortunate enough to have gardens and those allocated new plots in 1990 and 1991 resented the long hours they now had to devote to digging and planting. Rumors of worsening shortages and impending famine forced them to take gardening more seriously than ever before. Those without plots of land sometimes stole the crops from those who had, driven by the expectation that the winters of 1990 and 1991 would be hungry ones. Perestroika had resulted in depleted food supplies deriving from disrupted supply lines and the refusal of many regions to send produce elsewhere. This situation was now affecting deeply entrenched behavior patterns.

A persistent rumor circulating about the sugar shortage was that the *kooperatory*, owners of private cooperative businesses, were to blame. According to one variant, the *kooperatory* had paid large amounts of money for sugar at the back doors of state shops, leaving none for humble citizens. Fueled by the much-remarked-on reluctance of Russian people to see others prosper when they do not, this rumor spread with vigor, despite evidence to the contrary. Resentment at the good fortune of some businesspersons and dislike of the high prices charged by them perpetuated accusations that their incomes were dishonest.

Shortages of other crops were, in part, created by failures to bring in harvests. In 1990, a low percentage of the grain harvest was gathered, despite it being a relatively good one.[19] There was inadequate labor power to harvest the potato crop as well, a circumstance not helped by many students refusing to fulfill their previous duty of helping the farmers. Changes in students' attitudes to voluntary labor, the possibility of expressing them (thanks to glasnost), and the fresh political will to do so had repercussions for the economy.[20] And because of problems of organization and transportation, many of the potatoes that had been picked were left in the fields to rot. As the command-administrative system ceased to function as before, effective structures and mechanisms did not develop to replace it. The telephone calls from above that in the past had prompted fast action, often at the very last moment, no longer prevailed. In this context of recognized shortages, the phrase "There is nothing in the shops" (even when there was) was one element in the collective identity crisis suffered by a people who through glasnost had learned, or had received public confirmation, that their country seriously lagged behind the West, after years of having been told the opposite.

Embittered by shortages and anxious about the consequences of more economic reforms, two new "folk devils" appeared in daily discourse. The first, not without justification, was the apparat. Its members were accused of hoarding state property for resale at private prices. Many believed that the apparat would become the new business class, doing deals at the expense of the people. Some evidence subsequently supported this fear. The second devil was a vague "mafia" or "mafias." Mafias were blamed for several offenses, especially sabotage. One story held that goods were not in short supply but rather were purposely hidden or dumped in the woods to rot. The mafia, whomever it included, was responsible. Another story claimed that trainloads of goods were standing unloaded in stations. Again the mafia was at fault. Some citizens included the apparat in the mafia, whereas others had pictures of criminal gangs and different ethnic groups. Control over price-setting by identifiable groups in some private food markets reinforced the image that mafias did exist and had an important effect on the economy. The point here is that a firm belief existed that someone was always operating at the expense of the people, be it the *kooperatory,* apparat, or mafia.

In 1990, Gorbachev and his colleagues could not agree about the necessary policies for economic reform. Gorbachev's support for the Shatalin plan and then his subsequent reluctance to adopt it when its opponents applied extreme pressure heightened confusion about economic direction.[21] As many citizens reached the view that perestroika was seemingly an economic and political muddle resulting from contradictory and partial reforms, Western specialists informed them that perestroika, whatever it had been, was now over. Failure to push ahead in 1990 with either the Shatalin plan or the Ryzhkov plan meant that perestroika had come to a halt.[22]

Those who remained more optimistic in 1990 and 1991 about perestroika's possibilities refrained from asking, "Why do we need perestroika?" and instead wondered, "How can we make perestroika work?" There was a growing consensus among radicals that "those who yesterday announced perestroika must today resign."[23] In this view, perestroika might work if the leadership changed. The instigators of perestroika were increasingly seen by radical reformers as its opponents, now holding it back and preventing its logic from unfolding. To some democrats, the Gorbachev leadership offered contradictory and partial reforms punctuated by authoritarian solutions. Gorbachev's assumption of the executive presidency in March 1990 had fueled fears about his desire to accumulate powers, especially since he had not been popularly elected. For democratic critics, this violated the spirit of perestroika.

But many, including democrats, feared the political instability that presidential elections might unleash. Ultimately, elections for the presidency were perceived as desirable but too destabilizing to permit. Many critics of authoritarianism also saw the need for a more coherent executive and firm leadership at a time of growing protest, ferment, and executive vacuum. Additional anxiety was prompted by the sudden arrival of troops in selected republics in January 1991 to enforce the draft, track down army deserters, and trace those who had opted for alternative services (as allowed in the Baltic states).[24]

A fractioning of the leadership ultimately helped reduce its credibility and effectiveness. The consequences of perestroika and democratization, and Gorbachev's handling of them, led committed reformers to desert him. They felt alienated from a leader they had once backed and began to formulate alternative ideas about how best to proceed. The resignations of Eduard Shevardnadze, foreign minister, in December 1990 and Kazimira Prunskene, prime minister of Lithuania, in January 1991 showed that even centrists feared creeping authoritarianism and felt increasingly powerless to achieve the economic and political goals that they themselves had set.[25] Many worried that the army, the KGB, and leaders of industry were exerting pressure on Gorbachev and paralyzing his commitment to reform. In this context of unease and rising tension, reformers such as Gavriil Popov drafted alternative strategies for economic policy, political reform, and national self-determination.[26] More defiant nationalist movements, such as Rukh in Ukraine and Sajudis in Lithuania, set out to build new independent democratic states.[27] Then in July 1991, Aleksandr Yakovlev left Gorbachev's team of advisers and together with Shevardnadze committed himself to the new Movement for Democratic Reforms. Once Gorbachev's loyal ally, Yakovlev now felt that the CPSU was a serious brake on reform.[28] The CPSU was even losing legitimacy among its previous adherents. And Boris Yeltsin, acting in his capacity as popularly elected president of Russia, in July 1991 stepped up the attack on the party by decreeing that all party cells in the workplace be disbanded.[29]

By mid-1991, Gorbachev's erstwhile supporters were pushing for more radical reforms than Gorbachev was prepared to countenance. After the failed attempt by the putschists in August to hold the Union together through the State of Emergency, Estonia's declaration of immediate independence was followed by those of other republics. A changed political situation demanded fresh policies. The political orientations of a significantly large enough number of actors were such that they were no longer willing to accept counterproductive restraints on reform. For many democrats, economic failures made building a market economy more compelling than before. Indeed, "market" became the myth of salvation.

By the early 1990s, the level of social frustration had become very high. Citizens seemed to scold each other more than usual, push and shove with greater force, and frequently utter words of despair. Some clung to the myth of the Great Soviet Past, while others embraced the Glorious Western Present.[30] The black-and-white images of "bad capitalism" and "good socialism," championed in earlier days by official ideology, were replaced in popular culture by similarly crude images of "golden past" and "bleak present," which competed with "hopeless socialism" and "wonderful capitalism." Nuances and subtleties were hard to find.

These dichotomies entered the cinema, too. The extremely popular and controversial film *Tak Zhit' Nel'zia* (No Way to Live) (banned by the party authorities in Kirgizia) portrayed a violent and hard life in the Soviet Union, contrasting it with a comfortable one in the West.[31] In one part, the film compared militiamen, ill-equipped to perform their jobs and living in squalid and overcrowded housing, with policemen in the United States and West Germany, who could draw expensive guns quickly and who lived in pleasant housing. The film was a good example of crude glasnost—exposure of new issues without rigorous analysis. Problems of the New York City police force, such as corruption and an over-preparedness to use firearms, were not addressed; militiamen who did not live in cramped communal housing in the USSR were not shown. Emphasis fell on the poverty, inefficiencies, and weaknesses of the militia and its inability to tackle crime in a society that was becoming more violent, brutal, and mean. The film provoked moral shock and fear, creating a picture of an inadequate society that could not protect its citizens or properly administer justice and punishment. Moscow audiences gasped at the apparent slickness of police forces in the United States and the FRG, groaned at scenes of violence on home turf, muttered disapprovingly at interviews with Soviet criminals, and laughed and tutted at images of incompetence in the country's own militia.[32]

In this context of breakdown in economic distribution, uncertainty, and growing despair, how "the moment" was interpreted differed tremendously. Various social groups in early 1989 were talking of impending civil war. Radical reformers in September 1990 feared an army coup as troops moved near Moscow. Their demand for an explanation was met with two justifications: Troops were there to pick potatoes and to prepare for the 7 November demonstration (more than a month away!).[33] While democrats feared authoritarian clampdown, Leninists worried about instability, political disintegration, insecurity, a loss of privileges, and an end to socialist values. Patterns of discourse about reform were varied, changing, and increasingly heated.

Political Chaos, Confusion, and Conflict

Economic failure and growing social tension were accompanied in late 1989 and 1990 by political chaos, confusion, and strong nationalism. Although the power of the newly elected soviets was theoretically increasing, people's deputies frequently did not have copies of the draft laws on which they were voting. Draft laws came from the apparat and at best were improved only occasionally by astute lawyers such as Iurii Baturin, Mikhail Fedotov, and Vladimir Entin, who drew up "initiative author's drafts" (they hesitated to call them "alternative draft laws"), which they published privately at their own expense and distributed to people's deputies so that informed debate could take place and more polished clauses be adopted. This applied in the cases of the Law on the Press and the Law on Archives.[34]

The work of people's deputies was difficult in 1989 and 1990 for several reasons. At the city level, budgets gave insufficient money for the policies envisaged. Mayors such as Gavriil Popov and Anatolii Sobchak had limited financial possibilities, were constrained by bureaucratic restrictions of the old system still effectively in place, and were not helped by many of the old guard not yet removed from administrative positions. Deputies also lacked the political experience to tolerate the instabilities of democracy, and Sobchak in particular complained in 1990 that disagreements and political splits prevented him from accomplishing anything.[35] To remedy the situation, he suggested working in a more decisive manner through a smaller Presidium, a move thought by his critics to show authoritarian tendencies.[36] Sobchak's dilemma was that the variety of groups represented on the Lensovet frequently thwarted effective decision making. And the lack of party discipline, along with other factors, prevented the emergence of an effective party system. Legislative and executive chaos was among the consequences.

Decision making and policy implementation were also difficult at the local level. Elections in 1990 had returned deputies to district soviets. These deputies, however, were unsure of their powers and spheres of responsibility. Political struggles raged between district soviets and city soviets over property ownership, control of the militia, and other issues. Many, too, found "democracy" difficult to practice. Chaotic sessions, unruly commission meetings, and lengthy, unproductive debates were common.

Moreover, what democratization meant for different political groups and theorists varied enormously from 1988 to 1991. Socialists, greens, and anarchists condemned Popov and Sobchak as "bourgeois democrats," declaring that "we are different democrats," championing self-management, and fighting against the introduction of capitalist markets.[37] Conservatives in the party leadership, such as Egor Ligachev, disapproved of free markets, too, and saw bourgeois democratization as threatening the very fabric of socialist morality.[38] Democratization meant instability, unrealistic political demands, and disorder. Some Leninists warned of the rise of fascism. By contrast, members of the Democratic Union and owners of private cooperative businesses welcomed the ideas of free trade and saw democratization in the direction of a multi-party system as an associated and necessary development.

Gorbachev's own view of political reform changed substantially after 1985, temporarily maturing in the face of resistance to economic reforms and pressures for independence from the republics, but then rigidifying in

1990 and 1991 in light of political chaos and a reluctance to let independence proceed. Gorbachev had talked of socialist pluralism in 1987 and 1988, pluralism having been an ideologically taboo concept for many years.[39] But by 1990, even though he referred to pluralism without its socialist qualification, his critics saw him as betraying it, as subscribing to the concept in rhetoric only. By the end of 1990 and in early 1991, even though Gorbachev was perceived to be resorting to authoritarian methods again—his hands increasingly tied, some believed, by relentless pressures from conservatives in industry, defense, and agriculture and his actions restrained by his inability to rise above his own party background—a rejuvenated society continued to denigrate the political system in alternative political programs, at demonstrations, through fringe theater, and in jokes.

Glasnost, Democratization, Media, and Theater

Glasnost played an integral part in political transition and, predictably, was ultimately condemned by Leninists for having contributed to demagogy and chaos. Glasnost's strength grew after the Central Committee plenum of January 1987 and again after the Nineteenth Party Conference of June 1988. Its main contribution to the redefining of society and polity was that it enabled numerous non-topics of the past to develop into live issues. Subjects that had been taboo under Joseph Stalin, Nikita Khrushchev, and Leonid Brezhnev began to be aired in a wide range of newspapers, journals, and books, thereby undermining the lines, fabrications, and silences of the past. And topics that had already enjoyed lively or limited debate in the 1960s and 1970s, which were not entirely the decades of stagnation that Gorbachev called them, were now analyzed in even greater depth.

Like pluralism, terms such as "civil society," "social justice," "totalitarianism," and "Stalinist despotism" took on fresh meanings, at first, in 1987, tentatively, then with greater confidence in 1988 and 1989. Discourse on "old" and "new" issues was aided by the Resolution on Glasnost, adopted at the Nineteenth Party Conference, and by televised coverage in 1989 of the Congress of People's Deputies. Stormy debates spread in 1990 to newly elected soviets from republican to local levels. People's deputies reacted to discourse in the media and also influenced it.

The process of democratization and glasnost, notwithstanding their shortcomings and unevenness, facilitated and also required much freer discussion of social and political problems. Debates were also fueled by a more dynamic media, which began to provide far more roundtable discussions and probing investigative journalism. *Ogonek* (Flame), *Moskovskie Novosti* (Moscow News), *Komsomol'skaia Pravda* (Komsomol Truth), *Sobesednik* (Talking Partner), *Iunost'* (Youth), and others attracted larger readerships, and more lively television programs, such as "Vzgliad" (Viewpoint), "600 Sekund" (600 Seconds) and "Moskovskii Teletaip" (Moscow Teletype), earned riveted viewers for their exposure of long-hidden social problems.[40] Both the content and style of television changed. New, often revelatory information was imparted, and presentation was sometimes fast, punchy, and upbeat. Aleksandr Nevzorov's "600 Sekund" best typified this new television.[41]

Thanks to glasnost, plays by previously banned writers, such as Mikhail Bulgakov, were now performed. *Zoikina Kvartira* (Zoia's Flat) was staged at Moscow's Vakhtangov Theater, *Bagrovy Ostrov* (Purple Island) at Leningrad's Komissarzhevskaia, and *Blazhenstvo* (Blessing) at Moscow's new Sfera Studio. More politically charged plays, such as Mikhail Shatrov's *Brestkii Mir* (Brest Peace) were also shown at the Vakhtangov as early as 1987. Although *Brestkii Mir*'s portrayal of Nikolai Bukharin and Leon Trotsky was electric and earned the performances standing ovations, by 1990 rapidly moving agendas had already rendered the play tame and its content stale. More appropriate for the political context were amusing satires of the KGB and Stalin performed by Moscow University students' theater club, such as *Sinie Nochi KGB* (Dark Blue Nights of the KGB) and *Chernyi Chelovek* (Black Person). These, too, were soon dated.

In 1987 and 1988, receptive and eager audiences packed theaters. But by 1991, theaters were, at best, only half full. Demoralized, weary, and depressed citizens ceased to rush for tickets, worn down by the worsening pressures of daily life and locked into a psychology of despondence, despair, and lethargy. In April 1991, Franz Kafka's *Protsess* (The Trial) played to a miniscule audience of thirty at Moscow's Stanislavskii Theater on Gorky Street. The premier of Alexander Solzhenitsyn's *Olen' i Shalashovka* (The Male Novice and the Camp Tart) at old MXAT, directed by the famous Oleg Efremov, was just one-third full. This was remarkable since it was one of the first plays to be staged about life in a labor camp. Clearly, the thrill and exhilaration of glasnost were over. This seemed ironical given that during the preceding four years, critics of glasnost had attempted to dampen it for fear of its unsound influence on citizens. Now many people were ceasing to take note of its results, gripped by economic difficulties and mesmerized by the unbelievable price increases of 2 April 1991, which turned out to be mild in comparison with the tenfold increases that followed in January and February 1992.

Notwithstanding various attempts to curb debates in 1987, 1988, and 1989 by political actors such as Egor Ligachev, Vadim Medvedev, censors, and editorial boards, and despite efforts to keep discourse within the confines of traditional "socialist morality," by the early 1990s the lid had come off many issues, including the very sacrosanct topic of V. I. Lenin's responsibility for totalitarianism, terror, and seventy years of deformed socialism.[42]

While reformers applauded the new honesty in reporting, conservatives pointed to its destabilizing effects.

Openness did not proceed exponentially. Its route was halting, inconsistent, heterogeneous, reversible, and often extremely changeable. The law On Protecting the Honor and Dignity of the President surprised many, who immediately criticized it for going against the grain of liberalization. "In how many Western democracies is it an offense to insult the leader?" asked bewildered citizens.[43] This decree soured the atmosphere of glasnost and resulted in September 1990 in the old-style arrest of Valeriia Novodvorskaia, a leader of the Democratic Union who had to endure psychiatric tests, allegedly to establish her mental health.[44] Her arrest for criticizing Gorbachev in unacceptable terms and the curious assassination in the same month of the priest Aleksandr Men' served as constant reminders that glasnost and freedom of expression were fragile. Rumors in the capital were rife about whether the KGB, the Orthodox church, Pamiat, or a mad person was responsible for the murder of Men'.

Confidence in applying glasnost and the ability to seek redress for restrictions on freedom of speech were limited by judicial and social contexts. The absence of a legal state, despite a flood of rhetoric about its desirability, and the barely embryonic nature of a highly shaky civil society meant that legal protection of citizens' alleged freedoms was missing and that the space for exerting citizenship as a right or as a political activity was cramped and hazardous. Many fears and insecurities of the past complicated matters still further. Nonetheless, Gorbachev's advocacy of a combination of glasnost and democratization ensured the development of fresh discourses, which redefined society and polity in conceptual terms and led to political demands for changes in practice. In the process, new agendas were forged by new groups, movements, and political parties.

New Movements and New Agendas

Gorbachev's willingness to allow new informal groups and movements to form independent of the CPSU represented a significant break with the past. Those who automatically would have been labeled "enemy of the people" under Stalin and "dissident" under Khrushchev and Brezhnev now slowly were gaining legitimate political voices.

But, inevitably, from new movements came fresh interpretations of reality, new agendas, a concentration on different "problems," and an attempt to construct them as serious issues. Frequently, the aims of these movements went far beyond what Gorbachev deemed desirable. For instance, in Lithuania, how Sajudis assessed political reality and wished to redefine it in practice clashed with Gorbachev's proposals. In early 1989, Sajudis called for economic independence much louder than it had done in 1988. In fact, many of its members had political autonomy in mind. The movement was divided on the issue of timing—some wanted immediate political independence, while more cautious nationalists pragmatically emphasized a step-by-step approach, with economic independence first.[45] By 1990, Sajudis' agenda had become a more unanimous "sovereignty now," largely due to Gorbachev's handling of center-republic relations.

New movements championed a host of other issues, although nationalism was certainly among the most intractable and heated and was vitally connected to the key political question about the nature of the state. Ecologists pushed for protection of the environment.[46] Religious groups called for stronger moral foundations in society, advocating the need to combat atheism.[47] Ad hoc single-issue women's groups focused on the effect of military service on their sons, calling for benefits for veterans who had fought in Afghanistan and for investigations into the mysterious deaths of soldiers who were not in combat.[48] And among patriots preoccupied with Russian revival were those who produced anti-Semitic tracts, making Zionism a scapegoat for Russia's ills.[49]

Some agendas were shared by political actors in different movements, groups, and parties. Radical members of the CPSU and many social democrats and liberals outside the party pushed in 1988 for an end to the leading and guiding role of the CPSU. The Democratic Union had been calling for this change since its formation in 1988, although being a tiny group, the organization could not on its own exert sufficient pressure to ensure a favorable political outcome.[50] In the Congress of People's Deputies, members of the Inter-Regional Group made changes in the constitution one of their policy platforms.[51] But it was the split in the Lithuanian Communist Party that forced modification of Article 6 onto Gorbachev's agenda. Legislation in Lithuania, too, such as that on a multi-party system, outpaced the center.[52] Although Gorbachev had initially argued against the modification of Article 6, by 1990 he was being forced to embrace it.[53]

In this context, an informal press, tiny at first, began to flourish alongside the established one. Some papers and information bulletins came out sporadically because their producers often had difficulty procuring paper and finding presses willing to print these materials. Between 1987 and 1990, more newspapers, including weeklies, bimonthlies, and monthlies, appeared each year and enhanced tremendously press diversity, enlivening debate and controversy. They were vital to the process of redefining society and polity.

Sajudis put out *Soglasie* (Accord); the Latvian People's Front produced *Atmoda* (The Awakening), later renamed *Baltiiskoe Vremia* (Baltic Times); and the Estonian People's Front printed *Vestnik* (Herald). The Lithuanian Movement for Perestroika wrote *Kauno Aidas* (Kaunas Echo). More independent reporting was provided in *The Estonian Independent* and *The Lithuanian Review*. Both had English editions. *Atmoda*, too, began a special monthly English edition in 1989. Some new papers were put out in two languages, such as *Estl Elu: Estonian Life,* in Estonian and in English, and *Pilnigi Atklati: Sovershenno Otkrovenno* (Completely Frank), in Latvian and Russian. *Vpered* (Forward) was a new paper for Tartu, as was *Tartuskii Kur'er* (Tartu Courier). Newspapers of the Leningrad Popular Front included *Nevskii Kur'er* (Neva Courier), *Severo-Zapad* (North-West), and *Nabat* (Alarm, which became the organ of the Free Democratic Party of Russia).

New political parties produced an immense variety of newspapers. The Democratic Union put together *Uchreditel'noe Sobranie* (Constituent Assembly) in Leningrad, *Svobodnoe Slovo* (Free Speech) in Moscow, *Demokraticheskaia Svobodnaia Sibir'* (Democratic Free Siberia) in Novosibirsk, and many other publications. The Social Democratic Party of the Russian Federation compiled *Al'ternativa* (Alternative), while the Social-Democratic Association wrote *Esdek* (Social Democrat). *Novaia Zhizn'* (New Life) was also close to the Russian Social Democrats. The Russian section of the Latvian Social Democratic Party launched *Men'shevik* (Menshevik). *Demokraticheskaia Rossiia* (Democratic Russia) coined by the democratic forces of Russia, became the paper of the Democratic Party of Russia and then of Democratic Russia. The Democratic Party of Russia in 1991 put out *Demokraticheskaia Gazeta* (Democratic Newspaper). And *Grazhdanskoe Dostoinstvo* (Civic Dignity) became the weekly of the Union of Constitutional Democrats. In 1991, the Republican Party of the Russian Federation launched *Gospodin Narod* (Mr. Common Man). Under the slogan "Intellectuals of all countries unite," self-proclaimed supporters of the new soviets and the democratic intelligentsia produced *Novaia Rech'* (New Talk). The new workers' movement in the Kuzbass put out *Nasha Gazeta* (Our Paper).

Anarchists, too, made a visible contribution to political debates. Anarcho-syndicalists produced *Obshchina* (Commune) and *Volia* (Liberty), while the Anarcho-Communist Revolutionary Union put out *Chernoe Znamia* (Black Banner). The Moscow Union of Anarchists put together *Golos Anarkhizma* (Voice of Anarchism).

Calling for a moral dimension to the reform process, the Christian Democratic Union of Russia printed *Vestnik Khristianskoi Demokratii* (Christian Democratic Herald), while the Russian Christian Democratic Party put out *Khristianskaia Politika* (Christian Policy). A little later, the Russian Christian Democratic Movement compiled *Put'* (The Way). The Orel branch of the Russian Christian Democratic Movement produced *Slovo* (The Word), the Civilian Christian Democratic Direction put together *Narodnaia Khristianskaia Gazeta* (The Christian People's Newspaper), and the Church of the Russian Orthodox Christian Community sold *Slovo Khrista* (The Word of Christ). Evangelical Christian Baptists expressed their ideas in *Prot-*

estant, a newspaper that, in comparison with others, enjoyed extremely high-quality newsprint. A Jewish press appeared, too, such as *Litovskii Ierusalim* (Lithuanian Jerusalem) compiled by the Lithuanian Society of Jewish Culture, *Vestnik Evreiskoi Sovetskoi Kul'tury* (Herald of Jewish Soviet Culture), and *Evreiskaia Gazeta* (The Jewish Newspaper).

On the extreme right wing, the anti-zionist newspaper *Pamiat* (Memory) was produced in Novosibirsk under the slogan "Russia, Rus! Preserve yourself, preserve" and also in Moscow with the slogan "For faith, czar, and fatherland! Patriots of the world unite!" Another anti-Semitic paper was printed in Leningrad entitled *V Bloknot Patriota* (Patriot's Memo), which embraced the slogan "Watch out, zionism; watch out, zionism." *Informatsiia Dlia Razmyshleniia* (Food for Thought) provided a briefer anti-zionist information bulletin. *Volia Rossii* (Russia's Will), put together in Ekaterinburg, delivered similar anti-zionist messages.

Other papers preoccupied with the rebirth of Russia included *Vozrozhdenie Rossii* (Russian Rebirth), put out by the Russian People's Front; another *Vozrozhdenie Rossii,* the paper of the Leningrad oblast writers' organization; and *Otchizna* (Fatherland), released by the Leningrad Russian patriotic movement Otechestvo. *Voskresenie* (Resurrection) described itself as "a Russian independent paper"; *Vedomosti* (Gazette), a paper of Irkutsk *guberniia* (province), used the slogan "We need a great Russia"; and *Veche,* with its literary supplement *Zemskii Sobor* (Assembly of the Land), was published by Otechestvo. *Den'* (Day), describing itself as a paper of the "spiritual opposition," also championed the preservation and glorification of Russian culture. It sprang out of the conservative Russian Writers' Union, and its editor had close links with the general staff of the armed forces. The Ufa historical-patriotic council wrote *Sobornyia Vedomosti* (Church Assembly News), under the slogan "God is with us," and the Russian national-patriotic center in Vologda produced *Kulikovskaia Bitva* (The Battle of Kulikovo). The Rossiia group put out *Nasha Rossiia* (Our Russia). *Narodnye Novosti* (People's News), using the slogan "For God, Nation, and Labor" and appearing in 1991, was vitriolic in its attacks on intellectuals. The Liberal Democratic Party of the Soviet Union printed *Liberal* under the slogan "Through a pluralism of thought to the command of law," although its ideas were much closer to populist nationalism than to liberalism.

Patriotic papers incorporated various shades of monarchism. The most staunchly monarchist included *Prestol"* (The Throne), under the slogan "Orthodoxy, autocracy, nationality"; *Legitimist,* using the same czarist motto; *Dvuglavyi Orel"* (Double-headed Eagle), which called for "faith and loyalty"; the fortnightly *Vzgliad* (Viewpoint); and *Tsar' Kolokol"* (The Czar Bell), a fatter booklet of about sixty pages. Monarchism and anti-Semitism often blended together in these papers.

Those who defended traditional socialist values and who feared the implications of a market economy, such as the United Labor Front, produced *Chto Delat'?* (What Is to Be Done?). The Movement of Communist Initiative (supported by the Leningrad and other conservative communist regional committees) printed *Molniia* (Lightning). The Soiuz group put out *Politika* (Politics). Similar defenders of socialism and opponents of a breakup of the Union included the International Front of Workers of Latvia, whose paper *Edinstvo* (Unity) ran the slogan "For a Soviet socialist Latvia!" In *Vmeste i Naravne* (Together and Equal), the Socialist Federation of Workers of Lithuania took a more moderate line, advocating serious consideration of a union treaty. The Estonian *Interdvizhenie Estonii* (Estonian Intermovement) with its slogan "Proletarians of all countries, unite!", was much more hard-line, as was the Lithuanian *Interdvizhenie Litvy* (Lithuanian Intermovement), with its "Workers of Soviet republics, unite!" By contrast, reformist members of the CPSU in 1990 produced *Demokraticheskaia Platforma* (Democratic Platform).

Voters' groups made efforts to have their own papers, such as *Khronika* (Chronicle), which was put together by the All-Union Voters' Association. Weekly independent newspapers not tightly tied to one particular movement also appeared: *Sibirskii Kur'er* (Siberian Courier), *Ekspress-Khronika* (Express Chronicle), *Panorama, Grazhdanskii Referendum* (Citizen's Referendum), *Sodeistvie* (Aid), *Tainy Kremlevskogo Dvora* (Secrets of the Kremlin Court), and *Kur'er* (The Courier). Some included front-page slogans that stressed their independence. *Sodeistvie* described itself as "a non-party, nonconformist newspaper," and *Grazhdanskii Referendum* insisted it was "an independent, non-party paper."

Information bulletins flourished, too: *Baltiia* (The Baltic), a monthly digest of the Baltic press; *Sajudzio Zinios* (Herald of the Movement), information released by Sajudis; *Potentsial* (Potential), a Latvian information bulletin; *Armianskii Vestnik* (Armenian Herald), a monthly newspaper; *Fakt* (Fact), a weekly dealing with "the latest events"; *Informatsionnyi Biulleten'* (Information Bulletin), compiled by the Inter-Regional Group of people's deputies. Activists in different districts began to print local papers as well, such as *Kolpinskii Vestnik* (Kolpin Herald), the newspaper of Leningrad's Kolpinskii *raion,* and *U Nas na Iugo-Zapade* (Our South-West), founded in the southwest of Moscow by the *raikom.* Institutions also issued papers and journals, such as *Kuranty* (Chimes) and *Stolitsa* (The Capital) by the Mossovet, *Nevskoe Vremia* (Neva Times) by the Lensovet, *Rossiia* (Russia) by the Presidium of the Supreme Soviet of the RSFSR, and *Rossiiskaia Gazeta* (Russia's Newspaper) by the same Supreme Soviet. The radical Inter-Regional Group of people's deputies in the All-Union Supreme Soviet adopted the title *Narodnyi Deputat* (People's Deputy) for their paper. *Pravitel'stvennyi Vestnik* (Government Herald) was put out by the USSR's Cabinet of Ministers, and *Shchit i Mech* (Shield and Sword) was issued by the Ministry of Internal Affairs.

More commercially geared groups produced papers for those in business. The Union of United Cooperative Workers, for instance, wrote *Kommersant* (Businessman), and the Tallinn business club produced *Biznesmen* (Businessmen). *Delovye Liudi* (Business People) catered to those wishing to join the business world, and *Delovaia Zhenshchina* (Business Woman) targeted aspiring businesswomen. Glossy color papers also emerged, such as *PS: Baltic Review,* which advertised cars, showed fashions, displayed gourmet dishes, and carried naked pinups.

Groups describing themselves as "social," rather than "political," also developed a varied press. Sodruzhestvo, for example, produced *Pozitsiia* (Position), and the Committee of Social Defense compiled *Golos* (Voice). Complete with headings in the color green, Rebirth wrote *Zelenyi Ostrov* (Green Island). Other green publications included *Ekologicheskii Vestnik* (Ecological Herald), *Tretii Put'* (The Third Way), *Spasenie* (Rescue), *Ekologicheskaia Gazeta* (Ecological Gazette), and *Nabat* (Alarm). More narrowly focused groups, such as the Association for the Struggle Against AIDS, printed *SPID-Info* (AIDS-Info). The Association for the Struggle Against Sexually Transmitted Diseases put out *Venera Press* (Venus Press). Those interested in crime compiled *Kriminal'naia Khronika* (Criminal Chronicle). As reflections on private life grew, *Chastnaia Zhizn'* (Private Life) appeared, complete with a lonely hearts page and luring front-page headlines such as "Marry a foreigner ... a dream? No—reality!"[54]

In 1990 and 1991, various women's papers appeared, such as *Moskvichka* (Moscow Woman), *Leningradka* (Leningrad Woman), *Zhenshchina Do i Posle 18* (Women Under and Over 18), *Sudarushka* (Good Lady), and *Delovaia Zhenshchina.* Ol'ga Lipovskaia in Leningrad had been compiling *Zhenskoe Chtenie* (Women's Reading) earlier, but it had only a tiny print run of thirty to forty copies.[55]

In 1990, the range of pornographic materials on sale noticeably increased. They fall outside the scope of this book but included *Seks Daigest* (Sex Digest), *Bania* (The Bathhouse), *Sovershenno Intimno* (Totally Intimate), *Kagliostro* (Cagliostro), *Vse o Sekse* (Everything About Sex), *Seks-anekdoty* (Sex Stories), *Tekhnika Seksa* (Sexual Technique), and *Kama-sutra.*

Some of these newspapers, such as *Svobodnoe Slovo,* appeared as early as 1988. Many more came out in 1989 and 1990; then another fresh surge occurred in early 1991. One of the best independent daily newspapers, *Nezavisimaia Gazeta* (Independent Newspaper), began in 1991 with a loan from the Mossovet, its founder. New trade union papers also went on sale, such as *Solidarnost'* (Solidarity), put together by Moscow trade unions, and *Prolog* (Prologue), compiled by the Federation of Independent Trade Unions of Russia. And news of Moscow's outlying districts started in late August in *Podmoskovnye Izvestiia* (Moscow Area News).

The titles just listed represent a tiny selection of the new Russian-language newspapers. Hundreds of other papers were also produced in the languages of the republics. Initially, they were sold rather cautiously, under threat of arrest, on the Arbat and near Pushkin Square in Moscow and in Kazan Square in Leningrad. In 1989, some sellers kept their papers in closed brief-cases, all the while glancing nervously around, until a potential purchaser approached. During 1990, these papers and bulletins spread more openly in Moscow to Kalinin Prospekt. Then the party committee in the October district granted permission for them to be sold legally. Okt'iabrskaia metro station, and to a lesser extent Shabolovskaia, became a hive of activity. Right-wing and monarchist papers, however, were much less frequently spotted here than democratic, green, Christian democratic, and pornographic materials.

By 1990, and more obviously in 1991, many of these new publications were being sold in kiosks on the streets, in underpasses, in metro stations, and in hotel lobbies. New newspapers became highly visible in city centers. The furtiveness of 1989 was over, and the process of purchasing became more acceptable and routine. In 1989 and 1990, most new newspapers sold for fifty kopecks or one ruble, with pornographic materials fetching three rubles, even five. In 1991, consistent with the general price increases of 1 April, many papers went up from fifty kopecks to one ruble or from one ruble to two or three. As the notion of *biznes* (business) caught on, the same paper could be found selling at different prices. In August and September 1991, *SPID-Info* was being sold for three different amounts: one ruble twenty kopecks, two rubles, and occasionally three rubles, depending on the seller. Likewise, *Nezavisimaia Gazeta* was sold in kiosks at its stated price of forty kopecks or near escalators inside the metro for one ruble. Yeltsin's shock therapy sent the price of newspapers higher still. In February 1992, the official price of *Nezavisimaia Gazeta* in Moscow was one ruble twenty-five kopecks (and one ruble sixty kopecks outside the capital), but it was sold for more by those who resold it on the streets. Newspapers sold in the underpass by Pushkin Square now ranged from one to six rubles. By September, *Nezavisimaia Gazeta* had no fixed price and was generally being sold for five rubles.

The discourse and agendas of these papers varied according to their editors' interpretations of the current situation. Nevertheless, after 1989 the perception that the USSR was in crisis was a common theme. But assessments of the crisis and its consequences varied, as did suggested solutions.

Newspapers, Movements, and Conceptual Frameworks

The burst of new newspapers reflected a complex society divided over politics, economics, religion, and social change. As more information about the USSR became available, scholars in the West had to reflect again on the relevance of conceptual frameworks and research techniques applied to the study of state-socialist and other political systems. Significant changes in the Soviet political system made this reevaluation pressing. And the demise of communist regimes in Eastern Europe quickened the pace of interest. Were old approaches of utility? Which perspectives used in analyzing other systems might be relevant? Or should entirely new methodologies be adopted? These were the main questions.

Since the 1960s, studies of Soviet politics had been critical of the weaknesses of the totalitarian approach and sensitive to the importance of "groups" exerting pressures on the system or being consulted by political leaders.[56] The absence of a civil society, however, meant that the formation of groups was severely limited. Politically active groups tended to be products of the system, and their actions generally occurred in the context of highly restricted opportunities and possibilities. So although groups outside the top leadership were involved in the policy process, especially after the Brezhnev regime recognized that specialist advice was needed, the way in which democratic centralism had come to be practiced by the CPSU meant that the political leadership set priorities.[57] Policies were defined and formulated from above, notwithstanding disputes and conflicts among leaders, negotiations among bureaucrats, and pressures from specialists. Groups within the system might exert pressure or be co-opted, but the mass public generally remained outside the political arena. Millions of citizens were mobilized politically to show support for, and ritualized involvement in, the system, but they did not try on their own on a regular and predictable basis to contest it, transform it, or set its agendas.[58] Established structures through which to do this were wanting. A tiny number of active dissidents boldly committed to a diverse range of religious, nationalist, political, and other concerns were a thorn in the side of the regime. But they lacked political space for acceptable action.

Alternative discourses were prohibited in public, too. Sporadic attempts were made to register complaints and to put forward alternative views, but punishment generally followed. In 1962 in Novocherkassk, those who protested about price increases were either shot or deported. Members of the independent trade union movement, which tried to expose the irrationalities and corruption of industry, either lost their jobs or were arrested and sent to psychiatric hospitals.[59] Demonstrations by Crimean Tatars, or strikes by workers in Tol'iatti and Kiev, rarely went past the stage of circumscribed protest; they were not able in an authoritarian state-socialist system to reach or involve a broader attentive public.[60] Instruments of state control, such as a politicized legal system and the existence of the KGB and its network of informers, prevented or deterred any action beyond circumscribed protest, and the collectively constructed psychology of *Homo sovieticus* often held citizens back.[61] Harassment, arrest, detention, unfair trials, prison, psychiatric hospitals, and death were among the penalties.

Under Gorbachev, different viewpoints became legitimate, albeit initially within certain limits. Greater freedom of expression made for obvious conflicting arguments and different agendas. Once voiced openly, complex patterns became evident. For example, the "issue" of a redefinition of center-periphery relations was on many agendas in Moscow and in the capitals of the republics, but the details of the agenda in Vil'nius, Tbilisi, and Kishinev differed, and all three were at variance with the priorities expressed in Moscow.[62] The diversity of interpretations of the nationalities question alone was immense.[63]

Concepts and Definitions

Integral to this study of the redefining of society and polity are the concepts "discourse," "problem," "issue," and "agenda." Discourse is the central unit of analysis and refers to the terms, categories, images, suggestions, arguments, and interpretations of the problems under examination. Problems can exist in society for a long time but not necessarily be defined as such by political leaders. In the 1970s, homelessness, shantytowns, poverty, and a lack of contraception were some of the problems suffered by Soviet citizens. They were not, however, discussed in public political arenas. They were thus non-problems and non-topics. Only when a problem is identified and discussed widely in public does it exist. At this point, it is transformed into an issue. Homelessness became an issue at the end of the 1980s, as did many erstwhile non-problems, thanks to glasnost.[64]

Issues are both socially constructed and politically constructed. What journalists choose to investigate and publicize can influence what becomes an issue. To a large extent, they construct "news" by what they investigate and how they cover it. Pressure groups and aggrieved citizens may agitate for attention to problems affecting them, but their success in doing so depends on the receptivity and responsiveness of gatekeepers in journalism and in politics. Demonstrations that receive little or no press coverage cannot catch headlines or catapult overnight into social and political concerns. These observations apply to all political systems. However, in the case of the authoritarian state-socialist systems, the political controls affecting the construction of news and issues are considerably stronger. Under Gorbachev, the political construction from above of social and political issues became weaker because of democratization and glasnost. The tight ideological straitjacket that had for seventy years prevented an enormous number of genuine problems from becoming issues slackened. Thus, issues finally mushroomed.

Issues, however, have careers. Their fate depends on how they are constructed, who reacts to them and how, the political clout of backers and opponents, the availability of financial resources to tackle them, and the political willingness of leaders and policymakers to act and to implement necessary policies.[65]

An issue's career may be affected by which agendas it is on, how it is presented there, by whom it is supported, and which agendas it fails to make. The horrors of abortion clinics have been a problem for women for decades. They became an issue in the early 1980s in women's samizdat.[66] This agenda, however, was a powerless one. Few citizens were even aware of it, and male dissidents generally failed to take women's issues seriously. The official press and political arenas ignored the problem. It was not until the late 1980s that abortion became an issue. Then it reached the attentive public through articles in women's magazines such as *Rabotnitsa* (Working Woman) and youth newspapers such as *Sobesednik* (Talking Partner) and *Moskovskii Komsomolets* (Moscow Komsomol).[67] For action, however, the conditions in abortion clinics must appear on policy-making agendas, not just in critical articles. Attaining the status of issue does not guarantee satisfactory outcomes. How to improve the quality of care in abortion clinics was a low priority for the Supreme Soviets in 1990, even though women's magazines were calling for action. And it was insufficient for the Soviet Women's Committee or the *zhensovety* (women's councils) to be troubled by the issue. Even though each newly elected Supreme Soviet set up a commission to deal specifically with women's affairs, the family, and mother and child protection, it did not automatically follow that the abortion system would be overhauled. This required budgetary allocations and a radical change in the attitudes of hospital staff toward clients.

Taking a different direction, following developments in Poland, *Moskovskii Komsomolets* asked readers to sign an anti-abortion petition and post it to the European parliament.[68] Those in favor of a woman's right to decide immediately responded by demonstrating outside the newspaper's offices.[69] The controversy, however, now a visible issue, resulted neither in the banning of abortion nor in improvements in the service. Presentation of the issues had no immediate effect on policy outcomes; indeed, the issue did not reach formal agendas.

A variety of responses to numerous other issues also emerged in relatively powerless arenas. Many issues, involving both interested constituents who tried to mobilize opinion and policymakers, made their way onto more powerful agendas. But again, the presence of issues on government agendas did not always guarantee favorable outcomes for interested constituents, nor could it in the case of sharp conflict. Political will, workable compromises, and adequate resources were often lacking.

Political agendas may vary at all levels of government—All-Union, republic, region, town, and local district. Different political actors at each level may have different priorities. Thus, their agendas can be made up of different mixes of issues and imperatives. Social movements, organizations, and groups, which make demands on different administrative levels, add to the complexity. This does not render the concept of agenda redundant; it merely underlines that we should be aware of how simplistic talk of "*the* political agenda" is since it begs the question "Whose agenda?" In a heuristic sense, the term *agenda* alerts us to different perceptions, definitions, interpretations, and priorities. It aids the description of reality and heightens sensitivity to complexity but on its own cannot explain or offer quick answers.

I prefer in this book to examine discourse about new issues, rather than specific agendas, with a view to highlighting the diversity of social and political thought that developed as the momentum of change increased. This approach fills a gap in the literature by attempting to show how Soviet citizens made sense of reality around them—hence the focus on the images, concepts, and frameworks used by them. The intent is not to consider the outcome of issues or how the policy process responded to the problems identified. Indeed, to get close to political decision making and policy implementation in the years covered, case studies based on extremely thorough interviewing of the political actors involved would be required. Nonetheless, it is worth stressing here that the redefining of issues and the formation of formal and public agendas may, or may not, influence policy outcomes and certainly do not determine them. Moreover, different responses to controversial issues may provoke conflict without resolution, especially if resources are scarce and the political will to compromise is lacking. Non-decisions may then be among the outcomes. Or, in cases of zero-sum conflict, violence may be adopted as the only perceived way to further a cause. And, in addition, once issues have a presence on formal and/or public agendas, their content may radically alter over time and be redefined. Not only are agendas dynamic; so are the issues on them and how they are constructed and understood. Glasnost was one early facilitator of this dynamism.

NOTES

1. *Izvestiia*, 26 December 1991, p. 1. See, too, the front page of the previous day's *Izvestiia* for commentary on Gorbachev's last working day.

2. See *Pravda*, 6 February 1990, pp. 1–2.

3. *Materialy XXVII S"ezda KPSS* (Moscow, Politizdat, 1986), pp. 3–97; *Bakinskii Rabochii,* 1 October 1986, p. 1.

4. *Materialy XXVII S"ezda KPSS,* p. 60. See, too, Mikhail Gorbachev, *Perestroika i Novoe Myshlenie Dlia Nashei Strany i Dlia Vsevo Mira* (Moscow, Politizdat, 1987), p. 72.

5. For early remarks on the importance of criticism and self-criticism, see *Materialy XXVII S"ezda KPSS,* p. 80. Mention of new thinking is made in Gorbachev, *Perestroika,* p. 141.

6. Passivity was also deeply rooted in political culture, which predated socialism. Under the czars, Russians lacked legitimate political channels through which to express grievances. They also feared the secret police and were not encouraged to take initiative. See Richard Pipes, *Russia Under the Old Regime* (Harmondsworth, Penguin, 1977); Stephen White, *Political Culture and Soviet Politics* (London, Macmillan, 1979). Historians, however, have made the point that political culture did not preclude political activity. Nor should one automatically assume passivity. See Linda Edmondson, "Was there a movement for civil rights in Russia in 1905?" in Olga Crisp and Linda Edmondson, eds., *Civil Rights in Imperial Russia* (Oxford, Clarendon, 1989), pp. 269–275.

7. I. A. Goncharov, *Oblomov* (Moscow, Gosizdat Khudozhestvennoi Literatury, 1963).

8. Mikhail S. Gorbachev, "O khode realizatsi reshenii XXVII S"ezda KPSS i zadachakh po uglubleniiu perestroiki," *KPSS: XIX Vsesoiuznaia Konferentsiia Kommunisticheskoi Partii Sovetskogo Soiuza, 28 Iunia–1 Iiulia 1988 g: Stenograficheskii Otchet,* vol. 1 (Moscow, Politizdat, 1988), pp. 29–92.

9. A. V. Gromov and O. S. Kuzin, *Neformaly: Kto Est' Kto* (Moscow, Mysl', 1990); D. V. Ol'shanskii, *Neformaly: Gruppovoi Portret v Inter'ere* (Moscow, Pedagogika, 1990); V. I. V'iunitskii, *Neformaly: Kto Oni? Kuda Zovut?* (Moscow, Politizdat, 1990); Informatsionnyi Tsentr Moskovskogo Narodnogo Fronta, *Samodeiatel'nyi Obshchestvennye Organizatsii SSSR (Spravochnik)* (Moscow, 1988); Vladimir Brovkin, "Revolution from below: Informal political associations in Russia, 1988–1989," *Soviet Studies,* vol. 42, no. 2, 1990, pp. 233–257; Richard Sakwa, *Gorbachev and His Reforms, 1985–1990* (London, Philip Allen, 1990), pp. 200–230; Geoffrey Hosking, *The Awakening of the Soviet Union* (London, Mandarin, 1990), pp. 55–81, 170–185; Judith B. Sedaitis and Jim Butterfield, *Perestroika from Below: Social Movements in the Soviet Union* (Boulder, Westview, 1991).

10. *Izvestiia,* 16 October 1990, pp. 1–2.

11. *Zakon Soiuza Sovetskikh Sotsialisticheskikh Respublik o Vyborakh Narodnykh Deputatov SSSR* (Moscow, Izvestiia Sovetov Narodnykh Deputatov SSSR, 1988).

12. *Ogonek* readers gave diverse responses to this question. See *Ogonek,* no. 7, February 1988, pp. 4–5. For a humorous but serious commentary see Aleksandr Ivanov, "Nadeius," *Moskovskie Novosti,* no. 26, 26 June 1988, p. 12.

13. The sugar shortage was partly related to Gorbachev's anti-alcohol campaign, which had been launched in 1985. Difficulties in obtaining spirits resulted in increases in the production of *samogon,* or bootleg vodka. The *samogonchiki* were berated in the media for buying up vast quantities of sugar.

14. Information based on conversations in Moscow, 1990.

15. This reason was given on Moscow radio.

16. *Sovetskaia Abkhaziia,* 21 August 1990, p. 1.

17. *Sovetskaia Abkhaziia,* 25 August 1990, p. 1.

18. *Visitki* were frequently not asked to be shown, particularly for the purchase of basic staples. Thus, the law was incompletely enforced.

19. According to official Soviet statistics, the 1990 harvest was 218 million tons. This was an improvement over the 1988 and 1989 harvests of 195 million tons and 211 million tons, respectively. In 1991, the harvest fell disastrously to 165 million tons. For details, see *The Independent,* 31 October 1991, p. 1.

20. Discussions with students at Moscow University, autumn 1990. For a more general discussion of youth, refer to Jim Riordan, *Soviet Youth Culture* (London, Macmillan, 1989).

21. The Shatalin plan was put together by a group of economists who came to be known as the Shatalin group because they were headed by Stanislav Shatalin. The group included Nikolai Petrakov, Grigorii Iavlinskii, Mikhail Zadornov, Aleksei Mikhailov, and Boris Fedorov. The group produced "Transition to the market: Conception and program," together with twenty-one drafts of accompanying legal acts. Its goal was to attain rapid transition to a market economy and privatization. For details, refer to Anders Aslund, *Gorbachev's Struggle for Economic Reform,* 2d ed. (London, Pinter, 1991), pp. 208–212.

22. Distinct from the Shatalin plan, the government put together a different program worked out by Nikolai Ryzhkov, Leonid Abalkin, Valentin Pavlov, and others. Gorbachev was expected to support the Shatalin plan. Instead he vacillated, sought a compromise between the two plans, and then dropped both. See Aslund, *Gorbachev's Struggle for Economic Reform,* ibid.

23. *Kuranty,* 13 December 1990, p. 7.

24. *Moskovskie Novosti,* no. 3, 20 January 1991, p. 1.

25. Eduard Shevardnadze, *Moi Vybor: V Zashchitu Demokratii i Svobody* (Moscow, Novosti, 1991), pp. 287–331.

26. Gavriil Popov, "Perspektivy i realii," *Ogonek,* no. 50, December 1990, pp. 6–8; and continued under the same title in *Ogonek,* no. 51, December 1990, pp. 5–8.

27. For information about Sajudis, consult *Soglasie.* For details about Rukh, see Vladimir Paniotto, "The Ukrainian Movement for Perestroika," *Soviet Studies,* vol. 43, no. 1, 1991, pp. 177–181; Solomea Pavlychko, "Between feminism and nationalism: New women's groups in the Ukraine," in Mary Buckley, ed., *Perestroika and Soviet Women* (Cambridge, Cambridge University Press, 1992), pp. 92–95.

28. A. I. Yakovlev, "Nuzhen novyi shag," *Izvestiia,* 2 July 1991, p. 2.

29. *Kuranty,* 25 July 1991, p. 1; *Argumenty i Fakty,* no. 29, July 1991, p. 2.

30. Citizens did not explicitly refer to the Great Soviet Past or the Glorious Western Present. These are labels I devised to capture a range of arguments heard in 1990, which can be subsumed under them.

31. William G. Rosenberg noted how in 1918 workers in Petrograd declared, "Tak dal'she zhit' nel'zia" (We cannot live like this further). See his "Russian labor

and Bolshevik power after October," *Slavic Review*, vol. 44, no. 2, Summer 1985, p. 233. Similarly, in 1904–1905, according to Linda Edmondson, this was almost a cliché slogan of the Russian opposition. See her "Was there a movement for civil rights in Russia in 1905?" in Crisp and Edmondson, eds., *Civil Rights in Imperial Russia*, p. 267. Edmondson cited a banquet in 1904 at which "all the speeches were fired by a single burning conviction: that to live as we have done up to now is no longer possible."

32. Jokes about the incompetence of the police were not new to Soviet society. A popular one in recent years was as follows:

QUESTION: Why do militiamen go about in threes?

ANSWER: One can read but cannot write. Another can write but is unable to read. And the third, who can neither write nor read, must keep an eye on these intelligent ones.

See E. F. Orlov, ed., *Politicheskie Anekdoty* (Moscow: Galaktika, 1990), p. 22.

33. Relayed on radio at the time. Rumors in the capital were also rife.

34. Iu. M. Baturin, M. A. Fedotov, and V. L. Entin, *Zakon o Pechati i Drugikh Sredstvakh Massovoi Informatsii: Initsiativnyi Avtorskii Proekt* (Moscow, Iuridicheskaia Literatura, 1989); Iu. M. Baturin, B. S. Ilizarov, A. B. Kamenskii, M. A. Fedotov, E. I. Khan-Pira, O. B. Shchemeleva, and V. L. Entin, *Zakon ob Arkhivnom Dele i Arkhivakh: Initsiativnyi Avtorskii Proekt* (Moscow, Iuridicheskaia Literatura, 1990).

35. Andrei Chernov, "Neuzheli voda 'zatsvetet,'" *Moskovskie Novosti*, no. 19, 13 May 1990, p. 5; and Andrei Chernov, "2:1 pol'zu sil'noi ruki," *Moskovskie Novosti*, no. 41, 14 October 1990, p. 4.

36. Information given by people's deputies Aleksandr Lukin and Valerii Fadeev from the Liberal Group of the Moscow City Soviet. Talk given at the School for Slavonic and East European Studies, University of London, 17 October 1990.

37. Mary Buckley, "Brezhnev era takes on a rosy glow amid the economic gloom," *Glasgow Herald*, 13 November 1990, p. 13.

38. Egor Ligachev became a member of the Politburo in April 1985. Since 1983, he had been head of the Department of Party Organizational Work of the Central Committee. For a while he was de facto second secretary to Gorbachev and supervised ideology as well as party organization. In 1988, Ligachev was shunted into agriculture. For further details, see Archie Brown, ed., *The Soviet Union: A Biographical Dictionary* (London, Weidenfeld and Nicolson, 1990), pp. 216–217.

39. Archie Brown, "Political change in the Soviet Union," *World Policy Journal*, Summer 1989, p. 475; *Pravda*, 30 September 1987, p. 1.

40. *Moskovskie Novosti*, no. 8, 21 February 1988, p. 2.

41. For scrutiny of the role of Gosteleradio, see Ellen Mickiewicz, *Split Signals: Television and Politics in the Soviet Union* (New York, Oxford University Press, 1988); James Dingley, "Soviet Television and Glasnost'," in Julian Graffy and Geoffrey A. Hosking, eds., *Culture and the Media in the USSR Today* (London, Macmillan, 1989), pp. 6–25.

42. Vadim Medvedev was a member of the Politburo and Central Committee sec-

retary for ideology from September 1988 to July 1990. For further details, refer to Brown, ed., *The Soviet Union,* pp. 242–243.

43. This question was reiterated throughout late 1990 and 1991 in interviews with liberal historians in Moscow. Some historians in favor of reform supported the *ukaz* on the grounds that it was essential to instill respect for the president.

44. *Svobodnoe Slovo,* 12 March 1991, p. 1; Nataliia Gevorkian, "Valeriiu Novodvorskuiu obviniaiut v oskorblenii Presidenta," *Moskovskie Novosti,* no. 39, 30 September 1990, pp. 1, 5.

45. Discussions with members of Sajudis in Vilnius, March 1989. See also *Sajudzio Zinios,* information letter, no. 60, 28 January 1989; *Soglasie,* no. 4, 14 March 1989; *Soglasie,* no. 9, 12 June 1989; *Soglasie,* no. 14, 27 September 1989.

46. See "Greens: Ecological Catastrophe" in Chapter 9.

47. See "Christians: The Evil of Atheism" in Chapter 9.

48. The Committee of Soldiers' Mothers formed in Moscow and Leningrad in 1989. For details, see Ol'ga Lipovskaia, "New women's organisations," in Buckley, ed., *Perestroika and Soviet Women,* pp. 76–77. The Organization of Soldiers' Mothers of the Ukraine was set up in 1990. It called for a professional Ukrainian army of volunteers, not conscripts. See Pavlychko, "Between feminism and nationalism," pp. 94–95.

49. See the sections on patriots and monarchists in Chapter 9.

50. See, for instance, Demokraticheskii Soiuz, *Paket Dokumentov* (Moscow, 9 May 1988); and *Uchreditel'noe Sobranie,* no. 2, July 1989, p. 1.

51. *Narodnyi Deputat,* no. 34, 28 July 1989, p. 2.

52. *Sovetskaia Litva,* 21 December 1989, p. 1. For examples of Lithuanian legislation outpacing All-Union laws, see "Postanovlenie o politicheskikh partiiakh," *Vedomosti Verkhovnogo Soveta i Pravitel'stva Litovskoi Sovetskoi Sotsialisticheskoi Respubliki,* no. 36, 31 December 1989, p. 537; and "Zakon o grazhdanstve Litovskoi SSR," *Vedomosti Verkhovnogo Soveta i Pravitel'stva Litovskoi Sovetskoi Sotsialisticheskoi Respubliki,* no. 30, 3 November 1989, pp. 747–755.

53. *Pravda,* 6 February 1990, pp. 1–2.

54. *Chastnaia Zhizn',* no. 4, 1991, p. 1.

55. Mary Buckley, "Gender and reform," in Catherine Merridale and Chris Ward, eds., *Perestroika: The Historical Perspective* (Dunton Green, Edward Arnold, 1991), pp. 72–74.

56. At a time when the concept of totalitarianism became fashionable inside the USSR, it had already endured more than twenty years of criticism by Western social scientists for its inadequacies. For an incisive critique, see Robert Burrowes, "Totalitarianism: The revised standard version," *World Politics,* vol. 21, no. 2, January 1969, pp. 272–294. For early advocacy of the importance of groups, refer to H. Gordon Skilling and Franklyn Griffiths, eds., *Interest Groups and Soviet Politics* (Princeton, Princeton University Press, 1971).

57. How much access and influence groups have enjoyed is contentious. Access has varied according to historical period, issue, and the group concerned. See Peter Solomon, *Soviet Criminologists and Criminal Policy: Specialists in Policy-Making* (New York, Columbia University Press, 1978); Thane Gustafson, *Reform in Soviet*

Politics: Lessons of Recent Policies on Land and Water (Cambridge, Cambridge University Press, 1981); Susan Gross Solomon, ed., *Pluralism in the Soviet Union* (London, Macmillan, 1983).

58. For a discussion of low politics, refer to Seweryn Bialer, *Stalin's Successors: Leadership, Stability and Change in the Soviet Union* (Cambridge, Cambridge University Press, 1980).

59. Viktor Haynes and Olga Semyonova, *Workers Against the Gulag* (London, Pluto, 1979).

60. Edward Allworth, *Tatars of the Crimea* (Durham, N.C., Duke University Press, 1988). For a discussion of strikes, consult Betty Gitwitz, "Labor unrest in the Soviet Union," *Problems of Communism,* November-December 1982, pp. 25–42.

"Attentive public" refers to those in society who are especially interested in a given issue, or issues, and who are most informed. A distinction can be drawn between attentive public and the "general public," whose members may be the last to become involved in controversies and are less likely to sustain their interest in them.

61. Alexander Zinoviev, *Homo Sovieticus* (London, Victor Gollancz, 1985).

62. For further details on Georgian politics, see Jonathan Aves, "Opposition political organisations in Georgia," *Slovo,* vol. 3, no. 1, May 1990, pp. 18–39.

63. "Outsider groups" refers to formations outside the government.

64. For discussions of non-issues and non-decisions, refer to Peter Bachrach and Morton Baratz, "Two faces of power," *American Political Science Review,* vol. 56, no. 4, September 1962, pp. 947–952; Raymond E. Wolfinger, "Non-decisions and the study of local politics," *American Political Science Review,* vol. 65, no. 4, December 1971, pp. 1063–1080.

65. It had been argued that, despite variations in the "careers" of issues, they can usefully be seen as shaped by initiation, specification, expansion, and entrance. Initiation refers to the articulation of a grievance in very general terms by a group outside the formal governmental structure. Specification is the expression of the grievance into a specific demand. Expansion is the application of pressure or interest to attract the attention of decision-makers; without this, the issue will not get onto formal agendas. Entrance represents movement from the public agenda to the formal agenda. Inevitably the likelihood of success varies according to the nature of the political system. See Roger Cobb, Jennie-Keith Ross, and Marc Howard Ross, "Agenda building as a comparative political process," *American Political Science Review,* vol. 70, no. 1, March 1976, pp. 126–138.

66. Vera Golubeva, "The other side of the medal," in Women in Eastern Europe Group, trans., *Women and Russia: First Feminist Samizdat* (London, Sheba, 1980), pp. 51–56.

67. See the section on abortion in Chapter 4.

68. *Moskovskii Komsomolets,* 1 March 1991, p. 1.

69. *Moskovskii Komsomolets,* 5 March 1991, p. 1.

2

Interpretations of Glasnost

> *1990. Telephone conversation.*
> *"Vas', have you read today's* Sovetskaia Molodezh' *[Soviet Youth]? Something special is written there!"*
> *"Really, what?"*
> *"Oh, it's not for the telephone."*[1]

GLASNOST MEANS "PUBLICITY," or "openness," but not necessarily in a broad sense of "openness about everything." When, in 1986, Gorbachev began applying the term more frequently to economy, society, and polity, he viewed glasnost as relative to perestroika and as delimited by it. Glasnost was one means to the end of perestroika, there to serve its goals. Glasnost was not unbridled. It was not supposed to be a phenomenon in its own right; it was not meant to gallop ahead of officially defined perestroika or deviate from its track. Rather, perestroika and glasnost were linked, with the former calling the tune. Gorbachev told the Twenty-seventh Party Congress in February 1986 that measures for the "strengthening" and "broadening" of glasnost had to be adopted. He observed that "this question is political. Without glasnost there is not, and cannot be, democracy, political creativity of the people, or their participation in management."[2]

Glasnost: The Means to Perestroika

Gorbachev's vision was for glasnost to facilitate perestroika and to work in tandem with it, especially in shaking up those stuck in the "old ways." Glasnost would unmask the failings of the past and lead to more informed policy debates based on sounder information. Glasnost would identify problems that had to be dealt with and delimit issues. Glasnost would expose conservative opponents of perestroika who resisted implementing *khozraschet*. Glasnost would prompt workers to become more active, take initiative, and criticize the weaknesses of their bosses. Glasnost would ease "criticism and self-criticism" and lead to a "new psychology." Glasnost would contribute to the shake-up of a petrified political system, uncover deceptions of the past, and instill responsibility for the present. Glasnost would enliven the arts and contribute to the demise of dull socialist realism. Thus, glasnost would aid honesty in reporting, economic reform, political accountability, and cultural expression. Glasnost was essential if reality was to be redefined.

In 1987, official commitment to glasnost strengthened and so did readiness to apply it. This was particularly so after the January plenum of the Central Committee (delayed more than once because of disagreements about economic reforms) at which Gorbachev vigorously attacked those opposed to change. Against those who criticized the Politburo for "taking too drastic a turn," Gorbachev argued that the situation in the country was complex and in need of serious analysis: "Only a deep understanding of the situation can enable us to find correct solutions to complex tasks."[3] Glasnost was therefore vital.

Although Gorbachev had tried to push through more far-reaching political changes, such as the election of party officials, and failed, his message about glasnost was sufficiently loud for supporters to wield it with added confidence. Publications in 1987 and 1988 became much livelier. Novels, short stories, and academic articles even began to criticize Stalinism and debate the significance of the 1920s and 1930s, thereby aiding Gorbachev's call for a reform process based upon a sound knowledge of the past.[4] And many citizens wanted answers about Stalin's crimes, Bukharin's trial, the reasons for the Chernobyl nuclear accident, and a host of other questions. Much, however, was still not criticized openly, such as Lenin's leadership, violence in the Soviet army, and the repressiveness of the KGB. Nevertheless, the limits of acceptable debate broadened significantly in 1987 and more so in 1988. Changing political context and encouragement in official speeches affected the extent to which glasnost was applied.

The Nineteenth Party Conference of mid-1988 gave glasnost an additional spurt. Gorbachev called the conference to push democratization further, a move that was itself unprecedented for breaking the routine of Soviet politics. Although in the recent past, congresses had generally convened every five years, the last party conference had met almost a half-century earlier. Gorbachev was impatient to accelerate political reform and did not wish to wait until the next party congress, scheduled for 1991 (but in fact brought forward to 1990), to do so. He was also impatient to challenge continued conservative resistance to reform. To put his call for "radical" political reform to a specially convened conference was a remarkable, and imaginative, achievement. Although Gorbachev may not have received all that he wanted out of the Nineteenth Party Conference, and notwithstanding fierce debates and opposition to political reform, recommendations for a new electoral system were supported when put to a vote.[5] Nevertheless, many deputies may not have grasped the full implications of electoral change or anticipated the speed of its subsequent implementation. When in December 1988 the Supreme Soviet ratified a new and hastily prepared electoral law designed to revitalize and transform the soviets, an important precondition for the injection of glasnost into electoral campaigns and parliamentary debates was met.[6]

These developments were accompanied by the formation of numerous informal social and political groups, the mobilization of which was furthered by new emphases in CPSU policies. Quick to take initiative, citizens in the Baltic states set up people's fronts. These were mass movements that favored perestroika and were designed to promote it. Thus, Gorbachev welcomed them. By October 1988, the Lithuanian Movement for Perestroika was claiming to have 180,000 supporters.[7] New social groups, political clubs, and movements subsequently proliferated as the political momentum of democratization stepped up and as citizens became increasingly confident to act.

Although Gorbachev had hoped that movements championing perestroika would strengthen his hand against those in the CPSU who resisted reform, the demands that soon emanated from popular fronts went beyond the officially sanctioned goals of perestroika. Movements in each of the Baltic states, after declaring support for reforms, next called for economic independence and a restoration of civil rights. Pressure for political sovereignty followed. The election of nationalists to the Congress of People's Deputies in 1989 and then to the Supreme Soviets in the republics in late 1989 and 1990 gave their aspirations an institutionalized legitimacy and provided them with an authoritative platform from which to struggle for the implementation of election manifestos. As representatives of the people, they had mandates to fulfill. Glasnost in their speeches and declarations was frequently turned against the authority of the CPSU and then against that of the general secretary. But not only were the legal powers of the CPSU questioned; after March 1990 the authority of the president of the USSR was questionable since the legitimacy of the Union itself was suspect. A discourse had developed in the Baltic states that challenged Gorbachev's understanding of center-republic relations.

Glasnost Outstripping Perestroika

By 1988, glasnost was outstripping perestroika, or to put it in Gorbachev's more modest assessment to the Nineteenth Party Conference, "Perestroika has pushed glasnost to the forefront."[8] Yet Gorbachev wanted still more glasnost, convinced, as he was, of its value to reform. At the same time, he became anxious by what he viewed as its abuse. Although he recognized that "glasnost presupposes a pluralism of opinions on all questions of home and international policy, a free play of different points of view, and discussion," he also warned that "like any other feature of democracy, glasnost presupposes a high sense of responsibility. It is incompatible with any claim to monopoly of opinion, with imposition of dogmas in place of those that we have rejected. It is incompatible with group interests, and more so with any distortion of the facts and with any settling of personal scores."[9] In Gorbachev's view, whereas some had embraced glasnost too vigorously, especially those who were uncovering problems that he did not wish to become political issues, still others were hesitating to wield it at all: "At the same time, comrades, facts are still suppressed and criticisms punished—and we must say so bluntly at our Conference. We come up against this in party organizations, in work collectives, in social organizations, in the governmental apparatus, and in relations with the mass media." Some officials, he declared, were responding "furiously" to criticism or were trying to "gag" and "persecute" defenders of the truth.[10] Gorbachev was flanked by radicals keen for a more thorough application of glasnost and conservatives who resisted it.

In 1988, Gorbachev was riding on the crest of political developments; he appeared to be using them to his political advantage, was not yet overwhelmed by them or lagging behind them, and was focusing his main struggle against the conservatives who resisted reform. He remained wholeheartedly committed to glasnost. The Resolution on Glasnost adopted at the Nineteenth Party Conference began by stating that "further development of glasnost" was one of the conference's "most important political tasks" and would be "guided by the interests of socialism and perestroika." In fact, glasnost was a "sharp weapon" in the service of perestroika and should be deepened since "large amounts of information are still inaccessible to the general public, are not being used for accelerating socio-economic and cultural development or for enhancing the political culture of the people and administrative cadres."[11] Moreover, "there are attempts to restrain glasnost in Party, soviet and social organizations, work collectives, and the mass media."[12] These attempts had to be challenged.

Gorbachev unswervingly defended glasnost, even though by 1988 he must have been exasperated by many of its results, some of which were backfiring on him, particularly in the republics. Gorbachev was vexed, for instance, by an emergency session of the Estonian Supreme Soviet, which on 17 November 1988, proclaimed the "sovereignty" of Estonia. Deputies were angry about Gorbachev's planned amendments to the Soviet constitution, which, they argued, restricted the rights of republics. To prevent this, they supported the right of the Estonian Supreme Soviet to veto legislation from Moscow.[13] When the Lithuanian Supreme Soviet failed to follow the Estonian example, members of Sajudis, which had formed the month before, took to the streets.

By now, demonstrations were no longer a rarity in the Baltic states. They had begun in August 1987 to mark forty-seven years of Soviet annexation. Very quickly, demonstrators developed the confidence to carry national flags and to champion slogans such as "Down with occupation" and "We are for a free Latvia in the European Community."[14] Popular fronts that had formed to support perestroika soon demanded more far-reaching changes. For nationalists, unwanted domination by Russians was the issue. Quickly moving to the top of their agenda was the question "How soon independence?"[15] Problems that Gorbachev had identified, such as the sterility of an electoral system in which citizens had only one candidate for whom to vote, became redefined by other political actors into broader issues of center-republic relations. Discourse on reform became charged by historical grievances, which influenced how nationalists recast issues tabled by Gorbachev.

Democratization and glasnost enabled and enlivened the politicization of the people, out of which came nationalist demands, tensions among nationalities (not always involving Russians), conflicts in relations with Moscow, and challenges to the authority of the CPSU and its leadership. The resulting processes of decentralization and fragmentation were varied and complex, notwithstanding the common consequence of independence. How the leadership of the CPSU responded to nationalist demands affected subsequent nationalist developments; and a ripple effect across nationalities, often the result of political links that they established for support and coordination, boosted confidence to act, as did the collapse in 1989 of the Soviet hold over Eastern Europe. Once nationalism was established as an issue, however, glasnost's decisive role was reduced. Final outcomes depended on political struggles.

A complication for the CPSU leadership was that different demands and pressures came simultaneously from different parts of the union. Immediately after people's deputies in Estonia had argued in favor of veto power, on 18 November 1988, a one-day general strike in Erevan supported demands that Nagorno-Karabakh be transferred to Armenia from Azerbaidzhan.[16] Nagorno-Karabakh was an autonomous oblast within the republic of Azerbaidzhan, but the majority of the people living there were Armenian. Also disputed was the autonomous republic of Nakhichevan, which was part of Azerbaidzhan but was actually separated from the rest of Azerbaidzhan's territory by Armenia, which ran between them. The issues here concerned the administration of territory. Tensions had been building in the Caucasus throughout 1988 and had included bloody massacres.[17] Reprisals and revenge led to a spiral of clashes between bands of Azerbaidzhani and Armenian self-defense groups. Curfews were imposed but often ignored. By December 1988, forty-eight thousand Armenians were said to have fled from Azerbaidzhan to Armenia and forty thousand Azerbaidzhanis the other way.[18] A serious refugee problem resulted. In 1989, tensions escalated further, which Gorbachev was unable to control. The result was protracted civil war. Gorbachev's agenda became how best to restore law and order and quiet Armenian claims.

Different newspapers wielded different strengths of glasnost in covering these violent events. *Bakinskii Rabochii,* for instance, the daily paper of Azerbaidzhan's Communist Party, markedly changed its style of reporting during 1988 but all the time focused on the question of who was to blame for the disturbances. At the beginning of the year, the tragedy of the massacre in Sumgait was put down to "hooligans" and "bandits." Armenians and Azerbaidzhanis were described as peace-loving friends. The first secretary of Armenia at the time, Karen S. Demirchian, was quoted as saying, "Friendship of the Armenian and Azerbaidzhani peoples comes from the depths of centuries. ... I believe not one Armenian, not one Azerbaidzhani, would cast a shadow of doubt on this."[19] When tensions over Nagorno-Karabakh grew in June, *Bakinskii Rabochii* reported that Armenians living there had declared, "Comrades. We Armenians have lived for many years in Shushin district in harmony and peace with Azerbaidzhanis. We do not wish to change the border. But because some want to change it, we find we are ashamed to look in the eyes of our Azerbaidzhani brothers and sisters. None of us has ever suffered from nationalism."[20] The paper attempted to create a picture of different peoples living harmoniously, disrupted only by a minority of troublemakers. The seriousness of clashes was often played down, and honesty in reporting the scale of tension, and its implications, was lacking.

In June, the message from *Bakinskii Rabochii* shifted from "Most Armenians and Azerbaidzhanis are not bandits" to "Most are not nationalists." Now "nationalists" were being constructed as the new "folk devil." Abdul Rakhman Vezirov, Azerbaidzhan's first secretary, proclaimed that "anti-perestroika forces" were trying to compromise democratization and glasnost, inflame nationalism, and provoke debauchery and a revelry of passions. He linked nationalists to "social parasites" and to "drunkards" who distributed narcotics.[21] And he lumped together nationalists, parasites, and drunkards as anti-perestroika forces.

As the containment of conflict failed, blame shifted yet again. In November 1988, *Bakinskii Rabochii* charged that the culprits were Armenians, the official Armenian information service, and the Armenian republic. Armenian anti-perestroika forces were allegedly responsible for illegal activities in Nagorno-Karabakh and for the refugee problem.[22] In the space of a year, those responsible had changed from bandits, to nationalists, to Armenians. For those relying on *Bakinskii Rabochii* as a source of information,

Azerbaidzhanis were largely blameless. Thus, glasnost could be used to serve political ends and construct self-interested images as well as impart unbiased information or provide more honest reporting.

Another form of political behavior that Gorbachev viewed as disruptive of perestroika was strike action. Strikes, like demonstrations, became more frequent, particularly during and after 1989. In the Ukrainian Donbass and Siberian Kuzbass, protesting miners struck over living standards, the lack of soap, and working conditions. Gorbachev told people's deputies in Moscow that "people hostile to the Soviet system" were attempting "to manipulate" the strike.[23] In particular, the Democratic Union, which had set itself up as a political party to oppose the CPSU, earned Gorbachev's wrath for allegedly encouraging the strike. He devoted more attention to criticizing this party than its tiny size merited. A year later, aggrieved miners, convinced that they had been betrayed by a government that had not delivered its promises of 1989, used the strike as a more overtly political weapon, demanding Prime Minister Nikolai Ryzhkov's resignation and radical changes in the way in which the mines were run.[24]

In 1988 and in 1989, then, ideas that Gorbachev did not like were aired in society. They included independence from Moscow, demands for territory, and charges that political leaders were breaking their promises to workers. The Democratic Union impertinently went so far as to claim that Gorbachev was bolstering a totalitarian system, which irritated him.[25] In a context of democratization, competing interpretations of reality inevitably influenced political behavior and led to agitation, mobilization, and more pressure on the state.

Glasnost in the context of democratization had soon led to open demands for policies at variance with Gorbachev's political preferences and, in his view, harmful to them. And increasingly, Gorbachev labeled as unconstructive, unsocialist, irresponsible, and destabilizing those uses of glasnost that did not serve *his* changing conceptions of perestroika. By 1989, glasnost had become Janus-headed, probably to an extent unanticipated by Gorbachev, particularly in connection with the nationalities question, which he poorly understood, and with the growing attacks on Lenin—a sacrosanct target that Gorbachev had not intended to hit. Perestroika, after all, was supposed to be a "revolutionary process" in the spirit of Lenin.[26]

Glasnost Under Attack

While one perspective held that glasnost was functional to perestroika and necessary for democratization, another held that glasnost was undermining perestroika. Adopting a narrow view of perestroika as economic efficiency, conservatives saw glasnost as destructive if abused. Since 1988, they had been blaming anti-perestroika forces wielding glasnost for unrest in Azerbaidzhan, the Baltic states, and anywhere that nationalist sentiments were being expressed. Conservatives were quick to point out that the abuse of glasnost had brought disorder, unpredictability, and chaos to daily life. In some areas it had resulted in uncontrollable violence among ethnic groups that was conducive to panic and anxiety. Those on the right of the CPSU created an image of disarray that was shocking and morally abhorrent.

By 1990, glasnost's critics were aware that its cutting edge had plunged society into an identity crisis. Most economic, social, and political policies of the past had come under attack. Past achievements were proclaimed failures. What had previously been black was now white and vice versa. Cruder applications of glasnost had indeed turned the ideological slogans of the past on their heads, leaving no room for subtleties and nuances. One consequence was that for a growing number, official ideology was bankrupt; alienated and angry young people could be heard declaring that "this country is going nowhere." Glasnost had contributed to the development of a moral vacuum.[27]

In the autumn and winter of 1990, with moral outrage and panic about ethnic violence growing and anxiety about published crime statistics surfacing, Gorbachev moved to the right toward the conservatives. Several explanations could be advanced for Gorbachev's action: (1) the military/industrial complex, stricter Leninists in the CPSU, and the KGB had successfully prevented him from approving the Shatalin plan;[28] (2) Gorbachev allowed himself to succumb to their pressure because he, too, shared their fears about what the Shatalin plan would mean; (3) Gorbachev felt the political moment was not yet ripe for launching into a market system; or (4) Gorbachev's shift was a tactical one. Gorbachev's motives for vacillating about economic reform, one minute seeming to support the Shatalin plan, then backing off in search of milder measures, are hard to ascertain with certainty.[29] In Moscow at the time, commentators offered different interpretations.[30] Two main responses, however, were evident: criticism and frustration among keen reformers who wanted more decisive and radical economic change, and continued opposition to economic reform from hard-line stalwarts in the CPSU who feared the undermining of state socialism and a breakup of the Union. The latter viewed economic proposals that gave greater decision-making power to the republics as politically perilous. Economic reform was now inextricably linked to center-republic relations. Gorbachev's apparent vacillations about economic reform served to polarize views about their desirability.

The political context in which discussions about the Shatalin plan took place was relevant to its fate. Opponents of reform were particularly anxious about the weakened power and authority of the CPSU that had followed the convening of the Congress of People's Deputies in 1989. Although 87 percent of the deputies were members of the CPSU, communist policies were nevertheless the targets of many lively political debates.[31] Moreover, these sometimes caustic political exchanges were seen by millions of citizens, many of whom remained glued to their television screens, taking time off from work to watch what was happening in their new parliament. Automatic and unthinking praise for the CPSU wrapped in hollow rituals was over. Political reality was genuinely being redefined.

The waning de facto authority of the CPSU was further evident in January 1990 in grass-roots actions to throw out local party leaders in Chernigov, Tiumen, and Vladivostok.[32] Pressure to abolish Article 6 of the constitution (discussed in the previous chapter) had been building throughout 1989.[33] Gorbachev finally yielded and in February 1990 persuaded a plenum of the Central Committee that the leading role of the CPSU had to be modified.[34] Although Gorbachev's authority as general secretary was weakened by these developments, his formal powers were increased in 1990 on his becoming president.[35] In this post, too, however, there were problems since the presidency initially lacked an administrative machine. Rule by decree was the solution—but it was not always a popular one since it smacked for democrats of authoritarianism (even though decrees were not necessarily implemented). Gorbachev's new authority to enjoy increased powers was not highly respected by many of his critics.

Throughout 1990, Gorbachev was worried by growing political chaos in the country and by persistent demands from nationalists for an independence that he was not willing to grant. In some spheres, he believed that glasnost and democratization had overstepped their intended briefs, giving rise to unacceptable criticisms and unreasonable attacks on official policies. In an attempt to reduce such excesses, in November he appointed the unexciting Leonid Kravchenko to head Gosteleradio.[36] Kravchenko had previously been director of TASS, the official news agency. Television immediately became less interesting and in some respects appeared to return to old sterile molds. The popular program "Vzgliad," for example, was immediately taken off the air.[37] In the following March, Kravchenko fired certain journalists from Central Television in a dispute over censorship.[38] Resistance to controls over television had been building in the early months of 1991. About sixty cultural figures announced that they would boycott Central Television until censorship was lifted.[39] They were joined in February by the Moscow Organization of Cinema Workers.[40] Anger increased in March when the USSR State Broadcasting Company declared that the Lensovet could not transform Leningrad radio and television into an independent company.[41]

A year earlier, Gorbachev had also tried very hard, and unsuccessfully, to remove Vladislav Starkov, one of the editors of *Argumenty i Fakty* (Arguments and Facts).[42] This action was prompted by a survey published by Starkov that showed Andrei Sakharov was the most popular people's deputy. Gorbachev, appearing to find this politically undermining, overreacted. The promoter of glasnost felt that it was being used too directly against himself, and he became keen to contain and curb it. If journalists and political movements would not apply glasnost responsibly, then they would be made to do so. Gorbachev's crusade against Starkov was a particularly desperate one.

Gorbachev's displeasure at the coverage given by *Moskovskie Novosti* of events in Lithuania in January 1991 made many temporarily wonder how long freedom of the press would last. The paper printed a black border in mourning with the Baltic victims, referred to "Bloody Sunday," and used the heading "The crime of a regime that does not wish to leave the stage." By implication, Gorbachev was a criminal. *Moskovskie Novosti* also issued an appeal to reporters and journalists: "If you lack courage or the opportunity to tell the truth, at least do not tell lies!" adding "they are evident today."[43]

Gorbachev took exception to the charge of "criminal," began insisting that newspapers and television channels "reflect the full pluralism of opinions and appraisals," and observed in the USSR Supreme Soviet that "a decision could be taken right away to suspend the Law on the Press."[44] In quick retaliation, Iurii Kariakin, a people's deputy, observed that this had been done in 1918 "and after that we could not restore it for more than seventy years."[45]

Arguments against the curbing of glasnost raged in *Moskovskie Novosti* over the next two months. Mikhail Fedotov, deputy minister for the press and information of Russia and also one of the co-authors of the initiative draft on the press, pointed out that after passage of the Law on the Press, "almost immediately a whole series of regulations was published contradicting it." Although the law had eliminated censorship, the Council of Ministers had "restored it in temporary regulations on censorship," such as the requirement by Gosteleradio, the Ministry of Justice, and the Ministry of Communications that all parts of the media be registered. This had amounted to a reinstatement of "the old principles: banning and permitting at will." The result was a disregard for the law.[46] In the same edition, Oleg Poptsov, president of Russian Television and Radio, recounted how Gosteleradio had stopped Radio Russia from broadcasting on two channels, thereby putting one-third of Russia's population out of earshot of the first republican radio.[47]

Moskovskie Novosti kept the issue alive in a subsequent roundtable discussion around the theme "The free press will defend itself." Egor Yakovlev, the newspaper's editor, observed that should the Law on the Press be overturned, his paper would surely be closed. More hopefully, but incorrectly as it turned out, he predicted that "glasnost itself cannot be eliminated without a direct revolution, which is hardly possible."[48] Igor Golembiovskii, first deputy editor of *Izvestiia* (News), regretted that even this moderate paper was under attack.[49] Vladislav Starkov, still editor at *Argumenty i Fakty,* envisioned that with censorship either his paper would cease to be printed, or a commissar would arrive to watch over every word written.[50] Vitalii Korotich, editor of *Ogonek,* despaired that *Pravda* and *Sovetskaia Rossiia* (Soviet Russia) constructed "democrat" as "class enemy." They were delivering the messages that "democracy" meant "economic hardship" and "free press" amounted to "anarchy." The parasitic top echelons of power were coming together with lumpen obedient groups.[51] Len Karpinskii, political analyst for *Moskovskie Novosti,* observed that Gorbachev could mention possible suspension of the Law on the Press and then retreat but that even without acting himself, his words were a cue to party functionaries who had been dispatched to the provinces to promote support for conservative papers such as *Sovetskaia Rossiia* and *Krasnaia Zvezda* (Red Star).[52] On a positive note, Vladislav Fronin, editor of *Komsomol'skaia Pravda* (Komsomol Truth), argued that despite attempts to turn back the clock, a return to a situation "without glasnost" was impossible because journalists had radically changed their attitudes.[53]

Participants in the roundtable called for the democratic press to coordinate its efforts and set up a fund to help papers in difficulty. They agreed to defend the Law on the Press, to expose to readers the scheming and distortions of its opponents, and to hold similar roundtables to keep the issue alive.[54]

Fears about threats to glasnost were somewhat allayed as Gorbachev appeared to move back to the center in the spring of 1991. In April, a joint statement signed by Gorbachev and leaders of nine republics addressed various economic measures and also included reference to the need for greater independence and autonomy on the part of the republics.[55] Since Yeltsin's signature was on the document and only a week earlier he had been calling for Gorbachev's resignation, anxieties about the inability of the two leaders ever to work together subsided. But a ban on all acts of "civil disobedience" worried democrats and those to their left. Conservatives felt relief, as did some democrats who were concerned about stability and the dire economic consequences of miners' strikes. They believed that although glasnost in action was being curbed, it was with some realism.[56]

The use of glasnost strengthened again in mid-1991 with the opening of a new Russian television channel and a Russian radio station.[57] Relieved citizens observed that although other television channels under Kravchenko's eye had become extremely dull in the preceding months, now at least one channel could be relied on for troubleshooting. The enthusiasm of Muscovites for their new-look channel was temporarily dashed on 19 August 1991, when broadcasting came under KGB control. Classical music and films were punctuated only by declarations from the Emergency Committee.[58] A reinvigorated glasnost returned to broadcasting on 21 August as the coup crumbled. Thereafter television became more upbeat, replacing the stodgy style of the past as typified by the evening news program "Vremia" (Time) with the more lively news presentations in "Vesti" (News). Nevertheless, criticisms of the media did not cease. Some self-proclaimed democrats in September and October 1991 attacked Popov, Sobchak, and Yeltsin for their dictatorial tendencies and contended that Popov controlled the Moscow press to such an extent that nothing critical of him could be printed, except perhaps, according to one politician, "in about 5 percent of all newspapers."[59]

The Uses of Glasnost

From 1985 to 1991, the application of glasnost varied immensely according to issue, actor, and outlet. In 1985 and 1986, established newspapers and journals did not apply glasnost in identical fashion. Some editors and journalists found it easier to criticize officially defined problems central to perestroika, taking their cues safely from above. *Pravda* and *Sovetskaia Rossiia* fell into this category. They focused in particular on economic inefficiency and bureaucratization. Their agendas were the agendas of the CPSU. Other magazines and journals, such as *Ogonek, Moskovskie Novosti, Sobesednik,* and even *Komsomol'skaia Pravda,* had more daring editors who pushed glasnost to its perceived, or felt, limits. They were more willing to expose social problems, discuss political distortions of the past, and publish more daring and sensational material. A "liberal" and a "conservative" press could be identified.

After 1987, the picture became more complex. Glasnost enjoyed much stronger backing from Gorbachev. Enthusiasts applied it. The press, television, and radio became more exciting. Then during 1988 and 1989, the CPSU itself was more visibly split into three different camps of radicals (Yeltsin, Afanasyev), centrists (Gorbachev, Yakovlev, Shevardnadze, Ryzhkov), and conservatives (Ligachev, Chebrikov). Arguments from above no longer conveyed a united leadership. Throughout the history of the Soviet state, of course, members of a given Politburo had always held differing views, as was evident from the emphases and nuances of their speeches. But during 1988, more obviously in 1989, and quite blatantly in 1990, cues from above radically changed their character. A message from Yeltsin was not identical to a message from Gorbachev. Diversity replaced conformist unity. But until Yeltsin's election to the Congress of People's Deputies in 1989, his cues lacked institutional force.[60] When later, in 1990, he was chosen by the parliament of the Russian Federation to be its chair, the legitimacy of his cues was considerably strengthened, as it was again after his election in June 1991 as president of Russia.[61]

By 1989, the notion of a "cue" in the traditional sense in which it had been applied to Soviet politics was redundant. Journalists, political actors, and citizens increasingly acted as they chose to, no longer waiting for a nod from on high. Indeed, from 1988 onward, and a little earlier in the Baltic states, citizens were more actively helping define the nature of political issues, to which the leadership was forced to respond. An embryonic civil society began to exert pressure on the state, forcing fresh agendas or contesting and renegotiating official ones. As political reform proceeded, the political space for contesting past lines expanded, albeit in fits and starts, rushes and regressions, and became an increasingly *legitimate* political space. Candidates standing for election, for instance, put forward a mixed array of ideas about policy, many of which contested past priorities and visions. Alternatives were suggested and debated, even though possibilities for their eventual implementation were often slim. In the process, political discourse became richer and more conflictual.

As criticisms of the Soviet past mounted during 1988 and 1989, so did remarks about the need for "responsible glasnost." Centrists, such as Gorbachev, repeatedly linked glasnost to the Leninist tradition: Criticisms that countered socialist democracy and socialist pluralism were irresponsible. Stricter Leninists emphasized glasnost's negative consequences—empty rhetoric and disarray. Against these perspectives, radicals eager for faster reform maintained that glasnost was not Lenin's invention. Moreover, genuine glasnost demanded a transformed political and economic setting in which to flourish. We can therefore identify three main interpretations of glasnost that had crystallized by 1990: Glasnost was Leninist; glasnost was, not Leninist, but unfettered inquiry; glasnost was destabilizing.

Adherents of each perspective, however, could change the emphasis of their arguments. The limits Gorbachev had placed on glasnost in 1986 soon broadened for several reasons, including the need to tackle conservatives with information about past mistakes and subsequently to keep up with more radical pressures for wider, or fewer, limits to glasnost. Then Gorbachev's enthusiasm for glasnost significantly diminished because some of its consequences challenged his own authority; the authority of the CPSU, to which he was still loyal (and unable to override); the credibility of socialist values (which he would not drop); and the legitimacy of the powers of the Union. As politics polarized in 1990 and 1991, some democrats became louder champions of glasnost because they believed that violations of the Law on the Press were threatening it. Other democrats worried about political chaos and disintegration and considered that there was a need for firmer executive control and a clampdown on some activities and issues, at least in the short term. A growing vacuum at the center of Soviet politics in 1990 and 1991 resulted in a sharper polarization of views about glasnost than had existed three years earlier. But by mid-1991, as a political center reappeared, the polarity of views about glasnost had been reduced, although its broad spectrum remained. After the failed coup of 1991, despite Gorbachev's continued, albeit brief, commitment on 23 August to socialism and to a revitalized CPSU (which was quite out of keeping with the popular mood among opponents of the state of emergency), the notion that glasnost should be Leninist was undermined, except among supporters of the coup and committed communists.

Glasnost as Leninist and Positive

Since 1985, Gorbachev had been regularly linking perestroika and glasnost to the spirit of Lenin. At the January plenum of the Central Committee in 1987, he announced that "we must recall once again Lenin's stand on the question of maximum democracy" and then quoted Lenin: "We must be guided by experience; we must allow complete freedom to the creative faculties of the masses."[62] Gorbachev was keen to emphasize that the human factor had to be activated through glasnost and that this was a Leninist approach. Fifteen months later at the Nineteenth Party Conference, he claimed that the people wanted "glasnost in all things, big and small," and that socialism gave "clear guidelines and objective criteria." He also insisted that the "heated discussions" of the conference had "reaffirmed the correctness of the historical choice of socialism made by our people in 1917."[63] At the Twenty-eighth Party Congress in 1990, Gorbachev stuck to this view, even though many social groups were now publicly and vehemently rejecting his link between glasnost and Leninism.[64] Lenin's legitimacy was being questioned to an extent of which Gorbachev did not seem aware. While taxi drivers could be heard saying, "The very worst thing in the whole of Russian history was that they didn't cut Lenin's throat in 1917";[65] nationalists were tearing down his statues; and political jokes about Lenin abounded, Gorbachev punctuated his speeches with "speaking in Leninist words" and "the laws of the Marxist dialectic."[66] A strong case can be made that Gorbachev's categories were out of tune with popular moods.

Like others, Gorbachev talked about "freedom." But whereas his critics to the left were still calling for it, Gorbachev announced that "the main positive achievement is that socialism has received freedom" and that "spiritual rebirth is necessary to society, like oxygen."[67] For Gorbachev, freedom and rebirth were Leninist in nature and glasnost served Leninism. For his democratic critics, freedom was linked, not to Leninism, the Marxist dialectic, or socialism, but to a rejection of all three. Gorbachev's critics sought oxygen in an un-Leninist glasnost. So, too, did some of his supporters, who believed that Gorbachev was the best leader for the moment but that in future years glasnost would go beyond the boundaries that Gorbachev wished to impose on it.

Echoing Gorbachev's arguments but often going a little further, sixty-four supporters of Gorbachev contributed to an anthology entitled *Sud'ba Glasnosti—Sud'ba Perestroiki* (The Fate of Glasnost—The Fate of Perestroika), published in 1990.[68] They championed glasnost as vital to the success of perestroika and occasionally quoted Lenin and party congresses for justification. The writer, people's deputy, and member of Gorbachev's Presidential Council, Chingiz Aitmatov, stressed that glasnost meant "full, fully-fledged information about all societal, social, and cultural events, a *real* portrayal of existence." He suggested that "if glasnost is TRUTH, then it should have no limitations." But for it to become a norm of life, then citizens must be educated into "the culture of glasnost."[69] V. Serikov, a hero of socialist labor, declared glasnost to be "one of the first signs of a civilized, democratic society."[70] Likewise, N. Bodnaruk, deputy editor of *Izvestiia,* argued that glasnost was essential for a "full-blooded" society, for progress, and for prosperity. Glasnost in society was like air to the body. In particular, it was necessary for the "normal journalist."[71] The words *normal* and *civilized* were increasingly part of political discourse. Vladimir Iadov, then director of the Institute of Sociology, summed it up with "glasnost—a normal way of life in a modern, civilized society."[72] For Iu. Manaenkov, erstwhile first secretary of Lipetsk *obkom* and later secretary of the Central Committee, glasnost affected the "atmosphere of life." Harm did not come from glasnost but from its absence. It could best be protected by a legal state.[73] For decades, argued Dmitrii Volkogonov, a professor, formal glasnost had existed and had given rise to an inner slavery and a fear of the truth. Now glasnost was "freedom of conscience, freedom of will, the expression of genuine citizenship and responsibility." Glasnost should not be a gift or a luxury but a natural element of life. However, "we do not have enough direct democracy: plebiscites, referenda, intelligent surveys."[74] A. Sukharev, general procurator and people's deputy, portrayed glasnost as the result of perestroika and as its main guarantor. But, he noted, glasnost gave satisfaction when it delivered results. He called for mechanisms to allow citizens to get "from state organs any information necessary for the practical realization of their rights," excluding state secrets.[75] Vitalii Korotich, editor of *Ogonek,* argued that glasnost was crucial for "people's control" and that since the Twenty-seventh Party Congress and Nineteenth Party Conference had conveyed the message that "we have no zones closed to criticism," then "we must develop the system of control. Our higher echelons of power are closed to public attention."[76] Korotich believed that it was time to scrutinize top leaders. If he could interview Margaret Thatcher and learn how she shopped and how she prepared breakfast for her husband, why should he not approach Soviet leaders in a similar way?[77]

Academics concerned with linking glasnost to specific issues such as the "demonopolization of information," the Law on the Press, and "pluralism of social interests" expressed similar views in *Glasnost': Mneniia, Poiski, Politika* (Glasnost: Opinions, Searches, Policy).[78] The lawyers Iurii Baturin, Nikolai Deev, Mikhail Fedotov, Vladimir Entin, and others made a strong case for legal protection for glasnost. Quotations from Marx and Lenin punctuated their text, but often perhaps more out of ritual political necessity than profound adherence to their ideas.

Some texts in 1989, however, still quoted Lenin with abundant enthusiasm. For instance, G. Mukhina's *V. I. Lenin o Glasnosti* (V. I. Lenin on Glasnost) held that glasnost was the antithesis of "lies, hypocrisy and dishonesty" and could best be understood through a Leninist approach as "an important principle of politics and an instrument in the activities of the socialist state and the Communist Party." Glasnost was the "creative spirit" of Leninist ideas.[79] Moreover, "a Leninist understanding of glasnost in the broad sense of the word is a necessary condition for the revolutionary renewal of society on the path of socialist revolution and socialist construction" and for control of the CPSU by the CPSU.[80] The notion of glasnost could be traced back to Lenin himself, whose selected quotes on criticism, truth, and enlightenment were woven into the text. Glasnost, said Mukhina, was best understood through Leninism and was best limited in its application to Leninism.[81]

Contributors to *Sud'ba Glasnosti—Sud'ba Perestroiki* and to *Glasnost': Mneniia, Poiski, Politika* were not nearly so ardent in their Leninism. So among writings within this general category of "glasnost is Leninist," there was a wide span of ideas. For many, the nod to Lenin may have been ritual rather than commitment.

Writings at the more conservative end of this rubric linked the effectiveness of glasnost to its use by the CPSU and, reciprocally, the renewal of the CPSU to its willingness to adopt glasnost. Here the message became, "Where criticism and self-criticism subside, there party life is deformed, creating a situation of complacency and impunity. It leads to stagnation in work and a degeneration of workers."[82] To overcome this condition, Lenin's words on the duty of communists would have to be taken to heart: "not to cover up the weaknesses of their movement, but openly to criticize them, in order quickly and radically to be delivered from them."[83] In a similar vein, back in 1990, Aleksandr Yakovlev had couched "the question of the party" as at the center of "ideological struggle."[84] For many in 1989 and 1990, the future role of the CPSU was the main political issue, and so the purpose of glasnost was relative to what the party became. But for radicals, the nature of the CPSU was an issue of the past that they had outgrown. Their agendas were more dynamic and their thoughts were elsewhere. Radicals rejected what the CPSU stood for, criticized it vehemently, but found it harder to agree on common constructive strategies. They were, however, united in their call for more and unharnessed glasnost.

Glasnost as Unfettered Inquiry

Against Gorbachev, many socialists, social democrats, and liberals argued that glasnost should not be constricted by Leninism, itself already discredited in their eyes. If genuine democratization was to take place, glasnost would have to be freer. Leonid Batkin and Valerii Chalidze provided the most eloquent arguments from this perspective, which included criticisms of glasnost being inadequate.

Batkin noted that "the literal meaning of the word *glasnost* is very simple. From its old root—voice, sounding loud and distinct, for everyone. From this came towncrier (herald), loudly broadcast on the squares of ancient towns."[85] In short, glasnost predated Lenin. Moreover, the Leninist state was best characterized by "an information vacuum" or by "an absence of glasnost," which enveloped management and decision making, bolstering "the diktat of the party apparat." Glasnost was the "main preliminary condition for profound changes," but two problems were associated with it. First, it was not accompanied by tangible results in economic and social policies. Unfortunately, "to reconcile oneself to scarcity and an unfree existence at a time of glasnost is incomparably more difficult than without it." Glasnost made hard times appear harder since everyone could complain. Second, glasnost suffered from being incomplete. Not everyone at the top of hierarchies used it, and not all problems had been touched by it. The provincial press hesitated to embrace it. Articles were still refused publication, and films continued to be banned. Skeptics pointed out that "not in the first weeks of apocalyptic Chernobyl, nor after the tragedies of Sumgait and Tbilisi, nor even during the favorable changes in the composition of the Soviet leadership in October 1988, was there a trace of glasnost. This badly complicated, for example, the solving of Caucasian clashes."[86] Rather than congratulate the government for having given freedom to the people, as Gorbachev did at the Twenty-eighth Party Congress, Batkin called for a quick and steady "transition from glasnost to guaranteed freedom of speech."[87] Glasnost was admirable but insufficient.

Entering the debate on glasnost from the United States, the émigré Valerii Chalidze suggested that "perestroika began with glasnost," which had provided a "hurricane of new information about the crimes of the state in the past, about Western life and present-day problems."[88] But the sheer abundance of this information frightened people because it was too much to digest after years of knowing so little. Nevertheless, like Batkin, Chalidze saw glasnost as insufficient and as extremely unsteady in its course, sometimes sliding backward. Chalidze cited the example of Nina Andreeva's letter to *Sovetskaia Rossiia,* which in 1988 had called for "a revival of Stalinist ideology." With Ligachev's help, this letter was reprinted in many newspapers, with the result that "glasnost receded for two weeks."[89] Oscillations in glasnost underlined that "in the USSR the past patriarchal relationship of the state to the people has not gone."[90] Glasnost should not be confused with freedom of speech and freedom of the press, said Chalidze, because "glasnost does not ensure these freedoms, but permits them to be used more widely than before." Chalidze stressed that glasnost was a policy: "It is government permission to speak more freely and also contraction of the sphere of censor's prohibitions." So "where there is freedom of the press, it is a boon, and the limits of the boon depend on the tactics of power."[91] Thus, the passage of the Law on the Press was crucial in the development of glasnost.[92]

Some of the arguments that glasnost was not Leninist were also put forward in 1989 by those who felt constrained to cite glasnost's Leninist credentials, such as some of the academics, lawyers, and writers cited in the previous section. They all defended glasnost and sought its legal protection. The difference, however, was that writers such as Batkin and Chalidze boldly condemned Leninism, criticized the party-state that perpetuated its cult, and advocated a broader glasnost much sooner.

Glasnost as Disorienting and Destabilizing

By contrast, the critics of glasnost felt threatened by it and wished to halt its advance. They generally opposed economic and political reforms and defended traditional Soviet socialism. Glasnost undermined the values they upheld and criticized the system they supported. Thus, nothing positive was likely to result from its use. Quite the contrary, it was destructive and upsetting. It posed questions that did not need to be asked, confused people, and spread ideologically unsound ideas throughout society. It was therefore destructive, immoral, and ultimately destabilizing. Members of the KGB, members of the army, and hard-liners such as Egor Ligachev voiced arguments along these lines. Everything they stood for was epitomized in the letter "I cannot renounce principles" by Nina Andreeva, a Leningrad teacher.[93] This letter quickly came to symbolize the so-called right wing.

Andreeva complained that "I have been reading and rereading sensational articles. What, for example, can revelations about 'counter-revolution in the USSR around the 1930s' give young people, apart from disorientation? Or revelations about 'the guilt' of Stalin for the coming to power in Germany of fascism and Hitler? Or the public 'calculations' of the number of 'Stalinists' in different generations and social groups?"[94] She insisted that many recent discussions of the past should not have taken place. They were incompatible with a more appropriate "class-based vision of the world" and were often no more than "political stories, base gossip, and controversial fantasies." "Left-wing liberals," with their overt cosmopolitanism, were preoccupied with seeing only mistakes and crimes in the past, ignoring the great achievements. Moreover, the topic of political repression had "grown out of all proportion

in the perceptions of some young people, overshadowing an objective attempt to understand the past." All this had resulted among students in "a
strengthening of nihilistic moods," "muddled ideas," "a confusion of political orientations," and "ideological omnivorousness."[95] They were even at-
tacking the concept of the dictatorship of the proletariat. In sum, glasnost
had given rise to ideologically damaging ideas.

Socialist realism was being compromised, too. Andreeva criticized the
plays of Mikhail Shatrov for ignoring the objective laws of history, for playing up subjective factors when he should have been looking at class, and for
making the "biased" accusations that Stalin was responsible for the murders
of Trotsky and Kirov! Andreeva concluded that glasnost was being "manipulated" and that non-socialist pluralism was the result. This was particularly
harmful for young people since Marxism-Leninism was no longer guiding
actions "in the spiritual sphere."[96]

Andreeva's ideas were supported by Egor Ligachev, Viktor Chebrikov,
Lev Zaikov, Boris Gidaspov, and many other traditionalists in the CPSU. As
political actors, however, they could not be quite so blunt about their fears
of glasnost. Andreeva was a useful mouthpiece. But their speeches, too, were
interlaced with remarks about the negative results of too much openness.

Conservative political leaders adopted the technique of first praising
glasnost's benefits and then emphasizing its unsavory consequences.
Ligachev, for example, in a speech in March 1987 to the artistic community
in Saratov, declared that "so as not to repeat the mistakes of the past, artistic
unions need wide glasnost and further democratization."[97] But he quickly
added that:

> There are also negative phenomena. Some newspapers and journals have con-
> centrated their attention only on the publication of materials reflecting the mis-
> takes of the past. But that is only a part of the truth. There is another side of the
> truth—above all, that our people, under the leadership of the party, accom-
> plished the Great October socialist revolution, whose seventieth anniversary we
> are preparing to mark; were victorious in the Great Patriotic War; constructed a
> socialist society; successfully led creative work; actively fought for peace
> throughout the world. The truth about accomplishments and contradictions
> must be complete.[98]

Ligachev's notion of "complete truth" did not explicitly allow for "competing interpretations." What he was effectively saying was that criticism of
the past was unconstructive and should be played down. Like Andreeva a
year later, Ligachev went on to warn against lavishing excessive praise on
works that had only recently been published. He reminded his audience that
the leading classics by Maksim Gorky, Vladimir Mayakovsky, and Mikhail
Sholokhov should not be pushed to one side.[99] By implication, glasnost
should not undermine approved experimentalism and socialist realism. The

subtext was that plays by Shatrov and others were overrated and did not deserve the limelight.

Until he was obliged to leave political life at the Twenty-eighth Party Congress in 1990, Ligachev repeated these themes in different speeches.[100] Talking in August 1988 to the *aktiv* (gathering of party activists) in Gorky, he remarked that "nihilism in relation to the past engenders the same relationship to the present. The links of time and of generation are lost." By inference, criticism of the past could be both excessive and destructive for the present. Staying close to old and new ideological categories, he asserted that socialism could develop only through a "dialectical unity of the policy of renewal and continuity."[101] He did, however, concede the need for a new humanitarianism, but only if it was linked to a "class approach." As Ligachev put it, there were "deep interconnections" between "a humanitarian and a class approach."[102] But class dominated and defined what humanitarian could be. Above all, socialism could not be abandoned. Ligachev's discourse, like Andreeva's, was locked into the terminology of "class," "proletariat," "dialectic," and "socialist revolution." Glasnost did not really fit in.

Gorbachev's anxieties about glasnost were also evident in 1990 and 1991. In 1987 and 1988, unlike Ligachev, Gorbachev had been extremely upbeat about the necessity for openness. He had always believed that it should be "responsible" but had nevertheless seen it as a means or motor for renewal and democratization. At the end of 1990, his emphasis changed. In his December speech to the Congress of People's Deputies, Gorbachev criticized intellectuals for wasting energy on "elucidating relations with the past" and arguing among themselves. This was a "disservice to society" and was used "for exciting destructive passions, destabilizing social consciousness." In a crisis situation, he argued, intellectuals should not fan the flames of ethnic confrontation but rather should help pacify the people. Intellectuals were not always "balanced and responsible" in their statements.[103]

Sounding more like Andreeva and Ligachev than his earlier self, Gorbachev unleashed fury on the media: "I share, in every way, the alarm of many intellectuals, their unease, at the influx of a mass of operators into broadcasting, the cinema, and the press. They abuse the title of intellectual; abuse freedom of creativity; do hackwork; produce vulgar, low-standard, inhumane work, loosening social morals, discrediting the meaning of culture."[104] For these declared reasons, "criteria of conduct" would be specified and upheld.[105] The chief instigator of glasnost in the mid-1980s wished to limit it five years later. Conservatives on the right applauded; democrats on the left became convinced that democratization had been betrayed. Other democrats and centrists felt the need for regulation in some spheres. For instance, Gorbachev's order On Working Out Urgent Measures to Safeguard Morality earned some approval for its attempt to address pornography, pseudomedical literature, and erotic films. A commission was set up under the Ministry of Culture to investigate international law and to safeguard morality.[106] But many radical reformers were concerned that attempts to control pornography would spill into other spheres, thereby limiting the scope of glasnost. Their feeling of betrayal soon turned into outrage at what many labeled "criminal" murders by the army in January 1991 in Lithuania and Latvia. Persistent disappointments led on 10 March to a rally of more than two hundred thousand in Manezh Square to demand Gorbachev's resignation.[107] This was not where Gorbachev had envisaged glasnost and democratization would lead.

Conclusion

Glasnost was a political weapon whose career was fragile and halting at first, then heady and controversial. Combined with democratization and harnessed by it, glasnost fueled processes of national self-determination, fragmentation, and ultimately disintegration of the Union. The cutting edge of its power, particularly after 1989, became more lethal for opponents after their various attempts to silence glasnost or discredit it. Journalists in early 1991 fought attempts to limit their use of glasnost, which for them had come to mean freedom of speech. But whereas the nature of glasnost had been a live issue from 1986 to 1991, the prominence of this topic receded during 1991 as political discourse became increasingly preoccupied with issues of crisis resolution and state power. By then, glasnost for reformers was a given that had to stay. They would fight back whenever leaders attempted to curb it. Ultimately glasnost became one tool among many in political conflicts about the legitimacy of the historic choice of socialism versus the need for a market economy and parliamentary democracy.

The spectrum of the aforementioned views about the role and relevance of glasnost reflected broad political responses to reform in a sharply divided society. Opponents of change feared glasnost not simply for exposing growing crime, social problems, unjust privileges enjoyed by the CPSU, and details of the purges and gulags, but also for giving a voice to alternative viewpoints and for contributing to the mobilization of new political movements. Glasnost's revelations of failures in economic and social policy along with an emerging plurality of political views and political groups meant more space for political debate and conflict. Glasnost meant a questioning and redefining of past norms, values, myths, and propaganda. Glasnost facilitated enlivened discourses that reexamined patterns of authority and power. Instability and legitimacy crisis for the state were among its threats.

For its supporters, glasnost brought public recognition of economic, social, and political wrongs in need of correction. Glasnost thus served the po-

Published in the newspaper of the Lithuanian Movement for Perestroika just before Gorbachev reached the height of his unpopularity, this cartoon portrays the different pressures on Gorbachev coming simultaneously from various directions. Two of the tentacles represent Latvia and Lithuania and their demands for sovereignty. Other tentacles are Yeltsin, demanding faster reform, and *Kuz'michi*—Ligachev and Polozkov—both wishing to slow down perestroika (they shared the patronymic Kuz'mich). SOURCE: *Soglasie*, no. 27, 2–8 July 1990, p. 1.

litical ends of redefining and reshaping the running of economy, society, and polity. New strategies could gather credibility from exposure of the failures of previous ones. Glasnost's supporters, however, were divided over how much glasnost there should be and on which topics. Different political ends required different limits to openness. The more radical the preferences, the wider were the desired limits to glasnost. One perspective called for an end to all limits.

Glasnost was also manipulated to suit political ends. Journalists and political actors who claimed to apply it did not necessarily uncover "truth," but their version of it. They presented labels, images, frameworks, and myths that may have been fresh and contrary to past party lines but were also partial. How social problems and political concepts were redefined illustrates the complexity of the process.

NOTES

1. E. F. Orlov, *Politicheskie Anekdoty* (Moscow, Sovetskaia Molodezh, 1990), p. 23.

2. *Materialy XXVII S"ezda KPSS* (Moscow, Politizdat, 1986), p. 60.

3. Institut Marksizma-Leninizma pri TsK KPSS, *M. S. Gorbachev: Izbrannye Rechi i Stat'i*, vol. 4 (Moscow, Politizdat, 1987), p. 300.

4. Institut Marksizma-Leninizma pri TsK KPSS, *M. S. Gorbachev: Izbrannye Rechi i Stat'i*, vol. 5 (Moscow, Politizdat, 1988), pp. 397–402. There were several early references to Stalinism. Rybakov's *Children of the Arbat* was serialized. See Anatolii Rybakov, "Deti Arbata," *Druzhba Narodov*, no. 4, 1987, pp. 3–133; *Druzhba Narodov*, no. 5, 1987, pp. 67–163; *Druzhba Narodov*, no. 6, 1987, pp. 23–151. For a review of Abuladze's Georgian film about Stalin, *Repentance*, see L. G. Ionin, "… i vozovet proshedshee," *Sotsiologicheskie Issledovaniia*, no. 3, 1987, pp. 62–72. The review discussed "totalitarian equality," the anti-hero, and evil.

Mid-1988 saw interest in Stalinism spreading to the mainstream journal *Questions of History*. See Iu. N. Afanasyev, "Izbavit istoricheskuiu nauku ot mertviashchikh put stalinshchiny," *Voprosy Istorii*, no. 6, June 1988, pp.71–75; Dmitrii A. Volkogonov, "Stalinizm—eto kontseptsiia izvrashchennoi teorii i praktiki sotsializma," *Voprosy Istorii*, no. 6, June 1988, pp. 63–64. At the end of the year, a round-table discussion of the 1930s was published. See "Kruglyi stol: Sovetskii Soiuz v 30e gody," *Voprosy Istorii*, no. 12, December 1988, pp. 3–29. Those participating included E. G. Plimak, R. A. Medvedev, V. P. Danilov, L. N. Nezhinskii, V. A. Kumanov, and V. M. Kulish. D. A. Volkogonov continued his contribution to debate, interviewed by Dmitrii Kazuminy in "Stalin mertv, no ne umer eshche stalinizm," *Moskovskie Novosti*, no. 8, 25 February 1990, p. 8. There was a similar roundtable on the 1920s. Refer to "Kruglyi stol," pp. 3–58.

Other relevant articles and stories focused on particular aspects of Stalinism or raised general questions about the meaning of history for perestroika: I. Kliamkin, "Kakaia ulitsa vedet k khramu," *Novyi Mir*, no. 11, November 1989, pp. 150–188; V. Tendriakov, "Rasskazy," which included "Para gnebnykh," "Khleb dlia sobaki," and "Parania Donna Anna," *Novyi Mir*, no. 3, March 1988, pp. 3–61; Iurii Afanasyev, *Pravda*, 26 July 1988, p. 3; "Varlam Shalamov: Proza, stikhi," *Novyi Mir*, no. 6, June 1988, pp. 106–149.

Personalities previously taboo were now also examined. For discussion of Tomskii, Riutin, and Bukharin, see I. S. Kulikova and B. Ia. Khazanov, "Mikhail Pavlovich Tomskii," *Voprosy Istorii*, no. 8, August 1988, pp. 64–83; Lev Razgon, "Nakonets," *Moskovskie Novosti*, no. 26, 26 June 1988, p. 11; A. Vaksberg, "Kak zhivoi s zhivyimi," *Literaturnaia Gazeta*, 29 June 1988, p. 13; L. K. Shkarenkov, "Nikolai Ivanovich Bukharin," *Voprosy Istorii*, no. 7, July 1988, pp. 59–78. Bukharin had finally been rehabilitated in 1988. See *Pravda*, 6 February 1988, p. 1.

For scrutiny of reassessments of history, consult R. W. Davies, *Soviet History in the Gorbachev Revolution* (London, Macmillan, 1989); Alec Nove, *Glasnost' in Action* (London, Unwin Hyman, 1989).

5. *XIX Vsesoiuznaia Konferentsiia Kommunisticheskoi Partii Sovetskogo Soiuza: Stenograficheskii Otchet,* 2 vols. (Moscow, Politizdat, 1988).

6. *Zakon Soiuza Sovetskikh Sotsialisticheskikh Respublik o Vyborakh Narodnykh Deputatov SSSR* (Moscow, Izvestiia Sovetov Narodnykh Deputatov SSSR, 1988).

7. *The Guardian,* 24 October 1988, p. 24.

8. Mikhail S. Gorbachev, "O khode realizatsii reshenie XXVII S"ezda KPSS i Zadachakh po Uglubleniiu Perestroiki," in *XIX Vsesoiuznaia Konferentsiia Kommunisticheskoi Partii,* vol. 1, p. 87.

9. Ibid., p. 88.

10. Ibid.

11. "Rezoliutsiia 'O gasnosti,'" *XIX Vsesoiuznaia Konferentsiia Kommunisticheskogo Partii,* vol. 2, pp. 166–167.

12. Ibid., p. 167.

13. A. Stepovoi, "Protivorechit deistvuiushchei konstitutsii SSSR," *Izvestiia,* 19 November 1988, p. 3. Two hundred fifty-eight deputies voted in favor of the declaration of sovereignty (which fell short of a call for independence), five abstained, and just one voted against. *The Independent,* 15 November 1988, p. 11; *The Independent,* 17 November 1988, p. 12; *The Sunday Times,* 20 November 1988, pp. A16, 3.

14. *The Guardian,* 8 October 1988, p. 7.

15. Information gathered in March 1989 in Vil'nius during conversations with members of Sajudis. For details, consult *Soglasie,* no. 26, 25 June–1 July 1990, pp. 3–5; *Soglasie,* no. 35, 27 August–2 September 1990, pp. 1, 3–4. For similar statements about independence for Latvia, see *Baltiiskoe Vremia,* no. 22, 11 June 1990, pp. 1–8.

16. This was not reported in *Zaria Vostoka* or *Bakinskii Rabochii.* Instead, see *The Sunday Times,* 20 November 1988, p. A16.

17. In February 1988, tensions led to a bloody massacre in Sumgait, north of Azerbaidzhan's capital, Baku, in which twenty-six Armenians died. For ideological pleas for "friendship among peoples," see *Bakinskii Rabochii,* 27 February 1988, pp. 1–2; *Bakinskii Rabochii,* 28 February 1988, p. 1. For announcement of a quieting situation, see *Bakinskii Rabochii,* 2 March 1988, p. 3. Subsequent clashes between Armenians and Azerbaidzhanis sporadically took place in Baku, Kirovabad, and Nakhichevan in Azerbaidzhan and in Erevan, Kalinino, Goris, and Stepanavan in Armenia. See *The Independent,* 1 December 1988, p. 17.

18. *The Independent,* 1 December 1988, p. 17; *Times,* 2 December 1988, p. 24.

19. *Bakinskii Rabochii,* 2 March 1988, p. 3.

20. *Bakinskii Rabochii,* 17 June 1988, p. 1.

21. *Bakinskii Rabochii,* 14 June 1988, p. 1.

22. *Bakinskii Rabochii,* 18 November 1988; *Bakinskii Rabochii,* 19 November 1988, p. 1.

23. *The Independent,* 20 July 1989, p. 10.

24. RFE/RL Research Institute, *Report on the USSR,* vol. 3, no. 17, 26 April 1991, p. 29; RFE/RL Research Institute, *Report on the USSR,* vol. 3, no. 18, 3 May 1991, p. 25.

25. *Uchreditel'noe Sobranie,* no. 2, 12 July 1989, p. 1.

26. Mikhail Gorbachev, *Perestroika i Novoe Myshlenie Dlia Nashei Strany i Dlia Vsevo Mira* (Moscow, Politizdat, 1987), pp. 20–21.

27. Many cynical Muscovites in their twenties and early thirties expressed this view to me in September 1990. For discussions of Soviet youth, see Jim Riordan, ed., *Soviet Youth Culture* (London, Macmillan, 1989); Hilary Pilkington, "Going out 'in style': Girls in youth cultural activity," in Mary Buckley, ed., *Perestroika and Soviet Women* (Cambridge, Cambridge University Press, 1992), pp. 54–71.

28. The Shatalin plan was also referred to as the 'five hundred days program' since it provided a detailed schedule of five hundred days for transition to a market economy. See footnotes 21 and 22 to Chapter 1.

29. For details of Gorbachev's vacillations, refer to Anders Aslund, *Gorbachev's Struggle for Economic Reform,* 2d ed. (London, Pinter, 1991), pp. 206–224.

30. Interviews in Moscow, 1990.

31. *Izvestiia,* 6 May 1989, p. 3.

32. For reporting on events in Tiumen, see *Izvestiia,* 19 January 1990, p. 3. Reflection on developments in Chernigov can be found in *Moskovskie Novosti,* no. 4, 28 January 1990, p. 5.

33. One of the clearest statements in favor of abolishing Article 6 came from the Inter-Regional Group, "Vlast' narody," *Narodnyi Deputat,* no. 34, 28 July 1989, pp. 1–2. This publication is distinct from the journal of the same name. The deputies had to turn to the Institute of Atomic Energy for use of the press "Sovetskii Fizik." The Democratic Union made its case against the leading role of the CPSU in the following: *Svobodnoe Slovo,* 8 August 1989; *Uchreditel'noe Sobranie,* no. 2, 12 July 1989; *Uchreditel'noe Sobranie,* no. 3, 11 August 1989; *Demokraticheskaia Svobodnaia Sibir',* no. 4, August 1990.

34. *Pravda,* 6–8 February 1990.

35. The presidency was approved at the February plenum. See ibid.

36. *Pravda,* 15 November 1990, p. 2.

37. Initially "Vzgliad" was not broadcast and was then taken off the air completely. See *Izvestiia,* 29 December 1990, p. 8; RFE/RL Research Institute, *Report on the USSR,* vol. 13, no. 1, 4 January 1991, p. 23; RFE/RL Research Institute, *Report on the USSR,* vol. 3, no. 3, 18 January 1991, pp. 44–45.

38. Tat'iana Mitkova, Evgenii Kiselev, and Iurii Rostov lost their jobs, followed by Vitalii Tishin. RFE/RL Research Institute, *Report on the USSR,* vol. 3, no. 13, 29 March 1991, p. 28.

39. RFE/RL Research Institute, *Report on the USSR,* vol. 3, no. 5, 1 February 1991, p. 51.

40. RFE/RL Research Institute, *Report on the USSR,* vol. 3, no. 7, 15 February 1991, p. 39.

41. RFE/RL Research Institute, *Report on the USSR,* vol. 3, no. 11, 15 March 1991, p. 43.

42. *Arguments and Facts International,* January 1990, pp. 2–3.

43. *Moskovskie Novosti,* no. 3, 20 January 1991, p. 1.

44. *Moskovskie Novosti,* no. 4, 27 January 1991, p. 6. The Law on the Press, which came into force on 1 August 1990, gave legality to many changes that had in fact already taken place. Nonetheless, it represented a significant break with the past.

For example, it permitted the expression of anti-communist sentiment and forbade censorship, except in limited cases of state secrets, war propaganda, and racism. It also gave courts a role in settling disputes.

45. Ibid.

46. *Moskovskie Novosti, no.* 6, 10 February 1991, p. 8.

47. Ibid, p. 9. The Russian radio program had gone on air on 10 December 1990. It was, however, provisionally using Gosteleradio's frequencies. In early February, Gosteleradio reduced the number of frequencies available to the program. When Gorbachev turned Gosteleradio into a new company, Kravchenko was retained at the head. See RFE/RL Research Institute, *Report on the USSR,* vol. 3, no. 7, 15 February 1991, p. 46.

48. *Moskovskie Novosti,* no. 10, 10 March 1991, p. 48.

49. Ibid.

50. Ibid.

51. Ibid.

52. Ibid.

53. Ibid.

54. Ibid., p. 9.

55. *Pravda,* 24 April 1991, p. 1.

56. Views expressed in interviews in Moscow, April 1991.

57. For interviews about the launch of Russian radio and television with its director, Anatolii Lysenko, and its chair, Oleg Poptsov, see *Moskovskie Novosti,* no. 19, 12 May 1991, p. 6. The article stressed that "unique material" would be presented "without any censorship."

58. This was not the case in Leningrad, where Sobchak retained control over one television channel.

59. Interviews with Aleksandr Krasnov and other people's deputies in the soviet of Krasnopresnenskii *raion,* Moscow, September 1991.

60. In December 1985, Yeltsin was appointed first secretary of the Moscow party committee. Soon after, he was named a candidate member of the Politburo. Many of his policies for Moscow, however, were deemed controversial, in particular the pace at which he fired those in top administrative positions in his battle against corruption. His request in 1987 at a plenum of the Central Committee that he be relieved of his position on the Politburo was granted at the next plenum in 1988. Before the end of 1987, he was removed, with some humiliation, from the post of first secretary of Moscow. For his own account and charges of cruelty against Gorbachev, see Boris N. Yeltsin, *Ispoved' Po Zadannuiu Temu* (Moscow, Ogonek-Variant, 1990).

61. *Moskovskie Novosti,* no. 23, 10 June 1990, p. 1; *Moskovskie Novosti,* no. 24, 17 June 1990, p. 7.

62. Institut Marksizma-Leninizma, *M. S. Gorbachev,* vol. 4, p. 317.

63. Gorbachev, "O khode," pp. 89–91.

64. Mikhail S. Gorbachev, "Politicheskii otchet Tsentral'nogo Komiteta KPSS XXVIII S"ezdy KPSS i zadachi partii," *Materialy XXVIII S"ezda Kommunisticheskoi Partii Sovetskogo Soiuza* (Moscow, Politizdat, 1990), pp. 36–37.

65. Harold Shukman, "Lenin or Alexander?" *Times Higher Education Supplement,* 2 March 1990, p. 15.

66. Gorbachev, "Politicheskii otchet," pp. 36–37.

67. Mikhail S. Gorbachev, "Vystuplenie po itogam obsuzhdeniia politicheskogo otcheta TsK KPSS XXVIII s"ezdu partii," *Materialy XXVIII S"ezda KPSS* (Moscow, Politizdat, 1990), p. 54.

68. M. M. Rassolov and V. V. Shinkarenko, eds., *Sud'ba Glasnosti—Sud'ba Perestroiki* (Moscow, Politizdat, 1990).

69. Chingiz Aitmatov, "Glasnost—eto pravda," in ibid., pp. 22–25.

70. V. Serikov, "Uchit'sia kul'ture dialoga," in ibid., p. 257.

71. N. Bodnaruk, "Neobkhodima kak vozdukh," in ibid., pp. 80–81.

72. V. Iadov, "Normal'nyi sposob zhizni," in ibid., p. 320.

73. Iu. Manaenkov, "Stepen' blagorodstva obshchestva," in ibid., pp. 202–203.

74. D. Volkogonov, "Pravda ne dolzhna byt' roskosh'iu," in ibid., p. 94.

75. A. Sukharev, "Bez dvoinykh standartov zakonnosti," in ibid., p. 264.

76. V. Korotich, "Glasnost zhazhdet zakonov," in ibid., p. 155.

77. Ibid., p. 156.

78. Iu. M. Baturin, *Glasnost': Mneniia, Poiski, Politika* (Moscow, Iuridicheskaia Literatura, 1989).

79. G. Mukhina, *V. I. Lenin o Glasnosti* (Moscow, Politizdat, 1989), p. 3.

80. Ibid., pp. 6–7.

81. Lenin was praised for giving special attention to the role of the press in developing glasnost. Ibid., p. 7.

82. V. A. Bobkov, *Vozrozhdenie Dukha Leninizma* (Moscow, Politizdat, 1989), p. 145.

83. Ibid.

84. A. I. Yakovlev, *Optimizatsiia Ideologicheskoi Raboty* (Moscow, Politizdat, 1990), p. 7.

85. Leonid Batkin, "Glasnost, svoboda pechati," in Iurii Afanasyev and Marc Ferro, eds., *Opyt Slovaria Novogo Myshleniia* (Moscow, Progress, 1989), p. 491.

86. Ibid., pp. 493–495.

87. Ibid., p. 496.

88. Valerii Chalidze, *Zaria Pravovoi Reformy* (Moscow, Progress, 1990), p. 84.

89. Ibid., p. 83.

90. Ibid., p. 85.

91. Ibid., p. 88.

92. Ibid., pp. 101–104.

93. Nina Andreeva, "Ne mogy postupat'sia printsipami," *Sovetskaia Rossiia*, 13 March 1988, p. 3.

94. Ibid.

95. Ibid.

96. Ibid.

97. E. K. Ligachev, *Izbrannye Rechi i Stat'i* (Moscow, Politizdat, 1989), p. 192.

98. Ibid.

99. Ibid., p. 193.

100. See John Gooding, "The XXVIII congress of the CPSU in perspective," *Soviet Studies*, vol. 43, no. 2, 1991, pp. 237–253.

101. Ligachev, *Izbrannye Rechi*, p. 284.

102. Ibid., p. 290.

103. *Bakinskii Rabochii*, 19 December 1990, p. 2.

104. Ibid.

105. Ibid.

106. *Izvestiia*, 6 December 1990, p. 3. The flood of pornography for sale on the streets did not decrease.

107. For commentary on discontent with Gorbachev in March and early April 1991 and growing support for Yeltsin, see *Demokraticheskaia Rossiia*, 5 April 1991, pp. 1–2, 4–6, 10.

3

Social Deviance and Social Collapse

WHEN JOURNALISTS AND academics applied glasnost to discussions of social problems, many official "success" stories of the past were redefined into tales of failure, deviance, immorality, and self-destruction. Glasnost in reporting brought acknowledgment that previously nonexistent problems, such as crime, prostitution, and rape, were alive, serious, and worsening. Questions long taboo, such as how many heroin addicts there were or why teenagers committed suicide, were now posed. Social deviance received more media coverage between 1987 and 1991 than it had enjoyed in the entire half-century from 1930 to 1980. Glasnost heralded a significant break with the past.

Glasnost performed three main roles. First, it exposed long-neglected problems, thereby constructing issues. This process incorporated some truth into social commentaries and provoked abrasive questioning about what had been ignored before. Second, glasnost delimited problems. Journalists specified their characteristics or suggested contours through images and moods. Sometimes they indicated links with other problems. Here there was space for inaccuracy as well as clarification. Third, in some hands glasnost resulted in more rigorous analyses of why particular problems existed and what could be done about them.

Most early reporting, however, focused on "what" and "how" rather than on "why." Description and exposé outweighed assessment and evaluation. Yet in many instances, description alone was a powerful tool. It unmasked past deceptions, corrected earlier omissions, and brought details to readers and viewers. It served to raise awareness.

But facts do not speak for themselves. The selection of and emphasis on certain facts can give rise to partial or biased interpretations. The omission or underplaying of other facts can result in distortion and misrepresentation. Although discovery, honesty, and criticism were among glasnost's achievements, manipulation, exaggeration, and persistent silence on some topics were some of its shortcomings. And not only did the degree of openness vary across social issues, but so did the nature of its application. The general picture was one of heterogeneity, notwithstanding some common treatments across issues. Although, for instance, more statistics became available on most topics, theft and murder were more readily discussed than rape and child abuse.

The impact of glasnost was powerful. Sudden coverage of a spate of social problems thrust numerous issues onto agendas all at once or in quick succession. Citizens enthusiastically devoured the burst of revelatory information, even complaining that there was too much to read. They began to reassess reality. But by 1990, excitement had numbed. Exposure, reexamination, and criticism led to fear and a sense of hopelessness. Citizens became anxious about personal safety and security. In a context of failed economic reform and political chaos, an exuberant glasnost exacerbated moral vacuum and uncertainty and fed exaggerations of social ills. Against the backdrop of relative silence in the past, the pace and intensity at which new issues appeared heightened this growing sense of social decay. There also developed a belief that a general, if undefined, social collapse was occurring. Moral vacuum and deviant behavior meant lawlessness. A sense of social instability, social uncertainty, and lack of social cohesion came to pervade the social fabric.

Glasnost, although worthy of praise, had upset stability and sense of place. It had undermined many of the beliefs and values of the past without offering a coherent set of new ones. Those who had been cynical before now became even more scathing about their lives and their political system.

Sounding more like urban Americans than Russian city dwellers of ten years earlier, Muscovites warned against walking alone at night. They advised against taking taxis on the grounds that drivers might rob passengers. Leningraders insisted that it was foolish to carry much money. In this context, it became fashionable for young men to carry tiny canisters of CS gas to defend themselves. Women's magazines gave advice on self-defense. Newspapers lamented that citizens could even be attacked outside their flats, scream for help, and be ignored by indifferent neighbors. The message from the media was that crime was rampant and growing and that citizens were becoming less responsible in responding to it. And Gorbachev's critics blamed perestroika for bringing crime, social tension, and despair.

Crime

The redefining of the place of crime in society contributed most to this growing sense of insecurity and social collapse. Until the Gorbachev era, crime had not been widely discussed. Then suddenly a barrage of information was released.

Several themes were given prominence in the process of redefinition: the extent of crime and its rapid growth, as illustrated by numerous statistics; the depravity of youths, as revealed by their disproportionate involvement in crime; the brutality of the social fabric, as evidenced by acts of violence and premeditated murders; the immorality and cruelty of criminals who would stoop to child kidnappings for financial gains; the links between crime and the economy, which had given rise to racketeers and corrupt law enforcers; the inadequacies of a legal system in which criminal codes did not address particular crimes or punished them too leniently; inadequate policing by world standards; the inability of Soviet political institutions to maintain law and order; and links between crime and crisis.

Concentration on these themes resulted in a portrayal of society as increasingly unstable. Ideology was turned on its head. One prominent image was that society was not civilized. Ironically, journalists rarely observed that societies now constructed as civilized, such as the United States, suffered much higher crime rates. But the press did admit that when in the past capitalist systems had released crime rates, Soviet ideology had immediately manipulated them. As *Izvestiia* put it: "Insofar as civilized countries were unashamed to reproach themselves, openly and fearlessly, for their social imperfections," commentators in socialist states took this as "confirmation" that crime was "bourgeois" in origin.[1] Moreover,

> in defiance of the facts, the theoreticians of "mature and developed" [socialism] stubbornly never stopped repeating that crime in our country had no socialist roots, that it was alien and explicable only as a vestige of the bourgeois past. In order for theory to be backed up by practice, the media were forced to lie. Supposedly, crime in our country was falling from year to year (the real figures were a strict secret).[2]

Whereas crime under Brezhnev was officially falling, under Gorbachev the opposite obtained.

Consistent with past Soviet practice, official crime statistics were not released for the first four years of Gorbachev's leadership. Then, making a significant historical break, journalists reported in 1989, "In the first quarter of the year, 509,000 crimes had been registered in the country, which is 31 percent up on the same period last year. The crime rate among minors rose by nearly 25 percent."[3] Thereafter articles in the press deplored yearly figures. Coverage of crime became both informative and sensational, generally delivering the message that with each year it was rising. Rarely, however, did articles point out the unreliability of crime statistics. Bold conclusions were often drawn, but these were methodologically dubious.

Between 1989 and 1991, citizens were bombarded with statistics. According to Minister of Internal Affairs Vadim Bakatin, the number of recorded crimes in 1989 increased by 31.8 percent compared with 1988 and by 17 percent in the first three months of 1990. The number of arrests increased in 1989 by 44 percent, and the number of criminals detained rose by 55 percent. In 1989, 1,304,000 people who had committed crimes were caught, and criminal charges were brought against 792,600. The number of juvenile delinquents increased by 15 percent, and they then made up 16 percent of all criminals. One out of every four criminals was a repeat offender. Bakatin revealed that to tackle the increase in crime, 5,800 special teams and mobile groups had been set up. He also noted that in 1989 the police had used firearms 3,891 times, about four times more often than in 1988.[4]

In 1991, the press poured out more figures. *Izvestiia* reported that approximately 809,000 people had been convicted of crimes in 1990, 20 percent more than the previous year. In the Union as a whole, there were 378 convictions per 100,000 people. Conviction rates, however, varied across republics, ranging from 465 per 100,000 in the RSFSR to lows of 144 in Azerbaidzhan and 165 in Armenia. Juvenile crime in 1990 rose, too, with 26.8 percent more teenage convictions than in the previous year.[5]

Numerous tables of recorded crimes committed in 1980, 1985, and 1989 were printed in academic journals such as *Sovetskoe Gosudarstvo i Pravo* (Soviet State and Law). Figures were broken down according to republic, showing the total number of crimes, the total number of crimes per 100,000 people, and the number of apprehended criminals. Figures were further dissected according to age group, social composition, and level of education. Data were also presented on the number of crimes committed in groups and by people under the influence of alcohol. "Criminological commentaries" often accompanied the statistics.[6]

But reporting often stopped short. It did not ask why conviction rates apparently varied. Were police forces more efficient in some republics than in others? Was crime genuinely lower where conviction rates were smaller? To what extent were crime statistics a true reflection of crime committed? And were processes of data collection comparable across republics? These and a host of other questions were generally not asked. Crime statistics worldwide are hazardous, based as they are on reported crime, which understates reality. How to interpret percentage increases in reported crime is especially difficult since in any given year a higher proportion of citizens may come forward than in the previous year, making comparison invalid. And in the Soviet context, citizens may have been more likely to report crimes as society became more open.

More focused reporting discussed different aspects of crime. Concentrating on crime among younger age groups, A. Illesh revealed that in 1987, 50 percent of crimes had been performed by those between the ages of fourteen and twenty-nine. In 1988 and 1989, this age group was responsible for 55 percent and 57 percent of reported crime, respectively. Every third speculator, hard-currency dealer, and extortionist was a young person. In Moscow, Belorussia, and Armenia, the crime rate among adolescents had risen sharply. And in Uzbekistan, young people were responsible for "up to 70 percent of all criminal assaults, burglaries of flats, and group hooliganism."[7]

The message was that most criminals were young people. This may, indeed, have been the case. But further questions went unanswered. How accurate were statistics on crime among youth? What prompted young people to resort to criminal activity? Was the system not meeting their aspirations? Did they perceive crime as the only route to living better? Was it positively correlated with social deprivation?

Whatever the accuracy of the figures, glasnost allowed them to be published. A deluge of information swept the country. But alongside the barrage of statistics came sensational reporting. Journalists told gruesome and shocking stories about violent crimes. The television program "600 Sekund" gave extremely fast, hard-hitting coverage of a range of brutal criminal incidents, interspersed with other news items. The speed of this new-style reporting overwhelmed audiences with information and created a frantic picture of a society in distress. Newspapers created the same image in numerous stories of fights among gangs of youths. A frequent suggestion was that young people were out of control, often seeking revenge and showing insolence toward authority.[8] The film *Tak Zhit' Nel'zia* (mentioned earlier) began with coverage of brutal assault, murder, and rape.[9] The film portrayed criminals as dangerous and unrepenting and as in need of punishment.

The idea that society was unsafe was reinforced by extensive coverage of murder and kidnapping. The press claimed that the number of premeditated murders in Russia, Ukraine, Kazakhstan, Latvia, Armenia, Tadzhikistan, and Kirgizia was increasing.[10] Reports revealed that in Central Asia and in the Caucasus, the kidnapping of young children was on the rise and that one-third of those kidnapped were killed.[11] Complying with the wishes of kidnappers, moreover, did not always pay off. The "returning of a child was no guarantee that the tragedy would not be repeated." An Uzbek family had one child kidnapped after another, and "the fourth was not given back."[12] Details about individual cases emphasized the cruelty and callousness of the crime. In exchange for their victims, kidnappers demanded money, authorizations for flats, and the admission of unqualified applicants to institutes.[13] Kidnapping thus locked into the widespread corrupt practices of obtaining goods and services illegitimately through social connections, influence, or threats.

The emotional level of reporting heightened in cases involving family members. Harrowing coverage was given to the story of Svetlana's anguish when she learned that her daughter, Ol'ia, had been taken away by Nikolai, the child's father.[14] The headline "They stole a child" was hard-hitting. A photograph, taken from behind, of a child wearing a bobble hat and scarf, with a small arm extended upward to hold the hand of an adult (with just the hand shown), suggested the vulnerability of children and the innocent trust they have in others. The parents had agreed to divorce and to keep on good terms for the sake of the child. One day the father appeared, told his mother-in-law that he was missing his daughter and had decided to take her for a walk. They did not return. Thereafter came Svetlana's sad pursuit of Ol'ia. A lawyer told her that unless she kidnapped her daughter, legal action would go in the father's favor because Ol'ia had been living with him since he had kidnapped her from Svetlana. The message of the story was that even in cases where both parents were intelligent and reasonable, not alcoholic or negligent, "kidnapping of one's own children [was] flourishing" and the kidnapper was rarely held responsible.[15] Journalists recommended that the courts address questions of custody and visitation rights.

The press put out several messages about kidnapping: It served corruption, it was a moral tragedy, and it required firmer legislation and police action. In addition, children were not safe from strangers or even from their own parents. Children were innocent victims vulnerable to the abuses of a corrupt adult world.

Investigative reporting on kidnapping reached the conclusion that criminal codes did not adequately address this crime. For instance, no clause covered it in the Georgian Criminal Code, even though the incidence of kidnapping was highest in Georgia. The Russian Criminal Code called for "deprivation of freedom" for up to seven years if the act was committed "for mercenary purposes or from other base motives" and a one-year sentence in the absence of motives. Yet many commentators considered Russian law too lax and criticized redrafted criminal codes for leaving the law "virtually unchanged."[16]

As well as harming children, the corrupt adult world produced the *reket* ("racket"). Descriptions of how individuals were affected by racketeers illustrated the point. *Ogonek* told the story of a thirty-year-old café owner. He claimed that "practically all cooperative cafés and restaurants, many seamstresses, and shops find themselves under the control of racketeers."[17] There were "criminal rackets" and "state rackets." Wherever money was being made, *rekety* made their presence felt and attempted to obtain for themselves part of others' legally earned profits. *Rekety* had always existed where business was done "under the table," but now the cooperative sector of the economy offered them new opportunities for extortion. Afraid, this particular man said, "In the course of a day, thousands of people pass through the café—how can I know who is carrying a knife or a bomb or who would kill? Does this mean that every cooperative must have three militiamen with guns sitting by the door?"[18] Such stories delivered the message that to survive, honest businesspeople had to deal with an unsavory criminal underworld. Thus, the reform process was distorted by criminality.

Reasons given for crime rarely traced it to social deprivation. Consistent with developing ideology, the prevalence of crime was initially linked to "the years of stagnation" under Brezhnev, which gave rise to parasites, black marketeers, drunkards, home brewers, and drug abusers.[19] By 1990, however, commentators such as Bakatin were arguing that "the slump in restructuring the economy" was partly to blame for increased social tension, as was the "politicization of society."[20] Bakatin observed that although politicization had its positive side, it also enabled "ideologues" to take advantage of social tension and to discredit the authorities. But then the authorities were sometimes corrupt, too. One "main difficulty" in combating organized crime was its protection "by corrupt functionaries in our law enforcement system as well as, of course, by degenerates from the party, state, and economic apparatus."[21]

Whatever the several causes of crime, results of its coverage included shock, disapproval, and a growing support in some quarters for "law and order." This support found frequent expression in more traditional publications, particularly *Pravda*, which asserted that society was inadequately policed. As discourse about "crisis" penetrated the media in 1990, one article claimed that in Paris there was 1 police officer per 180 inhabitants and in New York 1 per 150; but in Moscow and Minsk there was 1 police officer for every 1,700 and 2,000 residents, respectively.[22] The situation was worse than before because the volunteer helpers from the public (*druzhinniki*) had become much less enthusiastic. Apparently, their number had fallen from 14 million to 9 million.[23] Therefore, asked *Pravda*'s correspondent, "why not put part of the Soviet army into police uniforms?" In reply, Deputy Minister of Internal Affairs General Lisauskas answered, "We have raised such a question. After all, police regiments are topped up with soldiers doing their compulsory service. And I do not think the young men would be against serving in police units near home. But that is up to the Ministry of Defense. We would accept help from the military."[24]

By 1990, reporting was stressing that resolutions about fighting crime had not sufficiently helped. In April 1988, the Central Committee had passed the resolution On the Status of the Struggle Against Crime in the Country and Additional Measures to Prevent Lawbreaking. Party committees were criticized for their lack of vigilance and were urged to step up law and order. The soviets, trade unions, and Komsomol were encouraged to fight crime by liaising with the comrades courts.[25] But crime kept growing. These measures had failed. Then Gorbachev returned to the issue of crime at the Central Committee plenum of April 1989 when he called for "an uncompromising struggle against criminal elements" and castigated party and government bodies for their "slackening attention."[26] But by the end of 1990, the argument that the army should help the police had superseded Gorbachev's call. In February 1991, army help became reality.

In 1990 and 1991, Gorbachev's speeches more frequently referred to the need for law and order. He told the Fourth Congress of People's Deputies in December 1990 that "restoring order in the country is now most necessary for overcoming the crisis." Crime was one aspect of the "crisis tendencies" that gripped economy, society, polity, and relations between nationalities.[27] The presidential decree of 29 January 1991, On Cooperation of the Militia and Subdivisions of the Armed Forces of the USSR to Safeguard Law and Order and to Struggle Against Crime, was published in the press the following day.[28] The army was to help the militia maintain "social order on the streets and in public places."[29] Crime had become "more dangerous" and had taken on a "mass character," making such measures necessary. The decree was said to be consistent with the recent law On Supplementary Measures for Stabilizing the Economic and Socio-political Life of the Country, passed on 24 September 1990, and was also in keeping with the Supreme Soviet resolution of 23 November 1990, On the Situation in the Country.[30] At the same time, a special committee for coordinating the activities of law enforcement bodies was set up under the president, with Iurii Golik as its chairperson.

Consistent with these attempts to step up law and order, the KGB was given new powers to investigate foreign joint ventures and to establish two new crime-fighting committees. Then on 4 February 1991, Gorbachev issued another presidential decree, On Measures to Step Up the Struggle Against the Most Dangerous Crimes and Their Organized Forms. It called for the setting up within the USSR Ministry of Internal Affairs of a special chief administration for combating the most dangerous crimes, organized crimes, corruption, and drugs. Regional units were to be set up within two months to promote cooperation across republics.[31]

Gorbachev's critics accused him of harping on increases in crime so he could strengthen law and order and thereby maintain an authoritarian grip over society. His preoccupation with crime followed fast on his clawing for the presidency, powers once enjoyed by the Supreme Soviet. According to his critics, putting the army on the streets was just one aspect of a more general undermining of democracy. Within two weeks of the presidential decree, however, newspaper articles were stressing that so far there had been no obvious threat to democracy. *Moskovskaia Pravda* contended that the move was justified since in 1990 the number of street crimes had been 5.9 percent higher than in 1989. Moreover, in January 1991, street crime had jumped again, by 15.2 percent throughout the USSR and by a high 28.5 percent in Moscow. There were now eighty-seven joint patrols in the capital and three times this number on weekends. Their routes and locations were apparently decided only after consultation with the Ministry of Internal Affairs.[32] More skeptical of the policy's success, *Moskovskii Komsomolets* revealed that there were joint patrols in 449 towns but that not every district had them because "there are not enough soldiers now."[33] Here the message was that joint patrols were policing in spotty fashion.

Certainly, law and order were extremely high on Gorbachev's agenda early in 1991. And some of the old-style paranoia crept into the public statements of political figures. In February 1991, the newly appointed deputy KGB chief, Viktor Grushko, warned that Western intelligence agencies had increased their activities in the USSR since the end of the cold war.[34] Rumors that Western banks were trying to destabilize the Soviet economy by flooding it with fifty- and one-hundred-ruble notes circulated in February after Gorbachev suddenly withdrew these notes from circulation.[35]

Issues of policing were further complicated because they were inextricably intertwined with the nationalities question. Cooperation of republican interior ministries was vital for the struggle against crime. But interior ministries in Georgia and Moldavia had already declared themselves independent of Moscow and were answerable only to their republican Supreme Soviets.[36] Even worse for Moscow, Georgia's KGB was run by a nationalist, Otar Khatiashvili. He had earlier been removed from his post by Moscow for criticizing the killings by Soviet troops of demonstrators in Tbilisi in April 1989 but had later been reinstated by Georgian president Zviad Gamsakhurdia.[37] The fragmentation of police forces and also of the KGB was of concern to Gorbachev. Iurii Golik allegedly declared that such fragmentation was "naive and absurd," playing into the hands of criminals.[38]

Although crime in the narrow sense was a social issue, by 1991 it had taken on a distinctly political hue. Crime was part of the crisis engulfing Soviet society. Crime necessitated new political measures, new committees, and new modes of policing. Crime was an important aspect of economic collapse. It was also an ingredient in national ferment in intransigent republics. *Pravda* lamented that in 1990, 795 people had died and 3,660 had been injured as a result of mass disturbances and interethnic conflict.[39] And the way in which republics were run affected the nature of policing and attempts to crack down on crime.

How to tackle rising crime fed into arguments of both the right and left. It was used as a justification for more law and order and tighter regulations, particularly by those wishing for a return to the authoritarian ways of the past and their paranoid rhetoric. Democrats, in reply, could cite attempts to reduce crime, such as putting the army on the streets, as repressive and as examples of the undermining of democracy. Crime in 1991 was on the agenda of all political actors and was analyzed in accordance with their broader political programs and understanding of the crisis. In the space of just six years, the issue of crime had been thoroughly redefined. It was no longer a blight restricted to capitalist societies. Moreover, how to cope with it was increasingly controversial and was linked to other issues of economic and political transformation.

Drug Abuse

Like other crimes, drug abuse was not a public issue before perestroika. The problem was officially nonexistent. So when discussions about the pleasures and dangers of marijuana, mescaline, and LSD were commonplace in the West, they were absent from the media in Brezhnev's Soviet Union. As heroin addiction spread through Western states in the 1970s, the Soviet Union prided itself on not having this blight. Drug addiction, like crime, was portrayed as characteristic of capitalism's moral decay.

In the 1920s, there had been "a plethora of conferences, books, and articles" on drug addiction. Morphine had been popular before the revolution, then cocaine. But after 1930, the literature thinned considerably, and officials claimed that drug addiction was declining. An extremely narrow medical literature was produced after Khrushchev, and debate did not occur in the wider press.[40]

By the 1980s, heroin addiction was part of Soviet society, too, but its existence was initially hushed up. Once the growing strength of glasnost forced the problem into the open, however, it was presented as "an evil that experts acknowledge is growing around the world."[41] This early redefinition decoupled drug abuse from a particular socio-economic system.

Glasnost produced five main results in writings on drugs: exposure of the problem, categorizations of abuse, release of statistics, reflections on treatment, and serious discussions of the social, personal, and moral implications of drug abuse. Early articles written in 1987 were somewhat sensational in tone, just as articles on other crimes had been. Magazines printed arresting photographs of needles, treatment centers, and despairing addicts. There followed in 1988 a limited debate on how the authorities could best respond to marijuana and heroin. Journalists scrutinized and questioned medical treatment and punishment, while some even defended these practices. This debate continued intermittently in the press until 1990, when more systematic attempts were made to explain why individuals turned to drugs. Over time, discussions became more sophisticated.

In 1987, as glasnost strengthened, journalists A. Illesh and E. Shestinskii informed readers that drug abuse fell into two categories: "classical" and "vulgar." "Classical drug abuse" (*klassicheskaia narkomaniia*) referred to the use of plant substances, such as marijuana, whereas "vulgar drug abuse" (*vul'garnaia narkomaniia*) meant the taking of "new, homemade narcotic substances ... produced by processing preparations of various kinds ... similar to those that are produced industrially for medical purposes."[42] This distinction was similar to Western categories of "soft" and "hard" drugs. Glasnost was thus used to instruct readers in how to classify.

Statistics were released two years earlier than general crime rates. In November 1987, it was reported that whereas in 1984 vulgar drug abuse had accounted for 2 percent of all drugs used, in 1986 the figure had climbed to 12–16 percent and in 1987 had exceeded 30 percent.[43] Alarmed at the pace of change, officials apparently commented that "it's difficult to say what drug addicts will be using a year or two from now."[44] According to Illesh and Shestinskii writing one year later, hard drugs were particularly popular in the Baltic republics, central Russia, and Moscow and Leningrad.[45]

Like all crime statistics, those on drug abuse probably seriously understated the problem. Nevertheless, in the late 1980s they were being released, giving an indication of likely minimum levels. For instance, V. Pankin, the head of criminal investigations, revealed that at the beginning of 1988, 131,000 people had been on record for having tried drugs at least once. Of these, 50,000 had been put on the medical register as drug addicts.[46] By mid-1990, the official figure had increased to more than 117,000.[47] By October 1990, fresh estimates suggested that 1.5 million citizens had tried or were using drugs. Specialists in the Ministry of Internal Affairs believed that the drug business was growing and noted threefold increases in the amounts confiscated.[48] Claims were made that 80 percent of the Soviet drug business came from domestic sources and that 20 percent was imported.[49]

Discussions of medical treatment received by addicts made even more statistics available. In 1987, according to Illesh and Shestinskii, 77 percent of registered addicts underwent medical treatment, allegedly voluntarily. Of these, 15,000 broke their habit, 21,600 suffered administrative disciplinary action, and 4,000 failed to complete their treatment and so were sent to "treatment and labor centers."[50] Writing in 1988 in the troubleshooting magazine *Ogonek,* Irina Vedeneeva questioned the success rate of treatment, pointing out that authorities often did not keep track of discharged addicts. She claimed that even addicts who found themselves in the most sympathetic treatment centers, such as hospital number 17, suffered low rates of success. Only 10 percent of those who had undergone treatment did not return later for more help.[51]

The pattern of redefining drug abuse included numerous statistics that indicated a worsening social problem difficult to eradicate through treatment or policing. But again, few asked to what extent official figures came close to mirroring reality. Vedeneeva was an exception. And as in reporting on crime, special attention was devoted to young people, in this case to the spread of drugs among minors.

In 1990, the All-Union Society for Saving Children and Teenagers from Drugs reported that children in the nine to eleven age group were beginning to use drugs, whereas previously the fourteen to sixteen age band had been the youngest. Allegedly, 70 percent of drug addicts were between sixteen and twenty-nine, and 30 percent of these were younger than twenty-four. One of the messages delivered was that one-half of those who used drugs were likely to die before the age of thirty.[52]

Journalism presented a sad picture of dying children and teenagers. One resulting image was of the unnecessary death of the nation's youth. This image was particularly barbed since official ideology had always constructed young people as joyful builders of communism. Now they were dispirited dropouts with no apparent enthusiasm for the Motherland. Ideology was again stood on its head. Another image presented drug addicts as "parasites" and as "socially dangerous." Subscribers to these labels tended to support the arrest and punishment of addicts and strict regimes in psychiatric hospitals. They challenged the remedies put forward by "pseudohumanists" who advocated more sympathetic counseling in enlightened medical settings.[53]

Some writings dwelt on the difficulty of saving youth presented by the sterility of existing institutions, which lacked imaginative approaches. Although in 1987, according to a decree of the Presidium of the Supreme Soviet of the RSFSR, cure and rehabilitation centers took in youth for six months to two years, research indicated that success was limited. Young people endured "monotonous, uninteresting, and fatiguing" days of work, which did not inspire them to master any particular profession.[54] Improvements were needed in work therapy. Another problem seemed to be "the older the teenager, the lower the desire to be cured." Among sixteen-year-olds, 9.5 percent did not believe in the effectiveness of treatment. The figure rose to 22 percent among seventeen-year-olds and 27.3 percent among eighteen-year-olds.[55]

Another message delivered by the media was that in 1986 and 1987 the punishment of addicts had been harsh. In each year, thirty thousand drug users had faced criminal proceedings, and some had been imprisoned for the first time for possession of small amounts. By 1988, implementation of criminal codes had become more lenient. Addicts who did not involve others in their addiction were viewed as ill, rather than as criminals, and small-scale possession no longer resulted in automatic imprisonment.[56] But addicts were regularly convicted of related criminal acts, such as forged prescriptions and domestic theft. In 1987, there had been thirty-five recorded cases of addicts attempting to acquire drugs with forged prescriptions.[57] They had also broken into pharmacies; in response, by 1988, 96 percent had installed burglar alarms.[58] An estimated 35 percent of illegal drugs in cities leaked from hospitals, and in the first ten months of 1987, seventy-three medical employees had faced related charges. By the end of 1987, thirty-five drug dealers had also been arrested because police campaigns were being stepped up.[59] As in other countries, burglary, robbery, and murder were crimes performed by hardened addicts since they had to spend large amounts to satisfy their daily habits. From 1987 on, the press explicitly linked drug abuse to other crimes.

The press also imparted information about deficiencies in police investigation of narcotics. Pankin revealed that nine hundred people were active in such investigation, but, regrettably, many worked badly, assuming incorrectly that drug abuse did not exist in all regions.[60] In 1990, Illesh reiterated the point, suggesting that "there is practically nowhere left where this problem, to one degree or another, has not exerted an influence on the criminal situation."[61] The production of synthetic drugs, in particular, appeared to be on the increase, and "just in Leningrad alone, over the last five years, six(!) illegal industries have been liquidated."[62]

By 1990, the battle against drug abuse was being increasingly portrayed as a fight across borders requiring the cooperation of all republics as well as liaison with Interpol. Illesh regretted that republics and regions had different attitudes toward this cooperation. And the greater independence given to ministries of internal affairs in the republics complicated the situation, just as the divisive nationalities question made concerted action difficult. He concluded that "only a united anti-narcotics policy in all republics of the country and well-organized interaction between law enforcement agencies can give a noticeable result." He went on, "I am convinced that not one republic acting independently can overcome such an evil."[63] The Ministry of Internal Affairs of the USSR, he applauded, was now setting up a centralized inter-republican structure to fight narcotics. Thus, the battle against drugs was a political issue inextricably linked to the nationalities question and openly addressed by the media. As a result, advocates of Union had more material to cite against the cause of independence.

Discussions of cooperation between republics and political institutions included complaints about costs and dangers. For example, the guarding of poppy fields by police and dogs, paid for by the Department for Combating the Embezzlement of Socialist Property and Speculation, was a drain on resources. Although the poppies were important for their medicinal properties, was the cost of guarding them worth the result? "Chases, night ambushes, and the apprehension of addicts, often armed with knives and sawed-off guns," were common.[64] The suggestion was that everything connected to drug abuse involved violence.

Much reporting, then, focused on the threats addicts posed to society and the associated costs. In a very different mold, Irina Vedeneeva gave readers one of the first sympathetic, if sensational, accounts of the plight of addicts, conveyed through photographs as well as text. It began with two scared eyes surrounded by a blackened face and a syringe below. The eyes transmitted horror, despair, and dependence. Gruesome photographs of mutilated veins, injections, and outstretched hands asking for help reinforced the image of desperation and unmet need. An addict with head hung low sitting next to a chessboard whose pieces had been knocked over implied the impossibility of pursuing normal pleasures. Addicts standing in rows with hands on their heads indicated the maltreatment that took place in some hospitals and conveyed the message that their plight was misunderstood. Treatment appeared humiliating, degrading, impersonal, and inhuman. Addicts slumped over their food at a table showed alienation, distance, and depression. Feet sticking out on a trolley carrying a covered dead body showed where this story was likely to end.[65]

Vedeneeva's text began by telling someone's personal horror story. This technique gave the problem of drug dependence an immediacy and a quiet terror:

> It's true, the last time the daughter was in hospital number 17 (it was not so long ago) it seemed to her mother that treatment had helped—for the first time in her life. Her daughter came out, and in her eyes there was some light. But not for long. The light quickly went out. Clearly, it was too late.
>
> "She cannot walk any more, think, speak, even stand up and close the door. She remembers nothing," says her mother. "She only looks straight ahead, eyes empty, with indifference. She is not long for this world. Save others before it is too late."[66]

Vedeneeva argued that "we have a poor understanding of the problem, study it inadequately. Age, sex, social origin, region, reasons. ... We lack such research, and even if it does exist, specialists are unaware of it. Not having these data, we are doomed to a passive struggle with drug addiction and for a long time to come will have the same sad percentage of remissions."[67] Vedeneeva called for research and new methods of treatment. She maintained that a more individual approach geared to a person's own characteristics—age and sex, for instance—should be developed.

Data convincingly backed up her conclusions. Even in hospital number 17, treatment was not tailored to the needs of individuals. And in the notorious psychiatric hospital number 15, addicts of all ages were thrown together with the mentally ill and with alcoholics. The first impression gained by visitors was "an eerie squeaking from unoiled steel bolts of the door, gloomy nurses, the haggard faces of chronic alcoholics dressed in one-sized clothing." But most depressing was the hospital fence, which was "filthy, terrible, shabby."[68] Vedeneeva offered a picture reminiscent of Erving Goffman's *Asylums*.[69] The atmosphere evoked by her writing was one of discomfort and suffering; the message, that misunderstood individuals were being stripped of their identities in inhuman surroundings.

Glasnost permitted such painful stories to be told and also gave a voice to the victims. Quotations from addicts enhanced the sense of abuse in society at large. According to one, "I studied in the technicum. The director called me in and confidentially asked, 'Tell me honestly if you are injecting and I will do nothing to you. On the contrary, I will help you.' And foolishly I said honestly that I had tried it. I was sacked the next day."[70] In reporting this incident, Vedeneeva illustrated social indifference, hostility, and condemnation.

After these early exposés came attempts in academic journals to look at who turned to drugs and why. Regretting that inadequate scholarly attention had been devoted to analyzing the problem, R. Gotlib and L. Romanova set out to examine the reasons behind it and the "concrete social processes" involved.[71]

Research found that feelings of alienation, inertia, and pessimism were among the causes. Gotlib and Romanova suggested that undesirable characters involved with contraband and illegal earnings took advantage of vulnerable citizens experiencing these emotions. The authors blamed both categories of person on the period of stagnation.[72] The Brezhnev years had caused moral baseness and laziness. Disrespect for work, particularly among the young, was one result. Of those drug takers who committed other crimes as well, 34 percent did not work, and of these 71 percent had not worked for a long time. Eighty percent of female drug users did not work.[73]

These academics argued that socially undesirable characteristics, such as lack of a job, were relevant. These included poor examples set by parents, which were often repeated in their children, especially in "unhappy families." Here bad relations among family members and sometimes a lack of contact with outside institutions such as schools provided a context in which drug abuse could develop.[74]

Men doing temporary and seasonal work away from home were another category given to drug abuse. Their new "bachelor lifestyle," in which they were cut off from close friends and family, brought out their weaknesses. Other men away from home were glad to sever family ties or were hiding from alimony payments. Here "family nihilism" was to blame and often arose when men viewed the family as a burden.[75] The instabilities of single-parent families also contributed to drug abuse.[76] Consistent with ideology, the authors maintained that good families were a haven of protection. Absence from the family, broken families, or bad families accentuated human susceptibilities and destructive behavior patterns.

Not all their conclusions, however, coincided with ideology on the family, work, and period of stagnation. Gotlib and Romanova reported that more than 50 percent of their interviewees had said that their habit developed "thanks to the availability of hemp."[77] Many young people turned to drugs out of a desire to try "forbidden fruit." In one sample (of unreported size), 29.4 percent wanted to imitate those who did take drugs, 15 percent hoped to experience the widely acclaimed "euphoria" that would result, and 22 percent feared the label of "coward" if they did not indulge. Drugs were also more popular in certain settings than others. In ports, for instance, ships brought in the "evil," especially "from capitalist countries."[78] Here ideological resonance crept back in. Although more probing sociological analysis did commence under Gorbachev, it frequently incorporated old-style ideological concepts as well as new ones. In many cases, they sat uneasily side by side.

In 1989, journalists and academics finally admitted that drugs were a problem in the Soviet army, too. In the early years of glasnost, criticisms of the army had been taboo. As late as March 1989, journalists writing for the popular youth magazine *Iunost'* were regretting that their articles on suicide and violence in the army were still being censored internally.[79] Only the most troubleshooting publications, such as *Ogonek*, dared touch the army. In this context, Boris Kalachev's article "Drugs in the Army" was a pacesetter. It noted that "the phenomenon was far from new" and briefly traced its history from the end of the nineteenth century.[80] Then in a study of 1,132 men from Krasnodarsk *krai* (territory), Kalachev reported that more than 50 percent had taken drugs and that 6 percent had done so for the first time in the army. Demobilized men in Kiev claimed that hashish was the most common drug. But the pattern varied according to where men had served. Former *Afgantsy,* for instance, were more disposed to heroin and LSD. The main reasons given for turning to drugs were curiosity (59.7 percent), the desire to be like others (28.9 percent), and stress (3.8 percent).[81]

An all-union survey of 2,000 drug takers conducted in 1989 reinforced the picture of regional variations. Hashish was six times more likely to be a user's favorite drug in Tashkent than anywhere in Latvia. Morphine was especially popular in L'vov oblast, Latvia, Gorky oblast, and Moscow. When asked which drugs they took, 33.5 percent named hashish, 23.1 percent said morphine, 2.8 percent liked opium, 3.7 percent cited Promedol (a drug used to treat spasms), 5.4 percent took codeine tablets, and 3 percent took koknar. Some enjoyed two or more drugs. Sixty-four percent of younger drug takers sniffed glue, 64 percent drank benzine, 55 percent took acetone, 37 percent inhaled the cockroach spray Dikhlofos, 27.6 percent used dyes, 11.8 percent inhaled chloroform, 10 percent swallowed brake fluid, 3.4 percent enjoyed antifreeze, and 5.7 percent mentioned other substances.[82] This information was revelatory and shocking, reinforcing the image of depravity and self-destruction.

Although by the 1990s much more sophisticated work on drug abuse needed to be done, reporters were asking sharper questions than they had four years before. Nevertheless, ideological categories shaped the more conservative articles in *Pravda,* which still reprimanded work collectives and the Komsomol for insufficient vigilance. But more sensitive reporting showed that a reduction in drug abuse was not simply a crude question of vigilance.

Prostitution

Like crime and drug abuse, prostitution was rarely mentioned in the press until 1986. There had been some discussion in the 1920s, but thereafter prostitution became a non-issue. The general pattern of discourse was that whatever had been a "problem" in the 1920s was either "solved" or "declining" in the 1930s as a result of the great "achievements" of socialist construction.[83]

According to ideology, prostitution did not exist under Soviet socialism. It was characteristic of capitalist systems, where the right to work was not guaranteed and where unemployed women were "forced" into prostitution so they could eat. Then, beginning in 1986 and escalating in 1987, newspaper articles on prostitution admitted its existence, deplored its extent, and described the lives of prostitutes. The barrage of statistics that accompanied the opening of crime and drug abuse was absent since far fewer had been collected. Although spotty data were released in piecemeal fashion, articles focused on the immorality of prostitutes and how they could best be punished.[84]

Journalism in 1986 and 1987 shattered the old myth that prostitution existed only under capitalism. But why it existed under socialism was not thoroughly analyzed. At best, inadequate accounts argued that prostitution, like drug abuse, resulted from poor upbringing, single parenthood, divorce, and the Brezhnev years of stagnation.

Prostitution was the first "new" issue to be covered by newspapers such as *Komsomol'skaia Pravda, Sovetskaia Rossiia, Literaturnaia Gazeta* (Literary Gazette), *Nedelia* (Week), and *Trud* (Labor). Early reporting offered sensational exposés and moral messages rather than critical analyses of why prostitution existed or who chose to make it a profession. Underage schoolgirls who performed sexual favors in cars and then blackmailed their clients were held up as examples of the depravity of youth.[85] The number of cases of venereal disease had quadrupled among young people in Georgia between 1980 and 1986 because of prostitution.[86] Young women who "worked" hotels in tourist spots in Sochi by soliciting foreigners were an insult to society.[87] Madames who lured young women to work in brothels, taking advantage of their lack of residence permits and their poverty and later threatening to tell their parents that they were prostitutes, were corrupt.[88] Pimps who demanded seventy rubles a day "protection" money, and who beat up prostitutes who did not pay it, illustrated the seamy side of this life.[89] These early articles dwelt on moral degradation, deception, crime, violence, and venereal disease.

In 1986 and 1987, horror stories abounded, often complete with lurid details. Articles described "dynasties" of prostitutes who "worked together" and who included grandmothers of seventy years of age down to their granddaughters of fourteen.[90] Prostitution, journalism warned, could bring syphilis and result in drunkenness, paralysis, freezing in snowdrifts, and even the amputation of hands and feet. One prostitute had had her throat slit by a deranged man. Sometimes prostitutes even fought among themselves to defend their own turf and to prevent competition from rivals.[91] The press constructed a picture of violence, illness, and corruption. More fairy-tale journalism suggested that prostitutes often dreamed of being saved from their plight of loneliness and self-destruction by a gallant customer, prefera-bly a foreigner who would whisk them away to a more comfortable world.[92] The chances of this happening, however, were slim.

Nevertheless, the hope of being "rescued" plus the lure of higher earnings attracted more young women into prostitution. Many press articles that tried to deliver the message of its unattractiveness backfired and unwittingly encouraged women and girls to become prostitutes. The popular film *Interdevochka* (Hard-Currency Prostitute) on the screens in 1989, also sug-gested that bored women who turned to prostitution for excitement and bet-ter lives could indeed win a foreigner to take them to the West. Members of the Soviet audience criticized the heroine for her unhappiness once she had married a Swede and for her yearning for Russia. They suggested that it was her own fault that her new life in Sweden did not work out. She was herself to blame for not settling down and taking advantage of fresh opportuni-ties.[93] Like the disapproving messages of many press articles, the suggestions of *Interdevochka* were rejected by some Soviet youth. To them, press and film showed the advantages of prostitution. Women could make a large amount of money quickly, buy otherwise inaccessible clothes and food, and enjoy proximity to foreigners. Life could be more glamorous than working night shifts in a textile factory or milking cows for a pittance.

Academic writings appearing toward the end of 1987 furnished more sys-tematic explanations of prostitution. Research among prostitutes in Geor-gia, for instance, found that women saw discrepancies between the lives they dreamed of living and everyday reality. Images of elegant and successful women on television underlined the mediocrity of the respondents' lives. Unable to afford boots at 120 rubles a pair, some women found prostitution attractive as a supplementary income.[94] On average, young women then earned 50 rubles for their services. Older and downtrodden streetwalkers re-ceived as little as 5 or 10 rubles. For women earning between 80 and 120 ru-bles a month in a conventional job, 50 rubles for one client was highly at-tractive. Researchers discovered that many prostitutes spent their earnings on their children, housing, and food as well as on clothing and cosmetics for themselves. The increased financial opportunities open to women as a result of prostitution, especially at a time of growing economic hardship in a con-text of raised expectations, made it an attractive option for many.[95]

The Georgian survey looked at 532 prostitutes who had been on police files. Seventy percent were younger than thirty. Fifty-two percent were di-vorced, 34 percent had never been married, 8.5 percent were married, and 6 percent were widowed. Seventy-five percent of the women had at least a sec-ondary school education. They had "the most ordinary social origins" and were generally not part of the criminal world.[96] Their main aim was to supplement low wages. Modern consumerism had encouraged this goal, as had "the shattering of principles of social justice" and "the deformation of value orientations."[97] Academics concluded that prostitution was "a complex and multifaceted phenomenon" in need of further research to discover more precisely its extent, sources, and problems. They believed that sensible policy recommendations should be based upon more complete data.[98]

As panic about crime rose in 1989 and 1990, prostitution was increasingly discussed in tandem with other problems, such as illegal hard-currency deals and the purchase of goods from Westerners. Early articles had incorporated these points, but larger numbers of tourists in the USSR at a time when Gorbachev's popularity in the West was peaking and Soviet economic reform was failing meant that more visitors could supply citizens with goods that their own economy had promised but could not deliver. In late 1989, *Nedelia* reported that 4 million tourists had visited the USSR in 1986 and 6 million in 1988. This influx had allegedly contributed to increases in prostitution.[99] The subtext here was that immoral foreigners from capitalist systems shared the blame for the spread of prostitution. But so, too, did "imperfections in criminal and administrative legislation" that failed to influence the behavior of lawbreakers. Fines of two hundred rubles were not adequate deterrents for prostitutes since they earned much more.[100]

Gorbachev's attempt to steer the USSR toward a "socialist" market economy meant that the attractions of prostitution increased. Prostitution offered higher wages than most sectors of the economy at a time of growing unemployment for women. Money earned from prostitution helped cushion the steep price increases of April 1991 and meant easier access to the consumer goods that television now advertised but that were out of reach of most citizens. The temptation to become "a hard-currency prostitute" (*valutnaia prostitutka*) increased as the dollar penetrated the economy in 1990 and 1991, even more so in 1992 and 1993. Glossy television advertisements for holidays abroad, for which citizens had to pay in rubles and in hard currency at a time before the ruble was convertible, were an additional pressure.

As the crude idea that anything that happened in the West was "normal," legitimate, and worthy of emulation spread in popular culture, prostitution gained fresh legitimacy. The staging in August 1991 of Edward Albee's "Everything in the Garden" (*Vse v Sadu*) at the Sovremennik Theater in Moscow delivered the message that prostitution was common in New York families, where housewives strove to supplement their husbands' inadequate incomes to obtain a few small luxuries. The way the play was interpreted indicated that prostitution was acceptable and that it existed in stable nuclear families, in which husbands became accustomed to their wives' profession.

Recommendations for combating prostitution varied. One argument held that "this immoral business" could best be tackled by pooling the efforts of the police and the Komsomol. Together they could rid society of this "filth" (*griaz'*).[101] A similar position called for a "real war" against prostitution.[102] Another suggested that since prostitution was spreading "like an epidemic," it should be made a criminal offense with sterner punishments than the administrative measures already taken. Prostitutes could be issued with a warning and a fine of up to one hundred rubles in the first instance and up to two hundred rubles if the offense was repeated within the year. Critics questioned whether this was an adequate deterrent given that young prostitutes' earnings were much higher.[103] In fact, prostitutes were generally picked up by the militia for reasons other than prostitution—usually for loitering in hotels.[104] In the same vein was the opinion that such "moral degradation" had to be "criminally punishable."[105]

More enlightened approaches noted that repressive measures and legislation against prostitution did not deter it.[106] Young girls, especially those who had left their jobs and families, needed to be educated away from it.[107] Viewing prostitution across the centuries, Sergei Golod argued that neither legislative nor medical measures had ever fully solved it. Rather, "sociospiritual" changes were needed in society itself.[108] In a different vein, at the end of the 1980s some prostitutes were arguing that their profession should be legalized, an argument reminiscent of those made in the United States and in Western Europe ten years earlier.

In the space of just five years, prostitution became increasingly attractive to some young women for the financial benefits it offered at a time of growing economic uncertainty. The media images of a life destroyed by venereal disease, cruel pimps, immoral earnings, and shame did not automatically convince citizens that the risks outweighed the benefits. By the early 1990s, there was general agreement among policymakers and journalists that prostitution should be discouraged, although they differed about how this could best be achieved. One problem that made deterrence more pressing was the spread of AIDS.

AIDS

For most of the Soviet past, the press had not dwelt on the illnesses and diseases still suffered under socialism. Discussions were largely restricted to specialist medical journals. In the 1920s, popular journals and magazines had covered health problems and had provided information and advice on a range of diseases, including syphilis and gonorrhea.[109] But during the 1930s and after, such delicate misfortunes were not so readily reported.

Obviously AIDS could not have been discussed earlier since in the 1980s it was a new issue worldwide. Although the Soviet press did not immediately give AIDS the extensive coverage it received in Britain and the United States or devote as much space to it as to crime, drugs, and prostitution, journalists did discuss AIDS, notably in *Ogonek, Izvestiia, Komsomol'skaia Pravda, Meditsinskaia Gazeta* (Medical Newspaper), and *Pravda*. *Ogonek* provided the most probing investigative journalism. *Izvestiia* was a mine of useful information, interviewing specialists who imparted socially necessary facts. *Meditsinskaia Gazeta* reported on individual cases, while *Pravda* more coolly noted relevant new legislation.

The first newspaper articles on AIDS took the line that it was a dreadful disease that ought to be discussed openly.[110] Thereafter a range of views was expressed in letters to the press and in commentaries on those letters. On this topic, more than on crime, drugs, and prostitution, the press broadened discourse to include readers' opinions.

One strong reaction moralized about the disgrace of having AIDS, often blaming the victims for illicit conduct. This approach paralleled disparaging images of prostitutes. Talking about AIDS to journalist Novikov in *Komsomol'skaia Pravda*, Vadim Pokrovskii, director of the Central Epidemiology Research Institute and after 1989 director of the AIDS Center in Moscow, regretted having received the following letter:

> We, graduates of a medical institute (16 young men), are categorically opposed to the fight against the new "illness" AIDS! We intend to hinder the search for ways of combating this noble epidemic in every possible way. We are sure that within a short time AIDS will destroy all drug addicts, homosexuals, and prostitutes. We are confident that Hippocrates would have approved of our decision. Long live AIDS![111]

Pokrovskii deplored that fact that AIDS sufferers were being made scapegoats in such a way.

Two months later, Novikov reported that *Komsomol'skaia Pravda* had received a flood of letters in response. Competing views were printed. One citizen admitted that:

> I fully support the opinion of the sixteen young medics that AIDS is a cleansing agent of humanity that will save it from drug addicts, homosexuals, and prostitutes. You write that children are dying, but useful endeavors include victims, especially when you consider that there are too many people on the planet and that there is not enough food or housing, including in our own country.[112]

By contrast, critics of the provocative letter called on medicine to do all it could to diagnose, prevent, and cure AIDS. Others inquired whether AIDS was really as dangerous as was feared. One reader suggested that mandatory annual AIDS tests should be given and that the test result should be noted down in every citizen's passport. An African regretted that fear of AIDS had led mothers to tell their children not to go near blacks, saying, "Get away; you'll be infected with AIDS."[113]

As in Britain, articles explained how AIDS could be contracted. Interviewed in *Izvestiia*, Pokrovskii dispelled myths about AIDS and pointed out the risks of blood transfusions, unsterile needles, manicures, and pedicures. He confessed that "we do not know the real position about the possibilities for AIDS spreading in our country. We do not know how many prostitutes, drug addicts and homosexuals we have."[114] But the USSR did not launch an advertising campaign on television about how only the "tip of the AIDS iceberg" was visible, as was done in Britain in 1988. Nor did Soviet leaders openly warn against the dangers of casual sex, although individual articles put this message across. Nor did the USSR follow the example of Britain's 1989 newspaper advertisements that showed pictures of healthy-looking AIDS carriers today with exactly the same healthy outward appearance in several years' time. Not until 1991 did posters about AIDS appear inside metro trains in the capital. Temerity about sex education in the USSR did not provide a solid foundation on which to build education about AIDS. That was left to the informal publication *SPID-Info,* sold in metro stations and on the streets. In early 1990, it had a print run of 220,000.

SPID-Info answered a range of questions posed by readers, such as whether oral sex could lead to AIDS. Its column "Facts Against Rumors" dispelled social myths.[115] It delivered sane messages such as "Remember: Condoms prevent not only AIDS but also venereal disease."[116] Using visual images, *SPID-Info* published sad cartoons that conveyed the stresses of modern sex: Man meets woman. They dance. They go home. They are both terrified of AIDS, so their lovemaking is interrupted. He rushes off in search of condoms but cannot buy them anywhere. He returns to her accusation that he is not a real man. He hangs himself.[117] Although melodramatic, this exaggeration underlined how desperate the consequences of unprotected sex were. Alongside useful information about AIDS, *SPID-Info* published articles on the history of *Playboy* magazine, sex life in prison, and erotic pictures.[118] Whatever one's views about the desirability of erotica and pornography, *SPID-Info* filled a gap for young people. It imparted information about sex and sexually transmitted diseases that they could not easily find elsewhere and gave sound advice about protection against AIDS. Moreover, in a society that gave so little attention to the art of loving, much of the erotica was perhaps, not misplaced, but instructive.

By far the best investigative journalism on AIDS was published by Alla Alova in *Ogonek*. In June 1989, her stinging article "Better Not to Think About It" blasted across a simple message: "Tens, perhaps hundreds of thousands of our fellow citizens, our children, relatives, and friends will be infected with the AIDS virus—and not from tragic accidents and not from their own 'amoral behavior'—but only because until now we have had practically no disposable syringes, disposable drips, disposable catheters, disposable dilators, or disposable containers for storing blood."[119]

Alova went on to note that in two years' time, more than 3 billion dispos-able syringes were to be manufactured. "But how do we live through the next two years?" she asked. "This year only 150 million will be pro-duced."[120] In the meantime, needles would be used more than once, gener-ally without being sterilized. The situation was grave. Specialists' conserva-tive estimates suggested that in 1995 there would be 600,000 carriers of the virus and 6,000 ill and dying. By the year 2000, the figures would increase to 15 million and 200,000, respectively. Why, Alova rhetorically asked, in a sit-uation in which the people were roused to participate in political meetings were there no demonstrations outside the Ministry of Health or Gosplan? She constructed a picture of a system unresponsive to a deadly disease that was spreading. Innocent victims were overlooked, and obvious deterrents, such as more disposable syringes, were too slow in coming.[121]

Alova conducted an energetic interview with Aleksandr Kondrusev, dep-uty minister of health, pressing him to confront the fact that people now feared going to the dentist or doctor for simple procedures in case they caught AIDS.[122] Her article ended with a plea for hard currency from those who earned it, such as actors and rock groups. The money would go to an "anti-AIDS" campaign to purchase necessary hospital equipment.

Alova kept up the pressure by writing for *Ogonek* one month later. The front cover drew attention to "Account 70000015: 'Anti-AIDS' Foreign Economic Bank" against a background of syringes and red crosses.[123] Grip-ping headlines declared, "We can no longer write, 'Before it is too late.' ... It is too late."[124] Her appeal for donations was louder than before and was di-rectly linked again to the purchase of disposable syringes. As before, she named those who had already made pledges. The list included Evgenii Evtushenko, Vladimir Voinovich, Andrei Sakharov, Boris Yeltsin, Alfred Shnittke, and Tat'iana Tolstaia.[125]

In contrast to predictions published by Alova, official Soviet statistics on AIDS have been modest. By June 1987, there were 54 known AIDS carriers in the USSR, 15 of whom were thought to be connected in a chain of infec-tion.[126] By January 1989, the official number had increased to 102. This fig-ure included 27 infants who had contracted the disease in the hospital as a result of unsterilized needles.[127] The incident triggered an emergency screen-ing program of 3,000 children and provoked a burst of letters to the press about the low level of hygiene in hospitals.[128] Nursing mothers were subse-quently discovered to have contracted the disease from their offspring. By the end of 1989, 428 Soviet citizens were reported to have the AIDS virus, increasing to 440 in January 1990 and to 553 in October 1990.[129] Table 3.1 shows these official figures as presented in a statistical handbook on health. Inevitably, they seriously understated the problem.

According to Oleg Iurin, deputy director of the AIDS Center in Moscow, the official number of Soviet citizens who were HIV positive increased in

TABLE 3.1   The Prevalence of AIDS (at the end of each year)

Number	1988	1989	1990 (10 October)
Number infected with the AIDS virus on Soviet territory	480	899	1,104
Of those, Soviet citizens	113	428	553
Of those infected, number showing symptoms of the disease	8	26	51
Of those, Soviet citizens	5	23	48
Of those, number dead	3	14	28

Source: Goskomstat SSSR, *Okhrana Zdorov'ia v SSSR* (Moscow, Finansy i Statistika, 1990), p. 52.

August 1991 to 650.[130] But the true figure was higher. Iurin estimated that it was between 5,000 and 6,000. Among known cases in Moscow, homosexual males were in the majority. Unlike the picture in Western capitals, not one case was due to a sharing of needles among drug addicts. Iurin, however, feared that a convertible ruble might lead to a larger market in hard drugs, a consequence of which could be the introduction of AIDS into the Soviet drug-taking community.[131] So far, only 5 women were known to have AIDS, which they had contracted either by sleeping with a foreigner or by breast-feeding HIV-positive babies.[132]

Early reporting on AIDS (as previously seen) highlighted the lack of disposable syringes. Although this was indeed a real problem, Iurin stressed that it was not the main problem. After all, properly sterilized non-disposable needles would not result in infection. The issue was one of standards, not of disposability. He also volunteered that some greens had confused the issues by pointing out that the incidence of AIDS had increased since Chernobyl. But the relationship between them was coincidental, not causal. He felt that a lot of reporting about the lack of condoms had indirectly fueled sexual problems. Citizens, he suggested, had become used to the idea that condoms were not in the shops and so did not look for them. In fact, now in August 1991, condoms were on sale in pharmacies. Reluctance to search for them was reinforced by reluctance to use them.[133] In a similar vein, Pokrovskii, director of the AIDS Center, worried about the "lack of sexual culture" (*polovaia kul'tura*) at a time of "sexual revolution."[134] Moreover, the dangers of careless sex were heightened by increased contact with foreigners, which in combination provided "favorable soil for an influx of AIDS from abroad."[135]

The press kept readers informed of new legislation. The decree of the Presidium of the Supreme Soviet On Measures to Prevent Infection with the AIDS Virus was published in August 1987. It stated that Soviet citizens and foreigners living in the USSR could be obliged to undergo AIDS testing. Persons refusing voluntary examination, and suspected of carrying the virus, could be taken for testing "with the assistance, in necessary cases, of internal-affairs agencies."[136] Foreigners refusing to be tested could be expelled from the country. By January 1989, 450 foreign residents found to be infected had been deported.[137]

Prison sentences were also introduced for risking the infection of others and actually infecting others. Knowingly putting another person at risk "is punishable by deprivation of freedom for a term of up to five years." Actual infection of another by someone who knows he or she has the disease is punishable by up to eight years' imprisonment.[138] In May 1990, *Pravda* published the text of the new law On Preventive Measures Against AIDS.[139] Article 1 gave citizens the right to medical examination and obliged health-care institutions to ensure safe examinations. According to Article 3, those suspected of infection had to undergo tests. Refusal to do so could result in the person being escorted to the necessary medical establishment by the police. Article 8 gave the infected the right to free transportation to treatment centers, free treatment, and social assistance. Parents had the right to stay at hospitals with their infected children. Article 8 also declared job dismissal and denial of employment an "infringment" of the rights of AIDS carriers and those ill with the disease. Children could not legally be kept out of preschool institutions. Citizens should not suffer discriminatory treatment with regard to housing. Article 9 provided special pensions for citizens infected with the disease in the course of their work.[140] Anyone wishing information about the punishments and rights of AIDS sufferers could have turned to the daily press to find it.

Here, too, it was reported that a special budget for studying AIDS had been allocated and a central laboratory established, intended to become the country's main information center. According to Pokrovskii, in 1987 the anonymous AIDS testing center in Moscow received at least sixty people a day, sometimes as many as one hundred.[141] It was then a section within Moscow's epidemiology hospital. In 1989, it officially became an AIDS center with its own budget. In 1990, Leningrad's first polyclinic for diagnosing and preventing AIDS opened in hospital number 30. Prior to that, thousands had passed through Leningrad's anonymous testing center. One aim of the new clinic was to quell "AIDS-phobia" (*spidofobiia*), which the press suggested was gripping society. Here psychotherapy and legal advice supplemented medical testing.[142]

By 1991, according to Iurin, there were AIDS centers in every republic, in twenty-one regions, and in some towns. Budgets, however, were inadequate, as in health care generally. Chaos in politics and confusion across administrative levels (as discussed in Chapter 7) made coordinated policies on AIDS difficult. Iurin regretted that many bureaucrats were indifferent and that AIDS was the type of problem that could win temporary attention but then quickly fade. In addition, debates within epidemiology about appropriate ways to proceed often left people's deputies unsure about which opinion to believe. Pokrovskii himself was a deputy on the Supreme Soviet of the USSR, but this did not guarantee automatic acceptance of his views. In Iurin's assessment, there was inadequate trust in specialist knowledge.[143]

Press reports, letters to the press, and my conversations with citizens suggested that AIDS-phobia did develop in response to the coverage of AIDS. Just as by the early 1990s, crime had frightened many citizens about taking to the streets after dark, concern about AIDS affected attitudes toward routine medical and dental checkups. Women worried about pap smears. Citizens began to fear blood tests and injections. Although AIDS-phobia created a social panic different from that attending theft and violence, citizens were still left feeling vulnerable to an outside threat over which they had little control. Fear of the medical system and heightened fear of rape were two of the consequences.

Rape

Rape is one way of infecting another person with AIDS, but even in 1991 the two were still not being linked in the media. At best, the occasional article in 1987 argued that "it's time that we talked frankly about so-called sex crimes, more precisely about their roots," regretting that "we give the appearance that nothing of this kind exists."[144] Articles on rape were extremely rare, and so numerous relevant questions were not asked. The application of glasnost to this topic was neither enthusiastic nor thorough.

Although very little was said about rape in 1987 and 1988, especially in comparison with the sensational reporting about prostitution, the message delivered was similar to that about crime in general: Rape was increasing. Statistics were cited to illustrate this message. For example, readers were told that figures released by the Ministry of Internal Affairs in Belorussia in 1987 showed that rapes had increased by more than 50 percent in comparison with the same period a year earlier. These crimes were committed by more than two hundred men, of whom 43 percent were teenagers. More than seventy of the victims were minors, nearly 50 percent of whom were schoolgirls.[145] Evidence suggested that gang rapes were disturbingly common. The clear message was that "a part of our youth has lost its moral orientation."[146] Yet again, journalists presented an image of immoral young people.

As in reporting on crime rates, statistics were not questioned, nor were conclusions based on them. Certainly the claim that the incidence of rape was increasing was dubious. Official crime statistics are compiled from recorded incidents, which depend on the cooperation of citizens. Worldwide many women hesitate to report that they have been raped. But it is possible that once rape has been labeled as a social problem, and as society becomes more open, women previously reluctant to report may more readily do so.

But even if this was the case in the USSR, official statistics were unreliable, comparative statistics were suspect, and therefore the reported social composition of rapists was questionable.

Not until 1989 did a scholarly discussion of rape appear in *Sotsiolog- icheskie Issledovaniia*. Here, just as others had done with drugs and prostitution, Margarita Pozdniakova and Larisa Rybakova regretted that hitherto sociologists had not studied rape. They called for careful analysis into the behavior of victims and into the personalities, living conditions, and family lives of rapists,[147] especially in light of an increase in reported rapes from 16,765 in 1987 to 17,658 in 1988.[148] They were particularly alarmed by the suggestion that in 1986, 63 percent of reported rapes had been gang rapes.[149] Pozdniakova and Rybakova hoped that information would identify those groups most at risk and contribute to the elaboration of preventive measures.

From interviews in two penal colonies in Kazakhstan, they pieced together portraits of rapists. More than one-half of the rapists believed that "there are often exceptional circumstances that justify a man hitting a woman."[150] The authors viewed this as a contemptible attitude that increased the likelihood of rape. One-half of the teenagers did not even consider their behavior violent. Rather, they had been playing "sexual games" and expressed surprise that they had been called to the militia. In many cases, they had been consuming alcohol prior to the rape, particularly those involved in gang rapes.[151]

The victims, too, had often consented to drink alcohol "with men they did not know."[152] The article did not attempt to suggest that all victims were innocent. However, it stressed that the consequences of rape were generally devastating: "fear, pain, and shock."[153] In addition, most victims were gripped with shame. They endured "protracted depression, apathy, various phobias, long-term aggression, mistrust of those around them, a loss of self-respect, a feeling of being 'soiled.'"[154] For the first time, women's emotions and suffering after rape were made public and analyzed. Likewise, coverage was given to men's sense of innocence after rape and their disrespect for women. At last, the message came across, albeit to a tiny academic audience, that women were abused as sex objects. The popular press did not follow suit.

But self-defense for women and precautions against rape did become wider issues in 1989. *Rabotnitsa* used diagrams to show readers how to defend themselves. The first exercise, entitled "Counterattacking Leg" and printed in October 1990, instructed women how to hit the bottom half of men's bodies.[155] Then in December, the second exercise illustrated how to perfect "a blow with the arm." The elbow could be used to strike a man's face. The side of the hand could slice into his neck. His sides could be attacked if he first went for the woman's throat.[156] Continuing in the same vein, the January 1991 edition ran a column on "how to deter a rapist." Women were advised to carry a whistle at night, to walk down the middle of partly lit roads, and to cross the street and walk in the opposite direction if followed by a curb-crawling car.[157] Such practical advice filled a long-silent gap. Also, a translation of an American booklet on how to minimize the threat of rape was printed in the pages following the article by Pozdniakova and Rybakova. It instructed women on how to take wise precautions under the headings "Safety in Your Home," "Safety on the Street," and (less usefully in a Soviet context) "The Car and Your Safety."[158]

So by 1991, recommendations on how to deter rape had entered the discourse of women's magazines and academic publications. The main ones were as follows: First, women should learn how to defend themselves. Second, ties should be strengthened between educational institutions where rapes occurred, such as the technical colleges, and law enforcement agencies. Third, researchers looking into rape should liaise with the police in an attempt to deter attacks. Fourth, more attention should be paid to helping victims, learning from Western organizations such as the FRG's Help to Raped Women.[159] And fifth, rapists should be punished for their behavior but also receive appropriate counseling. In 1990, six rapists received the death sentence.[160]

The issue of rape made a sudden and modest entry into the Soviet press in 1987. By 1991, academics and journalists had recognized that much work in this area was new and superficial and in need of more serious thought. Despite slow progress on the ground in work with victims and attackers, intermittent calls were made between 1987 and 1991 for more research and practical help. But there was not a flood of articles, as there had been on crime in general.

At the beginning of the 1990s, rape lagged far behind other social issues in prominence. Much less was said about it in the press and in academic journals. Moreover, the few articles that were published were written by women. The dominance of journalism by men was probably a crucial reason for the silence surrounding the topic. The same pattern obtained in Western states in the 1960s and 1970s. It was only with the rise of radical feminism in the 1970s and 1980s (as distinct from liberal feminism and socialist feminism), with its preoccupation with violence against women, that rape and wife-beating came onto Western agendas. The lack of a large independent feminist movement in the USSR could also account for the dearth of public discussion. Male journalists appeared more content to cover prostitution than rape, where women could be described as the immoral actors and where their own sex was not the uninvited aggressor. Women colluded in the former activity but not in the latter.[161] Future discussion about rape is therefore likely to depend on energetic women forcing it onto mainstream agendas. More than likely, debate will develop first in women-only circles.

Child Abuse

Like rape, child abuse was rarely discussed between 1987 and 1989. Although during these years articles criticized children's homes and indicated how awful lives in them could be, they hesitated to talk about child abuse per se.[162] Instead, they castigated mothers for abandoning their children, thereby increasing the number in homes.[163] Reflecting traditional gender-role stereotypes, the articles did not apportion any blame to fathers. Glasnost, this attitude illustrated, was not always innovative but could apply traditional values in new ways. At best, the press made fleeting or euphemistic references to child abuse in discussions of broader topics. For example, coverage of the Children's Fund conference held in 1987 made a passing remark that in children's homes and in boarding schools "beating of children [was] the norm."[164] Elaboration and analysis, however, were wanting.

Not until 1990 did child abuse become slightly more public. Thereafter rare articles exposed the problem, defined what it meant, and illustrated the forms it took by referring to specific cases. *Pravda*, for example, carried an interview with Stanislav Doletskii, a pediatric surgeon who had coined the term *syndrome of dangerous treatment of children* (*sindrom opasnogo obrashcheniia s det'mi*), more neatly translated as "child abuse syndrome."[165] Doletskii revealed that "alas, there are very many examples. And, at times, the mind cannot cope with what one encounters."[166] He elaborated:

> A newly married couple got rid of a child whom very recently they had wanted. He interfered with their life. Another coupled "calmed" their crying baby by punching it—concussion. Children are burned with cigarettes. One serviceman beat his daughter so unmercifully that it was not then possible to look at the child's body without shuddering. How can one close one's eyes to phenomena that cease to be exceptional or rare?[167]

Most important, Doletskii informed readers. He showed how the range of abuse was wide, from physical violence to the administration of tranquilizers. He warned that the attempts of busy adults to quiet children with sleeping pills could have dire consequences.[168]

As in the West, child abuse was not new when it entered public discourse. And claims that it was increasing were impossible to verify, given that it had always been hushed up. We have only to cast our minds back to Gorky's *My Childhood* to recall the regular beatings endured by Russian children.[169] Doletskii, however, contended that today's child abuse syndrome could be partly explained by "decades of authoritarian upbringing," which had "devastated and withered children's living souls."[170] Mothers and fathers had been brought up themselves on slogans and in a distorted culture; they in turn had strangled and suppressed their children's personalities. So tensions in many families ran high.

This explanation was consistent with broader criticisms of the past. But although the Soviet education system had fostered discipline, rather than gentle encouragement, this was an insufficient explanation since child abuse existed in very different systems. Doletskii also held that child abuse was made worse by family instability, divorce, single parenthood, and alcoholism.[171] But although these may have been contributory factors, neither divorce nor single parenthood necessarily led to child abuse. Evidence of a causal link was wanting. It was all too easy to name these factors as possible causes since official ideology would have done the same.

Child abuse is likely to be an issue that will be more deeply scrutinized as the 1990s progress. Much more information, however, is needed. The intensely private nature of this abuse makes it relatively inaccessible. Cases of children who end up in the hospital because of near-fatal abuse can be tracked, as can more obvious cases of abuse in state children's homes, provided the authorities permit investigation. But the millions who may be suffering in silence will continue to be undetected. As with rape, unless the victims come forward the crime will remain locked in the private sphere. At the beginning of the 1990s, telephone hotlines for children had yet to be set up.

Suicide

Just as there were no sound ideological reasons in the Soviet past for craving drugs or for beating children, neither were there grounds for suicide. In the 1930s, research into the topic was "suspended," and the word *suicide* even disappeared from the *Great Soviet Encyclopedia* and the *Demographic Encyclopedial Dictionary.* After the end of the 1920s, statistics on suicide were not published.[172] Not until the 1970s was a center for the study of suicide set up in Moscow. Research then resumed.[173] But discussions did not reach more public arenas until the advent of glasnost.

Early coverage of suicide in 1987, like that of prostitution, was sensational rather than explanatory. Suicide was recognized but not analyzed. Consistent with the pattern of treating other social issues, journalists reported some of the statistics that had been released and told the sad tales of individual suicide cases.

The first available statistics were spotty. Not until 1990 did readers learn that fifty-four thousand people had died from suicide three years earlier.[174] Reporting did not immediately concentrate on the extent of the problem or on reasons for differential patterns of aggregate figures across republics. Instead, journalists wondered about the reasons for particular suicide attempts. Speculations, for example, about the reasons for the suicide of Valerii Legasov were printed in *Pravda.* Legasov was a scientist who had spent time at Chernobyl and had become obsessed with safety regulations. Did he commit suicide because he was not awarded the title of hero of socialist labor, which everyone expected him to win? Was the suicide a result of depression? Was it due to a large dose of radiation?[175] And in other cases was economic reform to blame? The agricultural worker Nazarov, like many others in the countryside, ended his life because he worked around the clock trying to be an independent farmer in a very hostile environment. The message delivered was that decollectivization was becoming a tragedy.[176]

Through these observations suicide was linked directly to contemporary problems—the dangers of Chernobyl, the unfairness of merit systems, and the difficulties of pursuing reform because of conservative resistance. Journalists constructed images of "good" citizens whose honorable efforts were thwarted by unwelcome attitudes and practices embedded in the system. Here glasnost indeed served perestroika.

And just as reporting on crime and drugs had devoted special space to young people, the same applied to suicide. Concentrating on the sixteen to twenty age group, journalists described the plight of cases such as twenty-year-old Igor' M, who tried to hang himself for performing badly at his institute, and nineteen-year-old Ol'ga D, who took 150 tablets because of "conflict with her parents" when she came home later than their 10 P.M. curfew and her father called her a "slut."[177] Even though firm policy recommendations were not made, a general questioning began about the relevance to suicide of interpersonal relations in the education system and at home. There was a growing sensitivity to the fact that teenage years can be emotionally difficult and that youngsters who attempt suicide are crying out for support and understanding.[178] In September 1988, a counseling service for teenagers opened in Moscow as well as a suicide hotline.[179]

One noticeably distinct feature of early reporting was a concern about self-immolation in Central Asia. Glasnost enabled journalists finally to acknowledge that in 1984 in Tadzhikistan there had been thirty known cases of suicide by fire, a figure that had increased to forty in 1986.[180] According to the press, "One girl's father would not allow her to go to school, and she could not bear it. A second's relatives, with whom she lived, tried to force her to marry. A third was beaten by her husband, was taunted by his relatives, and could not see any way out."[181]

The message given by *Komsomol'skaia Pravda* was that traditional customs that confined women clashed with modern Soviet notions of emancipated women and put Muslim women under tense emotional strain. Some saw suicide as the only salvation from disciplined and restricted lives. Daily life was often torture for women because "to go out onto the street without a veil is a disgrace. To the cinema—forbidden. To be seen with a boy is shameful. To disobey one's elders is not allowed. To study is a disgrace. To marry against one's parents' will is also shameful. For going out, a girl is put under lock and key. … Nearly all cases of self-immolation by young girls take place at home when relatives are present."[182] Several articles criticized "obsolete" customs that "caged" women, recommending that the problem be more openly discussed.[183]

Self-immolation was sometimes a consequence of abduction. Girls were generally expected to marry their abductor to minimize the shame heaped on themselves and their family. If they did not wish to marry, three options were open to them: suicide, running away from home, and legal action against the abductor. The first and second could result if the woman lacked parental support. The third went against the grain of Muslim customs and required emotional backing from parents.[184]

Exhausting lives for women was another reason given in the press for self-immolation. One woman taken to a burn center after attempting suicide declared that she was "simply tired of living."[185] *Pravda* reported that:

> a woman, barely having given birth to her most recent child, not in the least strong enough, must get out of bed and get involved with the domestic economy—with the cows, sheep, kitchen garden, and stove. This is on top of sleepless nights by the cradle and an endless washing of clothes, usually by hand. In addition, she must please her husband, her mother-in-law, and other relatives; prepare lunch; and cater to their whims.[186]

Some women in this predicament endured male violence, too, which was dismissed by neighbors as just a domestic argument.[187] Leading physically and mentally stressful lives, Muslim women, the press suggested, sought release through suicide.

Several interpretations of self-immolation coincided with official ideology, which for some time had castigated Muslim cultures for their "obsolete," feudal, and patriarchal ways. A sharp contrast with enlightened "Soviet" culture was thereby constructed. Muslims, however, viewed this dichotomy as especially Russian in tone and as insensitive. Another approach, consistent with the reform process, was to blame the party for its "old ways" of ignoring the problem.

In theory, party committees should have examined every case of self-immolation. In practice, they quickly closed investigations on the grounds that evidence was missing or the women did not file complaints before ending their lives.[188] In Uzbekistan, one journalist revealed, party organizations "shut their eyes to this, screen the essence of this disgraceful phenomenon with all sorts of far-fetched reasons."[189] Two hundred and seventy self-immolations had occurred in Uzbekistan in 1986 and 1987 "by women as a mark of protest against the debasement of their honor and human dignity." But the party did not take this protest seriously.[190] And neither, suggested *Meditsinskaia Gazeta*, did Islam. Mufti Babakhanov, chair of the Muslim Spiritual Administration of Central Asia and Kazakhstan, was quoted as saying that "the roots of this phenomenon lie in domestic disorders" and that women who committed self-immolation were not particularly religious. Allah did not forgive such a grave sin, and the guilty were doomed to torment in hell without funeral services.[191] Journalists and academics constructed party committees and Islam as "accomplices" to the "villains" who perpetuated traditional customs. Villains included fathers, husbands, abductors, mothers-in-law, and neighbors.

By the end of 1988, more serious attempts were being made to explain self-immolation and dispel old myths. According to *Kommunist Tadzhikistana* (Communist of Tadzhikistan), it did not occur only in remote and highly religious rural areas. In fact, most suicides took place in economically developed urban areas. Moreover, self-immolation was not restricted to young women but included all age groups. Suicide occurred because of the "discrepancy between the ideal and reality."[192] By 1991, however, rigorous analysis into self-immolation was still wanting. No one had yet asked whether in some cases it could be murder. Comparative analysis with self-immolation in India would have led directly to this question.[193]

The coverage given to self-immolation between 1986 and 1991 was not commensurate with the extent of the tragedy. Yet in comparison with other forms of suicide, it received proportionally more attention. Statistics published in 1990 showed that suicide was three times more likely among men than among women and that the suicide rates in Central Asia were much lower than in the Baltic republics.[194] Table 3.2 reveals that in 1986 Estonia suffered the highest rates, 27.4 successful suicides per 100,000 inhabitants. In rural Estonia, the figure reached 35.6 suicides per 100,000 inhabitants. By contrast, in Tadzhikistan, the republic most discussed in the early articles on self-immolation, there were 5.2 known suicides per 100,000 inhabitants. Most of these were in towns where the official suicide rate was 10.8 suicides per 100,000 inhabitants. The rural rate was as low as 2.4 suicides per 100,000 inhabitants. If we assume that the official figures were not wildly incorrect, then self-immolations were a tiny proportion of all suicides. And no one was asking why rural Estonia was so badly afflicted with the problem. Was data collection more efficient there? Or were other factors, such as Estonia's history and social composition, relevant?

It was left to more academic writings to explore the motives behind suicide. Aina Ambrumova and Lidiia Postovalova argued in *Sotsiologicheskie Issledovaniia* that "suicidal behavior" was the "result of a complex interrelationship" of "psycho-physiological, psychological, socio-economic, and socio-cultural factors," often the consequence of physical and emotional burdens, a reduction in tolerance on the part of others, and defective moral upbringing.[195] The "group at risk" was large and included elderly people, students in higher and secondary education, teenagers, migrants, divorcees, single people, and those suffering from chronic illnesses. Quite healthy peo-

TABLE 3.2   The Number of Suicides in 1986, by Republic (per 100,000 inhabitants)

Republic	Total Population	Urban	Rural
Estonia	27.4	24.5	35.6
Lithuania	25.3	21.3	32.5
Latvia	25.3	21.2	33.9
RSFSR	22.9	21.2	27.5
Moldavia	18.6	13.5	23.1
Ukraine	18.5	16.7	22.1
Belorussia	17.8	14.5	23.3
Kazakhstan	16.5	17.7	14.7
Kirgizia	9.2	12.1	7.2
Turkmenia	8.6	12.1	5.6
Uzbekistan	7.5	11.0	5.0
Tadzhikistan	5.2	10.8	2.4
Georgia	4.6	4.0	5.2
Azerbaidzhan	3.4	4.8	1.9
Armenia	1.8	1.9	1.6
USSR	18.8	18.4	19.4

Source: Adapted from Sergei Smidovich, "Samoubiistva v zerkale statistiki," *Sotsiologicheskie Issledovaniia,* no. 4, 1990, p. 75.

ple, they argued, could commit suicide when under stress. Much depended on how an individual responded to a frustration of her or his own needs.[196]

Ambrumova and Postovalova observed that suicide was a global phenomenon, particularly in industrially developed countries. They thoroughly debunked the ideological claim that it was characteristic of capitalism. They stressed that special preventive measures had to be taken and that rehabilitation centers needed to be set up with sensitivity to regional variations. Moscow was ahead of the rest of the country in this respect, having over the years set up anonymous centers to help those suffering stress. However, "scientific sluggishness, bureaucratic routine, insufficient attention to questions of community," held back progress.[197] Ambrumova and Postovalova called for more sociological research into regional variations in suicidal behavior to deepen understanding and aid preventive measures. They added that sociologists needed to probe behind the official statistics and not overlook attempted suicides. But above all, research should be linked to broader questions of "problems of the humanization of culture and the relationship of people to questions of life and death, good and evil."[198] Specialists had a "professional and moral duty" to fight suicide, as they had done at the beginning of the century. And "civic spirit" (*grazhdanstvennost'*) was needed for this.

The pattern of how suicide opened was similar to that of other social issues, culminating at the beginning of the 1990s with academics calling for more sophisticated inquiry. Like some writers on drug abuse, they identified the phenomenon studied as an evil best fought by humanizing culture.

Limits to the "New" Social Issues

Although a refreshing amount of new information was imparted between the late 1980s and the early 1990s, much was left unsaid. Journalists and academics cited statistics, with all their imperfections, and uncovered personal details of the lives of prostitutes, drug addicts, rape victims, and suicide cases, but huge gaps remained. Uses of glasnost brought revelation, commentary, and some debate, which sometimes prompted outrage. But glasnost was not automatically employed to produce rigorous analyses. Given the historical context, this is not surprising.

Discussions took place, first and foremost, in the mass media, where the aim of journalists was to point fingers. Investigative journalism in a country long denied freedom of inquiry produced a shower of information, often bitty and incomplete. Many journalists simply wanted to get issues, problems, and dilemmas across to the public, to generate awareness that they existed.

But in 1987, journalists were restricted by the paucity of information available to them. Censorship policies persisted. Although some editors, such as Vitalii Korotich of *Ogonek*, were more daring than others, sensitivity to censorship was acute.[199] Topics concerning the army, for instance, were still avoided in 1989 by most editors. And sensitivity to censorship fluctuated with the political moment. In early 1991, a more repressive atmosphere gripped the country. And the appointment of conservative individuals, such as Leonid Kravchenko, to gatekeeping posts in the media still had immense impact.[200]

The silences on some issues in 1987, 1988, and 1989 were also partly due to a lack of rigorous social science training. Citizens long schooled in ideological conformity were unlikely overnight to produce sophisticated questionnaires and dispassionate multivariate analyses. Not only was some information unavailable to them, but also methodological skills were frequently missing. Furthermore, social consciousness about some topics was very low. Traditional attitudes about gender roles often led journalists to blame rape victims for their situation. This, too, had been a problem in the West, and still is. Such views influenced opinions about whether rape was newsworthy at all and the sorts of questions asked about it.

Thus, the situation for society as a whole was one of inadequate information on most topics; persisting censorship—real or imagined; an uncertainty about what the political future held; and a thin distribution of practiced analytic skills. In this context, sensationalism and loud exposure, with all their defects, were both understandable and liberating in the short term. A burst of shocking stories about the seamy side of life was almost inevitable in a society where they had been denied for so long. What was released may not always have been pleasant, professionally presented, adequately analyzed, or soberly summed up, but it was creative journalism emerging out of one of the world's most sterile and fettered investigative settings.

Conclusion

The picture of society constructed by the media during the late 1980s contrasted sharply with images of the past, particularly those put across in the 1930s and 1940s. The "happy" socialist realism of those decades praised Stalin for the achievements of socialism and thanked him for making life so ecstatic. Citizens were either lawabiders who were enthusiastic to build socialism or enemies of the people who were destructive. Now glasnost showed, graphically and vividly, that joy was not the hallmark of Soviet life. "Deviant" citizens, including youth—once the promise of the Motherland— were indifferent to socialism. The picture was one of suffering, immorality, violence, disillusion, and neglect. In turn, citizens became more despondent about the life around them. Opinion surveys in 1990 revealed that fear and pessimism were now common emotions and that citizens were expressing high levels of anxiety and fatigue.[201] At the same time, competing proposals for dealing with social problems reflected a growing pluralism of thought.

NOTES

1. E. Zhbanov, "Proizvol i zakonnost'," *Izvestiia*, 13 July 1990, p. 3.

2. Ibid.

3. *Soviet News*, 26 April 1989, p. 139.

4. Interview with Bakatin in A. Chernenko and A. Cherniak, "V ramkakh zakona," *Pravda*, 17 April 1990, p. 3.

5. *Izvestiia*, 6 April 1991, p. 6.

6. A. E. Zhalinskii and G. M. Min'kovskii, "Prestupnost' v SSSR v 1989g: Statisticheskie dannye, kriminologicheskii kommentarii," *Sovetskoe Gosudarstvo i Pravo,* no. 6, 1990, pp. 82–91.

7. A. Illesh, "Nesovershennoletnie prestupniki," *Izvestiia*, 17 April 1990, p. 3.

8. N. Lukanovskii, "Narushiteliam raz"iasneno," *Pravda*, 31 August 1988, p. 6.

9. See "Reactions to the Failures of Economic Reform" in Chapter 1.

10. G. Ovcharenko, "U femidy net tain," *Pravda,* 27 January 1988, p. 6.

11. Evgenii Dodolev, "Semeinoe delo," *Nedelia,* no. 4, 25–31 January 1988, p. 12.

12. Ibid.

13. Ibid.

14. Elena Letskaia, "Ukrali rebenka," *Nedelia,* no. 14, 31 March–6 April 1986, p. 12.

15. Ibid.

16. Dodolev, "Semeinoe delo."

17. D. Likhanov, "V osade," *Ogonek,* no. 5, January 1989, pp. 18–19.

18. Ibid.

19. K. I. Mikul'skii, V. E. Rogovin, and S. S. Shatalin, *Sotsial'naia Politika KPSS* (Moscow, Politizdat, 1987), pp. 31–32.

20. Chernenko and Cherniak, "V ramkakh zakona."

21. Ibid.

22. B. Pippiia, "Sred' bela dnia," *Pravda,* 15 August 1990, p. 6.

23. Ibid.

24. Ibid.

25. *Pravda,* 13 April 1988, pp. 1–2.

26. *Soviet News,* 3 May 1989, p. 145.

27. *Bakinskii Rabochii,* 19 December 1990, p. 1.

28. *Pravda,* 30 January 1991, p. 1.

29. Ibid.

30. Ibid.

31. *Izvestiia,* 5 February 1991, p. 1.

32. D. Spiridonov, "Komu ugrozhaet patrul'?" *Moskovskaia Pravda,* 9 February 1991, p. 1.

33. *Moskovskii Komsomolets,* 13 February 1991, p. 1.

34. *The Independent,* 13 February 1991, p. 10.

35. Ibid.

36. Marc Champion, "Moscow tries to halt break-up of police," *The Independent,* 8 February 1991, p. 12.

37. Ibid.

38. Ibid.

39. *Pravda,* 15 February 1991, p. 6.

40. M. S. Conroy, "Abuse of drugs other than alcohol and tobacco in the Soviet Union," *Soviet Studies,* vol. 42, no. 3, 1990, pp. 447–480; John M. Kramer, "Drug abuse in the USSR," in Anthony Jones, Walter D. Connor, and David E. Powell, eds., *Soviet Social Problems* (Boulder, Westview, 1991), pp. 94–118; John M. Kramer, "Drug abuse in Eastern Europe: An emerging issue of public policy," *Slavic Review,* vol. 49, no. 1, Spring 1990, pp. 19–31.

41. A. Illesh and E. Shestinskii, "Eshche raz o narkomanii," *Izvestiia,* 23 November 1987, p. 4.

42. Ibid.

43. Ibid.

44. Ibid.

45. A. Illesh and E. Shestinskii, "Narkomaniia: Otchet daet militsiia," *Izvestiia,* 28 February 1988, p. 48.

46. Quoted in ibid.

47. S. Aleksandrov, "Nenaviazchivo protiv narkomanii," *Izvestiia,* 25 July 1990, p. 6.

48. *Izvestiia,* 29 August 1990, p. 6.

49. Aleksandrov, "Nenaviazchivo protiv narkomanii."

50. Illesh and Shestinskii, "Narkomaniia."

51. I. Vedeneeva, "U cherty," *Ogonek*, no. 8, February 1988, pp. 19–23.

52. Aleksandrov, "Nenaviazchivo protiv narkomanii."

53. Vedeneeva, "U cherty."

54. A. I. Grishko, "O narkomanii sredi podrostkov," *Sotsiologicheskie Issledovaniia*, no. 2, 1990, p. 101.

55. Ibid., p. 102.

56. Illesh and Shestinskii, "Narkomaniia."

57. Illesh and Shestinskii, "Eshche raz o narkomanii."

58. Illesh and Shestinskii, "Narkomaniia."

59. Illesh and Shestinskii, "Eshche raz o narkomanii."

60. Illesh and Shestinskii, "Narkomaniia."

61. A. Illesh, "Skol'ko u nas narkomanov," *Ivestiia*, 29 August 1990, p. 6.

62. Ibid.

63. Ibid.

64. G. Alimov, "Poslednie plantatsii," *Izvestiia*, 6 October 1987, p. 2.

65. Vedeneeva, "U cherty," pp. 19–23.

66. Ibid., p. 19.

67. Ibid., p. 23.

68. Ibid., p. 20.

69. Erving Goffman, *Asylums* (Harmondsworth, Penguin, 1968).

70. Vedeneeva, "U cherty," p. 22.

71. R. M. Gotlib and L. I. Romanova, "O nekotorykh prichinakh narkomanii," *Sovetskoe Gosudarstvo i Pravo*, no. 1, 1990, p. 67.

72. Ibid., p. 68.

73. Ibid., p. 72.

74. Ibid., pp. 69–70.

75. Ibid.

76. Ibid., p. 70.

77. Ibid., p. 72.

78. Ibid.

79. Discussions with journalists in the editorial offices of *Iunost'*, Moscow, March 1989.

80. B. F. Kalachev, "Narkotiki v armii," *Sotsiologicheskie Issledovaniia*, no. 4, 1989, pp. 56–61.

81. Ibid., p. 39. *Afgantsy* refers to the men who fought in Afghanistan.

82. A. A. Gabiani, "Narkotiki v srede uchashcheisia molodezhi," *Sotsiologicheskie Issledovaniia*, no. 9, 1990, pp. 84–89.

83. See Elizabeth Waters, "Restructuring the 'woman question': Perestroika and prostitution," *Feminist Review*, no. 33, Autumn 1989, pp. 3–19; Elizabeth Waters, "Victim or villain? Prostitution in post-revolutionary Russia," in Linda Edmondson, ed., *Women and Society in Russia and the Soviet Union* (Cambridge, Cambridge University Press, 1992), pp. 160–177; Andrea Stevenson Sanjian, "Prostitution, the press, and agenda-building in the Soviet policy process," in Jones, Connor, and Powell, eds., *Soviet Social Problems*, pp. 270–295.

84. Accurate statistics on prostitution are difficult to compile in all systems. Selected articles, however, have attempted estimates of its extent in particular cities. The files of one Moscow police chief covering fifteen years showed a record of three thousand five hundred prostitutes, aged fourteen to seventy. This is probably a gross understatement. See P. Kislinskaia, "'Legkoe povedenie' na vesakh pravosudiia," *Sovetskaia Rossiia,* 12 March 1987, p. 4.

85. V. Golovanov, "Avtomobil'nye devochki," *Literaturnaia Gazeta,* 16 September 1987, p. 13.

86. I. Inoveli, "Tiazhkoe vremia legkogo povedeniia," *Zaria Vostoka,* 25 September 1987, p. 4.

87. A. Pravov, "Pliazhnye devochki," *Komsomol'skaia Pravda,* 19 September 1987, p. 2.

88. B. Alekseev, "Nochnoi promysel'," *Nedelia,* no. 12, 23–29 March 1987, p. 15.

89. G. Kurov, "Ispoved' 'nochnoi babochki,'" *Sovetskaia Rossiia,* 19 March 1987, p. 4.

90. See Kislinskaia, "'Legkoe povedenie' na vesakh pravosudiia."

91. Ibid.

92. Pravov, "Pliazhnye devochki."

93. An interpretation reiterated in numerous conversations in Moscow, 1989 and 1990.

94. Anzor A. Gabiani and Maksim A. Manuil'skii, "Tsena 'liubvi,'" *Sotsiologicheskie Issledovaniia,* no. 6, 1987, pp. 61–68.

95. Ibid.

96. Ibid., p. 62.

97. Ibid.

98. Ibid.

99. V. Trushin, "Prestupniki i inostrantsy," *Nedelia,* no. 41, 9–15 October 1989, p. 11.

100. Ibid.

101. D. Mysiakov and P. Iakubovich, "'Dama' s podachkoi," *Komsomol'skaia Pravda,* 9 October 1986, p. 2.

102. V. Iurlov, "'Putany' iz Kirgizstana," *Sovetskaia Kirgizia,* 16 May 1987, p. 3.

103. M. Gurtovoi, "Pochem liubov"?" *Trud,* 31 July 1987, p. 4.

104. Ibid.

105. Kislinskaia, "'Legkoe povedenie' na vesakh pravosudiia."

106. Ia. I. Gilinskii, "Effktiven li zapret prostitutsii?" *Sotsiologicheskie Issledovaniia,* no. 2, 1988, pp. 65–70.

107. Kurov, "Ispoved' 'nochnoi babochki.'"

108. Sergei I. Golod, "Prostitutsiia v kontekste izmeneniia polovoi morali," *Sotsiologicheskie Issledovaniia,* no. 2, 1988, pp. 65–70.

109. In the 1920s, *Delegatka* sometimes discussed venereal disease, attempting to enlighten women about its dangers and characteristics. *Delegatka* was the journal of the department of mass work and agitation of the Moscow committee of the Bolshevik Party. It lasted from 1923 to 1931.

110. A. Novikov, "SPID," *Komsomol'skaia Pravda*, 1 August 1987, pp. 3–4.

111. Ibid. One hopes that this was intended as satire.

112. A. Novikov, "Eshche raz o SPIDe," *Komsomol'skaia Pravda*, 28 October 1987, p. 3.

113. Ibid.

114. K. Smirnov, "Spid bez sensatsii," *Izvestiia*, 16 June 1987, p. 3.

115. *SPID-Info*, 6 February 1990, p. 2.

116. Ibid.

117. *SPID-Info*, 6 February 1990, p. 7.

118. See, for instance, ibid., pp. 4–5; *SPID-Info*, 31 May 1990, p. 11; *SPID-Info*, no. 3, March 1991; *SPID-Info*, no. 4, April 1991, pp. 8, 13, 15. Later editions were numbered as well as dated, unlike early ones.

119. Alla Alova, "Luchshe ne dumat'?" *Ogonek*, no. 26, June 1989, p. 28.

120. Ibid., p. 28.

121. Ibid.

122. Ibid., pp. 28–30.

123. *Ogonek*, no. 31, July 1989, front cover.

124. Alla Alova, "Blagotvoritel'nyi valiutnyi schet 'Antispid,'" *Ogonek*, no. 31, July 1989, p. 7.

125. Ibid.

126. K. Smirnov, "SPID bez sensatsii," *Izvestiia*, 16 June 1987, p. 3.

127. This occurred in Elista, capital of the Malmyk Autonomous Republic. See Rupert Cornwall, "27 Soviet children infected with AIDS," *The Independent*, 28 January 1989, p. 12.

128. Angus Roxburgh, "Soviet AIDS scandal grows," *The Sunday Times*, 29 January 1989, p. 17.

129. *SPID-Info*, 6 February 1990, p. 2.

130. Interview with Oleg Iurin, Moscow AIDS center, August 1991.

131. Ibid.

132. Ibid.

133. Ibid.

134. Vadim Pokrovskii, "Uspet' chto-nibud' sdelat'," *Sovetskaia Rossiia*, 14 June 1991, p. 4.

135. Ibid.

136. *Izvestiia*, 26 August 1987, p. 2.

137. Cornwall, "27 Soviet children infected with AIDS."

138. *Izvestiia*, 26 August 1987, p. 2.

139. *Pravda*, 10 May 1990, p. 2.

140. Ibid.

141. Pokrovskii was interviewed by Smirnov, "SPID bez sensatsii."

142. F. Ivanov, "SPID: Otkryta pervaia poliklinika," *Izvestiia*, 10 March 1989, p. 2.

143. Interview with Oleg Iurin, Moscow AIDS center, August 1991.

144. G. Nerobeeva, "Ne nado opuskat' glaza," *Sovetskaia Belorussiia,* 6 December 1987, p. 2.

145. Ibid.

146. Ibid. The topic was especially sensitive since rapists were often still at school, at technical college, or at the university.

147. Margarita E. Pozdniakova and Larisa H. Rybakova, "Prestupnaia strast'," *Sotsiologicheskie Issledovaniia,* no. 4, 1989, pp. 62–70.

148. Ibid.

149. Ibid., p. 62.

150. Ibid., p. 64.

151. Ibid., pp. 64–65.

152. Ibid., p. 66.

153. Ibid., p. 68.

154. Ibid., p. 69.

155. *Rabotnitsa,* no. 10, October 1990, pullout section, p. 4.

156. *Rabotnitsa,* no. 12, December 1990, pullout section, p. 4.

157. *Rabotnitsa,* no. 1, January 1991, p. 31.

158. E. E. Mininga, trans., "Kak protivostoiat' ugroze iznasilovaniia?" *Sotsiologicheskie Issledovaniia,* no. 4, 1989, pp. 70–73.

159. Pozdniakova and Rybakova, "Prestupnaia strast'," p. 69.

160. *Izvestiia,* 6 April 1991, p. 6.

161. Moreover, prostitution had a titillating image, despite the usually grim reality. Rape, too, has recently taken on a similar character in some Western images. If this happens in Russia, too, it will not be to women's benefit.

162. E. Salina, "Poterpi malysh," *Nedelia,* no. 7, 13–19 February 1989, p. 21; T. Zelenskaia, "Pust' budet teplym detskii dom," *Izvestiia,* 7 July 1987, p. 3.

163. O. Kharlan, "Kogda otkaz bessovestnyi," *Izvestiia,* 5 May 1986, p. 3. For detailed analysis, see Elizabeth Waters, " 'Cuckoo-mothers' and 'apparatchiks': Glasnost and children's homes," in Mary Buckley, ed., *Perestroika and Soviet Women* (Cambridge, Cambridge University Press, 1992), pp. 123–141.

164. TASS, "Po zovu serdtsa," *Izvestiia,* 15 October 1987, p. 3.

165. V. Shchepkin, "Po isku detstva," *Pravda,* 1 March 1990, p. 3.

166. Ibid.

167. Ibid.

168. Ibid.

169. Maksim Gorky, *My Childhood* (Harmondsworth, Penguin, 1990).

170. Shchepkin, "Po isku detstva."

171. Ibid.

172. Aina G. Ambrumova and Lidiia I. Postovalova, "Motivy samoubiistv," *Sotsiologicheskie Issledovaniia,* no. 6, 1987, p. 53.

173. Ibid.

174. S. G. Smidovich, "Samoubiistva v zerkale statistiki," *Sotsiologicheskie Issledovaniia,* no. 4, 1990, pp. 74–87.

175. V. Gubarev, "Schast'e i tragediia Akademika Legasova," *Pravda,* 17 October 1988, p. 4.

176. D. Barchuk and A. Solov'ev, "Tragediia v Khmelevke," *Izvestiia,* 5 January 1990, p. 2.

177. A. Ryskin and V. Iakovlev, "Iz shesti vozmozhnykh," *Ogonek,* no. 48, November 1986, p. 31.

178. Ibid.

179. T. Khudiakova, "Doverie ne tol'ko po telefony," *Izvestiia,* 4 September 1988, p. 4.

180. A. Ganelin, "Pod parandzhoi," *Komsomol'skaia Pravda,* 8 August 1987, p. 4.

181. Ibid.

182. Ibid.

183. Ibid.; E. Gafarov, "Zhivye fakely," *Pravda,* 21 April 1988, p. 6; *Current Digest of the Soviet Press,* vol. 40, no. 44, 30 November 1988, pp. 16–17.

184. A. Grachev, "Kogda grustiny nevesty," *Pravda,* 29 April 1986, p. 6.

185. Gafarov, "Zhivye fakely."

186. Ibid.

187. Ibid.

188. Ibid.

189. V. Artmenko, "Ne ukhodia ot urokov pravdy," *Pravda,* 5 February 1988, p. 2.

190. Ibid.

191. I. Vetlugin, "Mir stanet prekrasen, esli vse my budem miloserdny drug k drugy," *Meditsinskaia Gazeta,* 23 November 1988, p. 4.

192. *Current Digest of the Soviet Press,* vol. 40, no. 44, 30 November 1988, p. 16. This is a translation of *Kommunist Tadzhikistana,* 11 September 1988, p. 2.

193. Dorothy Stein, "Burning widows, burning brides: The perils of daughterhood in India," *Pacific Affairs,* vol. 61, no. 3, Fall 1988, pp. 465–485.

194. Smidovich, "Samoubiistva v zerkale statistiki," p. 75.

195. Ambrumova and Postovalova, "Motivy samoubiistv," p. 53.

196. Ibid., pp. 53–54.

197. Ibid., pp. 58–59.

198. Ibid., pp. 59–60.

199. There was self-censorship within newspapers and set by editors. At the highest level, censorship came from the Central Committee.

200. For details about Kravchenko, see "Glasnost Under Attack" in Chapter 2.

201. *Komsomol'skaia Pravda,* 30 October 1990, p. 2; Iurii Levada, "Chego zhdem i chego boitsia," *Moskovskie Novosti,* no. 49, 9 December 1990, p. 9.

4

"New" Failures in Housing and Health Care

> QUESTION: *How in the Soviet Union can we solve the food problem and the housing problem?*
>
> ANSWER: *To solve the food problem, we must seal the border and stop exports. To solve the housing problem, we must open the border and allow people to leave.*

THE TECHNIQUES USED by the media in presenting criminal behavior to the general public were also used in redefining the problems of housing and healthcare: statistics, exposé, sensation, photographs, personal accounts, and links across problems. Applying these tools of glasnost, journalists delivered the new message that many of the "great achievements" of the state had frequently been fabrications, overstatements, or partial truths. Social services often suffered from ineptitude, corruption, and inadequate resources. Among their consequences were injustice and poverty.

Fresh approaches to housing and health care contrasted in three main ways with the opening of crime. First, some problems in state services had been previously recognized, such as housing shortages. Unlike the non-topics of drug abuse and rape, these were "old" problems. Journalists did not need to expose them from scratch, already enjoying a foundation of material on which to build. This meant that more probing coverage could be delivered sooner. But this condition did not apply to all issues concerning the state, some of which, such as infant mortality, had also suffered from official silence. So the degree of glasnost required by different aspects of state provision varied.

Second, numerous statistics had been released before, some for decades. They were available in statistical handbooks and frequently cited as indicators of socialist progress. But although some statistics were not novel, the way in which they had been presented needed to change for construction of more truthful pictures. Aggregate statistics that had previously blazoned laudable increases in the number of hospital beds and in the number of new apartment blocks had never been juxtaposed alongside maternal death rates or accompanied by discussions of the poor conditions inside hospitals and communal flats. This approach would have created very different pictures.

Third, the emotional consequences among citizens of the impact created by investigative journalism differed. Whereas discussions of deviant behavior in society provoked fear, examination of the inadequacies in housing stock, the nature of treatment in abortion clinics, and high infant mortality rates triggered shame at low living standards and poor conditions. Doubts were raised, too, about the likelihood of improving them quickly.

Taken together, more probing accounts than ever before of housing and health care underscored low living standards in general. The exponential curves of the past, which showed improvements on all social indicators, were evidently invalid. The new messages were that citizens endured indignities in communal flats, humiliations in abortion clinics, and destitution in shantytowns. Glasnost allowed journalists bluntly to name hardships and to criticize inadequate resources and the unresponsive, even hostile, attitudes of those in positions of authority. Glasnost enabled journalists to apportion blame. Thus, glasnost resulted in serious indictments of social policies accentuated by comparisons with the West.

Although public discussion of social problems arising from state provision and services had preceded glasnost, indictments had never before been so thorough. Since the Khrushchev years, and regularly under Brezhnev, the press had noted housing shortages, overcrowding in kindergartens, high rates of illness among children attending them, and long waiting lists for kindergarten places. But these were generally pitched as problems that would be solved as society moved toward communism. As social science research developed under Brezhnev, albeit haphazardly, lively debates took place on a range of officially recognized social issues with proposals for how these "non-antagonistic contradictions" could best be tackled.[1] Never, however, was there any public suggestion that such solutions required a fundamental overhaul of the system. The assumption underpinning all published analyses was that improvements would result within the prevailing system as it perfected itself. Soviet socialism itself was not questioned. At most, mistakes in the implementation of policies could be isolated for attack but not the general direction of party programs. Details could be selected for criticism but not broader intents. Glasnost broke this mold and led to critical appraisals of both the content and direction of policies.

Just how critical the appraisals were varied immensely according to year, writer, and outlet. As already discussed in Chapter 2, political context and editorial policy affected the parameters of acceptable glasnost. Some journalists and academics, in tune with Gorbachev's official line, targeted Brezhnev's so-called years of stagnation as the main culprit and went no further.[2] But by 1991, others on the right and left were feeling confident enough to challenge Gorbachev's policies, and radical reformers were questioning the entire edifice of Soviet state socialism. Thus, glasnost produced heterogeneous results. Similarly, the quality of the critique varied immensely. Sensationalism could be quite crude, as in exposés of life in slums where shock outweighed rigorous analysis. But, again, given the silences of the past, it is hard to see how reporting on some topics could not have been sensational. Perhaps what mattered most was which silences persisted in reporting and in academic inquiry—a question that affects journalism and analysis worldwide.

The aim of this chapter is to explore the treatment of selected issues concerning state provision: housing conditions, contraception, abortion, and infant mortality. This list is not exhaustive, but it is sufficient to indicate in some detail the sorts of approaches adopted.

Housing Conditions

Glasnost triggered different sorts of articles about housing. During 1986, 1987, and 1988, topics included differences in the supply and quality of housing across republics, the significance of waiting lists, and the corrupt allocation of living quarters. More sensational reporting looked at squalor, lack of hot water and heating, homelessness, and shantytowns. Never before had there been an admission of homelessness under socialism. That had always been a characteristic evil of capitalism, a system that gave no guarantees of work or shelter. Likewise, shantytowns were a revelation. And by 1990, reporting was including an idealization of the West. Thus, articles on housing began to contrast cramped rooms and apartments under socialism with the spaciousness of homes in capitalist systems. Once more, the old ideology was being inverted, remaining true to the crudities of earlier dichotomies.

The unsanitary and overcrowded conditions of housing received special attention. Journalists constructed a bleak picture linking poor conditions to broader questions of health and work performance. Passing references to the extent of squalor were particularly hard-hitting. Their brevity effectively underscored the point. For example, in Azerbaidzhan "nearly 50 per cent of all housing ha[d] outdoor sanitation (not connected to the main drains system) and no hot water."[3] In Sverdlovsk, according to official statistics, three hundred thousand people lived in slums, and "thousands of children ha[d] no elementary conveniences, [were] cold at night, or suffer[ed] from tuberculosis."[4] In Leningrad, communal flats "often [did] not have a bath or hot water, and the ceiling [was] crumbl[ing] in places and leak[ed]."[5] Newspapers imparted the information bluntly, then moved on. This technique of providing a succession of points, all appalling in different ways, hardened the blow of the assault. Some journalists achieved on paper the style that Aleksandr Nevzorov perfected on his television program "600 Sekund" (already discussed).

Reporting drew attention to squalor and overcrowding in a context in which one-quarter of urban dwellers still lived in communal flats. Here each family had one room and shared the bathroom and kitchen with other families. Those who lived in such conditions learned nothing fresh from investigative journalism other than that their plight was a relatively common one spanning cities and republics, albeit with regional variations. For the first time, however, they could see the emotional results of housing conditions brought to public attention. Glasnost enabled journalists to go beyond exposure of squalor and cramped conditions to probe their impact on individual psychology. One common theme during 1989 was that life in communal flats and in hostels often meant high levels of domestic tension and frayed nerves. According to *Izvestiia,* a thirty-year-old pilot who lived with his wife and two children in a room measuring just 9.6 square meters was under awful daily pressure. Another pilot living in an adjacent room also had two children, and the navigation officer on the other side had one. The hostel provided one kitchen for every four families. In the pilot's own words: "In the room there are crying, nappies; the oldest son, a schoolboy, cannot sleep; my wife moans. One cannot talk of relaxation. And tomorrow, in flight, on the plane, with passengers behind one's back, one must deliver them to a fixed destination, observing flight 'safety' and a high level of service."[6]

Apparently most pilots in the north lived in similar conditions. Individual portraits of stress made poignant comments about home and work life. By quoting sufferers' own perceptions of their predicament, journalists brought immediacy to it. This device conveyed that the problems were real, believable, and awful.

Ogonek produced a similar story, noting that air force pilots generally lived in "garrison" hostels, rather than in civilian accommodations, because the latter were impossible to find. But even here, single men were lucky if on arrival an empty bed could be found.[7] Photographs showed just how crowded the hostels were. In one room, five men grouped together in a corner surrounded by suitcases and chairs. Their coats hung on a makeshift pole, and washing dried alongside on a piece of string.[8] In another, three children slept in the same bed with washing overhead. At the end of their bed, the television was on. Looking into the camera, the unhappy face of their mother was framed by more washing, a tiny bowl in which to do it, and an upsidedown water bottle hanging on the wall. The image conveyed intolerable lack of space, unbearable clutter, and dampness. Another photograph played on the lack of privacy. Two men in the bathroom were cleaning their teeth. Two others stood behind them, waiting for their turn at the sinks.[9] Photographs made the written messages instantly credible and heightened their impact.

The technique of quoting the inhabitants on their problems also made them more believable. Simple decoration and maintenance, for example, were additional difficulties. The men complained that "not one room here has been decorated at the expense of the garrison. We buy wallpaper, paint, and other construction materials ourselves."[10] Their words alternated with the information that burst pipes were common; that the hostels' isolated spots lacked enough doctors, crèches, or kindergartens; and that there were no jobs for wives who wanted to work, so families had to struggle to survive on one income. The result was a powerful picture of intolerable living conditions.[11] Facts punctuated by quotations from those affected also gave reporting a dynamic rhythm. Even though this technique was not novel, the type of information that it conveyed was. This was a powerful way of stating that life under socialism could be distressing.

But journalism revealed that even more deplorable than Leningrad's communal flats and pilots' isolated hostels were the shantytowns of the Far East. How could citizens live a "normal life," asked *Izvestiia*, if their home was a mere shack built on a swamp and thrown together from assorted materials, including crates? Several thousand people were crammed into six hundred such slum dwellings in the city of Susuman. The shacks were dark and dirty inside. These squalid living conditions were linked to alcoholism and to unpredictable crimes. *Izvestiia* portrayed Arkadii Buchuk as the victim of his living conditions and troubled family life, narrating how one day he went on a drinking binge with friends and ended up kicking in a plywood door and shooting one of his mother's friends.[12] Journalism concentrated on individual cases for maximum impact, providing images of squalor leading either to passive despair or violent behavior. Citing relevant statistics, reporters uncovered that other towns shared Susuman's problems. In Magadan, for example, there were more than eight thousand such shacks.[13] The message put across by *Izvestiia* was that poor living conditions encouraged drunkenness, drug abuse, prostitution, and crime in general.

Reporting on housing conditions more readily drew links between poor accommodations and crime than did the growing literature on crime. But such assertions were often not convincingly demonstrated; journalists did not ask the methodologically necessary question of whether drunkenness, drug abuse, and prostitution also occurred in better living conditions. Certainly drunkenness was found at all levels of society. The key question was whether it was significantly more likely to occur in poverty. Journalists did not explore this possible correlation. Nor did they admit that drinking binges lasting several days have long been common in rural Russia, a fact substantiated by recently opened party archives that also indicate that murders were often among the consequences.[14] Binges cannot be put down to shantytowns alone, although their conditions may reinforce the need for escapism. Binges are a social phenomenon long integral to Russian male cultural patterns.[15] But journalists have not yet thoroughly applied glasnost to behavior in male subcultures.

Journalism certainly did not inspire hope that there were easy ways out of hostels, communal flats, and shantytowns. Instead, articles reiterated the long-recognized hurdle of enormous waiting lists everywhere for state flats. Journalists had cited statistics in the past but now incorporated them with an almost automatic regularity. As in discussions of crime, drugs, and suicide, readers were treated to an onslaught of figures. In 1988, for instance, *Bakinskii Rabochii* told its readers that in Azerbaidzhan, there were 133,000 families on lists. Of these, 20,000 had already been waiting more than ten years and were living in shabby hostels or ill-equipped buildings. Even invalids and veterans of the Great Patriotic War suffered these poor conditions. "We ought to be ashamed," commented Abdul Rakhman Vezirov, then Azerbaidzhan's first secretary.[16]

Some articles provided comparative statistics. *Izvestiia* reported that the shortest lists were in Moscow and Tashkent, where 12 percent of families were waiting their turn. At the other end of the spectrum, in Baku, Ashkabad, Kiev, and Riga, 26 percent of families were on the housing list compared to 28 percent in Minsk and a high 32 percent in Kishinev. These figures excluded families that wanted to move to Moscow or other cities but that lacked the residence permits or opportunities to do so.[17]

The move, then, from a communal flat or hostel to a state flat was not easy. But neither was access to communal housing automatically granted to the homeless, a topic that could not have been explored before homelessness was granted official existence. After 1986, fewer articles dealt with it than with other housing problems, and the statistics given were spotty and incomplete. Nonetheless, journalists delivered the message that communal housing, however bad, was much sought after by those with nowhere to live. Special coverage was given to students not wishing to leave the city of their education. In Leningrad, for example, every year one thousand graduates who had initially come from other towns joined the city's housing lists. Only between 5 and 10 percent of them, those with their own children, would be housed in one room within five years. In all, there were twenty thousand young specialists on the list. Galina Toktalieva's investigative journalism exposed the "homeless intelligentsia" and captured their anger and frustration. As Shura, one interviewee, put it, "I can show you single mothers. I can show you, and you will understand, why children are thrown into children's homes or simply into doorways."[18] As in the reporting of drug abuse and child kidnapping, photographs of victims sharpened the point.

Consistent with the new message that homelessness existed, the press began to print pictures of destitute, cold, and hungry citizens living on the streets and covered with dirty blankets. These photographs, however, did not appear until 1990 after a long buildup in reporting. *Moskovskie Novosti,* as usual at the forefront of investigative journalism, showed a man sitting helplessly on the ground, with one leg outstretched, his foot covered with an extra blanket. The way in which he positioned his leg suggested that he might be an invalid, but the reader had no confirmation of this. A blanket over the man's head conveyed cold. He held a disheveled dog close to him, implying a need for warmth and companionship. On the ground around him were garbage and pieces of cardboard. Graffiti behind heightened the sense of dereliction. The Kremlin in the distance introduced a contrast between an affluent world of power and privilege and a desperate one of neglect.[19] Such an image, already commonplace in Paris, London, or New York, gained its powerful impact in a Soviet newspaper from the fact that it had never been permitted before. Once again, the happy lives constructed by socialist realism were being seriously qualified.

Galling for many on housing lists and for those on the streets was the new public knowledge that flats in cities were often left empty or were unfairly allocated. *Pravda* reported in 1987 that the Central Committee of the CPSU had examined "serious violations of the principle of social justice," which were apparently common. City soviets left some flats empty in case party officials suddenly demanded accommodation. Examples were plentiful. Kharkov City Soviet, for example, ignored those on the waiting list and in 1986 gave sixty newly decorated flats to party and soviet officials. In turn, these people gave their old flats to their children's families.[20] The loud message was that officials were given preferential treatment and then abused their privileges. Here glasnost served perestroika's goal of uncovering corruption.

Other housing allocations were categorized as "gross violations." Disabled war veterans and the families of soldiers killed in combat were either left on lists or given flats on the outskirts of towns in new areas with few amenities and few inhabitants. Especially large numbers of veterans were on lists in Kharkov, Petropavlovsk, Erevan, and Sukhumi.[21] Journalists charged that allocations were both unjust and immoral. Some noted that the period of stagnation had undermined "socialist social justice" and had encouraged indifference. This conclusion also served perestroika's condemnation of the Brezhnev era.

Pressure for scarce housing in urban areas had always been exacerbated by population growth and by migration, not always legal, into cities from rural areas. This same rural outmigration, however, had resulted in empty homes scattered in the countryside. The press addressed this "new" issue.

According to *Sovetskaia Rossiia* in 1987, there were more than 725,000 empty rural homes in the USSR; almost 500,000 of these were in Russia. At the same time, 1 million Muscovites had requested private plots but had not yet been given them. In 1987, fewer than 10 percent of Moscow families enjoyed such plots.[22] Journalism pointed out that housing stock and land for cultivation existed, but in areas of low demand. In urban areas, where pressures were greatest, solutions were not on the horizon. In early 1991, however, city soviets began allocating rural plots in an attempt to meet the need of urban dwellers to grow their own food. As rumors of worsening food shortages, price increases, and famine spread, this need grew.

In the late 1980s, the pressure for housing intensified as a result of millions of homeless refugees, a situation that made the issue hard to ignore. In addressing it, journalists' use of statistics was especially effective since it created a picture of urgency. They told readers that the Chernobyl nuclear disaster had resulted in 1 million people in need of immediate resettlement. Experts felt this might soon increase to 10 million.[23] Another 1 million refugees had moved from Transcaucasia, Central Asia, and the Baltic republics. A further "looming problem" was that of demobilized troops from Eastern Europe. Already there were five hundred thousand, and the figure was expected to rise to 2 million.[24] Commentary delivered the message that "they represent one of the biggest headaches in terms of rehousing."[25] And in addition to these groups, there were hundreds of thousands who needed resettlement from areas of ecological disaster such as the dried-up Aral Sea.[26] Journalists constructed the image of millions of citizens desperate for shelter for very different reasons—some tragic, some not—but all with nowhere to go. The social infrastructure could not cope. Then demand escalated again in Russia in 1992 as newly independent states demanded that soldiers leave.

The need for housing had always far outstripped the ability of the state to provide it. Despite massive housing construction under Khrushchev and Brezhnev, supply never managed to catch up with demand. This was due to several factors. First, urbanization, especially after 1928, demanded new housing for millions. Factory workers arriving from the countryside generally lived in hostels attached to the workplace. The construction of more hostels addressed one problem but created others. Second, about one-quarter of all housing was destroyed during the Great Patriotic War. Third, hastily built five-story housing thrown up in the Khrushchev era was now considered cramped, of low standard, and frequently in need of replacement. Fourth, building standards generally had been criticized as shoddy and in need of immediate repair when first-time dwellers moved in. This was not helped by the siphoning off of construction materials to the black market. Fifth, the standards sought by citizens had increased over the years. One room for an entire family was no longer an acceptable norm. And with the breakdown of extended families, couples wanted their own separate flats and more space. High divorce rates complicated this further. Sixth, economic decline meant that the share of capital investment allocated to housing had fallen from 23 percent in 1956 to 12 percent in 1986.[27]

In the early 1990s, reporting turned to serious building problems and citizens' changing housing needs. An example of the former was a brand-new, nine-story building in Novomoskovsk that collapsed. Apparently, "new residents did not even manage to hammer one nail in the walls in any of the thirty-six new apartments." Builders wasted 2 million rubles, but fortunately no one was injured. Experts believed that the accident was due either to "a miscalculation of the firmness of the soil" or faulty foundations or both. The article concluded that "next to the collapsed building stands yet another new one. 'It is still standing,' worried experts stress."[28] Journalists revealed that carelessness, negligence, and lack of foresight in building design contributed to the housing crisis. They created a picture of incompetence in building—yet one more failure of state socialism. Poor construction practices contrasted with the more sophisticated demands of citizens.

The issues of damp, drainage, communal flats, shantytowns, and homelessness did not go away in the 1990s, but calls were made for what were, by comparison, luxuries: more personal space so that citizens could live like "normal" families in the West in larger flats. The idealization of life under capitalism in 1991 entered complaints about housing. Writing in *Ogonek*, S. Smolkin argued that in statistically average Western households everyone enjoyed his or her own room and there was a family lounge as well. Therefore, "one sees other members of the family only when one wants. One watches television only when there is the desire to and looks only at what does not spoil one's mood. One socializes with guests who are visiting relatives only if they are pleasant guests. And one invites home who one wants, not asking other inhabitants of the family nest."[29] As a consequence, "in the West, they get less irritated. They argue less. They sleep better. They tire less."[30] Ironically, Smolkin attributed a better life to "they," not distinguishing between country, class, race, or social group. He constructed an image of a "good life" in the West and a "bad life" in the USSR. "And naturally," he went on, "they more easily maintain a cheerful, healthy atmosphere of relations—both in the family and at work." Although living conditions in Western states were better on average than those in the USSR, these countries also suffered homelessness and poor housing, facts not recognized by *Ogonek*'s article. In addition, family conflict was not absent from the most spacious Western homes. The old tinsel of the wonders of Soviet socialism and the horrors of capitalism was now reversed. Seemingly, the West had no housing problems and lots of happy families, whereas the Soviet Union was plagued by overcrowding, which gave rise to irritable relationships. A common characteristic of reporting was to overlook the complexities and subtleties of problems in the West. The main aim was to construct a picture of undesirable Soviet conditions that sharply contrasted with alternative policies elsewhere. Coupled with the notion that Western ways were normal, policy suggestions linked to them were thereby legitimated (overlooking entirely any discussion of how "normal" varies according to the practices and values of different social groups). Smolkin's main proposal was that fewer one-room and two-room flats be built in Moscow since people needed more space. His justification was that experience elsewhere indicated that this was beneficial to the harmony of family life.

Consistent with the pattern of emphasizing a point through visual images, Smolkin's piece included a photograph of a tiny kitchen with two children at the door. Overhead, washing hung down to greet them. It was overcrowded.[31] But by 1991, this image was becoming hackneyed. The punch that it had delivered two years earlier was now numbed by repetition. The potency of photographic glasnost changed rapidly. More powerful, although not particularly original either, was a panoramic shot across the rooftops of nine-story apartment blocks that stretched way into the distance. One long, straight road ran through the middle of the endless tall buildings. The photograph, which could have been almost any suburb built during the Brezhnev era, evoked anonymity, monotony, repetition.[32] Life here, it seemed, could be only dull and dreary. The soullessness of the urban sprawl left the reader feeling that escape was somehow essential. But the article and photographs offered no way out.

By the early 1990s, then, reporting on the housing crisis was linking it to defense policy, ecology, tensions between nationalities, and building practices. Discussions highlighted the implications of this crisis for physical and mental health, family life, child care, employment, and crime. Journalists examined the immensely broad causes, consequences, and ramifications. The solution was obvious—more housing. How best to achieve this quickly in a country with huge budget deficits was uncertain. Despite the CPSU's bold commitment in its 1986 program to provide every family with its own home by the year 2000, it was obvious by 1990 that this goal was unattainable.[33] As Moscow's mayor Iurii Luzhkov put it in an interview with Egor Yakovlev, editor of *Moskovskie Novosti*, "Talk that the housing problem will be solved before the year 2000 is nothing but deceit of the people."[34] Subsequent economic and political chaos, particularly in 1992, meant that much housing construction was frozen. At a meeting of the "little soviet" of the Moscow City Soviet in March 1992, the chair of the housing commission reported that most construction work in Moscow had ceased because of lack of funds.[35] The new issue on the agenda was the privatization of both state and cooperative flats. This, however, was proceeding haphazardly amid confusion. Citizens in March 1992 had no idea what their tax obligations to local authorities would be if they decided to privatize.[36]

Contraception

Contraception was rarely mentioned in the press before 1987. Although Lenin supported birth control, his remarks about it are probably among his least quoted.[37] After the 1920s, the topic largely disappeared from public discussions. There was extremely brief mention in 1968 of the intrauterine device, extolling its virtues over contraceptive pills.[38] But silence generally hung over the topic and was not broken until glasnost. Greater openness meant that at last the dire lack of contraceptives was acknowledged and deplored. Women's magazines also uncovered the unsympathetic attitudes of many gynecologists to requests for information about contraception, a problem suffered particularly by teenage girls. Letters to the press gave poignancy to the associated emotions. In fact, readers' letters played a large role in framing the issue.

In 1987 and 1988, letters to *Komsomol'skaia Pravda, Rabotnitsa,* and *Meditsinskaia Gazeta* started to demand condoms. In response to Novikov's article on AIDS[39] (discussed in the last chapter), one Muscovite complained that condoms were very hard to find and suggested that condom slot machines be installed on the streets, at railway stations, and in hotels.[40] One woman observed, "We are developing complicated electronics. We sent rockets into space, but we cannot create the needed means of protection against unwanted pregnancies."[41]

Some pointed out how difficult it was to raise the subject, given the silence of the past: "Now how does one write about THAT? It's not done to direct attention to THAT." Rallying readers of *Meditsinskaia Gazeta* to say something, the author concluded, "So, perhaps, comrades, that's enough shyness. Speak frankly, are condoms needed or not?"[42] In response, one reader complained, "It's already a year since condoms were in pharmacies in L'vov; as a result, my wife and I became the victims of an unplanned pregnancy."[43] Another lamented, "In Belorussia it is not possible to buy these products. A black market has even appeared, and the price has soared one hundredfold."[44]

There were also letters that joked about the matter, illustrating the degree of desperation. According to one reader, "Some people are recommending using children's balloons instead of condoms."[45] Another noted that since sugar and washing powder were now rationed, why not condoms, too?[46] A third suggested that condoms be included on the shopping lists of products ordered through the workplace.[47] More flippantly, one letter writer called for more beautiful boxes for condoms and another for a change of name since not everyone liked to go into a shop and say, "Condoms."[48]

The absence of condoms inevitably caused concern about venereal disease. One reader from Borisoglebsk in Voronezh oblast noted that gonorrhea was prevalent.[49] Professionals elaborated similar points. According to Professor

Vladimir Kulakov, "Because of the spread of AIDS, the condom has become an important part of sexual life. Yet the condoms produced in our country (in two factories only!) are of such poor quality that they offer no reliable protection against pregnancy or the virus. As to the supply—it's laughable. Each male citizen in our country can count on four condoms per year."[50] Just 220 million condoms were produced annually—clearly not enough for a population of more than 281 million that lacked choice about contraceptive methods.[51] Open discussion of the issue incorporated previously unknown statistics indicating the overwhelming size of the shortage.

The problem of how to obtain contraceptives was exacerbated for young women by gynecologists who withheld information and advice. In a letter to *Sobesednik,* one sexually active fifteen-year-old wrote, "Although I look quite grown-up, there is a lot I do not know. So recently I went to the gynecologist. The elderly gynecologist nearly fell off his chair when I explained that I needed advice. He demanded my birth certificate and asked me to bring my parents along. ... So where can I get the information?"[52]

Fortunately, with relaxed censorship, advice columns in women's magazines began to fill the information gap on sex and contraception. In *Rabotnitsa* one doctor described it as his "sacred duty" to avert "the typical situation" in which an inexperienced girl finds herself pregnant and then is afraid to tell her mother. Contraception could prevent this painful scenario. In this doctor's opinion, "For the first 3 to 4 months when intimate relations have only just begun, pills are the most suitable method. With adaptation, once the young people have become used to each other, they can move on to barrier methods, to condoms. Subsequently, they can alternate these methods."[53]

In this new climate, past condemnations of contraceptive pills were attacked. *Nedelia* regretted that:

> unfortunately, in our country a strong prejudice grew against hormonal contraception; various fears are associated with it—from birth defects to cancer. This is not surprising; after all, neither doctors nor patients received reliable information about contraceptives in general or hormonal contraceptives in particular, and the scanty information that filtered into the press was totally negative. Detailed discussion of modern methods of contraception is not a topic of today's conversations.[54]

Elsewhere, old opinions were replaced by the belief that lower-dose pills were safe. But warnings were still issued that pills were not vitamins and were best taken for short periods only.[55] Journalists, however, pointed out how much debate was academic since in practice pills were not always available. Pharmacists often responded to requests with the remark that they had not stocked them "for a long time."[56]

The redefined attitude of advice columns was that even though sexual activity at a young age was not to be encouraged, advice was nevertheless necessary to prevent legal and illegal abortions and to deter early pregnancies—all of which harmed health. But making information available was not always easy. Kulakov recounted how:

> a while ago we bought a large consignment of contraceptive devices in Hungary. The firm sent us a brilliant information pamphlet, which, we thought, should have been immediately made available to the general public. Alas, our institute has no publishing rights, and all our efforts to have the pamphlet published elsewhere were in vain. So there is still no proper, easily accessible literature on the subject of contraception and family planning. So it is back to abortion which still kills hundreds of women every year.[57]

Despite glasnost, the amount of information about contraception that reached young girls was less than what was desired by professionals. And although glasnost enabled franker, much less moralizing public discussions of sex life, for many citizens the key issue was whether glasnost would result in the production of contraceptives to meet demand. Sharp criticism about the lack of contraceptives stemmed not only from fear of AIDS but also from doctors' worries about the ill-health that could result from women's distress at unwanted pregnancies and the subsequent "hell of abortion."[58]

Abortion

Abortion was (and still is) the main means of birth control in the USSR. It was first legalized in 1920 as a necessary evil, prohibited in 1936, and made legal again in 1955. Yet despite its legality, it was not publicly discussed until 1987.[59] Apart from a chilling description of the abortion clinics published in 1979 in the women's underground *Almanach,* little was said.[60]

With greater freedom of expression under Gorbachev, women and men began speaking out against "the world's cruelest abortion system."[61] Alarmingly high statistics were finally released, confirming what most Soviet specialists in the West had long suspected. Thus, like its application to other new social issues, glasnost generated statistical information and revealed personal stories of anxiety and suffering. The inhumanity of the system and the sheer extent of the problem became live issues. Until, however, contraception is made widely available, and until couples overcome their reluctance to use it, women of childbearing age are likely to continue resorting to abortion.

The main public revelation was that many Soviet women endured six or more abortions in a lifetime. According to Kulakov, "The Soviet Union holds a sad record: the highest number of abortions in the world. Every year, twenty-three thousand teenage girls (under seventeen years of age) have an abortion. Every year, for each 5.6 million births, there are 6.8 million abortions."[62] *Moskovskie Novosti* added the distressing, but probably exaggerated, figure that 90 percent of first pregnancies ended in abortion.[63] Equally horrific, *Nedelia* informed readers that only 15–18 percent of women in the Russian Republic had never had an abortion and that a further 15 percent had endured several abortions during the course of just one year.[64]

These statistics were often mentioned in passing, as supplements to general arguments. More systematic tables broken down according to republic were published for the first time in official statistical handbooks, as shown in Table 4.1. According to these, in 1985 there were 100.3 abortions for every 1,000 women between the ages of fifteen and forty-nine, totaling 7,034,000 abortions. This average was exceeded in the Russian Republic, reaching 123.6 abortions per 1,000 women. Lower figures in Uzbekistan, Azerbaidzhan, Tadzhikistan, Armenia, and Turkmenia of 46.9, 30.8, 39.5, 38.4, and 40.9 abortions per 1,000 women, respectively, could be accounted for by larger family size among Muslim populations and by the inclination to reproduce rather than to abort. Lithuania stood out among the Baltic states for its low abortion rate of 46.3 abortions per 1,000 women. This could be explained by the strength of Catholicism among Lithuanians; Catholics made up 80 percent of the republic's population.

Although abortions were legal, articles revealed that some women sought illegal abortions because they did not wish those working in official channels to be aware that they needed one. Others did so because pregnancy had gone beyond the legal limits for abortion. In some parts of the country, illegal "criminal" abortions accounted for 80 percent of all abortions.[65] And each year six hundred women died from botched abortions and many more suffered infertility and disability.[66] Therefore, official statistics seriously understated the number of abortions performed, and any attempts at comparative analysis were further complicated by regional variations in illegal ones.

Articles in *Meditsinskaia Gazeta* included attacks on those who performed illegal abortions, describing them as "mercenary." This medical paper exposed perpetrators of the practice and informed readers of the penalties involved. According to Article 116 of the Russian Criminal Code, the illegal performance of abortion by a physician was "punishable by corrective labor for a period of up to two years or by deprivation of the right to practice medicine."[67] Many women, however, preferred the individual treatment of a private operation to the bureaucratic and insensitive system provided by the state.

Glasnost prompted a burst of harrowing letters to the press exposing the psychological and physical pain associated with abortion in a humiliating system. According to women's accounts, the abortion system was harsh. Letters conveyed several messages: Women experienced disrespect from medical workers, tiresome queues for treatment, and filthy bed linen. The operation was performed without anesthetic, and little sympathy was given for

TABLE 4.1 The Number of Abortions, by Republic

Republic	Number of Abortions (in thousands)				Number of Abortions (per 1,000 women aged 15–49)			
	1975	1980	1985	1988	1975	1980	1985	1988
USSR	7,135	7,003	7,034	5,767	105.7	102.3	100.3	82.3
RSFSR	4,670	4,506	4,552	3,832	126.3	122.8	123.6	105.2
Ukraine	1,146	1,197	1,179	774	88.3	94.1	92.2	61.9
Belorussia	195	202	201	135	78.7	81.1	80.0	54.1
Uzbekistan	160	161	199	234	51.9	43.8	46.9	50.8
Kazakhstan	391	378	367	295	108.7	99.2	90.7	72.2
Georgia	95	89	69	74	74.0	67.7	52.4	56.5
Azerbaidzhan	59	62	54	40	43.1	39.0	30.8	22.4
Lithuania	46	45	42	35	53.0	50.9	46.3	38.0
Moldavia	93	96	103	95	89.7	90.7	96.0	88.3
Latvia	58	60	58	50	91.4	92.5	88.7	76.8
Kirgizia	64	65	69	68	84.1	76.6	73.8	67.7
Tadzhikistan	39	40	41	43	53.4	45.3	39.5	38.6
Armenia	45	32	34	27	60.5	38.8	38.4	30.2
Turkmenia	34	34	31	35	60.8	51.1	40.9	43.1
Estonia	40	36	35	30	107.1	96.7	91.4	77.3

Sources: Goskomstat SSSR, *Naselenie SSSR 1987: Statisticheskii Sbornik* (Moscow, Finansy i Statistika, 1988), p. 319; Goskomstat SSSR, *Naselenie SSSR 1988: Statisticheskii Ezhegodnik* (Moscow, Finansy i Statistika, 1989), p. 413.

the pain and ill-health that resulted. These letters created an image of patients' powerlessness in an inhuman system.

For the first time, what abortion entailed was defined for the public in some detail. Women had to pass through several queues, which necessitated taking time off work. Rudeness and insensitivity characterized each step, gradually wearing stressed women down further.[68] Then came the procedure itself:

> At ten in the morning the women waiting for an abortion were lined up at the door of the operating room. God save you from lingering, making a wrong move, or asking an inappropriate question.
>
> "What are you waiting for?" the doctor shouted at me as he was removing his bloodstained gloves, the very sight of which made me feel weak. "Have you completely lost your head to come into the operating room wearing socks? Take them off!" he said.
>
> My hands were shaking, my movements faltered, I felt scared, hurt, and on the verge of tears.
>
> "Hurry up, hurry up, I have had enough of this," the doctor spurred me on.
>
> After that I remember the clinking of instruments and pain, acute pain. They gave only enough anesthetic to make me too weak to moan. Well, anesthetic is expensive, I know.[69]

The client recalled how afterward she lay with an icepack on her stomach while the doctors "all went home. No one came to me, looked at me, or asked how I was feeling. I don't know, perhaps that is how they do things. Perhaps, really, there were a lot of us and few of them."[70] Personal accounts such as this, in which women described in simple, step-by-step terms what had happened to them, not only brought openness to a horrific reality previously swept under the carpet but also provided graphic pictures of humiliation and degradation in a brutal system. Soviet socialism was meant, not to be brutal, but to be officially caring. Glasnost in women's stories served to erode one more ideological falsehood.

Other letters confirmed this picture: "They only give anesthetic for abortions in exceptional circumstances. Of course, anesthetic is needed more by sick people. Agreed. Woman is by nature patient. Silence tolerates any pain. But it would be better if she did not have to suffer."[71] Anesthetic could apparently be bought by paying fifty rubles for an *abort po blatu*.[72] But reports indicated that the *blat* conveyor belt was just as crowded as the official one. Letters to the press also provided gruesome warnings: "Most important of all, don't forget all the necessary items: a dressing gown, slippers, and two sheets because in our hospital there is not enough bed linen. There were forty of us in two wards with one bed among three. In the toilet there was not even anywhere to wash our hands. There were no tap and no washbasin."[73]

The insanitary and crowded conditions of many Soviet hospitals rendered the procedure traumatic. In response to such letters to *Rabotnitsa*, A. Barabanov, then deputy minister of health, commented, "It is painful to read these letters—as one of the leaders in the field of health, as a doctor, as a man. At last, I cannot but feel personal responsibility, personal blame for—let's call things by their real names—the pitiful condition of the protection of women's health. In recent years we really forgot about the necessity to give priority to the development of this important service."[74] What Barabanov omitted to say was that this service for women had always been neglected.

Writing in *Sobesednik*, Tat'iana Belaia called for a declaration of war against abortion. Lambasting the system for failing to produce contraception, she stressed that abortions were terrible, painful, and shameful. The queues, insolence, and lack of anesthetic were deplorable. Her burst of valid accusations was powerfully accompanied by three photographs. In the first, an outstretched palm, presumably a doctor's, held the miniscule hand of an aborted fetus. With a poster in the background that read, "Children—the flowers of our life!" the image suggested the cruelty of abortion and the murder of a valuable treasure. Underneath, the photograph of a woman on her back with a frightful look on her face indicated the pain of abortion. At the bottom of the page, a lone woman leaned against the wall in a dreary hospital corridor, presumably awaiting her turn, watching two women walk ahead of her. The picture evoked emptiness and a haunting dread about what was to happen.[75] Inevitably, this sort of information was seized upon by right-to-lifers. In uncovering abortion, journalism served two contradictory functions: It exposed a serious problem while calling for an improved system, but it also provided abortion's opponents with reasons why it should be banned. Honesty about the details of abortion contributed to the issue's politicization.

In this context, it was not long before opponents of abortion began to speak out. Catholics in Lithuania and in the western Ukraine criticized it.[76] Then in March 1991, *Moskovskii Komsomolets,* with a circulation of 1,538,288, called upon readers to write to the European parliament in support of a petition against abortion. Under the heading "Together with Europe," the journal noted that "it has become clear that in our country, as abroad, there are many opponents of abortion for religious and other considerations. And today the real opportunity has appeared for them to say a decisive 'no' to abortion, uniting with like-minded people from European countries."[77]

Selectively citing "European" opposition to abortion for legitimacy (and ignoring European supporters), the journal declared that abortion was an "act of violence and murder of a tiny being." Abortion was also "violence against the body and against the dignity of woman." The text asserted that in Europe the mass murder of 2 million children a year was taking place. Abortion was a "crime against humanity, a sin before God."[78] Given the indignities of the Soviet abortion system, we can see why many opposed it. But large numbers still supported it, seeking a more dignified system. Representatives from the Free Association of Feminist Organizations (SAFO), the Radical Party, and the Anarchist-Radical Union of Youth expressed their hostility to the petition by demonstrating outside the editorial offices of *Moskovskie Komsomolets* with placards declaring, "No to sexism" and "No to Vatican officialdom."[79]

By the early 1990s, glasnost had enabled the opponents and defenders of abortion to air their views. As in Western Europe, and as in Poland and Czechoslovakia since the revolutions of 1989, abortion was becoming a more volatile political issue.[80] Conflicting categorizations of abortion required diametrically opposed policies.

Once glasnost exposed the indignities of the abortion system, long known to most citizens, public shame resulted because women, idolized as the symbol of life, motherland, and goodness, were being poorly treated in clinics. The socialist state had never provided its women with sufficient contraceptives, and it dealt bureaucratically with their unwanted pregnancies in an indifferent and overburdened medical system. No social panic resulted, no fear, just embarrassment, shame, and a sense of failure. The USSR had been a world superpower, but its womenfolk had to abort more frequently than most women in other countries. This, in the 1990s, was not something of which to be proud. Neither were the USSR's high infant mortality rates.

Infant Mortality

Just as statistics on abortion had not been released in the past, neither had infant mortality rates. Glasnost resulted in their incorporation into yearly statistical handbooks and prompted discussion about why infant mortality was so high. Early articles in 1987 and 1988 focused on poor prenatal care, unsanitary conditions in maternity homes, frequent births, and ecological factors. Many of these causes were new topics in themselves, thereby heightening the shock of the general picture. By 1990, however, an additional factor had been incorporated into the story. Intrauterine starvation and poverty in Turkmenia appeared to account, in part, for a high number of child deaths. When child starvation in Turkmenia was raised in the USSR Supreme Soviet's Council of Nationalities, a "parliamentary incident" took place as objecting deputies from Turkmenia had to be calmed.[81]

Newly published statistics showed that in some republics, in particular Turkmenia, Tadzhikistan, Uzbekistan, Azerbaidzhan, and Kirgizia, the death rate of children up to one year of age was alarmingly high. According to Table 4.2, the worst infant mortality rates were found in Turkmenia, where, unlike in other republics, differences between urban and rural rates were negligible. In 1986 in Turkmenian towns, there were 56.5 deaths per 1,000 births up to the age of one; in the countryside, 59.3 deaths per 1,000 births. The urban-rural gap was more striking elsewhere. The lowest infant mortality rates were in Lithuania. Here in 1986, in towns there were 10.5 deaths per 1,000 births up to one year of age. The rural figure was slightly higher at 13.9 deaths per 1,000 births.

Particularly worrying was the fact that infant mortality rates in some republics were not improving. Turkmenia's urban infant mortality rate from 1975 to 1988 showed minor fluctuations, none of which was large enough to modify the general pattern. Even where there was improvement, it was often slight, as in the RSFSR. One of the best records for improvement was in Lithuania. Here rural mortality rates fell from 22.5 deaths per 1,000 births in 1975 to 13.9 per 1,000 in 1986. Curiously, statistical tables on infant mortality and abortion for 1988 showed lower rates across the board. Were official attempts being made to show "improvements"? Were procedures for gathering statistics changed? Or was "progress" genuine?

But statistics for all years may be deceptive. Medical workers often covered up child deaths since in many cases their negligence was to blame. Thanks to glasnost this was now made public. Infant mortality rates were

TABLE 4.2   Infant Mortality Rates in Selected Republics (the number of children dying up to age one, per 1,000 births)

Republic	1975	1980	1981	1982	1983	1984	1985	1986	1988
RSFSR									
Total population	23.7	22.1	21.5	20.4	20.1	20.9	20.7	19.3	18.9
Urban	22.5	21.2	20.3	19.5	19.2	19.9	19.8	18.8	18.2
Rural	26.2	24.0	24.3	22.4	22.4	23.4	22.8	20.4	20.4
Uzbekistan									
Total population	53.8	47.0	43.8	42.0	43.1	45.1	45.3	46.2	43.3
Urban	53.6	44.4	42.3	40.7	40.7	40.3	38.5	40.6	37.7
Rural	53.8	48.1	44.5	42.6	44.3	47.5	48.7	48.8	46.0
Georgia									
Total population	32.7	25.4	29.7	25.4	23.9	23.9	24.0	25.5	21.9
Urban	29.4	24.3	25.6	24.7	24.6	25.7	27.3	27.6	24.8
Rural	35.8	26.5	34.0	26.0	23.1	22.0	20.6	23.1	18.7
Lithuania									
Total population	19.6	14.5	16.6	15.1	14.1	13.4	14.2	11.6	11.5
Urban	17.8	12.9	14.5	13.7	13.4	11.8	13.2	10.5	11.4
Rural	22.5	17.3	20.5	17.8	15.6	16.6	16.3	13.9	11.7
Turkmenia									
Total population	56.5	53.6	55.9	52.5	53.2	51.2	52.4	58.2	53.3
Urban	54.4	57.4	55.7	54.7	55.3	49.1	49.0	56.5	52.5
Rural	58.0	51.0	56.1	50.9	51.8	52.6	54.7	59.3	54.2

Sources: Goskomstat SSSR, *Naselenie SSSR 1987: Statisticheskii Sbornik* (Moscow, Finansy i Statistika, 1988), pp. 345–346; Goskomstat SSSR, *Naselenie SSSR 1988: Statisticheskii Ezhegodnik* (Moscow: Finansy i Statistika, 1988), pp. 474–476.

thus higher than officially stated. *Nedelia* forcefully made the point that "often if an infant died or experienced a severe birth trauma, the mechanism for 'correcting' mistakes was adopted: The case history of the birth was rewritten or, more accurately, falsified to hide the mistake or other incorrect actions."[82] Such revelations called into question the accuracy of statistics and the validity of comparisons across republics.

During 1987 came official recognition that infant mortality rates were worse in the USSR than in capitalist countries.[83] The reasons given included poor conditions in maternity homes and inadequate prenatal care. In 1987, *Nedelia, Izvestiia,* and *Pravda* described how infant deaths occurred. In some cases, the hospital's lack of oxygen caused the tragedy: "Marina is thirty-one. It was her first child. The boy was born without problems, but he was very weak. And now he's gone. They say that had there been oxygen in the maternity home and a postnatal unit, he would have survived. How can it be that there was no oxygen! Isn't there enough of it? It should be given, first of all, to maternity homes."[84]

In other cases, maternity clinics without hot water and sewage systems were to blame. Readers learned that in Turkmenia more than 60 percent of maternity clinics and children's hospitals lacked hot water. There was no water supply to 127 hospitals, and two-thirds of these lacked sewage systems. In the summer, epidemics such as viral hepatitis, jaundice, and intestinal infections were common.[85] Reports from Uzbekistan indicated that prenatal care was very poor, as in Turkmenia, and that there was a serious shortage of respiratory equipment for infant resuscitation.[86] According to *Pravda*, 76 percent of maternity hospitals in Kirgizia and 85 percent in Turkmenia lacked a central water supply, and almost 50 percent of Moldavia's maternity hospitals lacked sewage systems.[87] In sum, maternity hospitals were unsafe!

Many maternity homes in Turkmenia and elsewhere were also crowded to the point that beds were placed in corridors. One consequence of this overcrowding was that these homes could not be "closed for repairs and disinfection as the regulations require[d]." The Khodzhaabad maternity home had not been repaired for eight years.[88] Nor was the capital immune from these problems. Apparently, only nine of Moscow's thirty-eight obstetric hospitals were of the appropriate standard. The rest needed major repairs.[89]

Newly released maternal death rates fit this gloomy picture. *Pravda* regretted that from 1985 to 1991, 14,000 women had died in maternity hospitals. Statistical handbooks indicated that more than 2,000 women died during childbirth every year. In 1980, there were 56.4 maternal deaths per 100,000 births. The figure fell a little in 1985 to 47.7 and in 1989 to 43.8. As Table 4.3 shows, rates varied immensely across republics. In 1989, Lithuania had the lowest rate, with 28.7 deaths per 100,000 births, whereas Kazakhstan, Georgia, Latvia, and Turkmenia each had rates greater than 50. The widespread practice of falsifying statistics meant, however, that even these figures were questionable. To make rates look less formidable, women's deaths as a result of childbirth could have been classified as death from something else. The official statistics nevertheless indicated that yet another shocking problem existed and was worse than in capitalist systems.[90]

Journalists revealed that a contributory factor to infant and maternal mortality was women's poor health. Anemia was a significant factor among women in Central Asia, where frequent births were common. According to doctors, women in rural areas of Turkmenia gave birth, on average, every fifteen months. A 60 percent protein deficiency was common.

Undernourished mothers produced weak and underweight children. "Intrauterine starvation" (*vnutriutrobnoe golodanie*) was a "mass phenomenon," a disease of poverty. Doctors admitted that "hunger in Turkmenian families is no rarity. Mothers are hungry; children are hungry. It is far rarer for fathers to be so. ... The custom here is that the man is the warrior, the protector, and so the best morsel is always for him—even if it is the last morsel in the house."[91] Among the consequences of intrauterine starvation were five-month-old babies weighing little more than two kilos and an increasing percentage of children with mental abnormalities. Mothers who had en-

TABLE 4.3 Maternal Deaths, by Republic (number dying during pregnancy, birth, and after birth)

Republic	Total			Per 100,000 Births		
	1980	*1985*	*1989*	*1980*	*1985*	*1989*
USSR	2,737	2,561	2,219	56.4	47.7	43.8
RSFSR	1,498	1,282	1,059	68.0	54.0	49.0
Ukraine	333	308	226	44.8	40.4	32.7
Belorussia	45	28	38	29.1	17.0	24.8
Uzbekistan	250	330	286	46.3	48.6	42.8
Kazakhstan	198	190	203	55.6	47.9	53.1
Georgia	23	22	50	25.7	22.5	54.9
Azerbaidzhan	60	73	52	38.7	41.1	28.6
Lithuania	14	13	16	27.0	22.2	28.7
Moldavia	51	45	28	64.1	49.8	34.1
Latvia	9	12	22	25.3	30.2	56.5
Kirgizia	53	55	56	49.4	42.8	42.6
Tadzhikistan	138	108	78	94.2	59.1	38.9
Armenia	19	18	26	27.0	22.4	34.6
Turkmenia	40	66	69	40.8	56.8	55.2
Estonia	6	11	10	27.0	46.6	41.2

Source: Goskomstat SSSR, *Okhrana Zdorov'ia v SSSR* (Moscow: Finansy i Statistika, 1990), p. 16.

dured multiple births were also producing children with Down's syndrome and a host of other illnesses. Unlikely to ease these problems, one-quarter of obstetricians and one-third of pediatricians in rural Turkmenia were insufficiently qualified.[92] Doctors were also overworked. In Chechen-Ingushia, gynecologists supervised as many as 700 pregnant women when they should have been looking after no more than 150.[93]

In 1991, *Pravda* openly stated that between 50 and 70 percent of pregnant women suffered "various pathological changes" and that more than 50 percent of all newborn babies had health problems.[94] These problems were not restricted to Central Asia. And their seriousness was compounded in areas of high radiation levels, such as Chernobyl.

Women's poor working conditions aggravated the situation. Women agricultural workers were exposed to high levels of nitrates in fertilizers. Journalists finally made the link between abuse of inorganic fertilizers and infant mortality.[95] Analysis of mother's milk in Turkmenia showed that it contained pesticide residues.[96] Similarly, 46 percent of nursing mothers in Kirgizia who worked on tobacco farms had chlorine and phosphorus compounds in their milk.[97] And women's poor health meant that their milk dried up within two to three months of childbirth.[98]

By 1990, the press had made clear that high infant mortality rates would be reduced only by an end to starvation in Turkmenia, drastic improvements in sanitary conditions in hospitals, more medical equipment, better-qualified doctors, improved prenatal care, and better working conditions for pregnant women. Such high infant mortality rates were shameful for the Soviet state and, in the case of the Central Asian republics, closer to the predicament of developing countries. Journalists using glasnost delivered the message that Soviet health care had failed the country's children. The tasks required to alleviate infant mortality were overwhelming.

The Shame of Social Policy

The application of glasnost to problems of housing and health care provoked shame about living standards. But some problems appeared more hopeless than others. For infant mortality rates to improve in Central Asia, so much had to change: Hunger had to cease, lifestyles had to be altered, and an overhaul of the hospital system was imperative. By contrast, concerted efforts in other spheres could mean positive results sooner. Although the abortion system was disgraceful, the changes it had to undergo for a better service were more straightforward. Likewise, the causes of the limited contraceptive supply were far fewer than the several interrelated ones affecting infant and maternal mortality and easier to address. But the housing crisis, like that of infant mortality, was multifaceted and multivariate in causes and in consequences.

Glasnost underlined that the tasks for social policy in the 1990s, and indeed for the rest of this century and beyond, were enormous. Social policy had not guaranteed adequate health care, not even for mothers and children, or provided housing of a moderate standard for everyone. The poor in Central Asia's rural areas suffered most. The loud "successes" of the socialist state were far more modest than ideology had trumpeted. The solution to problems of social policy demanded massive efforts and more resources, the prospect of which, with the failure of economic reform, was bleak. And the chaos and poverty created in 1992 by Yeltsin's crash program of economic reform left citizens unsure of what the future could bring. Confusion surrounding the privatization of housing and the possible privatization of medicine made many wonder if they could even afford shelter and basic medical care.

NOTES

1. The opening in 1968 of the Institute of Sociological Research in Moscow ensured that some topics would receive attention, notwithstanding the political ups and downs of the institute and of professional sociology. See Ann Weinberg, *The Development of Sociology in the Soviet Union* (London, Routledge and Kegan Paul, 1974).

2. See K. I. Mikul'skii, V. Z. Rogovin, and S. S. Shatalin, *Sotsial'naia Politika KPSS* (Moscow, Politizdat, 1987).

3. Vladimir Kulakov, "Birth rights," *Pravda International,* vol. 3, no. 2, p. 10.

4. *Moscow News,* no. 15, 14–21 April 1991, p. 2.

5. Galina Toktalieva, "Piatyi ugol kazennogo doma," *Sobesednik,* no. 39, September 1989, p. 6.

6. N. Lugov, "Pilot na zemle," *Izvestiia,* 23 January 1989, p. 1.

7. Mikhail Mamaev, "Polet vo vcherashnii den'," *Ogonek,* no. 24, June 1989, pp. 14–17.

8. Ibid., p. 15.

9. Ibid., p. 16.

10. Ibid., p. 15.

11. Ibid.

12. R. Bikmukhametov, "Vystrely v polnoch'," *Izvestiia,* 1 August 1988, p. 4.

13. Ibid.

14. TsPA (Central Party Archive, Moscow), fond 17, opis' 10, delo 139.

15. Drinking binges have long been common at harvest time. Ibid.

16. *Bakinskii Rabochii,* 15 November 1988, pp. 1–2.

17. V. Tolstov, "Kak obespecheny zhil'em krupneishie goroda strany," *Izvestiia,* 4 September 1988, p. 2.

18. Toktalieva, "Piatyi ugol kazennogo doma."

19. *Moskovskie Novosti,* no. 50, 16 December 1990, p. 6.

20. *Pravda,* 1 October 1987, pp. 1–2.

21. Ibid.

22. E. Maksimovskii, "Derevenskii dom gorozhana," *Sovetskaia Rossiia,* 2 August 1987, p. 1.

23. Viacheslav Storozhenko, "Zemlia dlia obezdolennykh," *Moskovskie Novosti,* no. 27, 8 July 1990, p. 10.

24. Ibid.

25. Ibid.

26. Ibid.

27. For further discussion of Soviet housing, refer to Gregory D. Andruz, *Housing and Urban Development in the USSR* (London, Macmillan, 1984); Henry W. Morton, "What have Soviet leaders done about the housing crisis?" in Henry W. Morton and Rudolf Tokes, eds., *Soviet Politics and Society in the 1970s* (New York, Free Press, 1974), pp. 163–199.

28. *Moskovskie Novosti,* no. 15, 14 April 1991, p. 2.

29. S. Smolkin, "Kommunal'noe myshlenie: Nadezhno li nashe zhilishche?" *Ogonek,* no. 5, January 1991, p. 10.

30. Ibid.

31. Ibid., p. 11.

32. Ibid., p. 9.

33. *Materialy XXVII S"ezda KPSS* (Moscow, Politizdat, 1986), p. 153.

34. Egor Yakovlev, "Kto skazhet 'net'—chinovnik ili my sam?" *Moskovskie Novosti,* no. 35, 2 September 1990, p. 14.

35. Moscow City Soviet, 25 March 1992.

36. Television programs in March 1992 explained to viewers what privatization entailed and which legal details had not yet been decided.

37. V. I. Lenin, "The working class and neo-Malthusianism," in *The Woman Question: Selections from the Writings of Karl Marx, Frederick Engels, V. I. Lenin, and Joseph Stalin* (New York, International Publishers, 1975), p. 84.

38. *Literaturnaia Gazeta,* 11 December 1968, p. 10. The article pointed out that 300,000 intrauterine devices had just been manufactured and that by the end of 1968 there would be a total of 1 million. Birth control pills would not be so widely used since "they can cause unpleasant side effects and sometimes serious complications." The article was written in response to an earlier piece, which had called for more contraceptives for women worldwide and which had attacked religious restrictions. Here contraceptives were described as "an important means to the liberation of women," and no distinction was drawn between the pill and the IUD. Both were praised as nearly 100 percent effective. See G. Speranskii, "Zhizn' oprovergaet dogmy,"*Literaturnaia Gazeta,* 2 October 1968, p. 12.

39. A. Novikov, "SPID," *Komsomol'skaia Pravda,* 1 August 1987, pp. 3–4.

40. *Komsomol'skaia Pravda,* 28 October 1987, p. 3.

41. *Rabotnitsa,* no. 7, July 1987, p. 13.

42. G. Denisova, "Pro eto samoe," *Meditsinskaia Gazeta,* 4 March 1988, p. 4.

43. "Razgovor na delikatnuiu temy: Otkliki na fel'eton 'Pro eto samoe,'" *Meditsinskaia Gazeta,* 10 June 1988, p. 4.

44. Ibid.

45. Ibid.

46. Ibid.

47. Ibid.

48. Ibid.

49. Ibid.

50. Kulakov, "Birth rights," p. 11.

51. Ibid.

52. *Sobesednik,* no. 47, November 1988, p. 10.

53. *Rabotnitsa,* no. 2, February 1990, p. 30.

54. Larisa Remennik, "Zhizn', ubitaia v tebe," *Nedelia,* no. 38, 21–27 September 1987, p. 12.

55. *Rabotnitsa,* no. 2, February 1990, p. 30.

56. *Sobesednik,* no. 47, November 1988, p. 11.

57. Kulakov, "Birth rights," p. 11.

58. Larisa Kuznetsova, "What every woman wants?" *Soviet Weekly,* 26 November 1988, p. 15.

59. For the little that was said about abortion from 1920 to the 1980s, see Mary Buckley, *Women and Ideology in the Soviet Union* (Ann Arbor, University of Michigan Press, 1989), pp. 37–40, 129–133, 156–159. For examination of policy, see Wendy Goldman, "Women, abortion, and the state, 1917–36," in Barbara Evans Clements, Barbara Alpern Engel, and Christine D. Worobec, eds., *Russia's Women: Accommodation, Resistance, Transformation* (Berkeley and Los Angeles, University of California Press, 1991), pp. 243–266.

60. Vera Golubeva, "The other side of the medal," in Women in Eastern Europe Group, trans., *Woman and Russia: First Feminist Samizdat* (London, Sheba, 1980), pp. 51–56.

61. Kuznetsova, "What every woman wants?"

62. Kulakov, "Birth rights." In the United States, there were 425 abortions for every 1,000 live births.

63. Ekaterina Nikolaeva, "Ne khochu zhalet', chto Ia—zhenshchina," *Moskovskie Novosti*, no. 4, 22 January 1989, p. 10.

64. Remennik, "Zhizn', ubitaia v tebe."

65. Ibid. To try reducing the number of "late" back-street abortions, the USSR Ministry of Health extended the legal termination date to twenty-eight weeks.

66. Kulakov, "Birth rights."

67. Iu. Sergeev, "Otvetstvennost' za nezakonnoe proizvodstvo aborta," *Meditsinskaia Gazeta*, 16 July 1986, p. 3.

68. Nikolaeva, "Ne khochu zhalet', chto Ia—zhenshchina."

69. Ibid.

70. Ibid.

71. *Rabotnitsa*, no. 7, July 1987, p. 13.

72. Tat'iana Belaia, *Sobesednik*, no. 47, November 1988, p. 11. An *abort po blatu* is an abortion acquired through extra payments.

73. *Rabotnitsa*, no. 7, July 1987, p. 12.

74. Ibid.

75. Tat'iana Belaia, "Budem otkrovenny?" *Sobesednik*, no. 47, November 1988, p. 11.

76. Mary Buckley, "Gender and reform," in Catherine Merridale and Chris Ward, eds., *Perestroika: The Historical Perspective* (Dunton Green, Edward Arnold, 1991), pp. 70–71; Solomea Pavlychko, "Between feminism and nationalism: New women's groups in the Ukraine," in Mary Buckley, ed., *Perestroika and Soviet Women* (Cambridge, Cambridge University Press, 1992), pp. 90–95.

77. *Moskovskii Komsomolets*, 1 March 1991, p. 2.

78. Ibid.

79. *Moskovskii Komsomolets*, 5 March 1991, p. 1.

80. Ol'ga Lipovskaia, "New women's organisations," in Buckley, ed., *Perestroika and Soviet Women*, p. 79.

81. P. Voshchanov and A. Bushev, "Zdes' legko obryvaetsia detskaia zhizn'," *Komsomol'skaia Pravda*, 25 April 1990, p. 2.

82. G. Rubanovich, S. Guseva, and A. Cherviakov, "Otvechat' za svoe zdorov'e: Lozh' ne vo spasenie," *Nedelia*, no. 15, 13–19 April 1987, p. 18.

83. In 1988, compared with the USSR's rate of 53.3 child deaths up to age one per 1,000 deaths, the figure was 5.8 in Sweden, 9.0 in the United Kingdom, 9.9 in the United States, 11.9 in Cuba, 46.6 in Guatemala, 75.6 in Turkey, and 101.7 in Pakistan. See United Nations, *Demographic Yearbook 1989* (New York, United Nations, 1991), pp. 342–362.

84. E. Mushkina, "Chelovek rodilsia," *Nedelia*, no. 7, 16–22 February 1987, pp. 16–17.

85. M. Volkov, "Aisberg v pustyne," *Pravda*, 31 August 1987, p. 4.

86. *Izvestiia*, 28 February 1987, p. 2.

87. *Pravda*, 11 February 1991, p. 4.

88. A. Kostikova, "Za chastokolom reshenii," *Pravda*, 7 February 1987, p. 3.

89. *Pravda*, 11 February 1991, p. 4.

90. Comparative figures showed maternal mortality to be lower in capitalist systems. In 1987–1988, the rate was 4.1 in Canada, 4.8 in Sweden, 5.9 in Britain, 6.6 in the United States, 12.0 in Japan, 48.3 in Chile, and 173.6 in Ecuador. State-socialist systems also showed varying rates: 11.6 in Poland and 49.0 in Cuba. See United Nations, *Demographic Yearbook 1989*, pp. 364–367.

91. Voshchanov and Bushev, "Zdes' legko obryvaetsia detskaia zhizn'."

92. Ibid.

93. Mushkina, "Chelovek rodilsia."

94. *Pravda*, 11 February 1991, p. 4.

95. Volkov, "Aisberg v pustyne."

96. Voshchanov and Bushev, "Zdes' legko obryvaetsia detskaia zhizn'."

97. *Pravda*, 11 February 1991, p. 4.

98. Voshchanov and Bushev, "Zdes' legko obryvaetsia detskaia zhizn'."

5

Pluralism Redefined

*T*HE APPLICATION OF GLASNOST to social problems had accustomed citizens to public revelation and reassessment. Roundtable discussions, investigative journalism, and more probing academic inquiries indicated that official lines of the past could now be challenged and reformulated. Glasnost, however, was not applied simultaneously in discussions of politics. Reinterpretations of pluralism, democracy, and civil society came later and were initially much more tentative. The redefinition of polity lacked the heady rush of exposé that had characterized the sensational treatment of some social problems.

There are four main reasons for these differences. First, social problems could be opened without an accompanying critique of the political system. They were less immediately subversive than debates about the significance of pluralism, the meaning of democracy, and the absence of a civil society. Nonetheless, these critiques were potentially undermining because biting evaluations of social policy could be linked back to the leadership of the CPSU. And the exposure of social problems schooled society in the skills of rethinking and questioning—also potentially subversive to polity. But such revelations did not entail demands right away for a different political system or for serious modifications of the prevailing one.

Second, it was consistent with Gorbachev's priorities for reform that social issues were approached first. Initially, glasnost was applied to economy and society, with a view to exposing policy failures and enlivening the human factor. At the Twenty-seventh Party Congress, emphasis did not fall on democratization. That enjoyed greater prominence in Gorbachev's speeches in 1987 and was not prioritized until 1988 at the Nineteenth Party Conference. Consequently, the formulation of political "problems" into "issues" came later, consistent with variations in the leadership's timing of reforms. The sequence of priorities affected which topics could legitimately come onto formal agendas, when, and with what emphasis. Reactions from society could affect, challenge, and recast how issues of pluralism and democracy were defined. But initially, in an authoritarian system, top-down reforms meant that what arrived on formal agendas was very much shaped by Gorbachev and by his interactions with other CPSU leaders.

Third, the treatment of the political concepts that were crucial to the reform process was much more cautious because, in part, scathing condemnations of the lack of pluralism in the USSR had destabilizing political implications. An immediate and relentless critique would have raised sensitive questions concerning legitimate authority. But more weight in accounting for the gentle opening of pluralism must be given to the contradictory nature of Gorbachev's reforms. The general secretary wanted democratization within the system, reform of the CPSU, and, at best, a limited pluralism that did not challenge the legitimacy of the CPSU's hegemony. Gorbachev did not wish to see radical transformations of the entire political system. Reforming the electoral system must at the time have seemed radical enough. Moreover, Gorbachev was of the CPSU, committed to it, and, unlike more radical reformers, unable to surmount or leave it, even after becoming president. This condition restricted his visions of political reform.

Fourth, stricter Leninists who resisted both economic and political reform held back the pace of political debate. Their objections to pluralism meant that Gorbachev's support for socialist pluralism had to be guarded for reasons of political tactics as well as his own preferences. And the fact that for decades pluralism had been vociferously condemned meant that a sudden call for it amounted to a volte-face. Its rehabilitation had to be handled carefully.

For years, *pliuralizm* had been ideologically unacceptable; then after 1987 it became increasingly fashionable among reformers, although their readiness to use the term was often halting. Many of its adherents, particularly during 1988 and 1989, wrapped the concept in qualifications, seemingly providing themselves with old-style ideological protection. Bolder arguments in pluralism's defense were made from 1989 to 1991. Whereas centrists, including Gorbachev, stressed the need for pluralism to have socialist credentials and to be responsible, more enthusiastic advocates linked it to choice, a multi-party system, and a dynamic glasnost. In response, conservative opponents of reform hurled abuse at a pluralism of opinions for defaming sacred cows—Lenin, the October Revolution, and the Motherland. For reformers, pluralism was an essential element of democratization. For conservatives, it meant the propagation of bourgeois values and was therefore a threat to ideological purity and stability. Moreover, pluralism could erode the leading role of the CPSU, take power away from the *nomenklatura* (nomenclature), and end a multitude of party privileges. These made it worth fighting against. So by the early 1990s, competing views of pluralism were being more readily expressed, in sharp contrast to the dull uniformity of the past. Approaches to the concept, however, were not isolated from broader concerns about how reform should, or should not, proceed.

Pluralism Condemned or Ignored

For seventy years of Soviet history, political actors, ideologists, and academics had either condemned or ignored the concept of pluralism. They had attacked it on two main grounds. First, in politics it was linked to reformism and democratic socialism. Both were undesirable since they were "revisionist" and impure. The argument ran that those who advocated democratic socialism for capitalist systems failed to understand that capitalism could never become democratic; and those who championed democratic socialism for socialist systems poorly understood the objective laws of history. Moreover, attempts at reformism and democratic socialism had led to counter-revolutionary developments, such as the Prague Spring of 1968 and Eurocommunism. Official lines held that the path taken by Soviet socialist construction was the correct one and was therefore not in need of reform. In addition, a one-party system operating according to the principle of democratic centralism guaranteed firm direction with adequate democracy. Many parties would mean unsound policies, disorder, and lack of direction. Pluralism in the Soviet context would amount to a misguided bourgeois deviation.

Second, as a typically bourgeois strain within Western sociology and political science, the pluralist approach to the study of political systems was "anti-revolutionary" and "anti-democratic." It failed to comprehend reality and the objective laws of history. Above all, it was biased because underpinning its misconceived concepts was a belief in liberal democracy. The questions it posed were narrow, ahistorical, and apolitical. As such, the pluralist approach added nothing constructive to knowledge. Rather, it distorted reality.

Democratic Socialism—Enemy of Socialism

In the 1940s, ideology propagated the view that democratic socialism was a "bourgeois reactionary ideology disseminated by the betrayers of socialism and directed toward the defense of aggressive expansionist politics of the anglo-american imperialist bloc."[1] One of its goals was to deceive the working people; hence the slogan "Democratic socialism—enemy of socialism."[2]

Democratic socialism meant a reformism that championed "a combination of socialism with capitalism, a reconciliation of the proletariat with the bourgeoisie."[3] Its adherents were right-wing socialists who poured "malicious slander" on socialist construction in the USSR. Abroad, Léon Blum, John Maynard Keynes, and Ernest Bevin were guilty of reformism and therefore were defenders, first and foremost, of capital.[4]

Heroic language of the 1930s and 1940s boomed that reformism would soon be dead because of the great success of Soviet socialist construction:

"As the consciousness and solidarity of workers of all countries becomes higher," and as "all the brighter glitters the Great example of the Soviet Union before the working class," so "all the harder is it for the servants of the bourgeoisie to perform their treacherous activity."[5] This Great example was redefined in the late 1980s as "deformed," "abnormal," and "uncivilized." And not just discourse but also action challenged the "glitter." The working class, through taking to the streets, rejected it, then affirmed the rejection through the ballot box. It turned out that those loyal to communist ideals were in the minority in Hungary, the GDR, and Czechoslovakia, although they were in a much stronger position in Bulgaria and Romania.[6] The objective laws of history were being rewritten by proletarian agents—an irony in light of earlier Stalinist assertions.[7]

Democratic Socialism and the Laws of History

Another line of attack against reformism and democratic socialism typical of the late 1950s and 1960s was that they had nothing to do with scientific socialism. Ideologists criticized advocates of democratic socialism for having a so-called neutral world outlook or for casting themselves as neutral social democrats. Social democracy was not neutral; rather, it was connected to the "reactionary direction of modern bourgeois philosophy and sociology, summoned to defend monopoly capital."[8] By contrast, scientific socialism recognized objective laws of history and served only the interests of working people. Critics of social democracy were, of course, right that it was not neutral. But to cast it primarily as a defense of monopoly capital was both crude and overstated. Likewise, the claim that scientific socialism served the interests of the working people was hardly substantiated by the privileged lives of the *nomenklatura*.[9]

Attacks on pluralism and democratic socialism persisted throughout the 1970s. Academics dismissed "plurality" (*pliuralistichnost'*) as a "foggy," "misty," or "obscure" concept, noting that it was used in theoretical texts wrongly arguing that capitalism could be reformed. Plurality masked the inability of capitalist systems to transform into something more just or more democratic.[10] Democratic socialism was depicted as the embodiment of *pliuralizm* (although pluralism often went undefined). Academics characterized the history of the concept of democratic socialism as one of the "opportunism," "revisionism," and "anti-communism" characteristic of Eduard Bernstein and Karl Kautsky. The charge was that both plurality and pluralism were entirely misplaced concepts since "our epoch is the epoch of revolutionary transition from capitalism to socialism and communism, happening under the banner of Marxism-Leninism."[11] The message was that pluralism had no objective place.

Democratic Centralism, Not Pluralism

More sophisticated attempts at dissecting the concept often lapsed into similar diatribes against capitalism and into defenses of democratic centralism.
Georgii Shakhnazarov, for example, at the end of the 1970s noted pluralism's Latin root and illustrated different emphases in argument among those
who subscribed to the pluralist approach.[12] He correctly noted that pluralism obscured the existence of "a powerful monopolistic elite—a narrow
group of people concentrating in their hands a gigantic share of social
wealth and political power."[13] He refused, however, to acknowledge possible differences or conflicts of interest among members of this group since together they made up "the dictatorship of the bourgeoisie."[14] Shakhnazarov
went on to argue that "bourgeois sociology asserts that under socialism a
multitude of interests demand political pluralism. All the experience of the
development of socialism refutes this fantasy."[15] Political pluralism had no
place under socialism, in Shakhnazarov's view, because the principle of
democratic centralism brought a unity of interests and ideas to economic
and social structure. Moreover, "facilitating a high effectiveness of the functioning of the political system," democratic centralism "provides for a regulation of objective processes and for the solution of contradictions through
cooperation, not conflict."[16]

Just ten years later, it was evident that democratic centralism did not guarantee sweet unity. Soviet socialism was unable to solve many problems
through cooperation since conflict was endemic. Shakhnazarov's claim that
democratic centralism "is an optimal combination of the interests of the
whole and part, of society and individual, of state and citizen, of center and
locality" reflected the strictures of official ideology but not socialist reality.[17]
And he knew this.

Dissident Defense of Democratic Socialism

Those who defended democratic socialism in the 1970s were branded
"counter-revolutionary," "anti-Soviet," and "dissident." Some, such as Roy
Medvedev, applied the term to socialist systems and called for their transformation into genuine socialist democracies with all power returning to the
soviets. But his condemnation of the USSR for its "sham socialism," "barracks socialism," and "pseudosocialism" was unacceptable to the leadership.
He wanted to inject truth, honesty, and humane values into Soviet socialism
and believed that this was possible by changing the system from within.[18]
For many dissidents in the 1960s and 1970s, the struggle for socialist
democracy was a legal one occurring within the framework of the constitution. They believed that the rights enshrined in the constitution were laudable but that the system did not honor them. The aim of these dissidents was
to push for a genuine implementation of the constitution.

By 1987, many of the ideas expressed by Medvedev almost twenty years earlier in his *On Socialist Democracy* had been officially adopted by Gorbachev and had become commonplace. For instance, Medvedev had condemned the Stalinist past but regretted that "even today the shadow remains and a great deal is left to be put right." He charged that the regime "is still not that of a socialist democracy" because "elitist methods continue to prevail in the running of the country and of the party." Public control over the system was "minimal or non-existent." Elections were a mere "formality" because "there is no element of contest, although contest is in fact completely compatible with a socialist society." And since elections to party bodies from the district level to the very top were also a formality, the party leadership "does not feel itself compelled to answer for its actions either to the party or to the people. Even now there are no normal democratic procedures for regularly replacing the country's political leadership."[19] In the 1970s, these ideas were politically dangerous, even though Medvedev was calling, not for the overthrow of socialism, but for its democratization and for fidelity to the constitution. Gorbachev's goal at the Nineteenth Party Conference was to win party approval for changes similar to those Medvedev had advocated.

Both Medvedev and Gorbachev were committed to a reformed socialism.[20] Medvedev's vision, like that of many dissidents, was a humane socialism without repression, harassment, privilege, or political unaccountability. It meant freedom to speak one's mind and to know the truth about the past. In a 1970 letter to Leonid Brezhnev, Aleksei Kosygin, and Nikolai Podgorny, Medvedev, Andrei Sakharov, and Valeri Turchin appealed for "further democratization." They recommended that it "be gradual in order to avoid possible complications and disruptions" but nonetheless "thoroughgoing." Problems of "freedom of information, the open airing of views, and the free clash of ideas" had to be addressed. They warned that "without fundamental democratization, our society will not be able to solve the problems now facing it and will not be able to develop in a normal manner."[21] In 1988, this assessment was Gorbachev's, too.

Others dissidents in the 1960s and 1970s made similar arguments. The Union of Communards held that a one-party state contradicted the Marxist idea of a socialist society. Genuine socialist democracy required a legal opposition and a multi-party system.[22] Ivan Iakhimovich suggested that Stalinists feared their own people more than the imperialists. This explained "the continuous brainwashing" and "the use of methods of intimidation and blackmail, the rude violation of the constitution, the extreme bureaucratization of the state, the immense network of spying, of informing, of prisons and concentration camps." These practices were Stalinist, not Leninist. Democratic socialism would be Leninist.[23] Gorbachev's many calls for loyalty to socialism also derived from Lenin. But had Gorbachev openly voiced in the 1970s the views he expressed in the 1980s, he, too, would have been reprimanded and punished.[24]

Pluralist Society in Contemporary Ideological Struggles

In 1985 and 1986, academic discourse on pluralism barely broke out of old molds. Before Gorbachev himself embraced the term, V. Il'in talked about "sharp contradictions between socialist and bourgeois ideology," "a deepening of the general crisis of capitalism," "a strengthening of the aggressiveness of imperialism," and the serious need for "a perfection of all systems of communist education, in particular, an increase in the level of ideological work."[25] Part of this ideological work required a clearer definition of pluralism. Il'in complained that the essence of pluralism had not been specified. Some saw it as synonymous with liberalism; others, as a blend of liberalism and conservatism. The current task was to produce a more polished working definition.[26]

To fill this gap, Il'in suggested that pluralism was "a conception concerned with world outlook (principle)" that rejected "unity of the world (community, integrity, reciprocity, and so forth)" and in practice advocated a variety of independent spheres. Il'in argued that pluralism championed as much freedom, decentralization, variety, and autonomy as possible and supported only as much discipline, unity, and organization as was necessary. Thus, pluralism was "the most important component" of the political platform of the petty bourgeoisie. It was closer to modern liberalism than to classical liberalism because it included a category of "separation of powers." But the principle of pluralism was "an important component in different sorts of bourgeois ideology." And if pluralism seriously competed with another initial category, such as "freedom," then pluralism could hypertrophy, as in anarchism, or could be present in a "truncated form" subordinate to a leading category, such as conservatism.[27]

Il'in's work was a curious blend of the old rhetoric against bourgeois ideology combined with a new concern to do it justice and unpack its complexities. Paradoxically, ideological ax-grinding sat alongside an attempt to define with greater clarity one of the concepts against which ideology still railed. The result was a somewhat confusing tract straining to break out of the ideological conformity trapping it. Not until the official adoption of socialist pluralism by Gorbachev could academics easily drop, if they so wished, their harangues against pluralism.

Socialist Pluralism on Public Agendas

Not until the late 1980s was the "socialist monopolism" of the past blamed for stagnation and the new "socialist pluralism" praised as a necessary means to a more democratic end. Concepts that ideology had once slated as reactionary, unsound, and shortsighted were now welcomed as progressive, laudable, and enlightened. Reassessments of academic writings, too, led to the conclusion that bourgeois social science was sometimes correct in its identification of competing elites.

Once officially recognized after 1987 as a concept that could legitimately be applied to the USSR at a time of political transition, pluralism was predictably viewed differently by various political actors and theorists. A few stayed close to the old lines of the past, hesitant to shift. Others reflected on "socialist pluralism" *tout court,* reluctant to dispose of the socialist component. Among advocates of socialist pluralism were those who wished to retain the leading and guiding role of the CPSU and those who argued for its demise in favor of a multi-party system. Still others tossed out socialism altogether, eager for more radical political change. And diehard conservatives vehemently attacked pluralism in their opposition to new bourgeois tendencies in economics and to chaos and indiscipline in politics.

The pluralist agenda was highly contentious. Opinions about it went to the heart of preferences about the nature of politics and about the meaning of citizenship, democracy, socialism, and justice; they also had serious implications for the future course of the USSR at a time when its present was volatile and uncertain. And opinions expressed in public altered as the political context made it easier for them to change. Many who in 1987 had hesitated to embrace socialist pluralism without tying it to the leading and guiding role of the CPSU were, in 1990, prepared to decouple them.

As conceptions of socialist democracy and democracy broadened, spurred on by popular fronts, democratic movements, and nationalism, political pluralism was seen by radical reformers as an essential component. In addition, reformers within the CPSU were increasingly predisposed to compete with others for political power. They formed the Democratic Platform inside the party. And as the authority of the CPSU visibly waned, evident in January 1990 when rank-and-file members threw out their party bosses for corruption and also manifest by thousands tossing away their party cards, the demise of the one-party state, unless propped up by force, seemed inevitable.[28] An enormous demonstration in Moscow in February 1990 calling for an end to Article 6 would have made its retention appear not merely anachronistic but also absurdly undemocratic at a time of so much rhetoric about democracy.[29] Agreement of the Central Committee in February to modify Article 6, followed in October by approval of the Law on Public Associations, laid the legal foundation of a multi-party system.[30] This was what advocates of pluralism wanted.

Gorbachev's Changing View of Pluralism

According to Archie Brown, Gorbachev took the "bold step" of adopting in public the notion of socialist pluralism before anyone else did. A prominent leader, rather than an academic, had to do this because "revisionist" developments among communists in both Eastern and Western Europe since 1968 had brought the concept under especially heavy political fire. Gorbachev first mentioned socialist pluralism, almost in passing, in July 1987 in a conversation with writers. He referred to broadening the authorship of articles in the Soviet press so that "the whole of socialist pluralism, so to speak, is present."[31] Soon afterward, in September 1987, the front page of *Pravda* twice quoted Gorbachev using the term positively in discussions with French politicians. Here he stressed that "our pluralism is based on our socialist values" and "the whole tradition of our domestic policy comes from Lenin." Pluralism was therefore not separate from socialism or distinct from Leninism: "We do not reject socialism. We want to make it better. So we say, 'More socialism.'"[32]

In 1988 and 1989, Gorbachev integrated the concept into several speeches. In April 1988, to visiting U.S. businessmen he remarked, "We feel the positive results of today's socialist pluralism of ideas. It promises us an unprecedented increase in the intellectual potential of society."[33] The next month, when talking to bosses in the media and in ideological work, he commented that in their meetings a full pluralism of ideas was expressed, which was a basis "for reflection, for better understanding, for sharpening and formulating one's ideas."[34] However, the limits to glasnost were set within the boundaries of a socialist pluralism of ideas.[35] Pluralism had to be socialist pluralism, and it had to be Leninist. Gorbachev stressed, "The Leninist sense of socialism gives the opportunity of providing a pluralism of ideas, a pluralism of interests and needs, and facilitates the realization of these interests and needs."[36] But he did not elaborate how.

In his Report to the Nineteenth Party Conference, Gorbachev reiterated these ideas: "Glasnost presupposes a pluralism of ideas on any question of domestic or foreign policy, a free comparison of different viewpoints, discussions. And only through this approach can glasnost fulfill its social role of serving the interests of the people, of socialism."[37] Pluralism meant different views but ones that served socialism. There was a firm boundary between socialist and non-socialist views. In his closing remarks to the conference, once again Gorbachev declared that "we affirm a pluralism of ideas; we reject a spiritual monopoly." But he quickly added that everything "must come from the interests of the people, must consolidate the humane values of socialism."[38] By implication, the expression of non-socialist values was taking pluralism too far. Thus, pluralism should be bridled and constrained. In fact, it would not be genuine pluralism at all.

Socialist pluralism was also positively referred to in the Resolution on Glasnost, which was adopted at the Nineteenth Party Conference: "The conference sees glasnost as a necessary condition for socialist self-government of the people, for constitutional rights, freedoms, and duties of citizens; as a means of collating and accumulating the entire diversity of interests and the socialist plurality of opinions that exist in Soviet society."[39] Apparently, Gorbachev had no intention of backing unfettered freedom of speech. In his remarks on reforming the political system, he warned; "Democracy is incompatible with willfulness, irresponsibility, or dissoluteness."[40] By implication, pluralism that was not socialist was irresponsible and immoral.

These themes of the need for a pluralism of ideas, but one occurring within socialist limits, found further expression in Gorbachev's conversation in July with General Wojciech Jaruzelski.[41] And when talking to Polish intellectuals, Gorbachev's language stiffened: "A struggle is taking place, a struggle in the form of discussions, of political dialogues, a comparison of positions. Shots are not ringing out, but the struggle is serious, a struggle within the limits of a socialist pluralism of ideas."[42] A less colorful reference to "a socialist pluralism of ideas of actions" was made by Gorbachev in November 1988 to the Supreme Soviet.[43]

Gorbachev's positive references to socialist pluralism continued in 1989 in a speech to scientific and cultural workers,[44] at a meeting with workers in Kiev,[45] and in concluding remarks to the First Congress of People's Deputies.[46] As before, his socialist limits to pluralism persisted. Gorbachev's insistence that pluralism be responsible and socialist inevitably fueled his view that a political opposition was undesirable and that a multi-party system was unnecessary.

Despite Gorbachev's embrace of socialist pluralism and notwithstanding his eventual agreement in 1990, after much pressure, that the leading and guiding role of the CPSU should be modified, his speeches in July at the Twenty-eighth Party Congress suggested a rather contradictory attitude toward a multi-party system. With ease, he condemned Stalinism for denying the existence of civil society; he also formally welcomed "genuine democracy with free choice" and "many parties."[47] But at the same time, he warned that political reform was "complex" and affected the interests of millions of people in different strata and groups. Growing politicization, he feared, could take on "a chaotic character."[48] Gorbachev referred positively to many parties but was anxious about a competition of interests giving rise to disorder. The possible consequences of pluralism troubled him. For this reason, he considered strong executive power necessary to restrain centrifugal tendencies. The new-style presidency had, since March 1990, given him this. But after the party congress, he asked the Congress of People's Deputies to extend presidential powers still further—this time to overrule the Supreme Soviets of the republics.[49] His critics viewed this move as undemocratic, effectively constraining pluralism. Gorbachev retorted that it was the only way he could push through economic reform at a time of chaos.

After Gorbachev's powers had again been extended in December 1990 at the expense of the power of the Supreme Soviet and through a revamping of top Soviet institutions, people's deputy Galina Starovoitova contended that so much power was now concentrated in Gorbachev's hands that, in fact, "a quiet state revolution" (*tikhii gosudarstvennii perevorot*) had taken place, unnoticed by the West.[50] Andrei Sakharov, she pointed out, had warned that one day perestroika would have to be defended against its instigators; the time had now come. Starovoitova remarked that leaders who advocated reform, such as Gavriil Popov, Anatolii Sobchak, and Boris Yeltsin, had "responsibility without power" (*otvetstvennost' bez vlasti*) because Gorbachev would not allow them the latter.[51]

Gorbachev's approach to the reform of the CPSU added weight to his critics' views. Had Gorbachev genuinely supported a multi-party system, would he have asked whether the CPSU should be a "vanguard" or a "parliamentary" party?[52] Party documents justified the former status in terms of the "need to return to a Leninist understanding of the party as a vanguard force of society."[53] Was this, he rhetorically asked, tantamount to demanding an exclusive position, merely exchanging the term *leading role* for *vanguard?* Clarity, he suggested, showed that such a role did not mean dictating to society but rather winning the battle to defend workers' interests. In this sense, he claimed, the CPSU would therefore be a parliamentary party.[54]

Gorbachev's logic was strange here. He began by asking "vanguard" *or* "parliamentary," thereby suggesting different types of party. He ended up concluding that the former was, in fact, the latter. Why did he pose the question at all? Why not simply say "parliamentary" if that was what he meant? The Leninist tradition, however, if it was to be retained, demanded something more assertive than "parliamentary." The old notions of "battle" and "struggle" died hard. This was why, in remaining faithful to the goal of conquering the "active battle for the interests of workers," the CPSU was straining to be in the vanguard.

Moreover, the CPSU had always known best—hence its status as vanguard. Nevertheless, Gorbachev claimed that the main positive result of glasnost was that "society received freedom," which was essential since "the spiritual rebirth of society [was] necessary, like oxygen."[55] But in his hesitation to shed vanguard completely, he kept intact the implication of "directing" others, being "ahead" of them, and knowing what was "best." Wherein was society's freedom to set agendas if a vanguard party knew best? Where was socialist pluralism?

In a similarly contradictory fashion, Gorbachev warned delegates that the CPSU found itself in a new society and therefore a renewed party was necessary. Then he affirmed, "We are not changing our line, our choice, of adhering to socialist values."[56] But the very notion of line and the refusal to reexamine values implied inflexibility in a "new" society. His critics concluded that Gorbachev wanted the old forms with new rhetoric. Gorbachev's stress on the importance of socialism appeared as strong in 1990 as it had been in 1987, when he had asserted that the limits to perestroika, glasnost, and democracy were those that "strengthened socialism."[57] He had even insisted that no one would be allowed to go against socialism and that, in any case, "90 percent of our people were born and grew up under socialism. They will not forego its achievements."[58] At a time when many citizens were making highly caustic remarks about socialism, Gorbachev's words indicated just how out of touch with everyday reality he was. In 1990, he could not, however, claim, as he had in 1987, that "there is no political opposition in the Soviet Union."[59] Although a well-organized and united opposition was indeed lacking, political movements, parties, and groups nevertheless perceived themselves as critics and opponents of the Gorbachev leadership and were advocating alternative programs and strategies.

The most popular counter-argument used in Gorbachev's defense was that he really did want a multi-party system but needed Leninist terminology to appease conservatives in the CPSU. For reasons of stability, he used old language and then in practice consented to more reform, each time leaving conservatives behind. Thus, a gap remained between word and deed, but at every step democracy won.

Evidence certainly showed him to be an astute politician, particularly before the end of 1990, sensitive to timing, prepared to retreat when he could not win (over agricultural reform and elections in 1986 and 1987), and ready to push forward when he felt the moment was ripe (convening the Nineteenth Party Conference in 1988). But in January 1989, Gorbachev told the twenty-eighth conference of the Moscow city party organization that "we live in a country with a one-party system—that's how it turned out historically." He then criticized "rogues and demagogues" for their "froth."[60] By implication, a multi-party system could degenerate into demagogy. The next month at a meeting with workers, he pronounced, "We must preserve a critical approach to work, to the past, openly solve all questions. But there is discussion and discussion. What, for example, are these discussions about a multi-party system? They are groundless." With three or four parties, citizens would not know where they were. What mattered most of all was the democratization of society, as supported by the CPSU.[61] This was one of Gorbachev's clearest statements against a multi-party system.

By 1990, instead of being ahead of political developments or able to ride on the crest of them, Gorbachev had fallen behind. He was pushed to curb the directing role of the CPSU. He was compelled to deal with questions of sovereignty by those who forced it onto the government's agenda. Glasnost, pluralism, and democratization were taking perestroika further than he had hoped. Interests were being expressed that threatened his remaining vision of a reconstructed USSR. He firmly told the republics, for instance, in the autumn of 1990 that they could not leave the Union and should sign a union treaty.[62] This was at a time when the Union Treaty was jeered at by many non-Russians and Russians alike. With food distribution uncertain, with local soviets and oblast soviets behaving, in the words of *Kommersant*'s editor Andrei Fadin, "like Supreme Soviets," the conservatives put pressure on Gorbachev for order.[63] Vladimir Kriuchkov, head of the KGB, declared in December 1990 that the KGB was prepared to defend the union and guarantee order.[64] At the same time, Gorbachev fired the moderate interior minister, Vadim Bakatin, replacing him with Boris Pugo, a Communist Party official previously in charge of party discipline.[65] More worrying for radical reformers, Gorbachev also appointed General Boris Gromov, a known hard-liner and formerly commander of the Soviet armed forces in Afghanistan, as first deputy interior minister.[66] This move by Gorbachev was widely interpreted as a shift to the right. When troops stormed Lithuania and Latvia in January 1991, evidence further bolstered this interpretation.[67]

By 1990, then, Gorbachev's attitude toward political pluralism had become contradictory and ambiguous. It was too late to retract his promise of pluralism, but he wanted to restrict, shape, and direct it and was under increasing pressure from the army, the KGB, and conservatives to do so. This pressure intensified as the tendency of soviets to disobey the administrative level above grew, thereby contributing to political chaos, and reasserted itself when Gorbachev appealed to the West for food aid.[68] Moreover, order, predictability, certainty, direction, and pride were sought not just by conservatives but also by many of the people. And Gorbachev's own CPSU background restrained his attitude toward pluralism; he always advocated a reformed party, not a proliferation of other parties.

By its very nature in an unstable context, a pluralism of opinions helped thwart many of these cravings for order and also defied manipulation. The best way to contain pluralism, many feared, was an army coup or authoritarian crackdown. Unfettered pluralism, ran the rumor, could herald anarchy or civil war.[69] By December 1990, as Gorbachev called for yet stronger presidential powers, Yeltsin was arguing that an authoritarian crackdown was in progress.[70] He accused Gorbachev of amassing more powers than those enjoyed by Stalin and Brezhnev. More calmly than Yeltsin but with troubled emotion, Shevardnadze warned of creeping authoritarianism when, in the same month, he resigned from his post of foreign minister.[71] Aleksandr Yakovlev later followed this example.[72]

In the winter of 1990–1991, Gorbachev's erstwhile supporters came to doubt their president's commitment to pluralism and democratization. Their fears were not allayed during 1991, although some political moments looked more hopeful than others. It was not until after August 1991 that Gorbachev was compelled to view pluralism differently.

From Socialist Monopoly to Socialist Pluralism

Although Gorbachev's commitment to a pluralism of ideas wavered with changing circumstances, firm advocates of pluralism consistently insisted that citizens should be the subjects of their own actions and not the objects of policy always designed from above. Writing in 1988, Leonid Kosals called for an end to the regulation of the masses, arguing that they did not need help from above or enlightenment. Rather, they would learn best by taking initiative unaided. Mistakes would inevitably be made, but the result would be the positive mobilization of the human factor.[73]

According to this perspective, conditions for the creation of socialist pluralism had not been favorable until perestroika. There had been "elements of pluralism" in Soviet society after the civil war, and these had been preserved until the end of the 1920s. They included many sectors in the economy (elements of economic pluralism); the existence of different points of view within Bolshevism (political pluralism); and different directions in art, culture, and science (cultural pluralism).[74] In the 1930s, however, these pluralist elements were eradicated. Under "socialist monopoly," informal socially useful activity was effectively banned—the conditions under which it could flourish were not allowed to exist. And out of socialist monopoly came stagnation.[75]

Perestroika, however, brought "demonopolization" (*demonopolizatsiia*), an indispensable prerequisite for the creation of socialist pluralism. Demonopolization referred to "the formation of a multitude of real, active, influencing subjects." The result would be "self-administering socialism" (*samoupravliaiushchii sotsializm*). Its success, however, required protective self-regulating mechanisms, which in Kosals' view could be established only through "radical changes in the functions of administrative organs (above all in party departments), changes in the very principles of their relations with below."[76] Kosals held that the decentralization of property and legal mechanisms for the resolution of conflicts were essential to the process of self-administration.

This approach was indeed credible. The opportunities for pluralism had changed over time. But genuine pluralism required supportive institutional structures and facilitating mechanisms that an authoritarian one-party state lacked. Roundtable debates involving social scientists and lawyers such as Igor Bestuzhev-Lada, I. Antonovich, Vladimir Guliev, and Boris Kurashvili pondered these themes in 1988, frequently reaching the pessimistic conclusion that pluralism's success in the immediate future was doubtful because the system made inadequate space for it.[77]

From Totalitarianism to Socialist Pluralism and a Multi-party System

While some blamed monopolism for stagnation, others in 1990 condemned the totalitarianism of Stalin, Khrushchev, and Brezhnev alike. Anatolii Butenko accused all three of repressiveness, playing down differences between them on the grounds that the consequences of their regimes for freedom of thought were identical.[78] Yet nuances were acknowledged: Butenko talked of a "Stalinist conformity of ideas" and a "Brezhnevite senselessness." But these totalitarian regimes all undermined the development of human potential; they squashed a pluralism of thought and therefore stifled personalities.[79] Butenko worked from the premise that people are "unique": "People have different mental abilities, and therefore each has one's own view, one's own judgment of this or that question, differing totally or in some respects, from the opinions of others. This is a natural independence of thought [*inakomyslie*]—the greatest gift of humanity, one's daily mental stock [*myslitel'nyi fond*], an inexhaustible reservoir of knowledge and judgment."[80]

Butenko's new stress on the variety of individuals and on independent thought moved away from the collectivism of the past. By implication, citizens did not need to be guided from above into socially appropriate views; they would make up their own minds unaided. The totalitarian regimes of the past had prevented this and had therefore deformed human beings. According to Butenko, "civilized" states did not judge individual positions. By implication, the Soviet state had never been civilized. In fact, "the party-state bureaucracy stubbornly never recognized this elementary democratic principle."[81]

Butenko distinguished between pluralism of thought and political pluralism. The latter was both the "product of a class society" and "a condition of its progress." The "essence" of political pluralism was an objective conditioning of different positions and different class interests expressed in the political sphere. Here Butenko supplemented the interests of a rigid class divide with the interests of other social divisions emanating from civil society. What ideologists of the past had condemned as a misguided way of viewing politics, Butenko was now adopting. He insisted that "a pluralism of interests in any society is unavoidable." Moreover, in civilized states it is protected. Therefore, in the USSR "neither repressive measures nor fear before freedom can be our allies."[82]

Having argued against repression and in favor of reform, Butenko stayed safely within the confines of socialist pluralism. He defended it as being in the interests of the people because it denied legitimacy to propaganda inciting war, aggression, racism, chauvinism, or discrimination against nationalities. Socialist pluralism operated according to the principle "Everything is permitted that is not forbidden."[83] True to his past style, Butenko theorized current political lines slightly ahead of others. Once a theorist during the Brezhnev years of developed socialism, he now became a theorist of socialist pluralism.

Butenko did, however, advocate a multi-party system as "the most developed form of political pluralism." "There is nothing more ridiculous," he castigated, "having recognized political pluralism and its development, then to deny a multi-party system."[84] He lamented that hitherto it was weakly developed, and he hoped that with time this system would strengthen. Yet he continually warned that multi-party systems had their pluses and minuses. They were advantageous because they allowed people to express choices, but their inadequacies included "the complexity and unwieldy nature" of organizations, the slow multi-step passage of socio-political programs, the inevitability of demagogy and of attempts to make fools of the people, and political intrigues and political maneuvering.[85] But Butenko failed to point out that political intrigues and maneuvers were not alien to state socialism either. Nor did he note that cumbersome political structures, mechanisms, and processes characterized the party-state apparat. Efficiency and speed had not been the hallmarks of Soviet socialism. Some of the flaws that he identified in multi-party systems were hardly unique to these systems.

Butenko's important tract was published first in *Narodnyi Deputat* and then in *Kommunist Gruzii* (Communist of Georgia).[86] Whereas most editions of *Kommunist* (Communist) published in the republics, such as *Kommunist Ukrainy* (Communist of Ukraine), *Kommunist Tadzhikistana*, and *Kommunist Moldovii* (Communist of Moldova), were still tedious in 1990, *Kommunist Gruzii* stood out for its forward thinking. Butenko's piece was printed here at a time of debate about Georgia's new electoral law, the details of which were finally adopted two months later.[87] The article fit the spirit of the Georgian political context.

Like Butenko, I. Podgorskii warned that "a multi-party system is not a panacea against misfortune."[88] And other skeptics dwelt in detail on the dangers of coalition politics. Citing the example of Italy, V. V'iunitskii made the point that "taking it in turn, ruling coalitions live from crisis to crisis, after which come more elections not giving anyone a majority."[89] The best form of multi-party system therefore seemed to be one that returned a single party with a majority.

In 1990, academics began reflecting on the relationship between concepts they had previously not discussed in print, such as multi-party system, choice, coalition, stability, rights, democracy, and consensus. Despite disagreements over definitions and implications, the political relevance of these discussions was that academics no longer publicly accepted the *monopolizm* that had made democracy impossible.[90] These discussions were also logical outcomes of serious consideration of what pluralism entailed. Discourse on pluralism had to lead to reflection on party systems.

Pluralism and Choice

Central to all defenses of a multi-party system is the concept of choice. It was therefore inevitable that choice would be incorporated into Soviet discourse.

In 1990, Podgorskii stated simply that "what is awful is when there is no choice."[91] Pluralism meant choice. But choice had not been possible in the past, stressed R. Ketkhudov and S. Ianovskaia, because individuals were viewed as "screws" or "cogs," as those who fulfilled tasks as objects of government. Subjects, by contrast, made decisions and were "representatives of the administrative-bureaucratic system," which over the decades held a monopoly on "truth." With the help of "cruel censors" and through battles with dissidents, they wielded "total control over social consciousness with the goal of forming a one-dimensional person."[92] The result was a dull conformity.

Conformity was maintained by "ideological stereotypes" embodied in slogans such as "The majority is always right," "The collective is higher than the individual," and "There are no indispensable people." "Unanimous" decisions, "unanimous" choices, and general "approval" were the norm. "Aggressive intolerance toward a strange opinion" and the "inability to take into account the view of the minority" gave rise to "conformist behavior." Conformity was "tightly connected to the morals of a person; to such characteristics as cowardice, irresponsibility, unscrupulousness, a perverted understanding of duty; and to an absence of veracity, of citizenship and feelings of human dignity, of high self-appraisal and self-respect."[93] The image constructed coincided with the stereotype of *Homo sovieticus*. Even though not all citizens were as conformist or as passive as this stereotype suggested, their opportunities for nonconformism in public were constrained by prevailing norms and values.

In short, the pressure to conform, which for decades had been integral to the way in which Soviet state and society were run, produced citizens who were unable to think independently. They lacked the strength of their convictions to make brave, enlightened, or responsible choices. This perspective also held that citizens were therefore not "normal" because their lives had for so long been "abnormal." Society was uncivilized—hence the pressing need to "reconstruct" individuals.

Pluralism as Objective Necessity

The argument that socialist pluralism was objectively necessary for successful political reform had firm advocates among political scientists and academic lawyers. Of these, Nikolai Deev and Nuriman Sharafetdinov offered one of the most thorough early redefinitions of pluralism. And unlike many others, they explicitly linked it to "democracy," "self-management," and "political power," illustrating how definitions of democracy affected one's view of pluralism.[94]

Deev and Sharafetdinov observed that pluralism had been approached in three ways. By 1989, the most widespread use of the term was referring to "a pluralism of thought, of views" (*pliuralizm mnenii, vzgliadov*), which the two authors dubbed "spiritual pluralism" (*dukhovnyi pliuralizm*). Rare, they noted, was reference to a "pluralism of needs and interests," which amounted to "social pluralism" (*sotsial'nyi pliuralizm*). And even rarer was discussion of its third aspect—"pluralism in politics" (*pliuralizm v politike*). They argued that spiritual pluralism and social pluralism were in need of "adequate political expression." The "key" to this was "the creation of a new-generation socialist model of soviet power and management" based on the idea of "humanism."[95]

Like Butenko and others, Deev and Sharafetdinov blamed an authoritarian, closed, and pyramidal system for the absence of pluralism, variety, and glasnost. They argued that institutions programmed to "centripetal tendencies ... did not reflect the real variety and contradictions of life." The result was a "sharp rejection" by orthodox doctrine of the idea of pluralism. Thus, Soviet power ignored the contradiction between society and state. And the will of the people was identified with conservative laws based on the principle of "only that is allowed that is permitted by law."[96] Instilled into social consciousness was an "undialectical" and "anti-democratic" stereotype of social development. It weakened people's social creativity and schooled society into one-sided and static thinking.

Deev and Sharafetdinov saw "variety, difference, and non-antagonistic contradictions" among social needs, class interests, nations, and other elements of social structure as the "contours" of the new socialist pluralism. These, they stressed, had to be protected by political-legal mechanisms, by a separation of power, and by a socialist legal state. In turn, these all needed "a universal and dynamic development of glasnost" because "pluralism is insolvent without glasnost."[97] They cast glasnost as "the ecology of pluralism," "the mechanism of comparing ideas and claims, the means of achieving 'transparency' in the mechanism of power and management." Conversely, glasnost itself could not be fully expressed without pluralism as an "instrument" of the expression of needs, interests, and views and as a "mechanism" for the institutional and structural guarantee of glasnost. They portrayed "pluralism-glasnost" as an organic relationship.[98] And just as Butenko argued that a pluralism of thought was normal, so Deev and Sharafetdinov described social pluralism as "natural." In economic relations, it was natural for participants to have different interests. Likewise, in the social sphere, different nations, peoples, classes, groups, and citizens expressed different needs. Regarding ideology, citizens offered competing views of social development and values that differed from official lines. Stalin's cult of personality and "totalitarian monism" had prevented these natural phenomena from flowering. The consequence was that "political life" did not exist. Indifference to a variety of interests "was one of the main reasons for stagnation in the development of society." In this context, the "political institutionalization of social pluralism" was vital.[99]

Here the radicalism of their thought ended. Deev and Sharafetdinov emphasized that the much-needed political institutionalization of social pluralism had to have limits. They were not calling for an end to democratic centralism but rather for "the liberation of the Leninist principle of democratic centralism from bureaucratic and centralist distortions from above."[100] They even contended that independent organizations and decentralization could coexist with democratic centralism. Keeping safely within official lines, Deev and Sharafetdinov indicated that democratic centralism guaranteed that social pluralism and glasnost did not violate constitutionally established socialist goals. This was the advantage of democratic socialism. They also suggested that the existence of many political parties in other socialist states had not contradicted the principle of democratic centralism. That, of course, was before the revolutions of 1989.[101] They quietly advocated a multi-party system but were constrained by party lines not to speak boldly.

Deev and Sharafetdinov made an important defense of freedom of thought and of association at a time when the leading and guiding role of the CPSU was still intact. They defended many parties and supported freedom of association. But they were careful not to attack either the CPSU or democratic centralism; they cast both in a positive light. In advocating pluralism and new political parties, they toned down their enthusiasm with the qualification "But this does not put the directing role of the Communist Party in doubt."[102]

Published in 1989, their work must have been written in 1988 or 1987. At that time, it was not easy for established academics to pour venom on the CPSU or on democratic centralism. If their remarks on the CPSU are put to one side (strikingly brief remarks in just one sentence), there remains an extremely strong plea for glasnost, democratization, and a multi-party system. Their advocacy of pluralism was essentially an attack on the current political system; it was a call for a fast end to excessive bureaucratic centralism and for a recognition of numerous different interests. Thus, theirs was a tract in defense of "the political."

A Renewal of Socialism Through Pluralism

Advocates of socialist pluralism were, by 1990, arguing that just as "pluralism cannot be fully realized without socialism," so, too, "socialism, ignoring pluralist principles of organization, is doomed to stagnation and even crisis."[103] In *Kommunist*, V. Pugachev maintained that the notion of pluralism was "based on a recognition of contradiction as a source of social progress." And from contradiction flowed an understanding of "conflict, opposition, and competition." All were desirable for social growth. Resolution of conflicts, however, had to be civilized, that is, according to the law. Pluralism did not extend to violent solutions, such as civil war or terrorism.[104] Pluralism also suggested the stimulation of a variety of forms of societal life. Moreover, pluralism could prevent a misuse of power by acting as a check on any given institution. Pugachev suggested that within the party itself, Lenin had seen the Orgburo, Politburo, and Central Committee as checks on one another. Pluralism did not have to contradict democratic centralism, although for many it may seem to at first glance.[105]

Like Gorbachev's statements on pluralism and reminiscent of Deev's and Sharafetdinov's cautious qualifications, Pugachev's remarks seemed contradictory. Pluralism was necessary for socialism, but within safe limits. Socialism needed pluralism, but not too much of it. Nonetheless, like Butenko, Podgorskii, Deev, and Sharafetdinov, Pugachev praised pluralism. He also championed pluralism, the market, and democracy as "universal achievements of civilization." However, he added the proviso that "pluralism works mainly in normal, peaceful conditions."[106] In the USSR, economic pluralism was timid and, along with pluralism in society, depended for success on democratization of the political system. The meaning of democratization, however, was contentious. Some comrades viewed a multi-party system as essential to democracy and to pluralism. Others, convinced that the conditions for a multi-party system were missing, found the idea of opposition parties "anti-socialist" and likely to result in serious social splits. Certainly the lack of democratic traditions in the context of "sharp social contradictions" gave rise to genuine fears of destabilization, anarchy, and destructive forms of political struggle.[107] Thus, the safest route was to follow the CPSU for stability and unity.

By implication, the USSR was not ripe for genuine pluralism. What mattered was a curbing of instability. This perspective was a common one from 1988 to 1990. Its adherents were loyal to cues from Gorbachev and keen to stress fidelity to Lenin. But radical reformers despised this view for what they took to be its empty rhetoric.

Democrats Enthusiastic for Pluralism

After 1988, political groups, movements, and parties committed to democracy began to fight for pluralism in practice. The process of democratization, in particular a revamped electoral system and the Law on Public Associations, gave a growing legitimacy to new political forces. Thus, the fight for pluralism became increasingly legitimate, too, notwithstanding the limits that the CPSU leadership wished to impose on it.

Self-proclaimed democrats generally stressed that pluralism was essential. The Democratic Union was the earliest of this group to call for pluralism, voicing the most confident defense. The Democratic Union's central argument was that, despite the divergence of views among members, "the principle of respect for the rights of individuals and the principle of pluralism unite us."[108] The Democratic Union cited Voltaire with approval: "I am deeply hostile to your idea, but I am prepared to sacrifice my life for your right to express it."[109] Pluralism was cast as a prerequisite for freedom and democracy. Official documents declared that "the essence of freedom is the right to be against."[110] The need for tolerance was implicit. The Democratic Union, however, came closer to its spirit than other parties.

Writing in *Svobodnoe Slovo*, Valeriia Novodvorskaia, one of the Democratic Union's leaders, declared pluralism to be a "programmatic goal," one that could not be reached through dictatorship. The prevailing partocracy, run by a "criminal clique," was shaped by a totalitarian system with "ill-fated leaders." The people had two tasks ahead of them: "the creation of a civil society and preparation of a campaign of civil disobedience."[111]

Civil society required that "no one has the right to decide for the people." Should a minority oppose the decisions of the majority, then there must be "legal possibilities for wide agitation for a different social order." In sum, minority rights deserved protection, and "people power must not become an ideological fiction."[112] Consistent with these arguments, the Democratic Union defended a multi-party system and parliamentarianism.

Members of the Democratic Union extended the principle of pluralism to the running of their party. At its fourth congress, four main internal factions were named: liberal democrats, social democrats, democratic communists, and christian democrats.[113] Pluralism extended to a confederal principle that gave republican branches of the party independence in how they ran their organizations. And since all decisions of the congress, the highest party body, were recommendatory only, politically significant disagreements were tolerated.[114] Even though commentators can cite the Democratic Union as a clear illustration of how a party should not function if it wishes to be effective, we can nonetheless appreciate why it functioned as it did. Its members were reacting strongly against the dominance of one party and against intolerance of competing ideas. The philosophy underpinning the group's politics was one of freedom of expression. Although it was far too small to become a mass party, having only about one thousand members in May 1990, the Democratic Union demonstrated among democrats the highest level of commitment to the idea of pluralism.[115]

Leninists Against Pluralism

Those who opposed pluralism supported discipline and one-party rule. Leninists, in particular, were suspicious of pluralism and feared that it would destabilize the unity of the Union and invite the growth of capitalist tendencies. One of the most vitriolic attacks came from the United Labor Front, which held its founding meeting in September 1989 in Sverdlovsk. Similar condemnations came from conservatives within the leadership of the CPSU, in particular Egor Ligachev, Viktor Chebrikov, Lev Zaikov, and Boris Gidaspov. Citizens such as Nina Andreeva, anxious about the results of democratization, also voiced their opposition in letters to the press.

In its newspaper *Chto Delat'?* the United Labor Front commented that "speculating on a pluralism of opinions and on glasnost, loud-mouthed 'supporters' of social interests defame the sacred name of Lenin and notions dear to every Soviet person like Motherland, October, patriotism."[116] Ironically, the United Labor Front itself could not have formed in pre-pluralist days. But then before perestroika it would not have needed to exist since its raison d'être was to defend Marxism-Leninism, state socialism, the KGB, the Ministry of Internal Affairs, and the army.

Whereas most new groups sought future directions, the United Labor Front praised achievements of the past. For this reason, it found pluralism a threat to solid communist values. It criticized a more relaxed press and glasnost for upsetting "the complexities of the current moment." Both pluralism and glasnost had fostered counter-revolutionary tendencies and had facilitated the emergence of a new Soviet bourgeoisie.[117]

Ligachev had expressed similar fears. Three years earlier in August 1987, he had warned that some enthusiasts of perestroika were really class opponents, hoping for "the departure of the Soviet Union from socialism in the direction of the market relations of the West, ideological pluralism, and Western democracy." But, he went on, "we will never turn away from the Leninist path, never give up the achievements of socialism."[118] By implication, a political opposition was unnecessary. Three months later, he emphasized that perestroika was initiated by the party "in the spirit of dialectical thinking" and that "in carrying out this work, we constantly turn to the lessons of Lenin, to the lessons of our history." The preservation of Leninism and its creative development were among these lessons.[119] At the Nineteenth Party Conference in 1988, he did not defend a multi-party system; rather, he cried, "Our strategic slogan—more socialism!"[120] In December 1988, he warned that Leninism did not mean private property and that perestroika was "the renewal and strengthening of socialism, the consolidation of the political stability of society."[121] Socialism was not pluralism.

Viktor Chebrikov, Lev Zaikov, and Boris Gidaspov made similar arguments. From late 1987 on, they railed against the press, informal groups, unbridled democracy, and a multi-party system. They even blamed Western intelligence services for promoting pluralism in the USSR through their support of nationalists.

In his capacity as head of the KGB, Chebrikov attended a celebration in September 1987 of the 110th anniversary of the birth of Felix Dzerzhinskii, head of the Cheka, the first Soviet secret police, which had been set up in

1917 to defend the revolution against counter-revolutionaries. In his speech to the gathering, Chebrikov proclaimed that perestroika as a revolutionary process would be defended "from any subversive intrigues" and should be based "on the creative development of Leninist ideas," for which, apparently, "Felix Eduardovich Dzerzhinskii wholeheartedly fought." Chebrikov advised everyone to look back "to the stormy events of the revolutionary years." After citing the Bolshevik fight against counter-revolution, foreign intervention, and hunger, and after praising cultural revolution and collectivization, he declared, "All this and many other achievements serve as inspiring examples for us." Perestroika, he suggested, should proceed in the spirit of Dzerzhinskii and October.[122] Although Chebrikov did not speak of pluralism per se, he praised one historical figure who had vigorously fought against it and who had helped squash members of outlawed political parties.

Two years later in a speech in Kishinev, Chebrikov castigated those trying "to speculate on the processes of broadening democracy, thereby pursuing their egoistic goals." Perestroika, he went on, had to be defended "from irresponsibility and extremism, from demagogy and adventurism." He blamed "informal associations" for bringing "harm" to society, which was "falling under the influence of extremists leading them down anti-social paths." Chebrikov criticized informal groups for "announcing support for perestroika but interfering with it in their activities." He concluded that "there are anti-socialist elements that are endeavoring to create an alternative political structure to the CPSU. Of course, one cannot but respond to such attempts and actions."[123] Chebrikov was implicitly saying that pluralism was harmful to society and trying to undermine socialism, that the CPSU alone should lead perestroika, and that many parties were unthinkable.

Lev Zaikov, first party secretary in Moscow from 1987 to 1989, echoed Chebrikov's opinions by arguing that "today we do not need discussion about a multi-party system but about consolidation of society on the basis of perestroika." He stressed that in so-called democracies, many parties often, in fact, supported one particular class. Currently harmful in the USSR were those who saw themselves in the vanguard but who were really pursuing ambition and adventurism, seeking "cheap popularity."[124]

Like Chebrikov and Zaikov, Boris Gidaspov, party leader in Leningrad, criticized new informal groups and sought inspiration from the October Revolution. Using old categories, he insisted that "on our banner is inscribed Lenin, October, socialism. We shall no longer be ourselves if we forego our socialist values, if we allow fierce pseudo-democrats to fool people with sugary fairy tales about 'people's capitalism,' unlimited democracy, and non-party glasnost."[125] What was vital was leadership by the CPSU. In response to a question in *Pravda* about the significance of glasnost and a pluralism of ideas, Gidaspov answered, "In the end, however many people there are, there could be as many viewpoints. ... We must fight for the authority of the party, above all, in actions."[126] Differences of opinion existed, but Gidaspov did not see them as useful or laudable; nor did he praise pluralism. Rather, he produced arguments that criticized its consequences. In addition, Gidaspov's scorn for the radicals made clear his derision for the results of a pluralism of opinions: "The so-called democratic community is frightening the population with various sorts of political catastrophes, the introduction of dictatorship, of martial law. All this, in their words, is allegedly the apparat scheming or, in their jargon, the partocracy."[127] But the party, one-party rule, and Leninism were sacrosanct. The message was that pluralism was destabilizing, confusing, and taken advantage of by dishonest and egoistic demagogues out to undermine the unity of the Union.

The now-famous letter written to *Sovetskaia Rossiia* by Nina Andreeva, a Leningrad chemistry teacher, was in a similar spirit but was more obviously and unapologetically Stalinist. Andreeva criticized the spread of "non-socialist pluralism," which had resulted from the manipulation of glasnost by those who lacked Marxist-Leninist principles. "Extremist elements capable of provocations" who had gained the upper hand in the leadership of new informal organizations were introducing unsound concepts into debates, such as " 'power sharing' on the basis of a 'parliamentary system,' 'free trade unions,' 'autonomous publishing houses,' and so on."[128] She regretted that "a politicization of these informal organizations on the basis of a by no means socialist pluralism ha[d] recently emerged."[129] Andreeva's central message was that the leading role of the party and the working class was essential and that "principles, comrades, must not be compromised on any pretext whatever."[130] Like Gidaspov a year later, she found attacks on the Soviet past excessive, often unjustifiable, and unconstructive. They disoriented Soviet youth and undermined the honor and dignity of socialism. Moreover, playwrights and authors such as Mikhail Shatrov and Anatolii Rybakov falsely discredited Soviet socialism by ignoring the objective laws of history. Criticisms of Stalin were one-sided; even Winston Churchill had praised him as an outstanding personality and a man of exceptional energy. Although criticism of mass repression was justified, an entirely negative and monochromatic treatment of Stalin was not.[131]

In sum, unprincipled "democrats" had taken advantage of glasnost and pluralism to challenge proletarian collectivism. By implication, pluralism was dangerous and immoral, and it had to be stopped. The leading role of the CPSU had to be defended, not undermined.

A slightly different attack on pluralism was voiced by Russians living in the Baltic states who felt that democratization was undermining their rights. In August 1989, the newspaper *Edinstvo* published an article entitled "Myths and Realities of Pluralism and Totalitarianism." It argued that there was much talk about "complete pluralism of thought" (*polnyi pliuralizm mnenii*) existing in the media but that in reality it did not. Instead, in Lithuania, there was "every kind of praise for the Lithuanian nation, culture, diligence, and other human qualities, basically characteristic of only the Lithuanian nation, a one-sidedness and clear single-mindedness against the Russian-speaking population, the so-called occupiers, Stalinists, and migrants."[132]

There was no point, the article continued, writing in Russian to official republican newspapers such as *Komsomol'skaia Pravda, Vechernie Novosti,* and even the city paper *Sovetskaia Klaipeda* since they were all mouthpieces of the nationalist movement Sajudis. Until recently, *Sovetskaia Litva* had allowed expression of views that coincided with those of members of Edinstvo. Now it, too, refrained from giving such views space and would not comment on why articles sent to it were not published.[133] Thus, the result was not pluralism but totalitarianism. *Interdvizhenie Litvy* carried similar messages, which grew in intensity as the breakup of the Union seemed inevitable. In June 1991, it quoted an attack by Nina Andreeva on *Gorbastroika* in her capacity as chair of the political *ispolkom* of Edinstvo. *Gorbastroika* was counter-revolutionary and a form of "bourgeois restoration"; it fostered anti-communism, anti-sovietism, and bourgeois nationalism and was undermining the unity of the Union.[134] By implication, pluralism was anti-communist and destabilizing.

Concern about the growth of popular fronts, nationalist movements, and new political parties, coupled with fears about transition to a market economy, led more than thirty right-wing groups to join in issuing a firm statement of resistance to reform (see Chapters 6 and 8). By 1991, Leninists were convinced that pluralism had contributed to dire "crisis," and some of them were prepared to terminate it by coercion.

Anarchists Against the State and Pluralism

Like Leninists, but for different reasons, anarchists derided so-called pluralism. They attacked it in 1990 as one element of "the period of liberalization" through which the USSR was passing. *Chernoe Znamia,* paper of the Anarcho-Communist Revolutionary Union, declared that "liberalism is outwardly a pluralism of opinions, a pompous propensity to go to meetings [*mitingovnost'*], and a poverty of influence."[135] A pluralism of views could not affect politics since Soviet liberalism amounted to a "manipulation of social consciousness." Above all, liberalism tried to "smooth over" class antagonisms.[136]

"Constitutional freedoms" that had been granted were, in fact, "a paper fiction." They guaranteed the people nothing. Instead, "a stinking heap of laws and resolutions" emerged, paralyzing "freedom and action."[137] The new freedom to attend meetings and to participate in demonstrations merely poured over "into the freedom to apply the militia's cudgels."[138] Thus, limited freedoms were greeted with oppression. Moreover, "political freedom is an illusion if it is not supported by economic and social liberation. So long as social inequality exists, there is nothing to say about freedom."[139]

Even though the concept of pluralism was enjoying wider coinage, anarchists argued that "statist tendencies were greatly strengthening."[140] One result was that the antagonism between people and state had reached its limit. The state was "interfering in all spheres of social life," thereby "deadening creative initiative." "Enslaved by the state," the individual had "no other choice but resistance to state dominance."[141] Notwithstanding class differences, all social strata should unite. *Chernoe Znamia* instructed that "we, anarchists, see a way out by instilling anarchist, anti-state consciousness." Only anarchism could "lead the workers to complete freedom, leaving no place for coercion, exploitation, and enslavement."[142] What constituted "anarchist consciousness" was not entirely clear. Pessimistically, anarcho-communists warned that "spontaneous and unconscious action rarely ha[d] a positive result."[143] Presumably, with "anarchist consciousness," the result would be different.

The Confederation of Anarcho-Syndicalists was also preoccupied by state power, although its members did not talk about a "period of liberalization." Their paper *Volia* argued in 1989 that a Bonapartist regime existed as part of a transition from marxist totalitarianism to "bourgeois bureaucratic authoritarianism."[144] The so-called legal state that was being advocated was, in fact, one characterized by civil war in the Caucasus. The "party-state apparat" was to blame for the situation.[145] Moreover, similar tragedies would occur elsewhere and totalitarianism would triumph unless "freedom, decentralization, self-administration, and non-violence" became the goals of all social forces, of all political, nationalist, and ecological movements.[146] The issue here was not really one of pluralism; indeed, the Confederation of Anarcho-Syndicalists did not adopt the concept. Rather, it was one of who held power—either the state or the people. The central message of *Volia* was "not Moscow, not centralized or local bureaucracy, not the army, but the people themselves must decide their fate." The relevant slogan was "Power to the people and not to parties!"[147]

Central concepts for these anarchists were state, people, and bureaucracy, not pluralism or a legal state. They tended to view pluralism, if at all, as an ideological trimming of either liberalization, Bonapartism, or a transforming bureaucracy. Pluralism as Gorbachev described it was a farce since all it entailed was a little more space to speak out in an otherwise oppressive system. And pluralism as choice, as advocated by Podgorskii, was really a deception so long as power resided within state structures. A multi-party system, defended by Butenko and many democrats, was also to be sneered at because power would remain in state institutions. The goal was, not plural-

In 1991, at a time of extremely rapid political change, anarchists continually warned the people not to be fooled by the promises of reformers in power. Accompanying an article on the meaning of freedom, this cartoon implies that glasnost is not genuine and that the state is always prepared to silence the voices it does not wish to hear. SOURCE: *Golos Anarkhizma*, no. 7, 1991, p. 3.

ism and a multi-party system, but "freedom" for the people. As ever, how this would be reached, and what it actually meant apart from decentralization and self-administration, was unclear.

The Moscow Union of Anarchists in its paper *Golos Anarkhizma* (Voice of Anarchism) elaborated a little further on what pluralism entailed. What mattered most of all was "complete political and civil freedom." Here freedom was defined as "the possibility for a person to act, to behave in a way desirable to the soul, that is, in a way most convenient for satisfying needs."[148] "Unlimited political freedom" came first on the organization's list of priorities since the people had endured more than seventy years "of vegetating in a bestial slave condition under the yoke of Bolshevik dictatorship." As a result, they had only a "vague notion" of what freedom was. In fact, politics signified "an art," and political freedom referred to "the opportunity for everyone to exert influence on the running of their own town, their own country; on what, how, and by whom social resources will be used." Whether money should be spent on tanks, kindergartens, roads, or hospitals should, in this view, be decided by the people.[149]

Integral to political freedom were freedom of speech, freedom to hold meetings, freedom to unite, and freedom to form parties. Without the freedom to unite, citizens remained "atomized, like dust in the wind." In this condition, everyone thought only of self and "the rest" became "victims" to deceive and use. Those who did not become victims were potentially "enemies" who might also trick and take advantage. Soviet society had become "a herd of egoistic rams, ready to gorge each other, indifferent, looking vacant, as they throttle, fleece, and slice their neighbors."[150] So long as the state kept society, parties, and unions under its control, this predicament would persist. Participation in most organizations was a "waste of time." Agitation on local issues, such as housing, pay, and prices, was, however, useful.[151] Conventional participation in politics, as advocated by democrats, was not what all anarchists supported since it invariably meant selling out to bureaucratic, bonapartist, bolshevik, or bourgeois interests. Political pluralism and a pluralism of opinions were thus vacuous if state structures defended particular class interests. Strike action, however, was an expression of political freedom, as was a more diffuse "social revolution."[152]

Like the Democratic Union, anarchists lacked political power and influence. Their contribution to discourse on pluralism, however, was a visible part of a growing pluralism of ideas. Moreover, their thoughts were distinctive and enjoyed some resonance among the young.

Pluralism in the Social Sciences

The concept of pluralism was also reconsidered under Gorbachev as a theoretical approach in the social sciences. In the past, the pluralist approach to the study of society and polity had always been condemned for attempting to create "the illusion of democracy" in capitalist systems when, in fact, it did not exist.[153] The pluralist perspective came under fire for being an "idealistic" and "romantic" model that hid the essence of class polarization. Its notion of competition among many elites was attacked by Soviet social scientists for obscuring a concentration of power in the hands of monopoly capital. Even if a pluralism of elites and opinions existed under capitalism, ownership of the means of production by the bourgeoisie meant that the elites were all bourgeois in nature, there to defend capital. Competition among them was therefore insignificant for an in-depth understanding of the bourgeois state.

The pluralist perspective was also flawed, ran the argument, because it depicted the bourgeois state as a neutral arbiter and therefore distorted the state's class nature.[154] The state was not impartial; it defended ruling capitalist interests and upheld and reinforced prevailing class divisions. It therefore safeguarded inequalities. The bourgeois state, unrecognized as such by the pluralist approach, was anti-revolutionary. In addition, "the connection of philosophical idealism and anti-communism created the methodological basis for a false reflection of reality, the goal of which was the justification and defense of the existing political reality of modern imperialism."[155] Thus, the pluralist perspective amounted to a justification of idealism, capitalism, and imperialism and a championing of anti-communism.

Another charge against the pluralist approach was that it refused to acknowledge how little difference there was among "bourgeois" political parties and paid scant attention to the decreasing effectiveness of multiparty systems, the citizens' lack of information on political matters, and the shrinking percentage of people who voted.[156] In sum, "pluralist" Western democracies did not actually function as the pluralist perspective indicated they would since "class," not "elite," was the key divide; and even when examined according to the perspective's own idealistic criteria, Western societies revealed low levels of political awareness as well as political apathy. Either way, they could not be said to be "democratic." And worst of all, the pluralist approach obscured class exploitation.

The pluralist approach was seen as an integral part of bourgeois social science. Otto Kuusinen's classic ideological text, *Fundamentals of Marxism-Leninism* (published in 1961), included a section entitled "Bankruptcy of Bourgeois Sociology." The central argument ran: "While historical materialism reveals the objective laws of social development and points the way to their comprehension and application in the interests of society, bourgeois sociology tries in all kinds of ways either to prove that there are no historical laws, or to distort the nature of these laws." In fact, bourgeois sociologists feared, and therefore ignored, the laws of history because they indicated the inevitability of capitalism's downfall and the triumph of socialism. Instead, such sociologists inaccurately portrayed historical events as "unique" and dwelt on the irrationality of human psychology, not seeing humans as "conscious beings."[157] Although Kuusinen's book did not systematically address the flaws of the pluralist approach, as did many texts published in the 1970s, it stressed class composition and historical inevitability. This emphasis was the dominant Soviet response to pluralism and to "bourgeois" Western social science. Indeed, by definition, social science in the West could not be anything but bourgeois.

The charge that bourgeois sociology focused on psychology, rather than on objective laws, was a common one. According to Villiam Smirnov, the appearance of theories of pluralism and pluralist democracy was "closely connected with the deep crisis gripping the capitalist system in the first decade of the twentieth century." In this context, investigators such as Sigmund Freud and Gustave le Bon set out to show the irrationality of humans, the negative influence of groups and crowds on their consciousness.[158] And E. Bagramov, commenting on the Ninth World Sociology Congress of 1978, declared that "if Marxist-Leninist science reveals the immutable laws of the development of mankind, then bourgeois sociology contradicts them, reducing everything to a spontaneous game of certain psychological or biological strengths."[159] Bagramov argued that one of bourgeois sociology's main goals was to discredit socialism. This was a foolish undertaking since "the world of socialism is widening and strengthening while the world of capitalism is narrowing and weakening."[160] So at the end of the 1970s, assertions about capitalism's inevitable decline and socialism's sure triumph were still pervading the literature on bourgeois social science.

By the 1980s, however, some were beginning to voice the view that not all Western social science should be condemned. In a book summing up the Eleventh World Congress of the International Political Science Association, Georgii Shakhnazarov noted that, although Western political science was essentially "anti-revolutionary" and "anti-democratic," some younger Western scholars were considering the real world and demonstrating an awareness that the "growth and consolidation of socialism, the success of liberation movements, and the strengthening of Marxist-Leninist science" demanded more objective analyses.[161] But like Bagramov, Shakhnazarov remained locked in slogans about the inevitable triumph of socialism and loyal to official ideology, despite his attempts to go a little beyond it. But for many social scientists, any attempts to do so would have lost them their jobs.

As belief in Marxism-Leninism shattered in Eastern Europe and increasingly came under fire in the USSR, social scientists more openly embraced methodologies once alien to Marxism. They sought social science training in Western universities and welcomed a host of new publications on Western sociology. What had once been rejected as mystifying and distorting work was now craved. Positivism, which had once been attacked, was now assessed more dispassionately. Statistical techniques, for so long poorly understood, rarely used, or badly applied, became more widely accepted. Social scientists sought to learn how to harness them. Opinion surveys, in particular, became much more popular.

By 1989, thanks to glasnost, more accurate writings on the history of sociology in the USSR had begun to appear. Iurii Levada, for instance, observed how "objective and critical rationality, characteristic of Western sociology, just like its pragmatic direction, found quite narrow application up to the 1930s, and was later forcibly removed from the stage."[162] Here Levada's use of "objective" was entirely different from Kuusinen's almost thirty years earlier. Now objectivity characterized Western social science, not Marx's historical materialism. Levada also recounted how in the 1960s struggles to give life to sociology as a discipline had suffered from official insistence that sociology result in the "scientific management" of society. Although more freely accepted today, the discipline of sociology still suffered from the inability to analyze the USSR since its categories and methods were unsuitable for generating models of current social reality, especially its crisis-ridden, destabilizing characteristics.[163] Levada's criticisms of the limits of social science for grasping social change were far more apt than those made by its opponents for most of the history of the Soviet state.

In 1989 and 1990, a burst of books and articles appeared on the general theme of "sociology and perestroika." Echoing Levada, social scientists argued that "socio-economic and political parameters" had determined the fate of sociology's development in the USSR. Like everything else, it had gone through "stages."[164] Now, however, sociology was "in crisis." Perestroika had prompted open thinking, and individuals had been freed of the "internal censor." Yet an "ambivalent feeling," characterized by "joy and suffering," had grown. This ambivalence was partly the result of the state of the country and partly the result of social scientists' ability to see different future scenarios, including a "war bureaucratic regime" like that of Mao Zedong's China or the Soviet Union in the 1930s and 1940s.[165] The ambivalence also stemmed from the awareness that, as a discipline, Soviet sociology lagged seriously behind "world standards."[166]

Although for some sociologists reflection on future variants was painful, the immediate result of glasnost in the social sciences was the introduction of new concepts and the pursuit of fresh theoretical directions. Emphasis moved away from the determination of historical laws and toward "the influence of the social subject."[167] Adopting this perspective, Vladimir Iadov argued that future developments depended directly on how social subjects—"society, people, party, state"—understood a situation and acted.[168] Iadov believed that the notion of "interest" had a place, too. Outcomes depended on "which interests dominated at the moment of passing laws" and during their implementation.[169] Iadov did not claim to be borrowing from pluralist perspectives, but he did, even if not consciously, incorporate notions of diverse interests competing for domination. These interests could be actively shaped by the behavior of individuals in society. In a similar vein, R. Ryvkina stressed that "social groups are the engine of social development and without their efforts changes in society cannot come about."[170] Both the dynamism of society and its inertia depended on how groups acted in any given historical period.[171]

Various other concepts began to find a more visible place in Soviet sociology. These included classification, factor, differentiation, social stratification, status, social consensus, social forces, processes, and phenomena.[172] Although sociologists may have found them useful terms in the 1970s, applying them had been ideologically difficult.[173] Those concerned with future scenarios adopted terms such as "transition mechanisms," "social diagnostics," "indicators," and "parameters."[174] Some social scientists appeared to react against the rigidities of historical materialism by dropping any notion of determining laws. Others attempted to incorporate new emphases into new laws. O. Shkaratan, for example, called for the formulation of "a law of growing diversity of action" linked to "the social structure of society." He believed this would be "a general historical and inter-formation law."[175] It was important to formulate such a law, he maintained, since "the path of development moves from simple to complex structures. In other words, the history of humanity is the growth of diversity of relationships, social groups, ways of life, and individuality."[176]

Above all, in the late 1980s and early 1990s, what differed about sociological concepts and questions was fresh emphasis on diverse social groups. New categories prompted discussions of groups as social actors. Gorbachev had given legitimacy to the human factor as an important concept from 1985 on. It invited discussion of how behavior patterns resisted reform. But it did much more than that by encouraging discourse about groups and individuals as actors who could influence policy and be receptive to it in different ways. Linked to notions of "pluralism of thought and opinions," the concept of the human factor resulted in more frequent public ruminations on individuality. And the need to know how citizens felt and acted resulted in the growing popularity of questionnaires and opinion surveys.

Social scientists, then, were finally confident enough to apply new concepts and think about new theoretical approaches. The pluralist approach was one of many that could be incorporated into the literature, borrowed from in parts, debated, or rejected. It was not wholeheartedly adopted; but neither was it condemned outright, as it had been throughout Soviet history. This was part of the growing sophistication of social science. But what continued to hold inquiry back, as many social scientists readily admitted, was lack of knowledge about different methodologies and techniques and lack of training in how to think critically. Hence, there was a willingness to receive advice from Western social scientists not only as part of trips to the West but also at home.

Pluralism and Transition

The Soviet transition period saw a span of opinions about the desirability of pluralism and about the significance of the waning of a one-party state. A comparable variety of views, fears, and hopes characterized the transition from dictatorship to democracy in Spain. A deeply embedded ideology critical of Masons and communists and hostile to a divided Spain had gradually to be undermined and new beliefs accepted.[177] The threat of army intervention in politics also hung over Spain in the mid-1970s and early 1980s, and anxiety about civil war was present.[178] As authoritarian systems become transformed, it seems inevitable that staunch defenders of the status quo ante will clash in various ways with those eager for change in new directions and that the threat of force is likely to be ever present until new political arrangements enjoy broad acceptability and legitimacy.

But here the similarities between Spain and the USSR end. Prior to Francisco Franco's death, Spain enjoyed economic modernization, growth, and increased prosperity. More exposure to "democratic" ideas occurred, too, either through higher education abroad, migrant work in other West European states, or contact with the thousands of vacationers coming to Spanish beaches.[179] A greater degree of loosening up took place in Franco's Spain than in Brezhnev's USSR. This is not to deny that Soviet social structure changed in the 1960s and 1970s or that some critical views were elliptically expressed in films, plays, and novels. Soviet youth, in particular, like Spanish youth, craved change.[180] But comparable economic growth was lacking, notwithstanding Spain's economic crisis of the mid-1970s. This exacerbated fears of the destabilizing effects of change in the USSR—unemployment, inflation, and poverty—which, in turn, fueled old ideological arguments about the purity of socialism. These fears obtained in Spain, too, but in a less total way.

A large number of Spanish citizens preferred authoritarian rule. They wanted unity rather than democratization accompanied by unacceptable nationalist demands. But they could also see a growing support for change in the population at large (expressed in referenda) and a relatively successful treatment of the "national question" by the government, which granted pre-autonomy status to the so-called historical nationalities of the Basque country, Catalonia, and Galicia and gave all regions the chance of adopting statutes of autonomy.[181] Delicate political maneuvering by King Juan Carlos enabled him to appease all sections of society with sufficient speed, backed up, as he was, by the mandate of successful referenda.[182] Gorbachev's political skills were not so adept, particularly in 1990 and 1991; they were hindered by the sheer size of the Soviet Union, by nationalist demands for outright independence, and by Gorbachev's reluctance to grant anything comparable to Spain's pre-autonomy statutes in time. The long tradition of the CPSU's leading role, rigid bureaucratic structures resistant to change, and corruption rendered the Soviet transition ultimately more chaotic, painful, and contentious. The political space for consensus and agreement was far less than in Spain, and the heritage of totalitarianism weighed heavily.

In a Soviet context of economic deterioration, poor distribution, growing inequalities, social unrest, political chaos, and fragmentation, there was a socio-economic and a political basis for pungent opposition to pluralism. Its critics' ideological and political opposition resonated with social groups afraid of the future for material reasons of employment and food supply. Fears of anarchy, chaos, instability, and civil war, fears deeply embedded in Russian political culture, enhanced the credibility of anti-pluralist arguments. Political culture can alter and be modified. But its well-worn characteristics shape and influence subsequent political developments. The lack of social and political infrastructures capable of giving democratization a firm underpinning was a crucial difference.

What, then, bolstered the pro-pluralist arguments? A Gorbachevian commitment to socialist pluralism because "we have no alternative" had worn thin by 1990, and at any rate Gorbachev's own political practice, unlike that of Juan Carlos, was to accumulate more and more power, thereby effectively restricting pluralism's institutional outlets, despite the fresh opportunities he had granted it. In economics, the need for a market and for an end to rigid planning could be twinned with arguments in favor of pluralism. But here opinion was fiercely divided—either the market was a panacea, or it was not. Fears of unemployment and of an uncertain future fueled doubters but also led some supporters to believe that salvation could come only through market mechanisms accompanied by pluralism as a necessary prerequisite. But others contended that market reforms might best proceed by authoritarian, non-pluralist methods. For still others, the strongest defense of pluralism in 1991 lay in the political arena—the need to end totalitarianism, to increase freedom, and to guarantee that a repetition of army interference in the Baltic states did not occur. But as political chaos beset the most democratic arenas, this argument was not always sustained by reality. Democratization in early 1991 seemed necessary, yet it was both fragile and daunting. Many people, even some committed democrats, could not see clearly what concrete benefits the reformed soviets would bring other than debate and criticism.

In this context of confusion, a popular yearning developed for a firm leader who could work economic, political, and social miracles. This had obtained more in the case of Portugal than of Spain. Here *Sebastianism* was a general craving for sudden political and social solutions brought about by one man—a new and great Sebastian. It was accompanied by *regenerationalism*, the desire to oust decadence and to regenerate glories.[183] But many of the Soviet people wanted only limited glories—goods and more decisive action. The questions became, "Would pluralism mean freedom with disarray and disintegration? Or could it produce freedom and something better?"

At a time of "identity crisis" for the Soviet state, no one could answer these questions convincingly, not even Popov in his stirring response to the ever-historic question "What is to be done?"[184] Unlike the situation in Poland, where after 1989 citizens initially accepted a market economy, high prices, and pluralism (serious reservations and indifference set in later), the predicament for the USSR was that before August 1991 the bulk of the population did not unquestioningly welcome pluralism.[185] There were sharp splits in society about its acceptability as well as indifference and cynicism among the politically passive and alienated. Moreover, political structures cramped its development. Not even a loose consensus about the future of the Soviet state existed or clear vision about center-republic relations.

From 1987 to 1991, unresolved issues of democratization, power, and citizenship meant that pluralism could not be comfortably defined, widely supported, or wholeheartedly promoted. Competing views of democratization's achievements, problems, and possibilities illustrated the gravity for political practice of controversies among leaders, political groups, people's deputies, and academics. Differing assessments of the performance of the newly elected soviets also fired debates about democracy, political chaos, and political crisis.

NOTES

1. F. Aleksandrov, *"Demokraticheskii Sotsializm": Reaktsionnaia Ideologiia Sovremennykh Pravykh Sotsialistov* (Moscow, Izdatel'stvo "Pravda," 1948), p. 3.

2. Ibid.

3. Ibid., p. 5.

4. Ibid., pp. 5–19.

5. Ibid., p. 32.

6. Judy Batt, "The end of communist rule in East-Central Europe," *Government and Opposition*, vol. 26, no. 3, Summer 1991, pp. 368–390; Arend Lijphart, "Democratization and constitutional choices in Czechoslovakia, Hungary, and Poland, 1989–91," *Journal of Theoretical Politics*, vol. 4, no. 2, April 1992, pp. 207–223.

7. For discussion of the persistence of communist ideas, see "Leninists: Crisis and the Loss of Leninism" in Chapter 8.

8. D. G. Bol'shov, *"Demokraticheskii Sotsializm" v Pleny Burzhuaznoi Ideologii* (Moscow, Znanie, 1961), p. 38.

9. For discussions of party privileges, consult Mervyn Mathews, *Privilege in the Soviet Union* (London, George Allen and Unwin, 1979); Roy Medvedev, *Let History Judge* (Manchester, Spokesman Books, 1976).

10. P. N. Fedoseev, S. V. Aleksandrov, G. L. Eganov et al., *Chto Takoe "Demokraticheskii Sotsializm"?* (Moscow, Politizdat, 1978), p. 20.

11. Ibid., p. 6.

12. G. Shakhnazarov, "O demokraticheskom tsentralizme i politicheskom pliuralizme," *Kommunist*, no. 10, July 1979, pp. 96–109. In 1974, Shakhnazarov became head of the Soviet Political Science Association. He was an adviser to Gorbachev and was elected in 1989 to the Congress of People's Deputies. For more information, consult Archie Brown, ed., *The Soviet Union: A Biographical Dictionary* (London, Weidenfeld and Nicolson, 1990), pp. 331–332.

13. Shakhnazarov, "O demokraticheskom tsentralizme," p. 98.

14. Ibid., p. 106.

15. Ibid., p. 102.

16. Ibid.

17. Ibid., p. 104.

18. George Sanders, ed., *Samizdat: Voices of the Soviet Opposition* (New York, Monad Press, 1974), p. 37. See, too, Stephen F. Cohen, *An End to Silence* (New York, Norton, 1982).

19. Roy A. Medvedev, *On Socialist Democracy,* trans. Ellen de Kadt (London, Macmillan, 1975), p. 37.

20. Roy Medvedev was elected to the Congress of People's Deputies in 1989. Since 1991, he has been a co-chair of the Socialist Party of Labor. See *Pravda,* 28 October 1991, p. 1; *Moskovskie Novosti,* no. 4, 26 January 1992, p. 7.

21. Sanders, ed., *Samizdat,* p. 400.

22. Ibid., pp. 235–239.

23. Ibid., p. 337.

24. Gorbachev had always insisted on the Leninist inspiration of perestroika. See his *Perestroika i Novoe Myshlenie Dlia Stranyi Dlia Vsevo Mira* (Moscow, Politizdat, 1987), pp. 20–21. He reiterated the importance of Marx, Engels, and Lenin in 1990 at the Twenty-eighth Party Congress. See *Materialy XXVIII S"ezda KPSS* (Moscow, Politizdat, 1990), p. 62.

25. V. I. Il'in, *O Meste i Roli Kontseptsii "Pliuralishicheskogo Obshchestva" v Sovremennoi Ideologicheskoi Bor'be* (Moscow, Ministerstvo Vysshego i Srednego Spetsial'nogo Obrazovaniia, 1986), p. 5.

26. Ibid.

27. Ibid., p. 6.

28. *Izvestiia,* 19 January 1990, p. 3; *Moskovskie Novosti,* no. 4, 28 January 1990, p. 5.

29. Iurii Gladysh, "Fevral'skii veter," *Demokraticheskaia Platforma,* no. 2, April 1990, pp. 1, 4–5.

30. *Izvestiia,* 16 October 1990, pp. 1–2.

31. Archie Brown, "Political change in the Soviet Union," *World Policy Journal,* Summer 1989, p. 475.

32. *Pravda,* 30 September 1987, p. 1.

33. Institut Marksizma-Leninizma pri TsK KPSS, *M. S. Gorbachev: Izbrannye Rechi i Stat'i,* vol. 6 (Moscow, Politizdat, 1989), p. 193.

34. Ibid., p. 205.

35. Ibid., p. 210.

36. Ibid., p. 212.

37. Ibid., p. 393.

38. Ibid., p. 411.

39. "Rezoliutsiia 'o glasnosti,'" *XIX Vsesoiuznaia Konferentsiia KPSS, 28 Iunia–1 Iulia 1988 goda; Stenograficheskii Otchet,* vol. 2 (Moscow, Politizdat, 1988), p. 166.

40. Mikhail S. Gorbachev, "O khode realisatsii reshenii XXVII S"ezda KPSS i zadachakh po uglubleniiu perestroiki," in ibid., p. 52.

41. Institut Marksizma-Leninizma, *M. S. Gorbachev,* p. 442.

42. Ibid., p. 464.

43. Institut Marksizma-Leninizma pri TsK KPSS, *M. S. Gorbachev: Izbrannye Rechi i Stat'i,* vol. 7 (Moscow, Politizdat, 1990), p. 169.

44. Ibid., p. 249.

45. Ibid., p. 340.

46. Ibid., p. 590.

47. *Materialy XXVIII S"ezda KPSS*, p. 4.

48. Ibid., p. 25.

49. Extended powers for the presidency permitted Gorbachev to stabilize the "sociopolitical life" through emergency measures for up to eighteen months. See *Izvestiia*, 26 September 1990, p. 1. As president, Gorbachev had enjoyed the right since March to declare a state of emergency and to introduce direct presidential rule. The initial right was geared to deal with situations of political instability. The extension in September was tailored to meet economic crisis.

50. A cabinet of ministers was created in December 1990, replacing the new Council of Ministers, which had formed in June 1989 and had slimmed down the old Council of Ministers. The Council of the Federation was also created in December 1990 and was composed of President Gorbachev, a vice-president and heads of state from the republics. Since the Presidential Council simultaneously ceased to exist, the Council of the Federation became the top decision-making body. As described in Chapter 3, a new Security Council under the president came into being as well with general responsibility for crime, public order, and defense. A government inspectorate, to be led by the vice-president, was given the unenviable and impossible task of seeing that laws and presidential decrees were implemented throughout the country. See *Sovetskaia Rossiia*, 27 December 1990, pp. 1, 3. These constitutional changes represented a further strengthening of executive power. Genadii Yanaev was chosen, amid controversy, as vice-president at the end of December. See *Bakinskii Rabochii*, 29 December 1990, p. 1.

51. Galina Starovoitova expressed this view at the conference Towards a New Community: Culture and Politics in Post-totalitarian Society, School for Slavonic and East European Studies, University of London, 8–14 December 1990.

52. *Materialy XXVIII S"ezda KPSS*, p. 39.

53. Ibid., p. 39.

54. Ibid., p. 40.

55. Ibid., pp. 53–54.

56. Ibid., p. 57.

57. *Pravda*, 30 September 1987, p. 2.

58. Ibid.

59. *Pravda*, 30 September 1990, p. 2.

60. Institut Marksizma-Leninizma, *M. S. Gorbachev*, vol. 7, p. 297.

61. Ibid., pp. 311–312.

62. *Materialy Plenuma Tsentral'nogo Komiteta KPSS, 8–9 Oktiabria 1990 g* (Moscow, Politizdat, 1990), pp. 11–12. See also Mikhail S. Gorbachev, "Politicheskii otchet tsentral'nogo komiteta KPSS XXVIII s"ezdu KPSS i zadachi partii," *Materialy VIII S"ezda KPSS* (Moscow, Politizdat, 1990), pp. 22–24.

63. Andrei Fadin expressed this view at the conference Towards a New Community: Culture and Politics in Post-totalitarian Society, School for Slavonic and East European Studies, University of London, 8–14 December 1990

64. *Bakinskii Rabochii,* 25 December 1990, p. 1. For commentary on Kriuchkov, see Len Karpinskii, "Pishite nam, pichite," *Moskovskie Novosti,* no. 51, 23 December 1990, p. 4.

65. Viktor Loshak, "Ministr ukhodit ne proshchaias," *Moskovskie Novosti,* no. 49, 9 December 1990, p. 6.

66. Ibid.

67. *Moskovskie Novosti,* no. 3, 20 January 1991; *Moskovskie Novosti,* no. 4, 27 January 1991.

68. This was an unpopular move on the domestic front since for many citizens it was an admission of failure and an affront to their pride. During 1990, feelings of awkwardness about food aid and opposition to it were expressed in numerous conversations.

69. There had been rumors of impending civil war since early 1989.

70. After Gosteleradio evicted Interfax, Yeltsin offered, in January 1991, to find it new accommodation. Yeltsin also offered to take "Vzgliad," banned by Gosteleradio, under the wing of Russian state radio and television. See RFE/RL Research Institute, *Report on the USSR,* vol. 3, no. 4, 25 January 1991, p. 27.

71. *Izvestiia,* 21 December 1990, p. 1. For commentary, see Egor Yakovlev, "V gostiakh u Eduarda Shevardnadze," *Moskovskie Novosti,* no. 1, 6 January 1991, p. 11.

72. Aleksandr Yakovlev, "Nuzhen novyi shag," *Izvestiia,* 2 July 1991, p. 2.

73. L. Ia. Kosals, *Sotsialisticheskii Monopolizm i Sotsialisticheskii Pliuralizm: Ot Zastoia k Razvitiiu* (Novosibirsk, Sibirskoe Otdelenie Institut Ekonomiki i Organizatsii Promyshlennogo Proizvodstva, 1988), p. 23.

74. Ibid., p. 22.

75. Ibid., pp. 22–23.

76. Ibid., p. 23.

77. See the roundtable on "Sotsialisticheskii pliuralizm," *Sotsiologicheskie Issledovaniia,* no. 5, 1988, pp. 6–24. For a little more optimism, refer to L. A. Gordon and Ia. S. Kapiliush, "Ot monolitnosti k pliuralizmu," *Sotsiologicheskie Issledovaniia,* no. 3, 1990, pp. 13–19.

78. A. P. Butenko, "Mnogopartiinost' v usloviiakh sotsializma," *Kommunist Gruzii,* no. 6, 1990, p. 48.

79. Ibid., pp. 48–50.

80. Ibid., p. 49.

81. Ibid.

82. Ibid., p. 51.

83. Ibid. See A. P. Butenko, "Eshche raz o protivorechiiakh sotsializma," *Voprosy Filosofii,* no. 2, 1984, pp. 116–123.

84. Ibid.

85. Ibid., p. 54.

86. A. P. Butenko, "Mnogopartiinost' v usloviiakh sotsializma," *Narodnyi Deputat,* no. 4, 1990, pp. 23–29.

87. *Zaria Vostoka,* 22 August 1990, pp. 1–3; *Sovetskaia Abkhaziia,* 29 August 1990, pp. 1–2.

88. I. Podgorskii, "Pliuralizm—eto vybor," *Kommunist Gruzii,* no. 4, 1990, p. 51.

89. V. V'iunitskii, "Mnogopartiinost'," *Dialog,* no. 10, July 1990, p. 9.

90. Podgorskii, "Pliuralizm—eto vybor."

91. Ibid., p. 52.

92. R. Ketkhudov and S. Ianovskaia, "Konformizm kak sotsial'noe iavlenie," *Kommunist Gruzii,* no. 3, 1990, p. 38.

93. Ibid., pp. 39–40.

94. N. N. Deev and N. F. Sharafetdinov, "Sotsialisticheskii pliuralizm: Otkrytye tekhnologii vlasti," in Iu. M. Baturin, ed., *Glasnost: Mneniia, Poiski, Politika* (Moscow, Iuridicheskaia Literatura, 1989), pp. 186–200.

95. Ibid., p. 186.

96. Ibid., pp. 186–187.

97. Ibid., p. 189.

98. Ibid., pp. 190–194.

99. Ibid., pp. 190–191.

100. Ibid., p. 193.

101. Ibid.

102. Ibid., p. 194.

103. V. Pugachev, "Cherez pliuralizm k obnovleniiu sotsializma," *Kommunist,* no. 8, May 1990, p. 72.

104. Ibid., p. 69.

105. Ibid., p. 70.

106. Ibid., p. 71.

107. Ibid., pp. 74–75.

108. Demokraticheskii Soiuz, *Paket Dokumentov* (Moscow, 9 May 1988), p. 5.

109. Ibid.

110. Ibid.

111. *Svobodnoe Slovo,* 8 August 1988, p. 2.

112. Demokraticheskii Soiuz, *Paket Dokumentov.*

113. I. P. Vasil'eva, "Demokraticheskii Soiuz v usloviiakh mnogopartiinosti: Raskol ili razmezhevanie?" *Sotsial'no-politicheskie Nauki,* no. 2, 1991, p. 118. Diversity was, in fact, broader since members included anarchists, socialist revolutionaries, and constitutional monarchists. These were not organized into factions. There were, however, regional factions.

114. Ibid., p. 119. Vasil'eva suggested that "reformers and realists" recognized the need to work within existing political institutions, such as the soviets. But a grouping called Grazhdanskii Put' preferred to work outside the system. At the third congress in Tallinn in January 1990, thirty-two local organizations chose not to participate in the forthcoming elections to republican and local soviets, while twenty-three decided to vote.

115. Ibid., p. 117.

116. *Chto Delat'?* no. 4, 1990, p. 1.

117. Ibid., p. 2.

118. E. K. Ligachev, *Izbrannye Rechi i Stat'i* (Moscow, Politizdat, 1989), p. 210. See footnote 38, Chapter 1.

119. Ibid., p. 214.

120. Ibid., p. 281.

121. Ibid., pp. 296–298.

122. *Pravda*, 11 September 1987, p. 2. In 1968, Viktor M. Chebrikov was appointed deputy chair of the KGB and in 1982 first deputy chair. In 1983, he became a candidate member of the Politburo, then a full member in April 1985. He supported Gorbachev's appointment as general secretary but became more critical of him over time. Gorbachev removed Chebrikov by apparently promoting him in 1988 to the Secretariat. Simultaneously, however, he lost his chair of the KGB. In 1989, he was pensioned off. See Brown, ed., *The Soviet Union*, p. 66.

123. *Pravda*, 11 February 1989, p. 2.

124. *Pravda*, 11 March 1989, p. 2.

125. *Pravda*, 28 November 1989, p. 2. In 1989, Boris Gidaspov was elected to the Congress of People's Deputies and in July replaced Iurii Solov'ev as Leningrad party leader. Gidaspov was soon labeled a conservative who resisted reform. Gidaspov's background was as an industrial chemist and corresponding member of the Academy of Sciences. See Brown, ed., *The Soviet Union*, p. 107.

126. *Pravda*, 28 November 1989, p. 2.

127. Ibid.

128. N. Andreeva, "Ne mogy postupat'sia printsipami," *Sovetskaia Rossiia*, 13 March 1988, p. 3.

129. Ibid.

130. Ibid.

131. Ibid.

132. *Edinstvo*, no. 7, August 1989, p. 5.

133. Ibid.

134. *Interdvizhenie Litvy*, no. 7, June 1991, p. 3.

135. *Chernoe Znamia*, no. 4, 1990, p. 1.

136. Ibid.

137. *Chernoe Znamia*, no. 3, 1990, p. 1.

138. Ibid.

139. Ibid.

140. *Chernoe Znamia*, no. 4, 1990, p. 1.

141. Ibid.

142. Ibid.

143. Ibid.

144. *Volia*, no. 2, 1989, p. 1.

145. *Volia*, no. 5, 1990, p. 2.

146. Ibid.

147. Ibid.

148. *Golos Anarkhizma*, no. 7, 1991, p. 3.

149. Ibid.

150. Ibid.

151. Ibid.

152. *Chernoe Znamia*, no. 3, 1990, p. 1.

153. Ol'ga Ostanina, *Kriticheskii Analiz Pliuralisticheskikh Kontseptsii Politicheskoi Vlasti v Sovremennoi Amerikanskoi Burzhuaznoi Sotsial'no-filosofskoi Literature* (Kirov, Ministerstvo Prosvesheniia RSFSR Kirosvkii Gosudarstvennyi Pedagogicheskii Institut, 1985), p. 3.

154. Asen Kozharov, *Monizm i Pliuralizm v Ideologii i Politike* (Moscow, Progress,1976), p. 278.

155. Ostanina, *Kriticheskii Analiz*, p. 19.

156. Ibid., pp. 3–17.

157. Otto Kuusinen, *Fundamentals of Marxism-Leninism* (London, Lawrence and Wishart, 1961), pp. 173–174.

158. V. V. Smirnov, "Teorii demokratii v burzhuaznoi politicheskoi nauke," in I. G. Tiulina and A. S. Kozhemiakova, eds., *Kritika Burzhuaznykh Politologicheskikh Kontseptsii (k Itogam XI Kongress Mezhdunarodnoi Assotsiatsii Politicheskikh Nauk)* (Moscow, 1982), p. 101.

159. E. Bagramov, "Sotsiologiia i puti obshchestvennogo razvitiia: K itogam IX vsemirnogo sotsiologicheskogo kongressa," *Kommunist,* no. 2, January 1979, p. 101.

160. Ibid., p. 102.

161. G. K. Shakhnazarov, "Predislovie," in Tiulina and Kozhemiakova, eds., *Kritika Burzhuaznykh Politologicheskikh Kontseptsii,* pp. 3–4. For an earlier statement, see his "O demokraticheskom tsentralizme i politicheskom pliuralizme," *Kommunist,* no. 10, July 1979, pp. 96–109.

162. Iurii Levada, "Sotsiologiia," in Iurii Afanasyev and Marc Ferro, eds., *50/50: Opyt Slovaria Novogo Myshleniia* (Moscow, Progress, 1989), p. 221.

163. Ibid., pp. 222–223.

164. A. V. Baranov, "Sotsiologiia i perestroika," in F. M. Borodkin, L. Ia. Kosals, and R. B. Ryvkina, eds., *Postizhenie* (Moscow, Progress, 1989), p. 9.

165. Ibid., p. 11.

166. R. V. Ryvkina, "Sovetskaia sotsiologiia i teoriia sotsial'noe stratefekatsii" in ibid., p. 17.

167. V. A. Iadov, ed., *Sotsiologiia Perestroiki* (Moscow, Nauka, 1990), p. 3.

168. Ibid.

169. Ibid. p. 4.

170. Ryvkina, "Sovetskaia sotsiologiia," p. 20.

171. Ibid.

172. L. A. Gordon, "Vozmozhen li pliuralizm v sovestskom obshchestve," in Borodkin, Kosals, and Ryvkina, eds., *Postizhenie,* pp. 137–165; R. V. Ryvkina, "Sovetskaia sotsiologiia," pp. 17–36; O. I. Shkartan, "Sotsial'naia struktura: Illiuzii i real'nost'" in Iadov, ed., *Sotsiologiia Perestroiki,* pp. 52–80; C. G. Kordonskii, "Obshchestvovedenie kak gosudarstvennyi institut," in Iadov, ed., *Sotsiologiia Perestroiki,* pp. 166–178.

173. Ann Weinberg, *The Development of Sociology in the Soviet Union* (London, Routledge and Kegan Paul, 1974); Vladimir Schlapentokh, *The Politics of Sociology in the Soviet Union* (Boulder, Westview, 1987).

174. A. I. Prigozhin, "Sushchnost' perekhodnykh protsessov," in Iadov, *Sotsiologiia Perestroiki,* pp. 97–118.

175. Shkaratan, "Sosial'naia struktura," p. 61.

176. Ibid.

177. Raymond Carr and Juan Pablo Fusi, *Spain: Dictatorship to Democracy* (London, George Allen and Unwin, 1981).

178. Kenneth Medhurst, "The military and the prospects for Spanish democracy," *West European Politics,* vol. 1, no. 1, February 1978, pp. 42–59.

179. Carr and Fusi, *Spain;* John Hooper, *The Spaniards* (Harmondsworth, Penguin, 1988).

180. Jim Riordan, *Soviet Youth Culture* (London, Macmillan, 1989).

181. Hooper, *The Spaniards,* pp. 256–266.

182. Carr and Fusi, *Spain,* pp. 207–242.

183. Richard Robinson, *Contemporary Portugal: A History* (London, George Allen and Unwin, 1979), pp. 32–34.

184. Gavriil Popov, "Perspektivy i realii," *Ogonek,* no. 50, December 1990, pp. 6–8; and continued under the same title in *Ogonek,* no. 51, December 1990, pp. 5–8.

185. Paul G. Lewis, "Saints and demons: Communism, post-communism, and political evolution in Poland," *Journal of Communist Studies,* vol. 8, no. 1, March 1992, pp. 41–62.

6

Democracy and Civil Society

WHEREAS OFFICIAL IDEOLOGY had long condemned pluralism, it had generally greeted democracy with positive acclaim. For decades, ideology had lauded Soviet socialism, in contrast to capitalism, as the most democratic political system. So the concept of democracy enjoyed a regular presence in discourse and flowed easily from the pens of ideologues and academics. Soviet socialism was officially defined as democratic because it represented the interests of the people as opposed to those of an exploiting minority. Democracy in the USSR was genuine, whereas bourgeois democracy in capitalist systems served only capital and was consequently unjust. Democracy under socialism, where state control served the people, was quite distinct and morally superior.

Democracy, then, was integral to socialism, whereas pluralism was alien to it. Democracy had never been the automatic target of Soviet discourse that pluralism had been. This is one reason redefinitions of polity dealt hesitantly with pluralism; it was a politically delicate concept. And precisely because pluralism had been ideologically taboo, visions of democracy without pluralism were less threatening to political legitimacy than any use of the term *pluralism*.

But democracy, too, had its inherited problems. Democratic socialism (as discussed in the previous chapter) had been scorned in the past as an enemy of socialism. It smacked of reformism; it was not revolutionary. It was something championed by so-called socialists who erroneously thought that the capitalist systems in which they lived could be improved without being fundamentally transformed. Their mistake was to believe that bourgeois democracy could become socialist democracy without socialist revolution.

Thus, democracy, in contrast to pluralism, was criticized only in some respects. Pluralism was ideologically unwholesome, whereas democracy was only partially so, depending on the context. Nonetheless, new assessments of democracy did confront ideological hurdles. In the past, apart from in dissident circles, socialism had been considered indisputably democratic. Gorbachev's political reforms, however, now prioritized *demokratizatsiia* (democratization). That Soviet socialism needed to democratize meant that discussions of the process had to confront just how flawed the system was. And arguments about what democracy was and how democratization could best proceed ultimately involved crucial issues of authority, power, and the legitimacy of the state. Reassessments of the past, of Stalinism, finally even of Leninism, ensued; they were inevitably heated.[1]

If the system, moreover, was to adopt some market mechanisms and increasingly look to liberal democracies for lessons in "checks and balances," was this a move toward the undesirable democratic socialism condemned so heavily before? As Sweden became a favorite, increasingly cited model of many reformers, this appeared so. Reformers did not find this appropriation of the Swedish model an ideological problem, but critics of reform did.

Initially, fresh definitions of democracy coming from the leadership brought mild modifications, just as remarks about socialist pluralism had been tentative and heavily qualified. But once redefining polity was on formal agendas, different reactions to democratization pushed the boundaries of discussion ever wider. At first, glasnost facilitated this process. But by 1990, glasnost was being taken for granted by enthusiasts. It was the developing agendas of new groups, movements, and parties that subsequently drove debate further.

By the summer of 1991, politicians, theorists, and lawyers had expressed a plethora of views about the political significance of democratization. They had also begun to assess the practical problems posed for democracy by the way in which the newly elected soviets were operating. Rather less energy was devoted to thinking about issues of representation and civil society. This chapter highlights some of the main arguments about democratization and looks more briefly at early discussions of civil society. The latter were crucial, if rarer, because they reflected the growing anxiety that without civil society, democracy would be impossible. The following chapter concentrates in greater detail on the reservations of people's deputies about the soviets and the extent to which they could be considered democratic.

The pace of change after August 1991 accelerated immensely to an extent unanticipated earlier that year or throughout the preceding seven. Nevertheless, many of the arguments, beliefs, and hopes about how politics ought to run had their roots in the ideas discussed here and in critical reactions to them. And also throughout 1992, many of the charges of "undemocratic" and "authoritarian" behavior leveled against Gorbachev in 1990 and 1991 were now directed at Yeltsin.

Жить стало лучше,
жить стало веселей !

Фото К. Завражина

"Life has become better, Life has become happier!" In early 1991, society was deeply divided between supporters of the CPSU and its critics. The cartoon satirizes some of Stalin's famous words in which he joyfully proclaimed that life under socialism was improving. Next to Stalin is the plaque of the Ministry of Social Protection of the RSFSR. Juxtaposed below are citizens delivering a different message in 1991. They shout that life is not better and that socialist protection has failed them. The contrast highlights the huge gap between official ideology and reality. SOURCE: *Svobodnoe Slovo,* 16 April 1991, p. 1.

Divisions over Democratization

The term *democracy* has been variously defined across centuries and across political systems. It has been acclaimed and attacked for various characteristics that it was deemed to possess.[2] The meanings given to *demokratiia* (democracy) in the USSR until August 1991 were not uniform either; and the reception given to embryonic *demokratizatsiia* was mixed. Political actors and citizens greeted it with euphoria, caution, indifference, fear, and opposition.

Gorbachev, who was instrumental in instigating democratization, believed that the process was fundamental to successful economic and political reform. Although how he viewed democratization and reform inevitably varied over time, Gorbachev was increasingly sensitive to the limits that he wished to impose on democracy and the opportunities he wished to provide. Democracy, for Gorbachev, incorporated a socialist pluralism but did not necessarily require a multi-party system.

In 1985 and 1986, Gorbachev did not tie democracy to pluralism or to civil society. He linked them at a theoretical level later, in 1987 and in 1990, respectively, as democratization progressed. But Gorbachev's utterances did not go far enough for those democrats who considered a multi-party system essential to successful democracy. Various shades of "democrat" criticized what they still took to be, in 1989 and in 1991, a "totalitarian" system. They knew which political arrangements they did not want and what general characteristics they would like to see develop, such as a depoliticization of the KGB; a separation of executive, legislative, and judicial powers; and the right of republics to secede from the Union.[3]

Strict Leninists, however, abhorred what the democrats wanted. Their preference was to limit the meaning of democracy to a reform of the CPSU. Other political parties were not necessary; in fact, they could only be ideologically unsound. Leninists also opposed the introduction of a market economy and the advent of an immoral and unequal bourgeois society. In an entirely different vein, anarchists, too, poured scorn on *demokratiia*. Democracy was a liberal sham granted from above that gave only grains of freedom. They championed freedom, which they defined as local self-administration. Different again were those who shunned democracy in the short term in favor of an authoritarian system designed to preserve the Union and to impose radical market reforms and market relations from above. Adherents of this view believed that a market economy was now vital but that only authoritarianism could deliver one. They, too, were worried that democracy meant disorder. If polity could not democratize in a stable way, for reasons of historical context, political culture, institutional mechanisms, and political conflict, then it should not.

Gorbachev: Democratization and Leninism

At the Twenty-seventh Party Congress in 1986, Gorbachev made no mention of *pliuralizm, grazhdanskoe obshchestvo* (civil society), or *pravovoe gosudarstvo* (a legal state).[4] His initial conception of perestroika did not extend to such democratic parameters. A multi-party system, new political movements and groups, and an end to the leading role of the CPSU were not in his vision. Rather, in 1986, when his main thoughts were on economic reform, the bulk of the Political Report to the Party Congress covered *uskorenie* (acceleration) of the economy, social policy, foreign policy, and the party. Less than 10 percent of his remarks were directed at "the further democratization of society and a deepening of socialist self-management of the people."[5] Gorbachev's comments on democratization said little more than that Lenin saw "the main strength of the development of new construction" in democracy and in the creativity of the working people. Democracy was "healthy and clean air," which could be found only in "the socialist social organism."[6] Rather than defining the concept of democracy, Gorbachev used vague analogies and was silent on policy proposals. The general idea he put across was that "acceleration in the development of society is unthinkable and impossible without the further development of socialist democracy in all its aspects and appearances."[7] Democracy was imperative, but what it entailed was not clear.

In 1986, Gorbachev did not yet advocate new-style elections, although he referred to, without specifying how, the party's duty "to strengthen the authority of elected deputies and also in every possible way to increase their responsibility before electors."[8] With hindsight, a gentle commitment to new elections could be read into this remark. Yet the desirability of increasing the authority and responsibility of soviets was not a new notion; it had been discussed during the Khrushchev era. Gorbachev's reference did not automatically offer a cue for an overhaul of the electoral system. In short, if Gorbachev had a precise intent, he did not reveal it.

Much clearer were his views on glasnost. He noted that to proceed, democratization needed glasnost and that democratization itself was "an important lever in strengthening socialist legality."[9] He drew tacit links between democracy, economic reform, initiative, glasnost, and socialist legality, although he did not define their precise nature. He said little about citizenship except to remark about the need for "equality of citizens before the law."[10] The section of Gorbachev's speech devoted to democratization also included praise for the Soviet army as a school of "civil responsibility, courage, and patriotism." Gorbachev argued that soldiers and officers should "always feel the care and attention of society."[11] These words could hardly have been reassuring for those wishing for an end to authoritarian rule.

In 1986, Gorbachev's public statements on democratization did not offer an exciting vision of radical change; nor could they. His suggestions had to be tempered and guarded so as not to offend too many conservatives too soon. Careful remarks about the need for more socialist democracy had to be made alongside quotations from Lenin and praise for the Soviet army so as not to cause alarm. In addition, the conventions of official political discourse limited what could be said. There were automatic categories into which leaders had to slot their statements. Otherwise they would not have been ideologically sound. Despite these political and ideological constraints, intellectuals wanting change were carefully reading between the lines. One hopeful interpretation of Gorbachev's remarks was that they marked the first, inevitably tentative, steps toward something new.

As economic reform proceeded slowly and amid much resistance, Gorbachev's conviction that political reform was essential grew. He felt the need to shake up the political system because attempts to give managers in industry more decision-making power and control over funds had been circumvented by bureaucrats in ministries behaving in "old ways." New *goszakazy* (state orders) had ended up taking 100 percent of factories' industrial output, depriving managers of the opportunity to take initiative about what to do with output not demanded by the state.[12] Ministers, Gorbachev believed, should be made politically accountable; they should be answerable to elected people's deputies in a revamped electoral system.

In January 1987, Gorbachev reiterated and extended these ideas at the Central Committee plenum (a meeting more than once delayed because of disagreements). He praised elections in the workplace and called for "a deepening democratization of the electoral system" and for "a more effective and real participation of voters in all stages of the pre-election and election campaigns."[13] The electoral system and its nomination procedures would be reexamined, and a new draft law should be debated by the people. In fact, in 1987 a limited experiment in voting took place, affecting only 2 percent of constituencies, in which voters enjoyed a choice of candidate.[14]

In his speech to the January plenum, Gorbachev also welcomed the fact that "criticism and self-criticism are broadening. The mass media are starting to work more actively. Soviet people feel good about the positive influence of glasnost, which is becoming a norm of society's life."[15] Glasnost, he declared, "is not simply a slogan but the essence of perestroika."[16]

Had Gorbachev foreseen where glasnost would lead, he might have expressed these words with less enthusiasm. Gorbachev's glasnost was always Leninist in inspiration. He repeatedly reiterated that "we must return to a Leninist formulation of the question of a maximum democracy of socialist construction."[17] Although Gorbachev's nod to Lenin could be interpreted in 1987 by generous radicals as necessary rhetoric to keep conservatives happy, by 1991 his persistent verbal loyalty to Lenin was seen as definitive evidence of Gorbachev's inability to rise above his party background and escape its organizing categories.

But in 1988, Gorbachev was genuinely and vigorously pushing for a shake-up of politics, as his remarkable achievement in convening the Nineteenth Party Conference illustrated. Here Gorbachev declared that individuals should be included in all the processes of perestroika. "Not the apparat," he insisted, "but the people are called on to play a decisive, revolutionary role."[18] Moreover, "the cornerstone of democratization is a rebirth of the soviets as full-blooded organs of people's power." An electoral system would be established to give "fuller expression to the variety of interests existing in our society."[19] Reforms should give "full power" to the soviets in the districts, towns, oblasts, and republics, thereby widening their rights.[20]

Few imagined in 1988 that two years later Gorbachev would be trying to reduce the power of the soviets. In a short period of time, he shifted from advocating an increase in legislative power at the expense of executive power to the opposite. The context of political instability in the republics, in Gorbachev's view, coupled with political chaos across administrative levels and between institutions, justified and required a strong executive presidency. Whereas critics to his "left" in 1990 and in 1991 feared more authoritarianism, Gorbachev felt that political expediency and pragmatism demanded strong executive powers. Gorbachev was also under pressure from critics on his "right" to maintain order and stability. As one lawyer put it, "Gorbachev's hands are tied by others."[21]

Nevertheless, throughout 1988 Gorbachev emphasized the importance of political reform. One of his strongest defenses was made in a speech to the Supreme Soviet, which approved at the end of the year the new electoral law. Reform of the political system was "an exceptionally complicated task," he declared, and renewal of the soviets and electoral reform were just "the first stage." The second "main stage" concerned "harmonious relations" between the union and the republics.[22] Gorbachev in 1988 could at last see the importance of the national question (indeed, hard not to given developments in the Baltic states, Azerbaidzhan, Armenia, and Georgia), but he did not yet realize its intractability and complexity.

Gorbachev, unlike many democrats, was not an enthusiastic champion of a multi-party system, as the last chapter showed. He expressed firm reservations in January 1989 at the twenty-seventh conference of the Moscow city party. Democratization applied to the CPSU and did not necessarily entail the flourishing of numerous other parties. The dangers were obvious—"demogogy and froth. These appear and disappear, but glasnost remains always."[23] These remarks nicely illustrate how Gorbachev's conception of democracy was limited. The people could criticize, but only to further officially defined perestroika. And glasnost did not require a multi-party system in which to flourish, nor should it imply one.

Civil society was not a concept that Gorbachev linked to democratization until 1990. At the Twenty-eighth Party Congress, he announced that "the Stalinist model of socialism" had been replaced by "a civil society of free people."[24] This meant that the political system had been "radically transformed" and "genuine democracy with free choices, many parties, and the rights of individuals confirmed." In addition, "real people's power [had been] reborn."[25] On the surface, Gorbachev went further than before by giving apparent support to a multi-party system. Civil society appeared to entail many parties. But Gorbachev did not give an operational definition of civil society, providing at best the foregoing connotative one. And in the same speech he warned against destructive forces seeking bourgeois construction. Civil society and many parties must not mean bourgeois parties. Civil society had to be socialist. Thus, Gorbachev's view of civil society was at variance with the views of many democratic reformers.

On his return to Moscow in August 1991 after being captive and isolated in the Crimea during the temporary state of emergency, Gorbachev, by now quite out of tune with the pace of change, reasserted his commitment to socialism and to the CPSU. His vision for democracy was still a socialist one in which the CPSU figured positively. Historical circumstance forced him speedily to reevaluate this position.

Democrats and Mass Parties

By 1991, there were various shades of democrat in the USSR. What made most of them differ from Gorbachev was their call for an end to the monopoly of communist ideology and for the creation of a mass democratic political party. The Declaration of the Democratic Party of Russia (DPR) in 1990, for example, stated that "our first priority is the revival of Russian statehood in the form of a sovereign democratic federal republic with a multi-party system." The DPR was "for the market and for free enterprise." It described itself as "a party of a parliamentary type, created for political struggle within the limits of the constitution."[26] In 1990, the DPR was busy calling for "the consolidation of all democratic forces to struggle for the constitutional overthrow of the party-apparat of the CPSU." The DPR was ready to work as a "bloc" with all democratic parties and movements to meet this goal.[27]

The movement Demokraticheskaia Rossiia (Democratic Russia) held its first congress in October 1990 but had come into existence earlier in the year as a general umbrella for democratic forces, or as a working alliance, in the battle against the CPSU. Democratic Russia grew out of the joint efforts of voters' associations and "Elections—90," which had been set up to coordinate the nomination of candidates who supported the Inter-Regional Group in the republican and local elections.[28] The Inter-Regional Group had been formed in the First Congress of People's Deputies, elected in March

1989. The group was led by Yeltsin and involved other democrats, such as historian Iurii Afanasyev; economist Gavriil Popov, who later became mayor of Moscow and held that post until 1992; and reformers from the Baltic and other republics. The Inter-Regional Group championed human rights, a new union treaty, and a mixed economy.[29]

Democratic Russia rallied behind reformist candidates and effectively ran Yeltsin's campaign for the Russian parliament. Thereafter it drew together a diverse array of democrats who had been elected to the soviets and who wanted to be part of a loose alliance that could orchestrate sustained opposition to the party-apparat. The organization attempted to coordinate their strategies and tactics and mobilize supporters in the population. Democratic Russia came to advocate a sovereign Russia and equal relations with surrounding republics.[30] Reform throughout the USSR, not an end to the union, was the initial aim.

Whatever their numerous differences over principle, self-proclaimed democrats saw *demokratiia* as their goal. Often this central concept went undefined beyond the general statements previously quoted about a multi-party parliamentary system. Most democrats advocated a separation of executive, legislative, and judicial powers but without specifying what this would look like. Above all, democracy was something the USSR did not have and democrats wanted. The aim was to get it. Only then, it seemed, would democrats address democracy's nuances. The main issue of the moment was how to weaken the CPSU's grip on power; next would come how to steer reform along the general lines of a market economy and establish a multi-party system with parliamentary rule. Some of the competing "democratic" strategies that emerged are outlined in Chapter 8. In 1990 and 1991, they were increasingly linked to finding a way out of the crisis.

Not all groups, movements, or parties with "democratic" in their name were looked on favorably by others. The Liberal Democratic Party, led by the populist Vladimir Zhirinovskii, for instance, was not noted for its democratic credentials. Although Zhirinovskii paid lip service to "a pluralism of thought" and legality, he did not define these terms or offer a genuine democratic program. Man, he advocated, should be the "head of the family," deciding himself "when he will marry, whether his wife will work, how many children they will have, where and how these children will study, what sort of house they will have and what will be in it and around it. Then there will not be any single elderly citizens or rejected children."[31] Zhirinovskii lacked any sense of women as citizens. He also offered highly unrealistic economic policies. Reform, he argued, would bring a boom in the agricultural sector and in construction, trade, and the service industry. Unemployment would be simply a "minimal" problem that functioned as a "medicine" for the economy. It would, in any case, be eased by "several million" Soviet citizens finding opportunities for employment in the West.[32] When he ran against

Yeltsin in 1991 in the elections for president of Russia, Zhirinovskii's campaign was one of crude populism appealing to nationalism and promising fairy-tale economics. He supported the coup of 1991, and his party was subsequently banned by Yeltsin.[33]

The Democratic Union was subjected to criticism for very different reasons. Although its programs advocated goals similar to those of other democrats, the party earned opprobrium for its methods. Its readiness in 1988 and 1989 to demonstrate and engage in civil disobedience meant that it quickly developed a reputation for confrontation and aggression, which did not go down well, particularly with more cautious groups such as Civilian Dignity. The Democratic Union's tactics were often perceived by other democrats to be unnecessarily provocative, risky, and unconstructive.[34] As a consequence, by 1990 some members of the Democratic Union were attempting to alter this image by toning down their confrontational style.[35] By then, however, other democrats who had previously been tentative in their willingness to demonstrate openly were seeing the political point of mass demonstrations at appropriate political moments. But now they criticized one faction of the Democratic Union for boycotting the elections of 1990, a move other democrats viewed as unproductive.[36]

Members of the Democratic Union produced the most theoretical reflections about the meaning of democracy. Although the political clout of this tiny party was minimal, the ideas emanating from it made a distinctive contribution to developing debates. From the outset, its official documents insisted that "democracy for us is, not a slogan or simple cry, but the form and essence of state construction based on political, economic, and spiritual pluralism; a multi-party system; a legal opposition press; and independent trade unions." Pluralism would be best obtained through "de-ideologization," the growth of civil society, and the establishment of a legal state.[37] But, above all, democracy had to be liberal democracy.

Unlike the newspapers and documents of other democratic parties, those of the Democratic Union showed a keen interest in the dangers of democracy without liberalism. Writing in *Svobodnoe Slovo*, the Democratic Union's Moscow paper, Leonid Karpov argued that the history of nineteenth-century Europe nicely illustrated struggles between democracy and liberalism, resulting in the victory of liberalism in the form of a legal state. Democracy, however, did not automatically mean liberal democracy. Herein lay its danger. Rather, "democracy not constrained by liberal principles can itself be a dictatorship or lead to dictatorship."[38] Majority rule could hurt a minority. "Pure" democracy, one not based on liberalism, was "democracy pregnant with dictatorship and totalitarianism." This was what Karl Popper and Friedrich von Hayek called "total democracy." Karpov stressed that it was "one step from democracy to totalitarianism."[39] Only a legal state defending the rights of individuals, rather than those of the majority, even though such rights were obtained through the majority, was acceptable democracy for the Democratic Union. This was a democracy defending natural rights, not the will of the majority or the state. Indeed, "this is the right to freedom, life, property, safety, etc."[40]

The Democratic Union had been championing the necessity for liberal democracy and civil society four years before the Movement for Democratic Reforms was launched. On 2 July 1991, erstwhile colleagues of Gorbachev, Aleksandr Yakovlev and Eduard Shevardnadze declared on the front page of *Izvestiia* their intent to launch the movement. They were both disenchanted and alarmed by Gorbachev's move to the right and by what they saw as an attack by the party leadership and the party apparat against "democratic transformation," against "economic and political freedoms."[41] Along with Arkadii Volskii, Gavriil Popov, Aleksandr Rutskoi, Anatolii Sobchak, Stanislav Shatalin, Ivan Silaev, and Nikolai Petrakov, their signatures appeared at the bottom of a statement that reaffirmed crisis. It declared that a "new situation" prevailed because "conservative forces [were] strengthening their position." This demanded "a new step to democratic development." Peasants should have land; workers, decent wages; intellectuals, a right to intellectual property; officers, pride in defending their homeland; believers, their church; and the people, their culture, traditions, history, and monuments. The signers of the statement advocated a "parliamentary republic," "law and order," "social and economic protection" of the people, and a "voluntary union of sovereign peoples."[42] This very pragmatically conceived response to a specific political situation was preoccupied mainly with concrete alternatives to what the government was offering. Thus, the new movement's discourse about democracy lacked the broader philosophical debates that occupied the Democratic Union.

In a separate article, Yakovlev elaborated the political predicament of the moment. Ultraconservatives, in particular the newly formed Russian Communist Party, were battling against democratization. Although a revolution had taken place in society, this was not the case in the CPSU. Moreover, democracy was "alien" to the "apparat's structures." It was time, Yakovlev maintained, to recognize that the CPSU had different groupings within it and "was pregnant with multi-parties." It was necessary "to work out measures that with maximum smoothness, with the help of society, transform this situation into a civilized multi-party system of a parliamentary type."[43] Many activists in Democratic Russia at this time were heard commenting, "I'm not sure what they are trying to achieve by this."[44] A suitable democratic movement already existed. Even many of those who had recently left the CPSU seemed genuinely puzzled by the initiative. So the Movement for Democratic Reforms was not greeted with widespread enthusiasm. At the time, it was just another new movement, although significant for being the brainchild of eminent politicians. For many democrats, however, that was precisely its weakness. Yakovlev and Shevardnadze were criticizing the CPSU too late to be considered truly authentic democrats.

After the failed coup of 1991, democrats gained the upper hand, with Yeltsin forcing the pace of change. Debates across the broad spectrum of democratic opinion now addressed issues of authoritarian rule, executive power, and the extent of social protection that should accompany a market economy. Many supporters of Democratic Russia, for instance, again attacked Popov and Sobchak, and now Yeltsin, for being authoritarian and undemocratic. They saw flaws in the leaders they had once backed. And because the Movement for Democratic Reforms supported Yeltsin, those to its left criticized it for backing authoritarians.[45]

Alongside debates and new fears came more democratic parties. In September 1991, for example, the Moscow branch of the Movement for Democratic Reforms met to adopt statutes and to elect delegates for a congress in October. Shevardnadze spoke of "political chaos," Yakovlev warned about Stalinists, and Popov called for the setting up of two or three democratic parties to counteract any reemergence of the CPSU. The Party for Democratic Reforms for Russia resulted from the session and held its first congress on 24 September. Shevardnadze and Yakovlev chose not to join it.[46]

A year before Yakovlev and Shevardnadze attempted to launch the Movement for Democratic Reforms, some members of the Democratic Platform within the CPSU (which radical reformist communists had formed in January 1990) decided to leave the party. They announced this at the Twenty-eighth Party Congress. Some of them formed the Republican Party of the Russian Federation under the leadership of Viacheslav Shostakovskii. Interviewed in *Moskovskie Novosti*, Shostakovskii observed that democrats in the CPSU had once hoped to oppose the party's conservatives by working within the party. But with the emergence of the hard-line Russian Communist Party, which formed on 21 June 1990, with Ivan Polozkov as leader, it had become clear that communists exhibiting their revanchist spirit would continue to be the main brake on democratic change.[47] Thus, developments on the right once more caused reformist-minded forces to set up fresh institutions as a way of striving to meet their goals, which now appeared unobtainable in existing structures. The Democratic Platform had hoped to turn the CPSU into a parliamentary party, shake out the conservatives, and benefit from the party's buildings and wealth but had failed. The Leninists had no intention of letting the Democratic Platform succeed. So to pursue goals, members of the Democratic Platform had to adopt alternative strategies.

During 1990 and 1991, political initiatives of different democrats frequently entailed the formation of a new group or movement with the specific aim of challenging, undermining, or resisting either the CPSU or more broadly conceived forces of the right. Effort was channeled into fighting *against,* and energy frequently concentrated on appropriate strategies and tactics for weakening another political actor. This meant that discourse about democratization was often geared to analysis of the political moment rather than to reflection about the meaning of democracy and the policies necessary to meet it. Analytic categories were shaped by ongoing battles and changing scenarios.

Leninists and Democratizing the CPSU

Whereas democrats wanted a redefined polity, Leninists dogmatically clung to the CPSU as the country's salvation. For them, democratization did not extend beyond renewal of the party. Anything more threatened to bring demagogy, instability, and uncertain direction. What mattered most was that the CPSU became truly Leninist again. In particular, this meant "democratizing work among cadres."[48] The message to the party faithful was to assimilate "V. I. Lenin's approach to the advancement of cadres" and "the Leninist tradition of solving cadre questions in the circumstances of party democratization" so as to "enjoy the trust of the people."[49] Some Leninists emphasized that they were indeed in favor of some change and tried to distance themselves from the image that they were resisting it. This approach led them to warn that "new democratic methods" of work would be established "with difficulty" and would "run up against conservatism and inertia, dogmatic thinking, and stereotypical actions."[50] These attitudes were something, they insisted, that applied to others. But most democrats believed that this characterization fit Leninists best.

The speeches of Egor Ligachev provide a clear example of the Leninist thinking that irritated democrats. Ligachev regularly contended that the CPSU should be the central object of democratization. At the Rostov oblast party conference in December 1988, he declared, "The Communist Party is the organizer and guarantor of the politics of perestroika. Restructuring itself, the party renews the life of society."[51] By implication, society would not enliven itself independently of the CPSU. Genuine democracy could exist only through a revitalized Communist Party in the same political system. "More socialism," Ligachev told a plenum of the Central Committee in February 1988, meant "more variety." When the truth was no longer dictated, many voices would be heard "through democratic means." An "open and honest confrontation of positions and arguments" would ensue.[52] But this confrontation would take place without radical change of the political system. A "widening of socialist democracy," not a multi-party system, was required, Ligachev informed the party *aktiv* in Gorky in August 1988.[53] So "confrontation" would, it seemed, be confined to the CPSU. Like Nina Andreeva, Ligachev believed that Marxist-Leninist ideology should continue to guide society—that in itself was democratic.[54] In sum, democracy was enshrined in the CPSU, in Soviet socialism, and in Marxism-Leninism.

After the selection of a new Politburo at the Twenty-eighth Party Congress, Ligachev's days in politics were over.[55] Leninist ideas, however, still enjoyed adherents. In 1991, an "announcement of socio-political organizations and movements of socialist choice" was published in the second edition of *Volia*.[56] More than thirty groups signed the statement including the Russian Communist Party, the United Labor Front, the Marxist Platform of the CPSU, the Moscow club of Communist-Leninists, Edinstvo, a group of deputies of the Mossovet, the Writers' Union of the RSFSR, and others. Together they declared that the "socio-political and socio-economic situation" in the country was "critical," as evidenced by "anarchy and chaos, ruin of the state, destitution, and bloodshed." Moreover, "political disagreements are acquiring an antagonistic character." In particular, "fascist forces had come to power in separate regions of the country. Calling themselves democrats, they propagate nationalism, chauvinism and shamelessly violate the rights of individuals." In response, the "patriotic and international forces of the country" should consolidate and vote in the referendum of 17 March in favor of retaining the Union of Soviet Socialist Republics.[57] Groups proclaiming "socialist choice" considered that genuine socialist democracy was under attack from fascists disguised as democrats.

The same edition of *Volia* carried an article entitled "Concerning the Treacherous Policy of B. Yeltsin." It argued that "the danger of a counter-revolutionary, anti-socialist revolution in Russia is growing and becoming more real. Its speeding up is prepared by frantic pseudo-democrats, headed by Yeltsin."[58] *Volia* charged that Yeltsin had been propelled into power by the people's dissatisfaction with perestroika. Yeltsin had given hope to millions of honest communists, but he was really out to satisfy his own political ambitions. Yeltsin later revealed his "perfidious policy, directed at the disintegration of the USSR as a great sovereign power."[59] Leninists reiterated their fears that glasnost and pseudo-democracy led to chaos, poverty, and the breakup of the Union. What was democratization for Gorbachev was counter-revolution for Leninists.

Many of the groups that had come together to declare their support for "socialist choice" echoed these sentiments in their own newspapers. In *Chto Delat'?* for example, the United Labor Front proclaimed, "With Lenin—not with Gorbachev!"[60] At its third congress in Moscow in March 1991, the United Labor Front expressed opposition to a transition to a market economy. The market was "anti-scientific, anti-people, and vicious." In supporting it, Gorbachev was being "opportunistic and capitulationist." Moreover, his policy was "disastrous for the party, the people, and the country." The United Labor Front's goal was "to defend the interests of workers," which meant challenging the market and its inevitable consequences of "unemployment, destitution, and a high cost of living." A democracy that was not socialist was against the people because it represented an economy that hurt workers.[61] Those who advocated such changes were, not proper democrats, but *demfashisty*—"dem-fascists."[62] The charge was leveled at Gorbachev and Yeltsin.

These ideas were more vigorously voiced after the price increases of 2 April 1991. Edinstvo issued a statement to the April plenum of the Central Committee of the CPSU in which it noted intensifying "class struggle" in the country "as a result of the deepening of contradictions between socialism and anti-communism"—a struggle reflected in the party itself. *Gorbastroika* was responsible for the crisis in the party and the crisis in society. *Gorbastroika* was a form of bourgeois restoration. Democracy, humanism, and renewal were part of the language of the bourgeoisie and capital and were not in the interests of the workers.[63] Edinstvo declared that Gorbachev's democratization was tantamount to a drift toward fascism. Therefore, "Edinstvo supports the setting up in the republics of Committees and Soviets of National Salvation, as organs of the genuine, constitutional power of workers standing against the destruction by nationalists and by anti-communists of the economic, political, and ideological foundations of socialist construction."[64] Without doubt, members of Edinstvo, the United Labor Front, the Russian Communist Party, and all signatories of the document supporting socialist choice would have greeted the coup of August with relief and support and responded to its failure with consternation.

After August and the subsequent banning of communist parties, committed communists did not all fall silent. Some regrouped under new names. For example, on 26 and 27 October, the First Congress of the Demokraticheskaia Partiia Kommunistov Rossii (Democratic Party of Communists of Russia) took place. In keeping with the spirit of the times, however, participants decided to change their organization's name to Narodnaia Partiia Svobodnoi Rossii (People's Party of Free Russia). Members adopted the slogans "Market prices—market wages," "Stop unemployment," and "Defend the weak."[65] And when, on 26 October, the Sotsialisticheskaia Partiia Trudiashchikhsia (Socialist Party of Workers) gathered, some present wanted "communist" to be included in the name.[66] On 7 November, what would have been the seventy-fourth anniversary of the October Revolution, communists loyal to Lenin staged demonstrations in newly renamed St. Petersburg and in Moscow, showing their respect for the Soviet socialism of the past. Revolutionary changes may have been taking place, but they certainly did not herald the end of communist beliefs on Russian soil. Demonstrators criticized Yeltsin and condemned the "fascism" that they claimed had engulfed them. In mid-November, consistent critic of Gorbachev and Yeltsin, Nina Andreeva, was chosen to be leader of a new Soviet communist party of Bolsheviks at its founding congress in St. Petersburg.[67] Then in De-

This cartoon portrays the USSR as a slow-moving snail. At a time when republics were assuming powers and engaging in a "war of laws" with the center, the Union lumbered on. The falling leaf suggests that perhaps the USSR is in the autumn of its life. The snail illustrates an article on the implications of Pavlov as prime minister for economic reform and for new powers for the republics. It prophetically concludes that Gorbachev "chose himself a dangerous partner." SOURCE: *Gospodin Narod*, no. 7, 1991, p. 1.

cember in Ekaterinburg, Russia's Communist Workers' Party was formed. It supported "proletarian democracy" and democratic centralism.[68]

August 1991, like November 1917, may have been an important historical cutoff date as far as system transformation was concerned, but it did not signify the death of socialist and communist thought. Many Leninists remained Leninists. They declared the banning of communist parties to be unconstitutional, lamented the formal demise of the CPSU, and regrouped into newly named communist parties. They did not perceive their struggle against market economy, bourgeois democracy, and fascism to be over.

Anarchists and Democracy as Manipulation

The democracy that the DPR and other members of Democratic Russia called for was despised by anarchists, too. Publications such as *Chernoe Znamia,* put out by the Anarcho-Communist Revolutionary Union, and *Volia,* the paper of the Confederation of Anarcho-Syndicalists, poured scorn on liberalism as "sanctioned from above" for offering just a few "political freedoms" while all the time manipulating social consciousness.[69] Cartoons showed "Glasnost!" "Democracy!" "Perestroika!" and "Legal state!" as empty slogans blaring out of the radio into the ear of a worker who had no food, only an empty bottle, and from whose pocket the state was taking ten rubles.[70] The Anarcho-Communist Revolutionary Union concluded that "the individual, enslaved by the state, already has no choice but to resist state power."[71] Everyone should come together to fight "state dictatorship," despite class differences.

Intellectuals, according to anarchists, were split. Since most of them depended for their livelihood on the state, they would not go further than "bourgeois democracy" in their demands. But the more advanced and radical section of the intelligentsia could see their "inseparable bond with the proletariat." They would form a revolutionary vanguard, thereby increasing the strength of the workers.[72]

Revolution, however, would not come about through elected people's deputies. In an article entitled "Mirror for the Supreme Soviet," *Volia* printed an extract from an anarchist theorist and professor of Moscow University, Aleksei Borov, writing at the beginning of the century. By implication, his remarks directed at the Duma were similarly applicable to the Supreme Soviet of 1990. Who were these "chosen people" sitting in parliament, he asked, having spent so much "time, energy, and money" to get there? They were not necessarily popular among the constituents they represented because popularity was "created by shameless advertisements and by the generosity of party committees." These parliamentarians, who were most likely "very far from the interests of those whom they represent[ed], barely knew the people's needs. Indeed, it was not necessary for politicians to know what the people needed. What mattered were the interests of their party and how best to make these interests come alive. The "legal machine" of the modern parliament, however, required more than the "good intentions" of politicians. Admittedly, some were trained in economics, but this meant abstract knowledge; they were "unfamiliar with the real, concrete, needs of the country." At best, they were meant for the archives, not for real life.[73] Numerous intellectuals in parliaments might be able to write well or speak eloquently or master the law, medicine, or art, but how could they, after years of study, "all, with surprising lightheartedness, cast aside their lawyer's desk or surgeon's knife when the opportunity to enter

"Glasnost! Democracy! Perestroika!" [from radio] "The legal state!" [taking 10 rubles from his pocket]   In 1990, as food shortages worsened, budget deficits increased, and fiscal crisis hit, comedians joked about Gorbachev's political slogans. Here the Anarcho-Communist Revolutionary Union joins in the ridicule. The cartoon suggests that the state gives ordinary workers nothing except rhetoric and steals from them through its economic reforms. SOURCE: *Chernoe Znamia*, no. 4, 1990, p. 1.

parliament present[ed] itself?"[74] They did not want to understand that governing the fate of the people was much more complicated than they imagined. Spencer was right to claim that, despite their intellectual expertise, parliaments generally exhibited lower mental and moral levels than the average prevailing in the country.[75]

Members of the Confederation of Anarcho-Syndicalists considered that these words rang true about the contemporary Supreme Soviet. Intellectuals did not know the needs of the people and hesitated to realize that they were poorly qualified to make national policy. The new Soviet "democracy" was fictitious, and its political actors were ill-equipped to perform the tasks that they had set themselves.[76] The Moscow Union of Anarchists portrayed the new democracy as the same as the old bureaucracy. The only difference was that the letters for "bureau" were being replaced by "demo." The substance, however, was the same.[77]

Whereas democrats put their political faith in elected deputies, political parties, and the development of a multi-party system, anarchists condemned all three, considering them a continuation of state power, which should be demolished, not praised. State power was oppressive, whether in the hands of the CPSU or the DPR. Genuine freedom would come only from local self-administration. But a question mark hung over how that would unfold.

Following the election, in June 1991, of Boris Yeltsin as president of Russia, there was euphoria among democrats. But the Moscow Union of Anarchists poured scorn on "the people's president" and stressed that there was little difference between new leaders and old ones. Democrats moving into power were just like the earlier bureaucrats now leaving. This was because the remaining core of state structures had not altered. SOURCE: *Golos Anarkhizma*, no. 7, 1991, p. 1.

Strong Leadership and Authoritarian Solutions

The rather vague local self-administration advocated by anarchists was viewed by many political scientists and politicians as a recipe for further chaos, fragmentation, ungovernability, and nihilism. They dismissed, in any case, the political importance of anarchist groups, which were tiny. But the threat of "anarchy" had troubled theorists since the last century. The spiraling disorder that could result from spontaneity and self-administration was a deep-seated fear in Russian political culture. And in a context of political collapse, analysts of different political persuasions argued that strong leadership and/or authoritarian solutions had constructive roles to play. Authoritarianism could temper unruly forces and permit positive changes to proceed without disturbance. But the characteristics, purposes, and time span of such strong leaderships varied with the analyst.

One adherent of firm leadership was political scientist Andranik Migranyan. In his view, strong leadership was needed "to push through marketizing reforms that would create an organized social and political base for institutionalized, democratic politics."[78] Migranyan conceived of strong leadership as the necessary means to a more democratic end. In 1989, Migranyan put the locus of this leadership at the center. But in 1990, after an escalation in nationalism in the republics and the growing illegitimacy of the center, he surmised that "perhaps only strong but charismatic leaders within each republic will be both powerful and legitimate enough to carry this off."[79]

A problem for Migranyan was that "a properly sequenced strategy of transition" was missing. As a consequence of democratization preceding a market economy, centrifugal forces had been released that lacked "institutionalized forms of conflict resolution into which to channel their demands." The result had been "a collapse of governmental authority throughout the country"—hence the very practical need for strong leadership.[80]

Against this view were those who considered strong leadership crucial in the battle against a market economy. Boris Kurashvili, head of the Political Research Department of the Institute of State and Law, argued in May 1991 that "only a firm authoritarian power can clothe and feed the people. Only it can organize production and save the country." Modernizers, using the CPSU as their base, should "resist the privatizers." Indeed, "the privatization of social property is a grandiose social venture," and "time is working against it." The Communist Party had a vital role to play since "not one serious party representing real forces exists, not even Travkin's party." In this context, ideas about a government of people's trust had no foundation and would be a "step toward an anti-people's government" and "a compromise without principle." "Roundtables" would not work. Certainly, armistices and compromises had their place, but first positions had to be clarified. Kurashvili held that "Gorbachev does not have a position. The modernizers have."[81] Kurashvili named Boris Gidaspov as one such modernizer. Kurashvili had also once had hopes for Vadim Bakatin, but he had now come out in favor of private property.[82]

Strong leadership was also the means, in Migranyan's view, to democracy and civil society; only strong leadership could build a market economy, a necessary prerequisite of democracy.[83] In Kurashvili's view, strong leadership could ultimately result in government for the people.

In a context of crisis and collapse, authoritarian means were seen as necessary for effective solutions. The solutions varied, but to many people a firm hand was the only efficient way to reach them.[84] Defenders of freedom and civil society, such as members of the Democratic Union and some supporters of Democratic Russia, viewed this conclusion with suspicion because their battles were against authoritarian solutions. Nonetheless, backing for a firm hand, albeit differently conceived, persisted during 1992.

One clash, then, in discourse about the appropriate means to achieve desired political and economic ends was between those who were convinced that authoritarianism was necessary for effective results and those who insisted that strong leadership prevented the necessary growth of civil society and thereby ruled out serious democratization. Both arguments emerged in the latter half of Gorbachev's leadership and persisted into the CIS. And just as there were diverse interpretations of what democracy entailed, so, too, there was no unanimity on what constituted civil society. Politicians and academics saw its characteristics, scope, and consequences differently.

Civil Society

Civil society was officially welcomed at the Twenty-eighth Congress in 1990. Prior to that it had not been a key concept in CPSU documents. Now an entire section of "Toward a Humane Democratic Socialism" was devoted to "civil society and legal state." The CPSU came out in favor of "the formation of a civil society in which no person exists for the sake of the state, but the state exists for the sake of the person."[85] It declared that "all social groups and communities have a guaranteed legal right and actual possibility to express and build their interests."[86] These interests would be protected by a "strengthening of a legal state, which excludes the dictatorship of any class, party, grouping, or administrative bureaucracy."[87] A legal state would be the guarantor of civil society. Abuse of power would be prevented by a separation of power among legal, administrative, and judicial functions.[88] Integral to this would be a democratic and open legislative process, a yearly accountability of the executive-administrative organs before the soviets, and an independent judiciary and procuracy.

With official party approval for civil society and a legal state, these concepts became more visible in journals such as *Kommunist* that had hitherto ignored them or, at best, had given them a low profile. Journals and papers that had already discussed these concepts, such as *Sovetskoe Gosudarstvo i Pravo* (Soviet Law and Government), *Narodnyi Deputat, Dialog* (Dialogue), and *Moskovskie Novosti,* continued to do so. Commentaries expressed various opinions about the significance of civil society.

At the end of 1990, philosopher Viktor Zotov noted that for decades social science, being dogmatic, had ignored the concepts of civil society and the legal state. But now it was possible to say that "the development of human civilization in many respects is defined by the development of civil society and a legal state."[89] In fact, "the more developed civil society is, the greater is the basis for democratic forms of the state. And, conversely, the less developed civil society is, the more likely is the existence of authoritarian and totalitarian regimes of state power."[90]

Fitting the style of *Kommunist,* Zotov traced the concept of civil society back to Karl Marx and Friedrich Engels and then went on to examine John Locke, Charles de Montesquieu, Immanuel Kant, Jean-Jacques Rousseau, V. I. Lenin, and Bogdan Kistiakovskii. Ultimately Zotov contended that autonomous civil society and the autonomous person as citizen stemmed from property relations and private property. He held that "private property is a great achievement and motor of human civilization. Without it there would not be such unique phenomena of world history as ancient Greece and Rome and the great epoch of the Renaissance."[91] These views were certainly free of past ideological restraints. Zotov also observed that present-day capitalist systems were very different from those of the past. Evidence showed "not only a legal but also a legal *social* state functioning in the conditions of society, which according to many parameters—standard and quality of life; social security (including pensions); organization of health, education, daily life, and leisure—finds itself much closer to the socialist ideal than any society calling itself socialist."[92] These words would never have passed the censor in the not-so-distant Soviet past. Zotov's article redefined the significance of property and shed old categories. He championed private property as an achievement that would bring higher standards of living and without which civil society and democracy would be impossible. Moreover, he delivered the message that capitalist systems had attained more humane results than socialist ones. Most amazing was that these arguments were found in *Kommunist* rather than in *Kommersant*.

Zotov concluded on the powerful note that "historical experience has shown that without a separation of powers, there is a usurpation of power."[93] Gorbachev's subsequent concentration of executive power, in the eyes of radical reformers, seemed to fit this bill.

Parties and Citizenship

Newspapers and pamphlets produced by some of the new political parties referred to civil society or indicated a sense of citizenship, whereas others did not use the term. The notion of active citizenship was generally missing from declarations and policy statements of right-wing parties and groups such as the RKP, Pamiat, patriots, monarchists, and the United Labor Front. Implicitly, the citizen was there to benefit from the wisdom of the state and its leaders, not to exert pressure on the state. The citizen was recipient, not instigator; subject, not citizen. The extreme form of this argument was expressed by supporters of czarism. According to *Tsar' Kolokol"*, czarist power guaranteed the direction and order of numerous peoples in one political body, which was ordained by God.[94] No discussion was devoted to the rights of individuals since they should be collectively cared for by an all-powerful autocrat who knew best. Members of Pamiat did talk of rights but generally of the collective rights of Russians rather than individual civil rights. Indeed, their anti-Semitism made them opponents of minority rights, rights that civil society should protect. The RKP and the United Labor Front were keen to defend workers' rights within a socialist state but certainly not "bourgeois" rights of an individualistic kind, as championed by ideologically unsound and morally lax capitalist societies.

By contrast, in its "Theses Toward a Program of Practical Activity," published in July 1989, the Inter-Regional Group of the Congress of People's Deputies took pains to itemize the rights its members felt citizens should be guaranteed.[95] The concepts of citizen and rights were closely twinned. Item three of the thesis on "Reform of the Political System," for example, declared that citizens should enjoy the "right and opportunity" freely to form social and socio-political professional and youth organizations. Implying the right of citizens to demonstrate and to strike, item four of the same thesis called for legal definitions of how strikes should be conducted and for analysis of "the mutual responsibility of citizens and state in mass actions."[96] The "Thesis on the Right to Receive and Disseminate Information" elaborated further rights. Discussion of what constituted civil society, however, was missing. That was left mainly to academic tracts and was not dwelt on in most political programs. Likewise, the theses of the Democratic Party of Russia focused on general aims and goals rather than on conceptual definitions.[97] (But then this is what one would expect of political programs.) And neither the theses of the Inter-Regional Group nor those of the DPR even used the term *civil society*. They specified desired rights but did not define what civil society was.

The Democratic Union was again the exception. In more philosophical tracts published in *Svobodnoe Slovo* and *Uchreditel'noe Sobranie*, members emphasized the importance of building a civil society. Valeriia Novodvorskaia argued that political and economic pluralism, her party's main goal, required a civil society and would not be achieved "through dictatorship." The aim of the Democratic Union, then, was to construct "the parallel structures of a civil society" within a totalitarian society. Through "civil protest" and "civil disobedience" this minority opposition party would sow the seeds of civil society and undermine totalitarianism.[98] Novodvorskaia insisted that "serious theoretical reformism is based on the very ideals of civil society and civil disobedience. Even parliamentary democracy in the West is based, not on social submission, but on ever readiness for rebellion. Civil society is on eternal guard and cannot disarm internally; otherwise state power would attack civil rights."[99] Civil society was essential for humanism, democracy, and freedom.

From the outset, the Democratic Union saw its own existence as "a necessary step toward the formation of the political infrastructure of civil society."[100] In the "transition period from totalitarianism to democracy, to political, economic, and moral pluralism—toward a society of free citizens in a free country," the Democratic Union was committed to propagating alternative values to those of the CPSU.[101] As a result, it was hoped that society would be enlightened and exert pressure on the state. The Democratic Union's tiny membership, estimated at one thousand in 1990, meant that the organization was not a political force destined to fulfill its own aim of being a serious opposition party to the CPSU.[102] Nonetheless, its members embraced concepts that many other reformers had yet to adopt. They were ahead of others in their ideas, definitions, and linkages across concepts. Only two years later did similar arguments begin to appear in journals such as *Sotsial'no-politicheskie Nauki* (Socio-political Sciences).[103] Not until 1991 did reformers begin to refer to civil society as essential to civil rights and an end to ideological monopoly. But some had a sounder grasp of the term, now a new politically correct buzzword, than others did.

Preconditions for and Consequences of Civil Society

Interviews I conducted with academics at the Institute of State and Law in 1990 produced several illuminating views and comments on the definition of and the practical steps needed to build civil society.[104] According to one lawyer, "Privatization of the economy is a precondition for civil society." Without the former, citizens could not enjoy, or understand, what a civil society was. Another insisted that a legal state needed a civil society in which to flower and therefore would not exist until civil society did. The best way to establish the latter was through political parties and the electoral mechanism. The pace of constructing civil society, however, would vary across the country. Central Asia, for instance, lacked many parties, enjoyed only limited political space, and had "a lower level of political culture." Only three trends in politics could be identified: communist, social democratic, and Muslim. Elsewhere, greater political variety indicated a richer political culture.

A third lawyer considered that civil society had begun to develop in 1988 but that citizens did not yet "feel" their citizenship. Rather, they experienced an awareness of being part of a society against the state. In turn, members of the state feared society's aggression toward the state and accentuated the conflict through their reactions. This accentuation then further contributed to the growth of civil society since citizens felt obliged to press their rights more forcefully. Nonetheless, this lawyer believed that civil society would develop slowly for several reasons: lack of an appropriate political culture, lack of knowledge about political procedure, an apparat that manipulated the system, and lack of defense for minority rights.

A fourth lawyer commented, "We have only recently understood what civil society is." It amounted to a society of free individuals in which, above all, "the state must defend civil society and not the other way round." Like other lawyers, he stressed that the development of civil society would take a long time but would be faster in the Baltic states than in Central Asia, where local leaders were like "sultans." In fact, many systems existed with different kinds of citizenship and with different stages of civil society; Voronezh, in Russia, for example, had one sort, and free economic zones would develop a different kind. The paths to civil society were democratization and the market, and a separation of powers and independent judges were essential. But, above all, fear should not pervade the system. "Levels" of civil society would emerge over time. A state of law (*gosudarstvo prava*), for instance, was not the same as a more developed legal state (*pravovoe gosudarstvo*). A state could legislate rights but not necessarily guarantee them. A more distant goal was a legal society (*pravovoe obshchestvo*), which would be a society guided by law.

On the same topic, a political scientist observed that "state socialism" had meant "citizenship *under* the state." So only through genuine elections could citizens be tied *to* the state. Only when the state represented the interests of citizens would society no longer be slave to the state. Another specialist in politics commented that in 1990 citizens were still prisoners of the state. The level of welfare guarantees was minimal, the state exerted pressure on individuals, and individual thought was constrained. Genuine citizenship should be active and lively and suffer less pressure than before. But civil society did not yet exist. The paths to it were de-statism and a division of power. The CPSU was so closely connected to the state that it was hard for academic analysis to talk of a civil society; in short, the party held on to the state. Not until one was separated from the other could civil society begin to grow. Stalin's terror had flattened interest groups. In civil society, a balancing of interests would take place. But prior to that, people had to know and define what their interests were. Economic freedom and equal rights to property were also necessary components of civil society. And, finally, many parties of different types were necessary. However, in 1990 these were "theatrical." Civil society required political pluralism, which this political scientist defined as an institutionalization of different interests. An end to Article 6 had been the first step. Next should come the protection of the minority from the tyranny of the majority. Then would follow a consensual model of democracy within a multi-party system. But until parties were institutionalized, civil society would not flower.

Here the worries of academics and the democratic deputies discussed in the next chapter coincided. Some deputies stressed that democratization would not be attainable until new parties matured and stabilized. This hinged to a large extent on elected representatives learning how to be democratic (how to practice democracy) and on the political system adopting more precise rules and divisions of function between institutions. The mechanisms of democracy had to be conceived, defined, learned, accepted, and implemented. Academics underscored that civil society, too, needed political parties to defend its different interests in political arenas. But at the same time, parties needed civil society to grow before such interests could be identified, formulated, articulated, and pressed. The development of each needed the other; but both were wanting. In turn, they were linked to private property and to a legal state. These different strands were organically inter-related. If one was missing, democratization would suffer.

Thus, the dilemma in mid-1991, according to many politicians and theorists, was that political parties needed civil society and civil society needed parties; both, however, were in embryonic forms. Moreover, both needed a democratization of political structures to flourish, yet both were part of the process of democratization.

State, Citizen, and Representation

Discourse on democracy and citizenship from 1987 to 1991 represented a radical break from the past. Official conceptions of the Soviet state, citizenship, and representation had remained largely static from the 1930s to the late 1980s. Admittedly, Khrushchev's attempt to de-Stalinize politics and society resulted in a fresh emphasis on democratization and social organizations.[105] Consistent with Marxist theory, the people were again invited to participate in the administration of their own affairs, albeit to a very limited degree. Stalin's totalitarian edifice was finally questioned, and the painful and halting transition into a less arbitrary authoritarianism was begun.[106] Under Brezhnev, new theoretical energy was devoted to unpacking what a "developed socialist society" meant for the state. At last, "non-antagonistic contradictions" or "problems" were acknowledged.[107] Soviet developed socialism suffered difficulties and imperfections. These had to be exposed and solved before communism could be reached.

But despite significant differences between the Stalin, Khrushchev, and Brezhnev years, and despite different phases within each leadership, the general nature of the relationship between state and society, between government and citizen, between law and subject, was fundamentally the same. A one-party state had since 1917 and 1918 outlawed other political parties. Since 1921, factionalism had been banned within that one party, thereby rigidifying the process of policy definition from above, institutionalizing the notion of a correct line, and making criticism of party policy ideologically difficult and costly. A secret police had since 1917 existed to defend the revolution against so-called counter-revolutionaries. Although terror, purges, and bloodshed were significantly different in the 1930s from other periods of Soviet history in both scale and arbitrariness, the instruments of repression were nevertheless always intact, further reinforcing "appropriate" conformist behavior in public arenas. The secret police may have been downgraded to a state committee under Khrushchev and in 1990 put under the supervision of Gorbachev's Presidential Council, but it was not abolished. Even after August 1991, citizens complained that the security service made its presence felt in unwelcome ways. As one deputy of the Mossovet whispered to me in an interview in October 1991, "Note that the KGB has been seized by the new leaders, but in many respects it has not radically changed. There are some rooms in this building where we know we are heard."[108]

Similarly, the lack of legal protection for individual rights has plagued citizens for the entire history of the Soviet state (previously, too, for centuries under czarism). No wonder feelings of vulnerability, fear, and paranoia have been common in the USSR and persisted until the decimation of the CPSU, particularly among the older generation. Even after August 1991, genuine anxieties about the reemergence of communist forces and about the power of secret services were reiterated. Speaking out in public, contesting official lines, and taking initiative had always been hard in a system with a KGB department in the workplace, informers in all organizations, and a politically controlled legal system. Lack of the rule of law and the insidious mental effect that concepts such as "enemy of the people" had in this political and legal context resulted in a citizenry that for decades was unable to become genuinely active. The paradox of Soviet citizenship was that citizens had extremely confined political and legal space in which to assume responsibilities or extract rights. More appropriately termed *subjects,* they were disciplined at school and in political meetings in the workplace to repeat appropriate political lines, even if the lines contradicted what had been said yesterday. The media reinforced political socialization even among citizens who sneered at obvious manipulations.

The "political" as an independent activity emanating from civil society and exerting pressure on the state was generally absent, notwithstanding sporadic protests, strikes, and citizens' mandates extracted in election campaigns. Political space for citizenship to challenge, negotiate, and contest in political arenas was extremely cramped. Citizens could, and did, put pressure on the state, but the channels open to them were limited, and there were no routine institutional possibilities for extensive political activity independent of initiatives from above. Citizenship as *activity* was wanting.[109]

Thus, fresh ideas about democracy and civil society that emerged in the Gorbachev years were potentially of immense practical importance. Reassessments of the relationship between citizen and state, society and government, executive and legislative, legal system and security service, questioned the prevailing system and prompted reflection on how the USSR should and could be run. The confined public discourse of the past visibly widened.

But by the end of 1990, many of those politicized and mobilized through Gorbachev's reforms believed that Gorbachev's commitment to democracy as they understood it was lukewarm. Gorbachev's enthusiasm for glasnost had diluted, and his circumspection about emergent political parties was evident. Intervention by Soviet troops in Lithuania in January 1991 confirmed these suspicions, even though a cloud of doubt hung over how the final decision to send troops was made. Precisely how Gorbachev had been involved

In 1991, it was in vogue to reprint occasional cartoons from Western newspapers. Taken from *The International Herald Tribune,* this representation nicely captures Gorbachev's diminished political status upon returning from the Crimea after the coup of August 1991 failed. SOURCE: *Pravda,* 31 August 1991, p. 4.

was unclear. As one cautious lawyer warned in an interview with me in Moscow in 1991, "We should not guess about the decision to go into Lithuania without adequate information." Sources close to the Kremlin believed that Gorbachev's hands had been tied on this and other issues. Many radicals were nevertheless impatient for "more democracy." And Gorbachev, like those to his right, was still talking of "more socialism."

Yet Gorbachev's discourse on democracy had not been static; it had been molded over time by a complex of factors, often pushed along by political forces that he unwittingly unleashed. Pressures could enhance his reforming tendencies, as in 1986, 1987, and 1988, or turn them back, as in late 1990 and early 1991. And although on 23 August, to a critical Russian parliament, Gorbachev defended socialism and the CPSU, the next day he acquiesced in dismantling its labyrinthine structure. A new era in post-Soviet politics had begun, and Gorbachev was chasing other people's agendas, which had left him far behind.

Conclusion

New definitions of such concepts as democracy, and redefined relationships between the concepts of democracy, property, and civil society carry the potential of influencing, shaping, and directing practice, but only if enough people in power can agree on the raison d'être of new arrangements, only if critics are too weak to oppose or undermine them, and only if broader circumstances and structures are such that their implementation is possible. Fresh conceptualizations and new theoretical approaches to the state can ultimately affect the running of the entire political system and therefore carry implications for political rights, duties, and responsibilities.

But fresh conceptions do not automatically lead to new practices. Durable and deeply ingrained mechanisms, procedures, political styles, and attitudes do not alter just because theoreticians, lawyers, policymakers, and politicians have new thoughts and alternative proposals. Even when attempts to modify old structures begin, old ways can distort, qualify, or redirect new intentions away from the designs of the instigators and the hopes of well-wishers.[110] And set in the broader historical context of growing political chaos in government and administration and of instability in relations between center and republics, many reflections on democracy, civil society, a legal state, and separation of powers can seem distant from the turbulence of reality. Before the August coup, elements of discourse increasingly appeared to be taking on the character of exotic reflections about the impossible.

NOTES

1. Treatment of Stalinism is not discussed here since it has been explored elsewhere. See R. W. Davies, *Soviet History in the Gorbachev Revolution* (London, Macmillan, 1989), pp 58–114; Alec Nove, *Glasnost' in Action: Cultural Renaissance in Russia* (Boston, Unwin Hyman, 1989), pp. 15–102.

2. For a general discussion of the term *democracy,* see David Held, "Democracy, the nation-state and the global system," in David Held, ed., *Political Theory Today* (Cambridge, Polity, 1991), pp. 197–235.

3. The right to secede was enshrined in the constitution. A useful source for the 1936 and 1977 constitutions is S. E. Finer, *Five Constitutions* (Harmondsworth, Penguin, 1979), pp. 117–194.

4. *Materialy XXVII S"ezda KPSS* (Moscow, Politizdat, 1986), pp. 33–97, 343–348.

5. Ibid., pp. 54–62.

6. Ibid., p. 54.

7. Ibid., pp. 54–55.

8. Ibid., p. 57.

9. Ibid., pp. 60–61.

10. Ibid., p. 61.

11. Ibid., p. 62.

12. Anders Aslund, *Gorbachev's Struggle for Economic Reform,* 2d ed. (London, Pinter, 1991), pp. 127–129.

13. Institut Marksizma-Leninizma pri TsK KPSS, *M. S. Gorbachev: Izbrannye Rechi i Stat'i,* vol. 4 (Moscow, Politizdat, 1987), p. 321.

14. J. Hahn, "An experiment in competition: The 1987 elections to the local soviets," *Slavic Review,* vol. 47, no. 3, Fall 1988, pp. 434–447.

15. Institut Marksizma-Leninizma, *M. S. Gorbachev,* p. 317.

16. Ibid., p. 320.

17. Ibid., pp. 346–347.

18. Institut Marksizma-Leninizma pri TsK KPSS, *M. S. Gorbachev: Izbrannye Rechi i Stat'i,* vol. 6 (Moscow: Politizdat, 1989), p. 399.

19. Ibid., p. 401.

20. Ibid.

21. Interview conducted in Moscow, April 1991.

22. Institut Marksizma-Leninizma pri TsK KPSS, *M. S. Gorbachev: Izbrannye Rechi i Stat'i,* vol. 7 (Moscow: Politizdat, 1990), p. 153.

23. Ibid., p. 297.

24. *Materialy XXVIII S"ezda KPSS* (Moscow, Politizdat, 1990), p. 4.

25. Ibid.

26. *Demokraticheskaia Rossiia,* no. 1, 1990, supplement.

27. Ibid.

28. These drew together the Moscow Popular Front, Memorial, the Social Democratic Club, Communists for Perestroika, and others. See Geoffrey Hosking, *The Awakening of the Soviet Union* (London, Mandarin, 1991), pp. 172–173. Further details are provided in Peter Duncan, "The Democratic Russia Movement," (Paper delivered at the annual conference of BASSEES, University of Birmingham, 28–30 March 1992).

29. The Inter-Regional Group printed its own newspaper, *Narodnyi Deputat,* which was distinct from the journal of the same name. The latter described itself as "a socio-political, problem-information journal of the Supreme Soviet of the USSR." In 1992, it dropped "the Supreme Soviet of the USSR."

30. *Demokraticheskaia Rossiia,* no. 1, 1990, supplement.

31. *Liberal,* nos. 2–3, November 1990, p. 3.

32. Ibid.

33. RFE/RL Research Institute, *Report on the USSR,* vol. 3, no. 36, 6 September 1991, p. 71. The party was banned on 23 August.

34. Information relayed by the Perspective Cooperative, Moscow, March 1989. Social scientists working in the cooperative were compiling an archive of informal newspapers.

35. Sergei Ivanenko, "Chem zanimat'sia, esli ne krichat' na mitingakh," *Moskovskie Novosti,* no. 50, 16 December 1990, p. 6.

36. The most detailed discussion of the Democratic Union is provided by I. P. Vasil'eva, "Demokraticheskii Soiuz v usloviakh mnogopartiinosti: Raskol ili razmezhevanie?" *Sotsial'no-politicheskie Nauki,* no. 2, 1991, pp. 117–126.

37. Demokraticheskii Soiuz, *Paket Dokumentov* (Moscow, 9 May 1988), p. 6.

38. *Svobodnoe Slovo,* 16 April 1991, p. 5.

39. Ibid.

40. Ibid., p. 6.

41. "Za ob"edinenie sil demokratii i reform," *Izvestiia,* 2 July 1991, p. 1.

42. Ibid.

43. Aleksandr Yakovlev, "Nyzhen novyi shag," *Izvestiia,* 2 July 1991, p. 2. For Shevardnadze's understanding of the situation in December 1990, see his *Moi Vybor: V Zashchitu Demokratii i Svobody* (Moscow, Novosti, 1991), pp. 237–331.

44. Conversations in Moscow, August 1991.

45. Information gathered from members of Demokraticheskaia Rossiia, Moscow, September–October 1991.

46. RFE/RL Research Institute, *Report on the USSR,* vol. 3, no. 40, 4 October 1991, p. 30.

47. "Net khuda bez dobra," *Moskovskie Novosti,* no. 29, 22 July 1990, p. 5.

48. V. A. Bobkov, *Vozrozhdenie Dukha Leninizma* (Moscow, Politizdat, 1989), p. 319.

49. Ibid., p. 344.

50. Ibid., p. 325.

51. E. K. Ligachev, *Izbrannye Rechi i Stat'i* (Moscow, Politizdat, 1989), p. 292.

52. Ibid., p. 225.

53. Ibid., p. 281.

54. Nina Andreeva, "Ne mogy postupat'sia printsipami," *Sovetskaia Rossiia,* 13 March 1988, p. 3.

55. For further details, see John Gooding, "The XXVIII congress of the CPSU in perspective," *Soviet Studies,* vol. 43, no. 2, 1991, pp. 237–254.

56. *Volia,* no. 2, March 1991, p. 1. This is a different *Volia* from the one put out by anarchists. In the nineteenth century, *volia* meant "liberty." Its contemporary meaning is "will."

57. Ibid.

58. Ibid., p. 3.

59. Ibid.

60. *Chto Delat'?* no. 8, 1991, p. 1.

61. Ibid.

62. Ibid., p. 2. Here "democratic" is shortened to "dem." In Russian, the pattern of shortening words and running them together with others is common.

63. *Interdvizhenie Litvy,* no. 7, June 1991, p. 1.

64. Ibid., p. 3.

65. *Pravda,* 28 October 1991, p. 1.

66. Ibid.

67. The congress drew 164 delegates from eighteen regions. See *Soviet Weekly,* 21 November 1991, p. 2.

68. Its founding congress was attended by five hundred delegates. See *Moskovskie Novosti,* no. 48, 1 December 1991, p. 9. New figures involved were General Al'bert Makashev and Professor Aleksei Sergeev.

69. *Chernoe Znamia,* no. 4, 1990, p. 1.

70. Ibid.

71. Ibid.

72. Ibid.

73. *Volia,* no. 4, 1 January 1990, p. 1.

74. Ibid.

75. Ibid.

76. Ibid.

77. *Golos Anarkhizma,* no. 7, 1991, p. 1.

78. Andranik Migranyan, "Gorbachev's leadership: A Soviet view," *Soviet Economy,* vol. 6, April-June 1990, p. 159.

79. Ibid.

80. Ibid., p. 156. See also his "Na puti k grazhdanskomu obshchestvu," *Sovetskaia Kul'tura,* 7 October 1989, p. 4; "Dol'giy put' k evropeiskomu domu," *Novyi Mir,* no. 7, July 1989, pp. 166–184; "Grazhdanskoe obshchestvo," in Iurii Afanasyev and Marc Ferro, eds., *50/50: Opyt Slovaria Novogo Myshleniia* (Moscow, Progress, 1989), pp. 446–448.

81. *Ruskii Kur'er,* May 1991, p. 5.

82. For details about Gidaspov, see footnote 125, Chapter 5. Vadim Bakatin was regional party secretary in Kirov from 1985 to 1987 and then in Kemerovo until 1988, when he became minister of internal affairs. In March 1990, he became a member of Gorbachev's shortlived Presidential Council. See Archie Brown, ed., *The Soviet Union: A Biographical Dictionary* (London, Weidenfeld and Nicolson, 1990), p. 25.

83. Migranyan, "Grazhdanskoe obshchestvo."

84. Throughout 1992, arguments about the need for a strong leader continued, particularly in debates about the new Russian constitution. For alternative versions see *Federatsiia,* nos. 14–15, 1992, pp. 9–24.

85. *Materialy XXVIII S"ezda KPSS,* p. 88.

86. Ibid.

87. Ibid., p. 89.

88. Ibid.

89. Viktor Zotov, "Grazhdanskoe obshchestvo i pravovoe gosudarstvo—pokazateli tsivilizovannosti," *Kommunist,* no. 17, November 1990, pp. 20–30.

90. Ibid., p. 22.

91. Ibid., pp. 23–24.

92. Ibid., p. 25.

93. Ibid., p. 29.

94. *Tsar' Kolokol"* (Moscow), no. 7, 1990, p. 2.

95. *Narodnyi Deputat,* no. 34, 28 July 1989, p. 2.

96. Ibid.

97. *Demokraticheskaia Rossiia,* no. 1, 1990, supplement.

98. *Svobodnoe Slovo,* 8 August 1989, p. 2.

99. Ibid.

100. Vasil'eva, "Demokraticheski Soiuz," p. 120.

101. Ibid.

102. Ibid., p. 117. Apparently this membership extended to more than 150 towns. Thirty percent of members were workers, 23 percent were employees, 20 percent were students, and 2 percent were peasants. The average age was thirty.

103. V. G. Smol'kov, "Problemy formirovaniia grazhdanskogo obshchestva," *Sotsial'no-politicheskie Nauki,* no. 4, 1991, pp. 9–16.

104. Interviews conducted at the Institute of State and Law, Moscow, September 1990.

105. For discussion of increased political participation under Khrushchev, refer to Jerry F. Hough and Merle Fainsod, eds., *How the Soviet Union Is Governed* (Cambridge, Mass., Harvard University Press, 1982), pp. 222–236; Roy Medvedev, *Khrushchev* (Oxford, Basil Blackwell, 1982), pp. 83–103, 207–222; T. H. Friedgut, *Political Participation in the USSR* (Princeton, Princeton University Press, 1979).

106. Scholarship has questioned the extent of totalitarian discipline under Stalin. Seweryn Bialer, for example, made a convincing case for different phases of Stalinism. See his *Stalin's Successors* (Cambridge, Cambridge University Press, 1980). Other scholars have provided evidence on chaos in the party: Merle Fainsod, *Smolensk Under Soviet Rule* (Boston, Unwin Hyman, 1989); J. Arch Getty, *Origins of the Great Purges* (Cambridge, Cambridge University Press, 1985); Lewis Siegelbaum, *Stakhanovism and the Politics of Productivity in the USSR, 1935–1941* (Cambridge, Cambridge University Press, 1988).

107. Alfred B. Evans, Jr., "Developed socialism in Soviet ideology," *Soviet Studies,* vol. 29, no. 3, 1977, pp. 409–428.

108. Interview in the Moscow City Soviet, October 1991.

109. Bernard Crick, *In Defence of Politics* (Harmondsworth, Penguin, 1964); T. H. Marshall, *Class, Citizenship and Social Development* (Garden City, N.Y., Doubleday, 1964); Sheldon S. Wolin, *Politics and Vision* (Boston, Little, Brown, 1960).

110. Peter Solomon made the amusing observation that one result was a *demokratizatsiia po nashemy* (democratization in our own way), Akademicheskaia Hotel, Moscow, May 1991.

7

Learning Democracy

They say that democracy is like a giraffe. Once you have seen it, you never forget it.

—A. Dobrynin
Soglasie, 1989

SINCE LATE 1989, analytic thinkers among reformers had been linking the fate of democratization to the development of civil society. To many people's deputies and journalists, however, these reflections were academic, distant from the daily world of politics. Scrutiny of the reformed soviets, putatively the most "democratic" institutions to date, revealed numerous problems. Many deputies readily volunteered that the soviets did not operate democratically and that serious barriers to successful democratization existed. Their assessments were tightly linked to surrounding practices.

Thus, discourse about democratization operated at two levels. One dwelt on theoretical considerations, and the second analyzed practical hurdles. But reflections were not always so neatly divided since theoretical concerns often affected how practice was viewed, and the actual running of the soviets stimulated further theoretical questions.

This chapter surveys prominent views held by people's deputies, journalists, and lawyers about the relevance of the soviets to democratization. By 1990, the nature of the soviets had become a crucial issue for those committed to political change. According to one perspective, the only realistic route to modification of the political system was through the soviets. Socialism could best be improved by creating genuine, competitively elected legislatures that represented the people. A second perspective held that changes in the soviets could lead to far-reaching transformations, including the establishment of parliamentary democracy. Underpinning both views was the conviction that how the soviets operated affected possibilities for democratization and the forms it might take.

The role of the soviets was also relevant to redefinitions of authority, power, and legitimacy. Successful democratization, stressed those adhering to the second perspective, required significantly more power for the soviets. A key political issue concerned not only how the soviets worked now but also how much better they might function if the relationship between executive and legislative powers shifted radically in their favor. Another vital aspect of democratization was whether deputies' groups and factions could operate as embryonic political parties and lead to a party system.

In the past, Sovietologists' access to politicians was effectively denied. A scholar without connections relied on written texts and speeches for material, not on interviews. "Consultations" with Soviet academics were possible, but even those during the Brezhnev era were not problem-free. And some difficulties persisted under Gorbachev. But democratization made access easier than before, especially after the historic election year of 1989; and glasnost meant that answers were less tightly constrained by official lines or by the deeply ingrained practice of whitewashing reality so as not to paint an unpatriotic picture before foreigners.

This book does not pretend to offer a random sample of deputies within or across soviets. That luxury was not available to me. It draws heavily on intensive interviews in a local soviet and in the Moscow City Soviet, access to which I felt privileged to be granted. Despite the relatively small number of deputies involved, I consider their perceptions an important part of the historical record.[1] They contribute to an understanding of how those involved in democratization assessed its problems, often in terms that Western analysts may not have anticipated or through prisms that they may not use. Since the interviews took place in the capital, the interpretations given here are Moscow-centric, although many of the difficulties named were common elsewhere. Material is inductively organized according to the themes and concerns given prominence by deputies and journalists in interviews and in the press. The purpose is to stay as close as possible to their categories, perceptions, and judgments.

Ideas and Context: Practical Problems for Democracy

For those with ideological objections to democratization, such as the Leninists discussed in the previous chapter, numerous developments and events, particularly between 1989 and August 1991, reinforced their conviction that it should be opposed. They disagreed with its principles and now deplored its results. The negative consequences of democratization included political chaos in the soviets, disorder in the republics, civil war in the Caucasus, and breakdowns in economic distribution. The drift toward bourgeois democracy and a market economy had already brought growing inequalities between rich and poor, horrendous price increases, and unemployment. Bolder commitment in 1991 to a future market economy heralded greater injustice, further inequalities, and general immorality.

Democrats, by contrast, supported many of the changes but were also un-happy about certain consequences of political reform. By 1990, it was clear to most political actors that the process of democratization was fraught with hazards. There was a loose consensus in early 1991 that chaos prevailed in politics. The symptoms were several and variously interpreted. Some poured scorn on the Congress of People's Deputies for achieving very little apart from empty talk and a strengthening of presidential power at the expense of its own. Others highlighted procedural difficulties, such as the impossibility of making decisions without a quorum. Observers of the new parties em-phasized how weak, inexperienced, and impecunious they were, all of which made the establishment of a multi-party system difficult. Some viewed these and other problems as temporary, as the inevitable teething troubles and growing pains of democracy in a transition period. Others wondered how long term they might be; perhaps they were deeply embedded in a Russian political culture that militated against democracy and that craved a firm hand from above. Personality clashes, personal rivalries, and political ambi-tions muddied the waters further. Factions within parties, splits, regroup-ings, and personal abuse were among the consequences.

A Weak Congress of People's Deputies

Against Gorbachev, critics to his left produced alternative views such as "Democratization is not democracy; glasnost is not yet freedom of speech; the Supreme Soviet is not yet a parliament."[2] Using this heading in June 1989, the Lithuanian paper *Soglasie* noted agreement with Andrei Sakharov that "the Congress gave practically nothing insofar as it did not change the essence of the system and only strengthened the personal power of the presi-dent."[3] At best, it exposed all the pressing problems that "lacerated" the multinational state and also showed voters a little of the "true face of the in-fluential conservative majority."[4] In more passionate words, Sakharov told the Congress of People's Deputies, "The Congress cannot suddenly feed the country. It cannot immediately solve national problems. It cannot immedi-ately liquidate the budget deficit. It cannot give us clean air, water, and for-ests at once. But it is obliged to create the political guarantees for solving these problems. It is precisely this that the country is expecting from us. All power to the Soviets!"[5]

A "key political task" for Sakharov was the delineation of powers. The Congress of People's Deputies had to seize the initiative immediately in keeping with "the great historical responsibility" before deputies.[6] "If the Congress of People's Deputies cannot take power into its hands here," warned Sakharov, "then there is not the tiniest hope that the Soviets in the republics, oblasts, *raions,* and rural areas can do it."[7] Unless the power of the soviets was strengthened, economic, social, ecological, and nationality problems would not be solved. Unless soviets in rural areas became powerful, land reform could not proceed. The key to the Soviet future, said Sakharov, lay with the soviets.[8] But the Congress of People's Deputies hesitated to give soviets sufficient power. By implication, democracy would not result and reform would flounder.

Two years later, deputies at all levels, but particularly at the local level, were complaining that their work was hindered since a division of responsibilities across different levels of soviet had not been demarcated. Thus, democracy could not easily function until "spheres of competence" (*sferii kompetentnostei*) were clear.

Imprecise Powers

While Sakharov and others discussed the importance of legislative power to democracy and the need to delineate the relationship between executive and legislative power, other critics focused on the need to define more precisely the relationship across soviets at different levels of government. In particular, the need for clarification about the division of functions was felt acutely at all levels.

Republican Supreme Soviets, for instance, existed in what Oleg Bogomolov dubbed the "time of half-power."[9] Bogomolov argued that many of the problems being experienced by the Russian parliament stemmed "from the fact that its real power has been limited by the center on the basis of the Constitution now in force and several other laws and acts of the All-Union authorities." Thus, sovereignty was still a myth. This problem was compounded within Russia because parliament took "no part in important decisions" and did not control the whole of Russia's territory; "actual power ha[d] never gone from the party and state-bureaucratic apparat to democratic forces."[10] Ol'ga Bychkova similarly argued that Russia's declaration of sovereignty, adopted almost unanimously by the parliament on 12 June 1990, "marked the formal start of the 'war of laws' between the republic and the center."[11]

Since all fifteen republican parliaments declared sovereignty between September 1989 and November 1990, tensions between the All-Union Supreme Soviet and republican soviets were destined to intensify in the absence of legal clarifications and appropriate changes in political institutions.[12] What happened, in fact, was that republican Supreme Soviets asserted their authority against the center. Increasingly, they gave themselves powers to control economic policy and financial matters. A sufficient proportion of their populations, notwithstanding ethnic divides, viewed assumed expanded powers as legitimate since Supreme Soviets had been elected by the people.[13]

At the local level, too, clarity about political functions was needed. In discussions in April and May 1991 with deputies from Krasnopresnenskii *raion* and from the Mossovet, many complained that their responsibilities were not clearly defined in relation to the level above. Deputies in Krasnopresnenskii *raion* seemed to feel this more acutely than deputies in the Mossovet. As one deputy declared, "Our main problem is that not one law defines each level of competence. And laws are not implemented because of this. Everyone must know for what they are answerable." One result was a war of laws, which was exacerbated by the lack of a "legal culture."[14]

Aleksandr Krasnov, chair of the *raisovet* (district soviet), agreed that imprecise functions in 1991 were one of the central difficulties suffered by all districts. Without defined spheres of responsibility, work was difficult. In response to this problem, deputies from the local districts had formed an interdistrict council (*mezhraiony sovet*) where they came together to make collective decisions about how to respond to their undefined predicament. Krasnov revealed that "we talk a lot to districts in Leningrad and maintain close ties with them. They are in the same situation."[15] It seemed, however, that until legislation specified how powers were to be divided between districts and city, the districts would flounder in many policy areas. Evidence indicated that in many soviets deputies felt that they worked in institutions without power.

Claims on property provide a clear example of the problem. According to another deputy, "We want to take over several empty buildings in our *raion*. I am concerned about two in particular on Herzen Street. We sent a letter to the Mossovet but have been waiting a long time for an answer. Popov does not want to decide quickly. He is always like this."[16] She concluded that "the *raisovet* has achieved little so far because the roles of the city and the district have not yet been defined." Competition between city soviets and local soviets for the control of property was common in 1990 and 1991 and became increasingly intense because property was still subject to public control and deputies to a certain extent assessed their political clout by the amount of property for which they were responsible.

A firmly held view was that a delineation of functions was not just desirable but before long would be imperative. In the words of a deputy chair of the *raisovet*:

> Higher levels do not wish to give to lower levels. But we have already agreed that we must together take a decision about our different spheres. There is agreement about the principle. We sent in our recommendations four months ago after a conference of all the districts. Popov is not against agreement. In the end, it will be easier for him. There will only be more scandals so long as this is not decided.[17]

He went on to highlight the scandal that had occurred between the Mossovet and the Ministry of Internal Affairs over who should control the militia. This dispute concerned a different division of responsibility, but the principle was the same.[18] A more positive deputy believed that, "although the spheres between district and city are not yet defined, the general paths are already clear. They just need to be specified. Recommendations have already been sent to the Mossovet. We have contacts there. This will be settled."[19]

Deputies at the district level repeatedly put developments in a time frame, insisting that the roles of different soviets were in the process of being worked out. This could not be done immediately or quickly, they said, but needed refinement as deputies came to learn what was appropriate. The process had to be protracted. Discourse on this theme was studded with analogies. One realist commented, "We have been thrown into the sea and we cannot swim. We need to learn to swim at our own pace and in our own style. We need time for understanding."[20] Another optimistic deputy suggested that "we are slowly building a normal system of power. And they can throw us out in the next elections."[21] References to a normal and civilized system were widespread in 1990 and 1991. The argument ran that economy, polity, and society were neither normal nor civilized and that attaining normality required serious change, effort, and time. Normality could not be reached instantly. If voters did not like the resultant divisions of functions across soviets, then fresh deputies could be selected. In the meantime, deputies had to confront the issue of how best to delineate powers.

Deputies on the Mossovet viewed the issue with less urgency. According to one, "Definition of spheres of competence lies in the hands of deputies. No one has stopped us from sorting this out, but we have not really started to do it. We will do it when we decide to."[22] Whereas a sorting out of respective functions was seen as crucial in the local soviet ready to take on more powers, in the Mossovet it was of a lower priority. Another deputy indicated that "a division of functions is not our main problem. It is a problem, but not a basic one. The actual composition of the soviets is more serious. We lack party-mindedness. We have been without it for so long. This is the farce of our democracy. Parties are too new. They are not solid."[23]

Deputies identified problems according to their relative weight. Most named imprecise functions as a difficulty but varied in the importance they accorded it. The view that soviets without parties could not be democratic was frequently put forward in interviews and in the press. Some deputies believed that the significance of this issue outweighed that of undefined spheres of responsibility.

An entirely different interpretation held that whatever the status of administrative divisions across soviets, industry would complicate the work of people's deputies. This factor was paramount in affecting what the soviets

"Moscow and the oblast. Who will win?" In 1990 and 1991, disagreements and battles between different administrative levels often went unresolved. A "war of laws"
existed and a lack of precise rules about local government made agreements difficult.
This newspaper, which served the area around Moscow, portrays disputes between
Moscow *oblast* and the capital. The cartoon suggests that no one can win. Efforts
will be made; but resolution will not result. This was part of the chaos, confusion,
and paralysis of local government. SOURCE: *Podmoskovnye Izvestiia*, 28 September
1991, p. 1.

could achieve and made others pale by comparison. A deputy on the Moscow oblast soviet put it like this: "The problem concerns a division not only between the structures of the soviets but also between the soviets and the productive forces. Some industries have immense power. And take the example of a director of a state farm. He will proclaim, 'Here I am the state' [*Zdes' gosudarstvo eto Ia*]."[24]

Early newspaper articles of the Gorbachev era had underscored this problem. Those in charge of farms and factories were delightfully attacked in satirical reporting about their small kingdoms, petty power, conceit, and mindless boasting. Years without glasnost, argued journalist Ali Naibov, had meant that arrogance, conceit, and swaggering had gone unchallenged.[25] Arrogance was shown when a factory director in Azerbaidzhan challenged a journalist about interviewing "his" workers in "his" factory without "his" permission. Conceit was evident when a farm director denied the same journalist access to "his" farm and reported the journalist to the district party secretary. Self-importance was inevitably a characteristic of the district party secretary, too, when he turned on the journalist: "You come to my district, without asking my permission. Imagine that I had come to visit you at home, went into your refrigerator without your permission, got some food, and began to eat. You would be offended and rightly so. So why do you offend me?"[26]

The strength of the emotional effrontery felt by the factory and farm directors at intrusion into their domains underlines just one aspect of the complex difficulties reformist deputies faced when trying to deal with managers steeped in old ways. No wonder deputies viewed many directors of industry and agriculture as unhelpful bosses who overvalued their own importance in mini-kingdoms in which they did not wish others to interfere or to undermine their bloated authority. The division of functions across different levels of the soviets mattered little when it came to battling with these impenetrable "states." Whatever the level, resistance to reform could be strong.

So discourse indicated that many deputies viewed the lack of a precise division of functions as a problem for democratization. But it was one among many problems and often not the most serious. By contrast, a minority saw positive aspects to the problem. The very lack of precision gave those at the bottom of the system the opportunity to assert themselves. A lack of rules gave space for initiative and definition. One deputy insisted that "those at the lowest level can say what they feel they can do. We must start at the bottom."[27] She believed that this was the only democratic way to proceed, whatever the ensuing conflicts. Dissenters viewed this approach as a recipe for disorder and anarchy. Their critics retaliated that "it is not anarchy. Rather, we are just beginning to understand where we are and what our many problems are."[28] So again the message was that sensitivity to problems had to be learned through a slow process, which would inevitably include confusion and some disorder. They were integral to the process of learning democracy.

Writing in *Moskovskie Novosti* in March 1991, just one month before the discussions just quoted, Popov asserted that a "crisis of local authority" existed. Consequences included disorder and a war of laws. To remedy the situation, he contended that the omnipotence of the local soviets had to be abolished, spheres of direct administration from above had to be identified, the role of representatives from the center had to be defined, and the functions of local authority had to be delineated.[29] In the same edition, Sergei Alekseev, chair of the Committee of Constitutional Oversight, questioned the expediency of local soviets and criticized the "hundreds of parliaments actively engaged in the 'war of laws and war of sovereignties' but not preoccupied with real matters." If authority was not defined, different institutions could continue "endlessly to block each other," leading to a "condition of no power."[30] Whereas many deputies in *raisovety* argued for a delineation of powers in their favor, others such as Popov and Alekseev called for legal curbs on the legislative and executive powers of district soviets.

Thus, deputies' views about divisions of administrative responsibility across local, city, and oblast soviets varied. According to one view, an absence of legal clarification reinforced chaos in policy making and policy implementation. How could a working democracy be built if deputies, as representatives of the people, were not clear about their duties? Other interpretations held that more serious political problems for democracy lay elsewhere: in weak parties, political inexperience, the lack of a democratic culture, the inability to make decisions, obstructive bosses in industry, the frequent lack of a quorum, nihilism, and anarchy. Debate about what ought to be the precise functions of the soviets, and the consequences of imprecision, continued throughout 1990 and 1991 in journals such as *Dialog, Narodnyi Deputat,* and *Sovetskoe Gosudarstvo i Pravo.*[31]

When in 1991, prior to the coup, a reorganization of Moscow into prefectures was announced, people's deputies at the local level immediately felt threatened. Krasnov convened an urgent meeting on 12 August to which all chairpersons of Moscow's local soviets were invited.[32] They debated the liquidation of the *raiispolkom* (district soviet executive committee) and the apparent usurpation of the power of elected deputies by appointed prefects. In a decree of 30 July, Yeltsin had given Popov extensive powers, to which local deputies strongly objected.[33]

The anger of local deputies about their perceived powerlessness did not abate after August 1991. In my second round of interviews with deputies in Krasnopresnenskii *raion* at the end of September 1991, Krasnov contended that "Yeltsin has made Popov into a feudal king. We are moving from democracy back to feudalism."[34] Having been elected by local constituents, many deputies in the district argued that they were there to represent the people; this was legally correct and enshrined in the constitution. Appointed prefects, whose functions these deputies were still trying to fathom from official documents that had just landed on their desks, were usurping their power. One deputy stated bluntly, "Our power has been taken away."[35] Another added, "The main question is one of legality. All we can do at the moment is discuss tactics and decide how best to oppose Popov."[36] "We are in yet another transition period," said a third.[37]

Confusion about the functions of district soviets increased in September and October 1991. One deputy despaired that deputies did not know what they were supposed to be doing now. When I pointed out that this had been a problem when I had talked to him in the spring, he looked somewhat surprised and responded, "But it is much less clear now."[38] The memory of past confusions was already blurred.

Deputies active in Democratic Russia were hoping for elections to the local soviets in November 1991.[39] They believed that this might revive the authority of the soviets in the eyes of the electorate. When Yeltsin declared that elections would not take place, critical deputies viewed this as yet another example of his authoritarianism and unconstitutional "rule by decree." More crucially, it affirmed the growing impotence of the local soviets. The imprecise functions of local soviets seemed increasingly irrelevant to deputies if they lacked any power. As one put it in March 1992, "There is no power here or anywhere. We have bedlam."[40]

In 1992, the debating chamber of the local soviet in Krasnopresnenskii district was turned into a cinema for the local community. The session was defunct. When asked why he bothered to come into the *raisovet* once a week if it had no power, one deputy responded, "We cannot leave the soviet out of fear that someone else will come along."[41] Deputies sat in their old places defending a building that for them symbolized a time of greater, but fleeting democracy. They had glimpsed the giraffe, wanted it to return, but believed that at the district level it would not.

The Rush for Sovereignty, Ungovernability, Fragmentation, and Anarchy

Enthusiasm for self-determination, sometimes fierce, right down to the district level, was one aspect of the reaction against the old system of commands from above. A consequence of this enthusiasm was that small units claimed the right to make decisions because they had been elected by the local people to make decisions on issues often without consultation and discussion with higher units. Such actions may have satisfied a yearning for local control, but they did not always result in efficient or realistic results.

Рис. А. Дорофеева

"My sovereign hut—my castle." Throughout 1990 and 1991, republics declared their sovereignty from the Union. So too, within republics, did some autonomous republics, oblasts, and even tiny districts. This cartoon satirizes the inward-looking approach to political life that resulted. The unspoken question was whether this new trend across the vast Soviet land mass was viable. How far could reactions to the old administrative command system reasonably go? SOURCE: *Argumenty i Fakty,* no. 34, August 1991, p. 1.

Critics regretted that local bosses often emerged, refusing to cooperate with others.

Political scientist Andranik Migranyan referred to this process as a form of "collapse" within republics, as a "trend toward fragmentation" that mirrored "a broader collapse of power structures throughout the country."[42] In 1990, he observed:

> Within all but the smallest territories, component units are declaring their "sovereignty." Within cities, for example, districts defy city authorities and declare "local control" over property, licensing, even airspace! In practice, this has typically meant that small units want to keep all the benefits of power while passing upward all the burdens and responsibilities of power. The result is municipal ungovernability.[43]

It was, in fact, the local soviet in Krasnopresnenskii *raion* that had declared control over its property and airspace.[44] Like Migranyan, *Moskovskie Novosti* rebuked the *raisovet* for claiming control over its land and mineral wealth as well.[45] When interviewed, deputies in this district viewed such declarations as their undisputed right, as a message to administrative levels above that they could no longer dictate what was of importance to others. Deputies in the *raisovet* looked on their policies of local control as just defiance of the command-administrative system. Deputies believed they had the authority to make such decisions because they had been elected by the local people to make decisions on their behalf. Deputies were also proud of having raised the salaries of teachers and doctors in their district and considered this to be constitutionally legitimate.[46]

In 1990 and in 1991, the Soviet press carried several examples of what Migranyan saw as "ungovernability." *Kuranty* (Chimes), the newspaper of the Mossovet, reported that "five months ago Gorno-Altai autonomous oblast left Altai Krai, declaring itself an Autonomous Soviet Socialist Republic directly subordinate to Moscow." A "sovereign war" between the oblast and the *krai* resulted, and the economy of Gorno-Altai suffered. The clear message was that declarations of sovereignty were often not thought out and produced unconstructive and harmful results. Finally, out of practical necessity Gorno-Altai entered into economic agreements with Altai *krai* and with Kemerovo and Novosibirsk oblasts.[47]

Moskovskie Novosti, too, reported the "paralysis of power" resulting from a "parade of sovereignties" at the local level. Tiumen region, for example, was "heading for disintegration." Pereslavl'-Zalesskii had announced independence from decisions made by the Iaroslav regional soviet. Moscow's October district had proclaimed itself a free economic zone.[48] The Gagauz region had declared sovereignty from Moldova.[49] And the Tatar Autonomous Republic had called itself the Sovereign Republic of Tatarstan, supported by the demonstrators' slogan "Tataria for Tatars."[50] This clamor

Рис. Н. БЕЛЕВЦЕВА.

"Sovereignty! Sovereignty!" In 1991, inventive cartoonists became preoccupied with the implications of declarations of sovereignty. One suggestion was that new sovereign parts actually needed each other more than they realized because their functioning was interlinked. Breaking off and heading in different directions could bring unworkable results and was stubbornly shortsighted. SOURCE: *Izvestiia,* 7 January 1991, p. 1.

for sovereignty did not cease after August 1991. In November, Chechen-Ingushia declared independence, followed in March by Tatarstan through referendum.[51]

Other critics of fragmentation expressed the fear that excessive democratization led to anarchy. Such an anxiety (noted in the previous chapter) had deep roots in Russian political culture. Perhaps for this reason, many preferred to use the concept of anarchy rather than Migranyan's more modern ungovernability. P. Osipov, for example, a deputy in the USSR Supreme Soviet, regretted that his autonomous republic, Iakutiia, had proclaimed sovereignty. "I am against excessive 'sovereignization' because we could actually end up with the sovereignty of a rural soviet or street. Unfortunately, sometimes we do not differentiate between democracy and anarchy." Osipov believed that democracy demanded respect for the law and that the rush for sovereignty contributed to "legal nihilism."[52] *Moskovskie Novosti*, too, regularly lamented the result: a war of laws and a war of sovereignties.[53]

The Tyranny of the *Nomenklatura* and the Persisting Power of the Apparat

Those who advocated local self-determination often did so out of the conviction that the persisting power of the apparat had to be resisted. They subscribed to the view that many problems of the transition period could be blamed on the "tyranny of the *nomenklatura*" (*nomenklaturnyi proizvol*).

This charge was made about Moscow's Zheleznodorozhnyi *raion*, where in May 1991 the crisis situation was exacerbated by the refusal of its executive to reconstruct itself. Reporting on the *raion*, Sergei Stupar' noted that "unfortunately, during the years of perestroika, the administrative command system in the district was not dismantled."[54] As a result, twenty-five deputies had called for a vote of confidence in the chair of the *raisovet*, V. Lytsenko, previously a secretary of the *raikom*. Lytsenko, however, prevented the deputies from exercising this legal right and "hampered" discussion of the issue by removing it from the agenda. Apparently, "this is not the only occasion when Lytsenko and his apparat have broken the law." As a consequence, the *raisovet* was moving into "conditions of chaos and muddle."[55] Constructive suggestions for changing the way in which the *raisovet* worked were "sabotaged" by the apparat, including unwelcome decisions of the Presidium. Stupar' concluded that "the tyranny flourishing in the district ha[d] traditional forms. Those who [had] 'managed' the *raion* in the period of stagnation [were] still doing so today. The opinions and interests of the people [were] empty sounds to them."[56] An appeal was made to the Mossovet to examine the situation.

Others contended that the hold of the *nomenklatura* on policy was felt regardless of whether the *raisovet* had been "reconstructed." A member of the Moscow oblast soviet argued that "ministries are structures that still have control in all areas. They exert strong influence over the processes that interest the local soviets."[57] A more forceful case was made by a deputy of the Mossovet. "Today power consists of the KGB plus the industrial-war machine. We are just a decoration. We have no power. The Communist Party still exerts a powerful influence on everyone." She went on to claim that "nothing has changed. Democracy is not in power. It is a fairy-tale. We must define who owns property at each level. The industrial-war machine often decides what will be built where."[58]

A different sort of attack was directed at the power of the *ispolkom*. Whereas some soviets appeared to enjoy relatively harmonious relations with their executive committees, others did not. Sometimes this depended on the degree of turnover among personnel in the executive committee, and sometimes it varied according to the issue under scrutiny and the individuals involved. The picture was a complex one. Where turnover had taken place, new members were sometimes criticized for being inexperienced. Where it had not, members were accused of being "stale." Where some turnover has occurred, old and new members were castigated for not cooperating with each other. Sometimes, however, experienced administrators willing to adopt new ways did work well with newly appointed democrats, although the pattern was far from homogeneous across soviets.[59]

Some democrats, however, accused their *ispolkom* of representing the apparat. Others claimed that the *ispolkom* usurped the power of elected deputies. For example, some democrats in the Mossovet felt particularly irked in the spring of 1991 about price increases on public transport from five to fifteen kopecks. According to one deputy, "We did not vote on this. The *ispolkom* took the decision!"[60] When asked if this was really just the same as the *podmena* (substitution) of earlier years, another responded, "Yes, it is. It is *podmena*. And it hit our authority. It happened quickly and it hit hard."[61] He then pointed out that some *ispolkomy* had been abolished precisely because this sort of behavior had been anticipated. But the number was small: Less than 5 percent of soviets lacked an *ispolkom*.

Those journalists and deputies who were democrats generally perceived the continuation of old patterns of power as a brake on democratization. Communists who were chairs of soviets could hamper the work of elected bodies. Other institutions, such as ministries and the KGB, still exerted far greater control than soviets. And relationships between the soviet and its *ispolkom* were varied but frequently perceived as one of unequal power.

Ineffective Representation

While some deputies and commentators stressed the dangers of excessive local self-determination, others insisted on the paralysis generated by the apparat. Still others focused more closely on the difficulties all soviets shared in making decisions. In particular, their persistent failure to obtain a quorum had become a serious issue by 1990. In December, Liubov' Lokhmatova remarked in *Kuranty* that "a session of the Mossovet resembles a boat that can never lift anchor and push off from the dock. Its large crew is very discontented by this, but instead of everyone dispersing to their places and getting on with their work, they shout, make a noise, and constantly run along the shore."[62] Lokhmatova noted that in the morning there was a quorum but that by the end of the day there was not. This situation might continue for an entire month. How, she asked, could one explain the fact that "a considerable portion of the deputies" was absent. Two hundred and twenty might turn up for any given debate, but that was only one-half of the elected number, and those present might not regularly appear.[63]

In the same month, *Argumenty i Fakty* applied a similar criticism to the work of the All-Union Supreme Soviet. An article entitled "As a Rule ... They Don't Work" argued that when urgent measures were needed to ease the current situation in the country, decisions could not always be made because the Soviet parliament lacked a quorum. *Argumenty i Fakty* printed a list of deputies who had failed to turn up during September and November 1990 for more than 40 percent of registrations and votes. Thirty-nine deputies on the Council of Nationalities and twenty-six on the Council of the Republics fell into this category.[64]

Interviews with people's deputies produced varying explanations for the problem. These included the failure of elected representatives to appreciate in advance the extent of their duties, the boredom of attendance, and impatience with the verbosity of others. In early 1991, a deputy in Krasnopresnenskii *raion* suggested that "at first we did not understand the significance of a quorum. Some deputies did not realize how much time being a deputy would demand and so later asked to be released from their mandate. A famous pianist, for example, had done this. We have 125 deputies on our *raisovet*, but I estimate that only 38 work every day as deputies. The problem of the quorum is that deputies do not want to sacrifice the private for the public."[65] Another local deputy saw the situation differently:

> The lack of a quorum is often a consequence of other problems. Some deputies do not want to attend because of *slovobludie* [verbosity]. People talk too much! Others get tired and walk out because no constructive work is being done. To get a quorum, we need to raise the level of consciousness. What matters here is what is in people's heads and how they think. We ought to be ashamed in front of voters. "How can you talk so long," they ask, "and not even manage to decide the budget?"[66]

A deputy on the Mossovet put the same point differently. "At first, in the commission on youth we found it hard to work. We could not manage to finish our debates in time. Now we can. It was hard to take decisions."[67] In short, deputies had to learn how to debate and how to make decisions within specific periods of time. Deputies had to learn democracy.

Taking broader perspectives, others insisted that the inability of deputies to reach agreement made the lack of a quorum irrelevant. As one lawyer put it, "The lack of a quorum is not a problem so long as other real problems have not been solved. In sessions, deputies cannot even make decisions."[68]

Indeed, for years citizens had passively received commands from others, not having to take responsibility. Now they had to learn to do so and decide for themselves. They also had to acquire tolerance and develop the art of compromise.

Another hazard for democracy believed to render a lack of a quorum far less significant was the new tendency of deputies in local soviets to think that they worked in parliaments. The charge was reiterated that deputies often overestimated the scope of their tasks and their own importance, aspiring to solve problems for the entire country. Deputies in Krasnopresnenskii *raion*, criticized the same lawyer, had declared it a nuclear-free zone. And, how he asked, could a local soviet make a decision about its airspace without broader consultation?[69] Discourse on different problems in the soviets often returned to the issue of local control, suggesting that it outweighed and distorted other problems. More broadly, the lack of a legal culture was felt. "And this," insisted one deputy, "cannot be blamed on the apparat."[70] But many democrats disputed this assertion. The view predominated that, although the lack of a quorum was a problem, other difficulties were more grave and sometimes exacerbated the low turnout of deputies.

Nihilism in the Soviets

Nihilism was one of the reasons given for the difficulty of obtaining a quorum. According to a district deputy, it was one of the most serious problems facing the soviets:

> Nihilism is a movement. People began to expect nothing. They wanted to destroy and be destructive. It affected everyone. It was negative. It results in the feeling that we can do nothing. It still continues today. We make mistake after mistake. We lack a sufficient level of experience. I would say between 10 and 20 percent of the deputies in this *raion* are nihilistic. They used to criticize the past; now they criticize the present. Tomorrow they will criticize the future. It affects the quality of our work. It is hard to neutralize the nihilists. They are very active. They will always want to be at the microphone, and then they will not leave it. They want to agitate, but they should be more constructive.[71]

This deputy had once been a member of the CPSU and now viewed himself as independent. He stressed the importance of democracy but regretted that destructive criticism, rather than positive action, had been one of its results. As he perceived the situation, so long as a precise division of functions across soviets was wanting and areas of responsibility were not always clear, the feeling of helplessness would be reinforced, and nihilism would continue to be fostered. When asked what the achievements of his *raisovet* were, he looked blank and slowly responded, "We have fewer achievements than problems."[72]

Deputy Osipov voiced a similar concern about some members of the Inter-Regional Group of deputies, to which he belonged. Like many groups, it had its own center, right, and left. But "among its members are people's deputies who consider themselves extreme radicals. They always voice sharp criticisms. I will not name them; everyone knows who they are." He estimated that 80 percent of the group had an "even temper," implying that the more radical 20 percent did not.[73]

Throughout 1990, articles in the press regularly talked about disorder, crisis, and chaos in the soviets, in particular in the Leningrad City Soviet. Here deputies were castigated for numerous instances of poor behavior. When the voting machine was found to be out of order, technicians claimed a deputy must have intentionally short-circuited it. In an opening debate, Aleksandr Bogdanov hung the Russian tricolor in front of the Presidium. When Anatolii Sobchak invoked a law prohibiting the use of unofficial symbols, radicals supported Bogdanov in an ensuing debate, which was televised. Viewers saw Bogdanov criticize Sobchak for "policing" the soviet. Bogdanov then called for Leningrad to be called St. Petersburg again, and deputies subsequently voted for him to be removed. When the militia appeared, a skirmish ensued with Vladimir Skoibeda, another deputy.[74] To many viewers, this was nihilism in action.

Journalist Andrei Chernov reflected on the unattractiveness of "democratic" behavior, which was alienating many citizens from the new soviets: "The democrats fought for victory; they do not appear prepared to use it. No party in any civilized country would allow itself to stall the work of the speaker who has just been elected. Neither would it allow its members of parliament to behave in such a disorderly manner, with endless impromptu procedural moves during the session. And even worse, threatening a boycott ..."[75] (Had Chernov studied the political importance of taking advantage of procedural rules for blocking debate in the British House of Commons, he probably would have made this point rather differently.) Elaborating on the boycott, he went on, "That was on 6 April, when the chairman of the session, Petr Filippov, proposed discussion of the speech to be delivered by USSR people's deputy Nikolai Ivanov on Leningrad TV. About a hundred 'democrats' left the room in protest against the 'red tape.' On the same day, Ivanov spoke on television, but the political hysterics of the left wing gave the conservatives the excuse to talk about 'seizure of the television.'"[76]

What Chernov omitted to say here was that had people's deputies not arrived at the television station and effectively taken it over, the controversial Ivanov would not have gone on the air at all. Since Ivanov's and Tel'man Gdlian's investigations had exposed corruption in the CPSU and been hampered by attempts to silence them, the deputies' behavior, seen in this light, was expedient. The role Ivanov and Gdlian played in exposing corruption, however, was not clear-cut. They had been unable to produce irrefutable evi-

"Congress of People's Deputies of the RSFSR. Like children." Newly elected parliaments bore the brunt of many jokes. Here an independent social democratic newspaper pokes fun at disorder in the Russian parliament. A common criticism in 1990 was that deputies in Russia could not easily work with each other, did not know how to compromise, nor how to reach agreements. Among the consequences were diatribes at the microphone, an inability to listen to others, a hurling of insults, and occasional scuffles. Some critics argued that each deputy was a parliament unto him- or herself. Many citizens lamented that the immature behavior of elected politicians meant that democracy was a farce. They had said the same about the USSR Congress of People's Deputies, elected in 1989. SOURCE: *Novaia Zhizn'*, no. (14) 23, June 1990, p. 1.

dence about leaders of the CPSU, Ligachev in particular, and had become an embarrassment to some democrats.[77]

Yet the issue for Chernov was the appropriate behavior of elected deputies. He criticized both left and right: "Incidentally, the conservatives also neglected their duty. On 4 May the faction Renaissance of Leningrad announced that from now on it would not leave the hall but would abstain on all issues. The reason—the 'unjust' composition of the deputies' commissions, in which many conservatives had not been included."[78] He regretted that "into the parliamentary river from the left and right bank fly reinforced concrete blocks of boycott." If the crisis in the Lensovet "burst" like the banks of a river, water would rush out, just as Sobchak had warned.[79]

Some deputies and commentators readily identified as disorderly what others thought was nihilistic. Long, negative, and unconstructive diatribes at the microphone were most frequently cited as evidence of this trend. Sergei Trube, for instance, coordinator of the Sodruzhestvo faction of the Mossovet, told *Kuranty* that Sodruzhestvo had been formed for this very reason:

> The impetus for the formation of the faction began with the wish to increase the effectiveness of the session since we saw that a small group of deputies were taking up literally 95 percent of the time at the microphone and, in our opinion, brought nothing of worth to its work. We concluded that deputies had to group together according to various interests—political, social, even according to personal sympathies, to discuss the plans of the session's documents and then to give an account of the opinions of the faction.[80]

Deputies who "talked incessantly" and who "led the session to a dead end" had prompted the formation of factions so that like-minded politicians could exchange ideas and think through policies.[81]

Discourse condemned unconstructive and disorderly behavior on several grounds. First, it wasted time since deputies did not limit what they had to say. Second, bored listeners often walked out, contributing to the problem of attaining a quorum. Third, deputies assumed powers broader than their remit, enhancing legal and political conflicts. Fourth, the tendency to criticize automatically reduced the possibility of reaching mutually agreeable solutions. And fifth, theatrical political gestures reduced the credibility of elected representatives among the electorate. The message from the media and from deputies themselves was that there was still much to learn about how to practice the art of being democratic.

Factions Before Parties

The relationship between elections, the formation of deputies' groups, and the emergence of political parties was much discussed in 1990 and 1991. According to one interpretation, "Our elections did not proceed on a multi-party basis; therefore party factions are a thing of the future."[82] A different perspective, adopted by lawyer Mikhail Piskotin, held that, although most deputies' groups were not formed along party lines, they were nevertheless "an important step in the transition to a multi-party system."[83] Piskotin argued that "the very logic of political struggle [led] to the formation of factions" and that deputies' groups helped bring together the social forces and movements represented among deputies. In the long run, he believed this circumstance would mean a more rational organization of the soviets.[84]

Some deputies, however, viewed the formation of their groups as a reaction against already existing political blocs rather than as the development of embryonic parties. Igor' Krugovykh, a member of the CPSU since 1979 who was still loyal to it in May 1991, was active in the independent faction of the Mossovet. He described how it was set up as follows:

> At the beginning of the first session of the Mossovet, when two large groups of deputies—the bloc of communists and the Democratic Russia bloc—opposed each other, we, a group of deputies, declared that we would not join either of the blocs, and we created a faction of "independent" deputies. Our organizing principle—independent cooperation. We proceeded from the view that deputies are accountable only to their electors and that no directives from party organs were necessary. In our faction are members of the CPSU, non-party deputies, and believers.[85]

The independent faction of the Mossovet began with twenty deputies and increased to fifty-three. They officially registered themselves under the title of "independent center" since centrism was their first principle. Their second was "We do not stand against anyone. We are in favor of solutions."[86]

Deputies who wished to move away from the strict party lines of the past and devote attention to issues, found loosely organized deputies' groups attractive as a forum for clarifying their own views. Osipov stressed the flexibility of deputies' groups, which made them distinct from parties. The Inter-Regional deputies' group, for example, placed no whip on its members. Everyone voted according to conscience. There had been, however, a move to make decisions binding on members, "but the majority did not support this idea."[87]

Those toward the more conservative end of the Soviet political spectrum argued that deputies' groups contributed to clearer decision making, counteracting anarchic tendencies. Viktor Alksnis of the conservative Soiuz group observed that "distinct from the majority of the world's parliaments, in ours every deputy is a faction unto himself. When a decision is taken spontaneously, deputies make serious mistakes. It is necessary to move to the creation of factions and to solve all problems through consultation between them."[88]

The Supreme Soviet of the USSR had twelve parliamentary groups at the end of 1990. These are listed in Table 7.1, along with their memberships. They cover a wide political span from the relatively large Soiuz group on the right to a tiny cluster of six social democrats at the other end of the spectrum.[89] But deputies' groups also formed around specific issues, such as ecology and science, or around geographic location, such as the Urals group, rather than around broad political platforms. Thus, some, it could be argued, were much less like embryonic parties than others.

In response to the question "How many factions exist in your soviet?" different deputies in 1991 often gave different numbers, indicating rather hazy pictures. In the Supreme Soviet of the RSFSR, according to two deputies,

TABLE 7.1 Deputies' Groups in the Supreme Soviet of the USSR, December 1990

Deputies' Group	Number of Members
Soiuz (Union)	110
Za Konstructivnoe Vzaimodeistvie (For constructive cooperation)	104
Communists	94
Spravedlivost' (Justice)	71
Inter-Regional Group	59
Group for scientific-technical progress	54
Deputies from autonomous republics	52
Ecological group	43
Group of young people's deputies	27
Urals deputies' group	25
Group of war internationalists	17
Social democrats	6

Source: *Narodnyi Deputat*, no. 1, 1991, p. 15.

eleven groups had formed by the spring of 1991. But according to one of these deputies, they fell into two broad groupings of communist factions and the democratic movement. The second insisted that it was more useful to view them as three clusters—independents refusing to join a party, left/center groups, and the Rossiia group to the "right."[90] In *Moskovskie Novosti*, however, Ol'ga Bychkova reported in February 1991 that thirty groups had formed, two-thirds of them on a professional or territorial basis.[91] It seems that the deputies interviewed had separated in their minds broad political clusters from issue-specific groups.

Faster agreement was reached among deputies of the Mossovet and in Krasnopresnenskii *raisovet*.[92] In the former, ten factions had formed by 1991, but most deputies remained outside them. In Krasnopresnenskii *raion*, four factions had been set up by April 1991. Communists in Sodruzhestvo made up the largest group of forty. One member described it as "an amorphous faction."[93] Ten democrats and radicals had come together in Pozitsiia, while those oriented toward business and cooperatives met as members of Solidarnost'. Ten deputies who described themselves as liberals had formed Dialog. The factions, however, were all new and inexperienced. Dialog had met only three times when I interviewed its members. They saw its purpose as helping them clarify thoughts "before the session." "We discuss *how* we will vote in the session," said one member, "but no one is bound to vote in a particular way."[94] Another added, "It helps us work out a position on a question and how to formulate a response."[95] They viewed Dialog as an informal group, relaxed in its discussions, in contrast to Pozitsiia, which had "a harder line."[96] As in the Mossovet, most deputies were not members of factions.

In both the Supreme Soviet of the USSR and the Supreme Soviet of the RSFSR, politicians frequently attended the meetings of more than one deputies' group to hear what was being said and to acquire a feel for different groups. In this context, deputies came and went, and factions were loose and shifting in size, albeit with core members. Yet despite overlapping attendances, many viewed the groups as useful preliminary forms of political identification. In early 1991, however, it was decided in the Russian Supreme Soviet that deputies could not drift across groups but had to commit themselves to only one. Some deputies believed that this arrangement would contribute to political stability.[97]

By 1991, it had been widely recognized that the formation of parties would take time and the development of a party system even longer. Elections had taken place in 1989 and in 1990 without being tightly tied to party politics since only one strong party existed. Moreover, its legitimacy was waning and its membership falling. One result was that, although many newly elected deputies were members of the CPSU, loose factions or deputies' groups subsequently began to meet, often demarcated by political tendency or clusters of opinion. For some, these were pre-parties at best whose members needed to sort out their views, positions, goals, policies, and strategies. For others, they were a form of anti-party, or anti-movement, a resistance to the institutionalized positions and lines of the CPSU or to attacks on it by Democratic Russia. Many deputies resisted joining new parties, not wishing to be trapped in a structure that dictated policy, but they nonetheless sought some form of political identification and group belonging.

In the autumn of 1991, deputies in Krasnopresnenskii *raion* and in the Mossovet told me that factions had disbanded. Changed political circumstances had led to political regrouping.[98] During September and October, many deputies, particularly those active in, or sympathetic to, Democratic Russia, believed that a new polarization had taken place. The redefined battle was between erstwhile communists who had left the CPSU in 1990 or in 1991 before the coup and who saw themselves as democrats now and democrats, such as those in Democratic Russia, who were "more democratic." The latter were pushing for elections to the local soviets to take place in November 1991 and wished to wage the battle directly against the "new" leaders, such as Yeltsin, Popov, and Sobchak, whom they variously portrayed as "dictators," "new czars," and "totalitarians." They criticized Yeltsin for his "undemocratic" and "unconstitutional" rule by decree, just as they had Gorbachev before him.[99]

The first factions, then, had short lives. They arose in a historical context in which elected deputies were reacting either to the CPSU, Democratic Russia, or both. They also fulfilled the need of inexperienced deputies to define their views on issues, to formulate opinions about policies, and to sort out appropriate strategies.

Although factions did not re-form in the local soviets, which had been stripped of power by the prefectures, they quickly functioned again in the

Moscow City Soviet after it was clear that the hoped-for elections of November 1991 would not take place. By February 1992, sixteen deputies' factions and groups "on a clearly defined course" had officially registered.[100] As Table 7.2 shows, membership varied from as few as five to as many as sixty-three, with an average of fourteen per group. Democratic Russia was the largest faction, despite turbulence in membership of the broader movement.

Of these sixteen registered groups and factions, only five insisted that membership be exclusive. These were Moscow, the Liberal Faction, the Democratic Party of Russia, the Social Democratic Party of Russia, and the Christian Democratic Union of Russia.[101] As before, these clusters drew like-minded politicians together to clarify their thinking and work out policy positions. Many deputies, however, continued to view the role of these groups with skepticism, dismissing them as formal groupings registered on paper but with no effective function in practice. As one deputy remarked in March 1992, "They do nothing."[102] Nonetheless, in the complex and protracted process of democratizing Russia and forging parties, factions were one essential aspect, even if they were ill-formed, weak, controversial, and reflective of wider political chaos.

In his seminal work on parties and party systems, Giovanni Sartori noted that "the transition from faction to party rests on a parallel process: the even slower, more elusive, and more tortuous transition from intolerance to toleration, from toleration to dissent, and, with dissent, to believing in diversity."[103] It was indeed this painful parallel process of learning toleration, recognizing the legitimacy of dissent, and appreciating the importance of diversity that made democratization so difficult. It clashed with Russian and Soviet political cultures. It also ran up against a sharply divided society that included citizens who espoused diametrically opposed and irreconcilable views. Opponents found each other hard to tolerate. And even those of like political persuasions found compromises hard to reach. This was one reason for the instability of new political parties.

Unstable New Parties

After the initial enthusiasm and energy that poured into the formation of new parties, such as the Democratic Union, the Democratic Party of Russia, the Social Democratic Party, the Russian Christian Democratic Party, the Republican Party, and the Liberal Party, came factionalism, personal animosities, fights over principles, and splits. Often relatively weak parties with small followings became weaker. They found it difficult to set up the huge infrastructures necessary to cover the entire Union or even one republic. Finance and experience were missing; so were large memberships. And despite the honorable declarations of democrats to put past personal ambitions be-

TABLE 7.2   Registered Deputies' Factions and Groups in the Moscow City Soviet, 18 February 1992

Faction or Group	Number of Members
Christian Democratic Faction	4
Christian Democratic Union of Russia	2
Constitutional Democratic Party	5
Democratic Party of Russia	7
Democratic Russia	63
Greens	8
Independents	23
Labor Faction	14
Left Moscow	6
Liberal Faction	10
Moscow	44
People's Party of Free Russia	12
Rebirth	7
Republican Party of the Russian Federation	24
Social Democratic Party of Russia	4
Union of Communists	5

Source: Upravlenie Delami Mossoveta, Upravlenie Delami Merii, Otdel Informatsii, *Informatsionno-spravochnyi Material: O Nekotorykh Itogakh 7 Sessiia Mossoveta (Vtoraia Chast')* (Moscow, March 1992), p. 4.

hind them, new ones inevitably arose. The CPSU, despite its declining membership and waning credibility, remained by comparison institutionally strong, until the "revolution" after August 1991. But both before and after August, other parties struggled to attract significantly large followings. The biggest party before August was Nikolai Travkin's Democratic Party of Russia, with approximately twenty-five or thirty thousand members; the next in size was Viacheslav Shostakovskii's Republican Party, with approximately twenty thousand members.[104]

The nature of emerging parties, in a context lacking an institutionalized multi-party system, was one of flux and imprecision. Divisions and splits were common. The Democratic Union (as noted in Chapter 5) had clearly identifiable factions and disagreements over political strategies.[105] Christian Democrats spread themselves across five or more groupings; the two largest were the Russian Christian Democratic Movement and the Russian Christian Democratic Union. The latter emerged in late 1989 at the initiative of Aleksandr Ogorodnikov. But accusations of financial impropriety against Ogorodnikov led in March 1990 to a split. Ogorodnikov's accusers were then expelled from the party, and they launched a new paper, *Khristianskaia Politika* (Christian Policy). The Russian Christian Democratic Movement, probably larger than the Russian Christian Democratic Union, formed in 1990. Its members were immediately divided on whether it should be a movement or a party. After much debate and soul-searching, the Russian Christian Democratic Party was born in the summer of 1990 within the broader movement.[106]

The Russian Christian Democratic Movement became one of the participants in the broader Democratic Russia movement. Gavriil Popov and others were keen for a very large democratic political party to emerge from within Democratic Russia. Its component parts, however, were united only in their battle against the CPSU. Thereafter constitutional democrats, Russian democrats, social democrats, christian democrats, and others tended, with some exceptions, to identify first with their smaller group or party rather than with the larger movement. Other participants, such as the Antifascist Center and the Association of Car Lovers, had more specific concerns. Six days before the August coup, *Kuranty* declared, "Today it's not a secret: There are many differences among democrats. They talk of a split, even that Democratic Russia will die." Democratic Russia had been unable at that point to formulate a clear response to the new prefectures in Moscow.[107] It seemed that some members opposed them, while others gave their support. Members, too, were divided in their opinions of Popov.

And Popov, it seemed, was now a member of both Democratic Russia and the newer Movement for Democratic Reforms. Where were Popov's political allegiances, many wondered? "It is not clear," wrote Konstantin Katanian in *Kuranty*, "if the mayor has gone from one movement to the other" or if he prefers to be in both.[108] Likewise, Shatalin was a member of the Democratic Party of Russia and the Movement for Democratic Reforms. Since the DPR was part of Democratic Russia, Shatalin, too, was affiliated with two democratic movements. Katanian argued that "such imprecision does not help the organization of democratic movements and parties." Incoherence and confusion resulted from dual affiliations and "disorderly shifts." And although Democratic Russia was prepared to cooperate with those in the Movement for Democratic Reforms, "they are not intending to unite with them."[109] Thus, a very large, coherent, and united democratic movement was unlikely to emerge.

After the failed coup, latent tensions and disagreements within Democratic Russia worsened. In early October, Popov declared that its liberal wing supported a market economy with little concern for a security net, while its social democratic wing emphasized the importance of social protection.[110] Arguments about the desirable features of the future market economy divided democrats, as did debates about political union. Christian democrats and the Democratic Party of Russia, for example, supported the idea of federation, but the Republican Party advocated a breakup of the Union.[111] In November, at Democratic Russia's second congress, the Democratic Party of Russia, the Party of People's Freedom, and the Christian Democratic Movement announced their intent to leave the broad movement and set up a new coalition, the Democratic Forces of Russia. They left Democratic Russia because they opposed its support of independence for autonomous republics within Russia.[112] Differences over Yeltsin's policies and political style also became more marked. In late October, the Moscow branch of Democratic Russia severely criticized Yeltsin's leadership of Russia since his election as president—the very man they had supported so vigorously in the 1990 elections.[113] Arguments also broke out over whether politicians should also be entrepreneurs.

As the pace of economic and political change quickened, disputes among democrats increased. The several democratic groups and parties that had come together in Democratic Russia subsequently experienced splits and offshoots as new movements formed. Thus, democratic movements and parties fragmented as policy became more complex and variegated; there was no longer the one sharp unifying goal of ousting the CPSU.

In addition to overlapping memberships, splits, personal animosities, and shifting coalitions came the practical problem of how to disseminate ideas. A lack of paper meant that the newspapers of the new political parties suffered instant hardships. At a gathering held in April 1991 at Moscow University's School of Journalism, their editors drew attention to the difficulty of obtaining a sufficient paper supply. According to a liberal democrat, "We have problems of no money and no paper." A social democrat stressed how "it was difficult to start our paper. We relied heavily on support from members. We also suffer from the 'information blockade.'" He claimed that editors were deprived of crucial information by the government. Other papers seemed short of articles. "We publish practically everything we receive," said a member of the Christian Democratic Union of Russia. And sometimes the ideological orientation of a group worked against a successful dissemination of ideas. As a member of the Confederation of Anarcho-Syndicalists put it, "We are against the process of commercialization." But money was essential to the anarchists' endeavor to publish *Obshchina*. Their fundamental political beliefs clashed with the necessary mechanics of building a party or movement.[114]

Many deputies were sensitive to the weaknesses of new parties and felt that they hampered progress toward democracy. Party-mindedness was a prerequisite of democracy, and newspapers were one means of promoting it. The CPSU was viewed by many democrats as enjoying an unfair advantage of experience, established networks throughout the Union, property, money, and publications. Developed party-mindedness prevailed in one party only. The others had yet to learn it. Moreover, many deputies still hesitated to commit themselves to any particular party. As one commented, "I have been asked to join more than one party. But it is too soon. I always refuse. I want to see how things develop. Also, my constituents elected me as an independent. So I would be breaking my promises to them if I joined a party now."[115]

Discourse suggested several obstacles to the new parties increasing their memberships and becoming institutionalized. First, resources were meager; how well a party could organize and disseminate its ideas depended on money, and a party with international links inevitably benefited. Second, the state of the economy made an impact on how parties operated; paper shortage and inflation were but two examples. Third, political inexperience and intolerance negatively affected the ability of party members to reach working compromises; disagreements, the growth of factions, membership instability, splits over principle, and shifting coalitions were among the consequences. Fourth, that deputies had not been elected as members of new parties made it difficult for parties to play a role in the soviets other than as weak factions. Moreover, the diversity of factions and their tiny memberships meant that they could not play crucial roles in agenda-setting and policy making. And fifth, the reluctance of many deputies to join new parties reinforced their weakness. Many expressed the opinion that another round of elections was needed for parties to consolidate and grow. According to this interpretation, the fate of parties was inseparable from developments in the electoral system. In turn, many deputies in 1990 and 1991 believed that before fresh elections could take place, heated debates about competing drafts of the new Russian constitution and the nature of the new democracy had first to be resolved. Yet again, the relationship between executive and legislative powers was among the most contentious.

The New Soviets: Achievements and Weaknesses

Although interpretations of the significance of the predicaments in which the soviets found themselves varied, common agreement about key characteristics was evident. The new soviets were inevitably beset with difficulties. Rules and procedures had to be worked out, often in an ad hoc manner. Not everything could be decided in advance or anticipated. Precise functions were hazy, especially in spheres such as control over property. Skills and political experience had to be acquired. Decision making was not eased by a frequent lack of a quorum, lack of information, different views in the *ispolkom* and struggles with leaders in industry and in agriculture. How effective many commissions and committees in the soviets were generally depended on the leadership skills of their chairpersons, on how much time deputies were able to devote to these committees, and on available resources. Administration also became complicated by budgetary politics. Many oblasts had to draw up budgets before knowing how much money they would have to spend. And, in fact, most budgets were drawn up from positions of deficit. Zagorsk, deputies told me, suffered a 60-million-ruble deficit.[116] Some oblasts also found themselves suddenly responsible for small towns or industries that had once been directly under the control of a ministry but had since been dropped by that ministry. The oblast in which they were situated then had to step in and assume responsibility.[117] This became an additional financial burden.

Amid a maze of procedural, legal, financial, and political problems, deputies focused on the hazards and possibilities of the day-to-day running of government at different levels. For those committed to democracy, their concern was to make it work rather than reflect on what civil society actually meant. Some believed that civil society was a prerequisite of successful democracy. But their pressing practical task, one that was tangible and immediate, was to defend the power of the soviets and widen it.

One astute deputy in Krasnopresnenskii *raion*, an historian, remarked, "We got the sort of soviets that we deserved—soviets that you would expect from our system at this point. It would be unreasonable to expect anything else. Look at how long it took for democracy to develop in Britain."[118] Other deputies similarly pointed out that democracy elsewhere had taken centuries to build. Time was an essential ingredient. Russia had never possessed democratic structures, apart from temporary and partial examples such as the Veche in Kievan Rus, the Duma and Sobor in Muscovy, the zemstva after 1864, and the Duma after 1905.[119] Certainly, it would have been odd if in 1989 and 1990 smoothly running soviets had suddenly appeared. Their nature was to a large extent congruent with historical context and held back by political culture. And the dilemmas of the soviets were part of the unfolding political crisis.

NOTES

1. In the soviet of Krasnopresnenskii *raion*, Moscow, I interviewed the chair, two deputy chairs, and four other deputies. More informal conversations with others took place in the canteen. Three rounds of interviews took place: April 1991, September 1991, and March 1992. In the Mossovet, I talked to thirteen deputies, two of whom came from Moscow oblast. These discussions were held in May 1991. Return visits occurred in September 1991 and March 1992, but the same deputies were not reached. Just two interviews were arranged in the Russian parliament in May 1991.

2. *Soglasie*, no. 9, 12 June 1989, pp. 1–2.

3. Ibid.

4. Ibid.

5. Andrei Sakharov, *Mir, Progress, Prava Cheloveka: Stat'i i Vystupleniia* (Leningrad, Sovetsii Pisatel', 1990), p. 116.

6. Ibid., p. 112.

7. Ibid.

8. Ibid.

9. Oleg Bogomolov, "Vremia poluvlasti," *Moskovskie Novosti*, no. 8, 24 February 1991, p. 6.

10. Ibid.

11. Ol'ga Bychkova, "'Voina zakonov' i borb'ba fraktsii," *Moskovskie Novosti,* no. 8, 24 February 1991, p. 6.

12. See Graham Smith, "The state, nationalism and the nationalities question in the Soviet republics," in Catherine Merridale and Chris Ward, eds., *Perestroika: The Historical Perspective* (Dunton Green, Edward Arnold, 1991), pp. 202–216.

13. RFE/RL Research Institute, *Report on the USSR,* vol. 2, no. 36, 7 September 1990, p. 22; RFE/RL Research Institute, *Report on the USSR,* vol. 2, no. 43, 26 October 1990, p. 34; RFE/RL Research Institute, *Report on the USSR,* vol. 2, no. 44, 2 November 1990, p. 43.

14. Interview in the soviet of Krasnopresnenskii *raion,* April 1991.

15. Ibid.

16. Ibid.

17. Ibid.

18. For further details, see *Shchit i Mech,* 19 April 1991, p. 2.

19. Interview in the soviet of Krasnopresnenskii *raion,* April 1991.

20. Ibid.

21. Ibid.

22. Interview in Moscow City Soviet, May 1991.

23. Ibid.

24. Ibid.

25. Ali Naibov, "'Perestroika i nravstvennost': Chvanstvo," *Bakinskii Rabochii,* 30 August 1987, p. 1.

26. Ibid.

27. Interview in the Moscow City Soviet, May 1991.

28. Ibid.

29. Gavriil Popov, "Slishkom mnogo parlamentov: Nuzhen munitsipalitet," *Moskovskie Novosti,* no. 12, 24 March 1991, p. 9.

30. Sergei Alekseev, "Vsia vlast' ... komu!" *Moskovskie Novosti,* no. 12, 24 March 1991, p. 9.

31. See, for instance, N. Postovoi, "Chetko razgranichit' funktsii," *Narodnyi Deputat,* no. 4, 1991, pp. 19–26. Here the case was made that territorial, demographic, and economic factors had to be taken into account when deciding functions.

32. *Moskovskii Komsomolets,* 13 August 1991, p. 1.

33. Ibid.

34. Interview in the soviet of Krasnopresnenskii *raion,* September 1991.

35. Ibid.

36. Ibid.

37. Ibid.

38. Ibid.

39. Interview in the Moscow City Soviet, October 1991.

40. Interview in the soviet of Krasnopresnenskii *raion,* March 1992.

41. Ibid.

42. Andranik Migranyan, "Gorbachev's leadership: A Soviet view," *Soviet Economy,* vol. 6, April-June 1990, p. 156.

43. Ibid.

44. *Moskovskii Komsomolets,* 6 August 1991, p. 1.

45. "Diagnoz izvesten, konsilium prodolzhaetsia," *Moskovskie Novosti,* no. 12, 24 March 1991, p. 8.

46. *Moskovskie Komsomolets,* 6 August 1991, p. 1. This information was repeated in interviews in the *raisovet.*

47. *Kuranty,* 4 May 1991, p. 4. *Kuranty* is the paper of the Mossovet.

48. "Diagnoz izvesten."

49. *Moskovskie Novosti,* no. 17, 21–26 September 1991, p. 6; *Moskovskie Novosti,* no. 38, 22 September 1991, p. 6.

50. *Moskovskie Novosti,* no. 38, 23–30 September 1990, p. 6; *Moscow News,* no. 26, 30 June–7 July 1991, pp. 1, 5.

51. *Nezavisimaia Gazeta,* 21 March 1992, p. 1; *Nezavisimaia Gazeta,* 24 March 1992, p. 1. For Yeltsin's unsuccessful attempt to impose martial law in Chechen-Ingushia, see RFE/RL Research Institute, *Report on the USSR,* vol. 3, no. 47, 22 November 1991, p. 28.

52. *Narodnyi Deputat,* no. 1, 1991, p. 19.

53. Alekseev, "Vsia vlast' ... komu!"; Popov, "Slishkom mnogo parlamentov."

54. *Kuranty,* 4 May 1991, p. 4.

55. Ibid.

56. Ibid.

57. Interview with a deputy of the Moscow oblast soviet in the Moscow City Soviet, May 1991.

58. Ibid.

59. Information from several deputies in Krasnopresnenskii *raisovet* and in the Moscow City Soviet, April and May, 1991.

60. Interview in the Moscow City Soviet, May 1991.

61. Ibid. *Podmena* refers to "a tendency on the part of the CPSU organs and officials to usurp the functions and authority of the state, to interfere in the work of professional administrators, or otherwise deal with matters that are properly the province of the state or economic management." See Ronald J. Hill and Peter Frank, *The Soviet Communist Party,* 2d ed. (London, George Allen and Unwin, 1983), pp. 118–119.

62. Liubov' Lokhmatova, "Za kogo golosovali," *Kuranty,* 13 December 1990, p. 4.

63. Ibid.

64. *Argumenty i Fakty,* no. 50, December 1990, p. 3.

65. Interview in the soviet of Krasnopresnenskii *raion,* April 1991.

66. Ibid.

67. Interview in the Moscow City Soviet, May 1991.

68. Interview in the Institute of State and Law, Moscow, April 1991.

69. Ibid.

70. Interview in the soviet of Krasnopresnenskii *raion,* April 1991.

71. Ibid.

72. Ibid.

73. *Narodnyi Deputat,* no. 1, 1991, p. 18.

74. Andrei Chernov, "2:1 v pol'zu sil'noi ruki," *Moskovskie Novosti,* no. 41, 14 October 1990, p. 4.

75. Andrei Chernov, "Neuzheli voda 'zatsvetet,'" *Moskovskie Novosti,* no. 19, 13 May 1990, p. 5.

76. Ibid.

77. For the views of Gdlian and Ivanov, *Soznanie,* no. 17, 1991, pp. 1–2; *Soznanie,* no. 18, 1991, p. 1.

78. Chernov, "Neuzheli voda 'zatsvetet.'"

79. Ibid.

80. *Kuranty,* 18 May 1991, p. 4.

81. Ibid.

82. "Po puty k Parlamentskim frakstiiam," *Narodnyi Deputat,* no. 1, 1991, p. 16. This was a roundtable discussion. This particular perspective was put forward by A. Mokanu, deputy chair of Soviet of the Union of the Supreme Soviet of the USSR.

83. Ibid., p. 17. Piskotin was also editor of *Narodnyi Deputat.*

84. Ibid., pp. 17–18.

85. *Kuranty,* 18 May 1991, p. 4.

86. Ibid.

87. "Po puty k Parlamentskim frakstiiam," p. 17.

88. Ibid.

89. For details of the Soiuz group, consult Ol'ga Bychkova, "Nerushimyi Soiuz," *Moskovskie Novosti,* no. 49, 9 December 1990, p. 6.

90. Interview conducted in the parliament of the RSFSR, May 1991.

91. Ol'ga Bychkova, "'Voina zakonov' i bor'ba fraktsii," p. 6.

92. From interviews in the soviet of Krasnopresnenskii *raion* and in the Moscow City Soviet, April and May 1991.

93. Ibid.

94. Ibid.

95. Ibid.

96. Ibid.

97. Interview in the parliament of the RSFSR, May 1991.

98. Interview in the Moscow City Soviet and interviews in the *raisovet* of Krasnopresnenskii district, September and October 1991.

99. Ibid.

100. Upravlenie Delami Mossoveta, Upravlenie Delami Merii, Otdel Informatsii, *Informatsionno-spravochnyi Material: O Nekotorykh Itogakh 7 Sessiia Mossoveta (Vtoraia Chast')* (Moscow, March 1992), p. 4.

101. Ibid.

102. Interview in the Mossovet, March 1992.

103. Giovanni Sartori, *Parties and Party Systems: A Framework for Analysis,* vol. 1 (Cambridge, Cambridge University Press, 1976), p. 13.

104. Stephen White, *Gorbachev and After* (Cambridge, Cambridge University Press, 1991), pp. 58–59. See, too, *Moskovskie Novosti*, no. 4, 26 January 1992, p. 7. Membership statistics, however, are unreliable because parties tended to inflate them.

105. I. P. Vasil'eva, "Demokraticheskii Soiuz v usloviiakh mnogopartiinosti: Raskol ili razmezhevanie?" *Sotsial'no-politicheskie Nauki*, no. 2, 1991, pp. 117–126; Sergei Ivanenko, "Chem zanimat'sia, esli ne krichat' na mitingakh," *Moskovskie Novosti*, no. 50, 16 December 1990, p. 6.

106. John Anderson, "The orthodox fringe: Christian democracy in Russia" (Unpublished paper). Greater detail is given in I. P. Vasil'eva, "Rossiiskie khristianskie demokraty: Politicheskie vzgliady i idealy," *Sotsial'no-politicheskie Nauki*, no. 7, 1991, pp. 108–120.

107. Dmitrii Kataev, *Kuranty*, 13 August 1991, p. 5. For the views of Viktor Aksiuchits of the Russian Christian Democratic Movement and Mikhail Globachev, vice president of the Constitutional Democrats, see *Stolitsa*, no. 34, 1991, pp. 7–10.

108. Konstantin Katanian, *Kuranty*, 8 August 1991, p. 4.

109. Ibid.

110. RFE/RL Research Institute, *Report on the USSR*, vol. 3, no. 42, 18 October 1992, p. 43.

111. Ibid.

112. For further details, refer to RFE/RL Research Institute, *Report on the USSR*, vol. 3, no. 47, 22 November 1991, pp. 30–31.

113. RFE/RL Research Institute, *Report on the USSR*, vol. 3, no. 45, 8 November 1991, p. 23.

114. Talks delivered at the School of Journalism, Moscow University, April 1991.

115. Interview in the soviet of Krasnopresnenskii *raion*, April 1991.

116. Information from deputies in the soviet of Moscow oblast and the Moscow City Soviet, April 1991.

117. Ibid.

118. Interview in the soviet of Krasnopresnenskii *raion*, September 1991.

119. Richard Pipes, *Russia Under the Old Regime* (Harmondsworth, Penguin, 1977), pp. 27–111; Stephen White, *Political Culture and Soviet Politics* (London, Macmillan, 1979), pp. 22–30.

8

Crisis

BY 1990, THE WORDS CRISIS (*krizis*), collapse, (*krakh*), disintegration (*razval*), and despair (*otchaianie*) were being heard daily. They had penetrated most people's discourse—be it intellectual analysis, journalistic commentary, or a conversation on the street. These concepts studded political speeches and programs, they punctuated complaints in food queues, and they spilled out of radio and television broadcasts. The general theme of crisis displaced the prominence of reflections on pluralism and democratization and far surpassed them in the attention received. Crisis interested everyone, whereas pluralism had not. Crisis affected daily life in immediate ways, whereas democratization, although having made an impact on voting behavior, citizen representation, and participation in the workplace, was still more removed.

Consensus and Disagreement

Crisis existed, was perceived to exist, and was believed to be grave. On this there was consensus. Several crises had developed, deepened, and exacerbated one another. These included crises of economic distribution, fiscal policy, social stability, nationality, political power, and legitimacy of the Union. Above all, the state was in crisis as popularly elected Supreme Soviets in the republics assumed responsibilities that deputies in the All-Union Supreme Soviet did not always wish them to take on. Newly legitimate republican parliaments were seizing authority and granting themselves powers that they deemed illegitimate in the hands of the center. The Union was visibly disintegrating as powers shifted. Republics had been declaring sovereignty, and ethnic tensions and disputes appeared increasingly intractable.

When people's deputies in November 1990 called for an emergency debate in the All-Union Supreme Soviet on the prevailing crisis, their demand reflected the anxieties of most citizens.[1] When troops stormed Lithuania in January 1991, that sense of crisis heightened still further.[2] When in the spring of 1991, striking miners in the Kuzbass belittled Prime Minister Pavlov's calls for a return to work, defied a two-month strike ban, demanded the resignation of Gorbachev and his government, and threatened a general strike, they contributed to growing unease about a crisis spiraling out of control. But for the miners, crisis had made them stop work. The strike had become a political weapon for the expression of discontent.[3]

Crisis for Leninists differed greatly from crisis for the miners. In February, groups advocating "socialist choice" criticized Gorbachev for bringing anarchy and chaos and urged citizens in the referendum of 17 March to say "yes" to the preservation of union.[4] Leninists saw strikes, instability, and nationalism as key features of political crisis. They wanted these trends curbed, by force if necessary. Then in April, four months before the August coup, Soiuz called for a state of emergency to be imposed for six months.[5] In 1991, both those in favor of reform and those against it were advocating radical strategies spanning from general strike to martial law. Actions to deal with the crisis thus deepened it.

Although most agreed that crisis prevailed, they did not then concur about its precise nature, origins, characteristics, implications, and consequences. On these, political leaders such as Gorbachev, Popov, and Yeltsin were divided. So, too, with much greater diversity, were political parties, groups, and social movements across the spectrum. The interpretations of democrats, Leninists, patriots, monarchists, christians, greens, feminists, and anarchists illustrated, not just a society divided, but a heterogeneity of political preferences. Although none of these groups and movements was powerful enough on its own to unseat Gorbachev, taken together their views indicated a lack of confidence in the president and in the legitimacy of the system. Their very different analyses of crisis are presented here and in the next chapter, not because these groups were all powerful political actors (which they were not), but because their analyses illustrate the variety and complexity of thought in a society that had recently been awakened and politicized by glasnost and democratization. How these actors defined crisis showed tremendous differences in focus, argument, and solutions.

Social and political reality was being redefined by these groups in myriad ways. In the Soviet past, one party line had generally replaced an earlier one, and citizens were informed what it was. Redefinition, when it occurred, amounted to a switch from one proclamation to another in which most citizens did not participate. Now, with a growing pluralism of thought and action emboldened by democratization, citizens were actively and openly involved in analyzing social, economic, and political change. As a consequence, published political thought and analysis were becoming increasingly varied and confident.

Crisis and Myth

Anxiety about crisis also nurtured already existing myths. Many citizens complained that life had never been worse. The myth of the Great Soviet Past swept again through Russia. Under Stalin, Khrushchev, and Brezhnev, there had always been food. Society had never before endured such high crime rates or been torn by nationalist strife. Under Gorbachev, food supply was chaotic, crime was endemic, and the republics were in ferment; famine and civil war were likely. If one pointed out in reply that the food supply ten years earlier was characterized by shortages, that crime had always existed but had been covered up, and that Bolshevik efforts to establish rule in Central Asia in the 1920s had provoked a highly unstable *basmachestvo* (Basmachi revolt), adherents of the myth repeated their claims with fresh examples.[6] According to one schoolteacher, "Under Stalin, you could buy as much as two kilos of caviar at a time served from large jars standing on the counter."[7]

Those citizens, particularly the young, who were not convinced that there ever had been a Great Soviet Past latched on to the Glorious Western Present. According to this myth, there was no hope for a better life in the USSR. At best, it would come slowly, but too slowly to be worth the wait. Life under capitalism was superior. It offered larger apartments, cars, stereos, videos, fashionable clothes, and freedom of movement. In response to the observation that capitalism also suffered from homelessness and unemployment came the blind belief that for those who wanted to succeed, the opportunities were there. Many suggested that the homeless and the unemployed were themselves to blame for their plight; they had not tried hard enough and did not want to work. What mattered to those who echoed this view was how to secure a personal invitation to the West, from anyone. Believers in the Glorious Western Present naively asked hopeful questions such as "How much will it cost me to go to the London Business School?" or "How many millionaires are there in London?"

Like all myths, the Great Soviet Past and the Glorious Western Present carried grains of truth. The system had in the past generally delivered scarce goods in the end, particularly to privileged cities. To many, this meant a better system. Life in 1990 was much harder for Muscovites than before because many of the products that the capital had previously received at the expense of other parts of the Union were now being withheld. Regions began to keep for themselves scarce products that in the past they had been ordered to send to Moscow. The transition from administrative commands from above to other forms of management had also disrupted usual supply

Рис. М. ЛАРИЧЕВА.

"Push me to Sweden!" One increasingly popular image was that life in the West was better. "The Glorious Western Present" was openly revered from 1989 on. Its appeal grew as prices soared, the future seemed uncertain, and political chaos worsened. In 1991, the idea circulated that Russia was no place to bring up children. Certainly, the cost of having a child was suddenly prohibitive. During the same year, the birthrate in the capital fell by one-third. SOURCE: *Izvestiia*, 24 December 1991, p. 1.

lines; less legal backup supplies provided by *tolkachi* (pushers), on which most directors of industries relied, suffered, too, from unpredictability.[8] The system of distribution, rather than the amount of food produced, was at fault. Famines tend to be system-made, the result of leadership decisions, rather than of natural disasters, as Amartya Sen has convincingly demonstrated.[9] The Soviet Union led the world in the production of potatoes, apples, and barley. Objectively, shortages were not inevitable. The harvest in 1990 had been a relatively good one.[10] But collapse of the old order of dictate from above, unaccompanied by new smooth mechanisms of distribution, resulted in chaos. The old system was hardly efficient, waste was immense, and bottlenecks were common, but, as many commented, it had worked. Once it broke down, nothing coherent immediately replaced it. And although shortages and scarcities had always been problems, with a critical glasnost to expose them, they seemed far worse than before and in many areas were.

Because glasnost gave license to criticize, many citizens exaggerated economic difficulties. The phrase "There is nothing in the shops" was heard daily in Moscow in 1990—regardless of whether the shops were actually empty. An odd practice of emphasizing the negative, even when it did not apply, caught on. For example, a woman serving in a hotel snack bar announced apologetically to the queue, "We have nothing here," although before her were spread fish, sliced meat, sausages, salads, and cakes.[11] The supply was no worse or better than a year before. A research scientist with some knowledge of the outside world asked in defiant tone, "Do you know of any country poorer than ours? Perhaps just China?"[12] Even more inappropriate was Anatolii Sobchak's claim that the situation in Leningrad could be compared with the blockade of the city by the Nazis during World War II.[13] The new right to complain in public resulted in many citizens portraying the crisis as much worse than it was. Inaccuracy and distortion became common. Disparity between public statements and reality had always existed in the Soviet past, being one feature of official ideology. Although the ideology was now condemned, elements of this feature persisted in new discourses.

Indulgence in exaggeration was fostered by the identity crisis that engulfed the Union, particularly Russia, about the gravity of social problems; the crisis was heightened, too, by a growing sense of inferiority when standards of living were compared with those of the West. With much more information about liberal democracies now available, citizens agonized over the ideological lies of the past that had told them life under socialism had been better. They had not necessarily believed these lies, knowing that some were false, but they were now additionally depressed by previously unknown details of the scale of disparities, which were sometimes picked over with self-punishing care. There were also those who wished to deliver a loud message to the West that life was dire and that Western aid was needed. Here the device of exaggeration was employed for political ends.[14]

These remarks are not intended to belittle the hardships of daily life suffered in 1990 and 1991. They were real and worsened as food supplies deteriorated. In 1991, price increases and inflation intensified the difficulties. But how they were described by those who endured them did not always match reality. Myths were employed to illustrate that life had been better or that paradise was elsewhere. Elements of fantasy and escapism served cathartic functions. Jokes, too (as indicated in the Introduction), provided mechanisms of release and were integral to ways of coping. And exaggeration was employed for additional reasons: out of a new conformity, since many exaggerated; the need for sympathy; and the belief that what was said was, in fact, true.

Certainly the seriousness of crisis in 1990 meant that the concept was on most agendas—formal, informal, politically important, and politically powerless. The aim of Chapters 8 and 9 is to provide a survey of selected thought on crisis, beginning at the top of the political hierarchy with an examination of the ideas of Gorbachev and other politicians who explicitly addressed "crisis" and moving down to groups in society with little or no ability to influence political decision making.

Gorbachev: Contradictions of the Transition Period

Crisis was firmly on the official agendas of the CPSU. How Gorbachev characterized it, however, differed from what many democrats said, as did his solutions. To Gorbachev's critics, his observations were rhetoric rather than analysis, unimaginative regurgitations of commitment to perestroika with no clear strategies for salvation.

One of Gorbachev's opening questions to the Twenty-eighth Party Congress in July 1990 was "How can we overcome the crisis phenomena [*krizisnye iavleniia*] that are affecting the life of the people and provoking just dissatisfaction?"[15] He cast the problem as one beset with contradictions. Perestroika had "fundamentally changed our society" and would define what it became in the immediate future. But perestroika faced "a mass of unsolved problems."[16] To grasp them, he suggested that:

> it is important to understand the dialectic here. We cannot get away from the question "Why cannot the perestroika process, successfully begun, and which by historical measures has already given society so much, bring healing to many of society's illnesses?" The situation has in given senses become worse. First of all, it concerns the consumers' market and the economy as a whole, the social order, and relations between nationalities.[17]

In response to the question "What to do next?" he answered that it was necessary "to strengthen people's belief in perestroika" because many blamed it, quite wrongly, for contemporary problems.[18] Rather, the dilemma was that "we find ourselves in a transition period when neither the dismantling of the old system has been completed nor the constructing of the new."[19] "A combination of the old and new, the contradictions of the transition period, [and] the complicated interlacing of interests, of political calculations, of objective and subjective factors" were reasons for these crisis phenomena.[20] In this situation, "nationalist and all kinds of destructive forces" fomented disorder, and some wanted to push the country into "bourgeois construction" and onto "capitalist rails."[21]

Gorbachev's words offered no new assessments. The problems he identified were well-known, but he gave no convincing strategies for tackling them. Gorbachev remained locked into well-worn ideological categories—dialectic, old and new, transition, contradictions, objective and subjective factors, and bourgeois construction. These were not useful guides to redefinition and action. Like others, Gorbachev identified economic and nationality problems as pressing. But unlike those who advocated more radical reforms, such as Popov, Afanasyev, and Yeltsin, Gorbachev hesitated to argue that the political system as a whole was in crisis and in need of transformation. His solution to the crisis in 1990 was not to shake up the political system but to continue working within it. He was failing.

Gorbachev's solution to the problems of transition was to establish "measures for stabilization of the political and economic situation in the country, a strengthening of law and order."[22] As far as the national question went, this meant a new union treaty. Opposition to the treaty was voiced immediately by the Baltic states and Georgia, and by 1990, six republics had refused to sign one.[23] For them, Gorbachev's idea of a treaty did not go far enough or proceed fast enough. Rather than concede to objections or attempt further negotiations, Gorbachev stiffened his line. Refusal to obey all-union law, even where it was not recognized, would not be tolerated.[24]

Gorbachev's other main solution to the crisis in 1990 was to consolidate more power in his hands as president at a time of waning authority. He opposed processes that meant a disintegration of the Union and believed that firmer powers were necessary to counter them. Gorbachev's speech to the Congress of People's Deputies in November 1990 indicated that even stronger executive rule was his immediate solution. Gorbachev proposed the dissolution of the Presidential Council and the setting up of the Council of Security in the office of the president. He also called for more powers for the Council of the Federation, changing its role from an advisory body to "an effective structure to coordinate efforts between the center and the republics."[25] Gorbachev's supporters interpreted this change as a constructive and pragmatic response to the growing authority of the republics, while his critics condemned his action as more authoritarianism. Polarized political views among leaders meant that whatever Gorbachev advocated, criticisms would be forthcoming. This required tactical maneuvering on his part but ultimately appeared to paralyze Gorbachev's ability to impose his political will.

In response to the chaotic war of laws, Gorbachev somewhat desperately suggested that a presidential supervisory body be established to ensure that all laws, decrees, and decisions were implemented throughout the Union. The multitude of legislation made this an impossible task, and in any case this legislation, which was often contradictory, was already much ridiculed. Similarly, to combat crime and the black economy, Gorbachev insisted that a special body be set up in the office of the president.[26] But institutions at the top no longer enjoyed the de facto authority to guide policy implementation.

The tone of Gorbachev's speech in November was somewhat inflexible. To the consternation of radical reformers, he stressed the importance of paying special attention to the problems of the army and of caring for their families. The prestige of the army had to be maintained. Prior to that he had strongly warned that "I am decisively against the division of the state, against the reshaping of territory, against the destruction of centuries of ties among peoples. Now I think it is easier for me to talk: On bitter personal experience, the blood of our people has already flowed and we see that we cannot break up."[27]

Gorbachev made an odd leap of inference here. That blood had flowed did not necessarily mean that disintegration was precluded. What he was saying was that he did not want the Union to shatter and that, if necessary, force would be used to retain it. When in early January 1991, more than one thousand Soviet troops moved into Lithuania, it seemed that Gorbachev was prepared to crack down, although controversy raged about how much responsibility for the move Gorbachev actually bore. Certainly, sections of society welcomed the troops. The self-proclaimed Committee of National Salvation of pro-Soviet Russians subsequently vowed to take power in Lithuania and overthrow the elected government to ensure adherence to the Soviet constitution. Many striking Russian workers in the republic hoped to bring about direct presidential rule. But nationalists and reformers were hostile to the presence of troops. A divided society and polity responded in contrasting ways to Gorbachev's words and actions.

Gorbachev's authoritarianism was not restricted to the nationality question. As troops moved into Lithuania, the independent news agency Interfax, which was giving special coverage of Baltic affairs, was closed down.[28] Prior to that the popular television program "Vzgliad" was stopped from broadcasting since it had intended to cover Shevardnadze after his resignation speech, which warned of impending authoritarianism.[29] The appointment of Leonid Kravchenko as head of Gosteleradio (already mentioned in Chapter 2) subsequently led to less glasnost on television and to an increase in old-style reporting.[30]

By the spring of 1991, troubled by the consequences of miners' strikes, Gorbachev became more anxious about economic collapse and crime. To tackle both, he announced an anti-crisis program to stabilize the economy and tackle law and order.[31] Gorbachev now advocated transition to free-market prices by October 1992, expanded conversion of military factories to the production of consumer goods, and an acceleration of privatization. But if the goals were clear to Gorbachev, the mechanisms for achieving them were muddy for those who had to implement them. In early August 1991, one retired chief engineer of a munitions factory told me, "Those who run the factories still do not know how to convert them to consumer goods. Directors are waiting for instructions; no one is telling them what to do, so nothing is happening. They are sitting idle."[32] Crisis was compounded by confusion and inaction.

Many problems in the economy were the unintended consequences of Gorbachev's own contradictory reforms. For instance, some directors of industry, with increased freedom to make some decisions thanks to the Law on State Enterprise of 1986, had increased wages but regardless of productivity. This had contributed to cost-push inflation.[33] In addition, wages had increased at a time when the supply of goods for purchase decreased, even though perestroika in theory was meant to increase consumer satisfaction. Between 1985 and 1988, consumer good imports fell because of a lack of hard currency aggravated by a fall in oil prices on world markets. Gorbachev's early investment had also continued to favor heavy industry. And revenue from vodka sales had drastically fallen because of the highly unpopular anti-alcohol campaign. These consequences resulted in ruble overhang—more and more money chasing fewer goods.[34]

Economist Gertrude Schroeder noted that additions to deposit accounts rose from 15 billion rubles in 1984 to 41 billion in 1989. At the same time, official Soviet statistics showed that by 1989, only 50 out of 1,200 standard consumer items were readily available.[35] Schroeder argued that this left the country with three major economic crises—a disintegrating consumer market, a disrupted investment process, and a massive budget deficit. On top of all this, fiscal crisis ensued because of an increase in money supply. Soviet official statistics showed that gross national product dropped by 10 percent from January to June 1991, compared with the same period in the previous year; national income fell 12 percent; but money supply grew by 40 percent.[36] Gorbachev's anti-crisis program did not address these economic complexities.

Other aspects of this program earned Gorbachev more unpopularity in the republics and among workers. He proposed the suspension of republican, regional, and local laws that contradicted Soviet law and suggested that sanctions apply to republics refusing to sign the new Union Treaty. He also favored a moratorium on all strikes and demonstrations during working hours.[37] In sum, he advocated a firm hand. His predicament, which he did not see sharply enough, was that the political preferences and demands of other political actors were incompatible with his own. And their support bases were broadening, while his were diminishing.

For Gorbachev, crisis in 1990 and 1991 ultimately demanded stronger executive powers, even force. But in the eyes of his critics, Gorbachev's strategies to ease crises made them worse. In addition, Gorbachev's reluctance during 1990 and 1991 to admit that processes of disintegration were outpacing the political system, and were incongruent with it, meant that he failed to see the increasing obsolescence and waning legitimacy of all-union structures. Gorbachev's insistence on more powers for the all-union president and for passage of a union treaty were themselves crises for many democrats. Gorbachev's democratic credentials were increasingly suspect.

Popov: State, Nationality, and Economic Crises

Gavriil Popov, a trained economist, people's deputy, and briefly mayor of Moscow, had a sharper analytic grasp of the crisis than Gorbachev did and a more dispassionate one.[38] He appeared better able to distance himself from the system he was scrutinizing and to be less fettered by his party background. Like Gorbachev, Popov had his own political interests, but they seemed to cloud his analysis less. In 1990, Popov felt compelled to ask "What is to be done?" about three crises resulting from perestroika: a crisis of the state system, a nationality crisis, and an economic crisis.[39]

Popov claimed that several problems fed into a crisis situation. The All-Union Supreme Soviet demanded subordination from the republics, but the republic-level Supreme Soviets insisted on the priority of their own sovereignty. The Russian Republic rejected the program of the president of the USSR. Representatives from Russia who made up the majority of deputies in the country's parliament at the All-Union level voted for one program, while Russia's parliament voted for a different one. In Georgia, advocates of independence had won seats in the republican elections, while the president of Georgia rejected the idea of leaving the Union. And soviets at different levels of the system fought each other and also battled with their own executive committees, presidiums, and chairpersons. In sum, "there is direct evidence of a serious crisis of the entire contemporary state system."[40]

Another aspect of the crisis of the state system concerned the way in which the soviets operated: "Serious and deep debates are raging in the soviets; hundreds of pages of laws, decrees, and resolutions are being issued; but practical changes in the country as a result of all this legislation have not occurred."[41] The soviet system itself was in crisis. Popov likened it to a puppet theater lacking the mechanisms to bring policy to real life.[42]

The crisis of the political system was further complicated by the nationality crisis. The country had moved from conflicts between non-Russian nationalities to conflicts between non-Russians and Russians. Even within Russia itself, autonomous republic after autonomous republic declared the desire to become independent, even though borders did not neatly coincide with the distribution of nationalities. Popov warned that not one of the leaders of the army, KGB, or Ministry of Internal Affairs could maintain his job if Russian soldiers refused to fight in trouble spots.[43]

The first two crises added to the economic crisis. The administrative-command system operating from the center used to order republics to send scarce products to Moscow, but this power no longer existed. For example, Riazan oblast had sent only 2 percent of requested potatoes to Moscow. Failed deliveries of foodstuffs were followed by manufactured goods, then oil, coal, and cars. The overall result was economic paralysis.[44] Moscow lacked the power to address serious problems affecting it, a situation highlighted by another example: "Recently taxi drivers gathered around Moscow, honked their horns—there was no petrol. They did not even know the elementary thing that not one filling station in the city belonged to the Moscow City Soviet, which had no relationship with deliveries. The same applies to meat supplies and much else."[45] Whether supplies reached Moscow now depended on the willingness of others to send them.

These three crises together meant "a growing destabilization of society. Citizens had already received all political freedoms, could demand whatever they wanted from whomever they liked. But they still lacked the possibility to do anything for themselves."[46] "To put it bluntly," said Popov, "our shelves are empty, and our current system suggests one way out—go to meetings and demonstrations, make demands, threats."[47]

Popov suggested that "the worst consequence of bureaucratic socialism [was] social dependence previously coupled with passivity and now supplemented with stormy activism, turning into an exceptionally dangerous phenomenon."[48] In short, life was getting much worse, and demands were therefore becoming more radical. Perestroika itself was not to blame. Crisis situations were common in many countries, such as Czechoslovakia, Poland, and Germany.[49] Rather, "the root of all crises is one: The country lacks real perestroika."[50] The important question was which variant of perestroika would emerge as successful from current struggles—a democratic one or the apparat's?[51] A storm was raging between them. In Popov's view, the democratic variant called for denationalization of the economy, desovietization of politics, and defederalization of center-republic relations.

A "denationalization" (*denatsionalizatsiia*) of the economy, however, did not merely mean pluralistic forms of property ownership. Thought had to be given to percentages of economic spheres—such as 20 percent state ownership, 30 percent private ownership, and 50 percent collective ownership. But the guiding principle had to be private property. And denationalization of the economy had to be accompanied by a "desovietization" (*desovetizatsiia*) of politics. Popov argued that "the essence of perestroika in politics is the complete liquidation of the soviets and the creation of normal institutions of democracy: legislative power, judicial power, and executive power."[52] The ineffectiveness of the Mossovet and Lensovet could not be sufficiently explained by the CPSU's monopoly control. Although now run by democrats, they still retained the "decorative" function they had performed for more than seventy years.[53] The entire political system needed an overhaul.

Some elected deputies reacted negatively to Popov's advocacy of desovietization on the grounds that it was unconstitutional. As discussed in the previous chapter, Popov's subsequently established prefectural system for Moscow was decried as "authoritarian," turning back the process of democratization. Others believed that it filled a serious executive void.[54]

As far as the nationalities question was concerned, empire had to end and be replaced by "voluntary interstate associations" (*dobrovol'nye mezhgosudarstvennye assotsiatsii*).[55] Popov recognized that this was not a simple task. He believed that it was insufficient to grant sovereignty according to current borders, which was the apparat's way of proceeding, since Russians could be found in Estonia and in other republics, Poles lived in Lithuania, and Abkhazians in Georgia. Russia itself was a complex mix of nationalities, as was Kazakhstan. To address these complexities, boundaries should be declared invalid. Then the democratic variant of "defederalization" (*defederalizatsiia*) could take one of two courses during the transition period. The entire USSR could be declared a united state without borders, as it had effectively been throughout all the years of the dictatorship of the CPSU; after denationalization of the economy would follow defederalization. Or a referendum could be held immediately, and the boundaries of the republics could be fixed according to the result of the referendum (Popov was somewhat optimistic here about the ease of the matter). Republics such as Estonia and Moldavia might shrink in size as a result, but there would be fewer conflicts in the future. Denationalization would then proceed in each republic.[56]

If the apparat's variant of perestroika triumphed, then *defederalizatsiia, denationalizatsiia,* and *desovetizatsiia* would take place within the confines of bureaucratic state socialism directed by the CPSU and its subsidiary "social" organizations. If the democrat's variant of perestroika was successful, these three processes would be instigated by the rest of society, outside the CPSU. However, Popov believed that a dilemma existed for democrats: After seventy years of totalitarianism, society could not permit the democratic variant "now or in the near future."[57] This made the USSR distinct from the states of Eastern Europe. Democrats therefore had to enter into coalitions to fulfill the democratic program. "The apparat will bring strength, cadres, and experience to this coalition. It will involve the army, militia, and KGB. The democrats will bring the trust and support of the people to the coalition and facilitate backing in legislative and in other elected organs where they are in the majority."[58] Moreover, a coalition would enjoy the support of the West. And the apparat had experience, even if its authority was waning.

Popov conceded that a coalition would bring tensions and splits. The democrats would have difficulties with the extreme left wing, and tensions would develop between the apparat and its conservative wing. Thus, a coalition would not involve all democrats or the entire apparat but parts of each. But he firmly held that a coalition was the only strategy for democrats who wished for democracy in practice as well as in words.[59]

By the end of 1990, coalition had become for many the only apparent solution. Different arguments were marshaled to support it, but ultimately proponents considered coalition pragmatic, even if it was not necessarily desirable or easy. The idea of coalition talks was not a new one for democrats. It was one item adopted at the May conference of Democratic Russia. Its chair, Nikolai Travkin, however, had coalition "with other parties and political organizations" in mind rather than coalition with the apparat.[60] Nevertheless, need for a coalition of progressive forces had been one strand within democratic thinking since 1989. The issue was now becoming one of how wide the coalition should become. Should it, or should it not, embrace elements of the apparat?

Many reformers in 1989 had called for cooperation with the "progressive forces" within the CPSU. The Russian Popular Front, for instance, argued that the system was in crisis and that a "revolutionary situation" prevailed. The "neofeudal domination of the *nomenklatura*" kept the people in poverty. The solution was to overthrow the apparat.[61] The best way to do this, according to the Russian Popular Front, was to support perestroika and draw together honest communists, non-party people, and believers. Together they could press for federalism, not centralism; an economy geared to consumers; a free market; a convertible ruble; a gradual reduction in the state sector; an encouragement of private business; and independent banks.[62] Pragmatism called for cooperation with some members of the CPSU. Thus, receptivity to the idea of coalition already existed in the thinking of popular fronts and radical reformers. Similar ideas underpinned the subsequent formation of the Movement for Democratic Reforms launched in 1991 by Yakovlev, Shevardnadze, Popov, and others discussed in the previous chapter.[63]

In the summer of 1991, Popov intensified his call for immediate action. If the CPSU had "marked time" in the past, now democrats were doing so at their peril. The main problem was that "we disorganized the old system but have not yet destroyed it."[64] An entire batch of "general democratic tasks" had to be performed urgently. Those who opposed "bureaucratic socialism" needed to organize a political party because now the danger came from fascism, "a third force."[65] The threat came from "lumpen patriots, lumpen chauvinists, the lumpen proletariat, the lumpen intelligentsia, the lumpen functionary, the lumpen apparat."[66] The conservatives now lacked credibility, and democrats were insufficient in number, lacked unity, and lacked experience. If democrats did not come together in coalition, lumpen solutions could triumph. Out of the Movement for Democratic Reforms must come a new parliamentary party that would strengthen the democratic movement, not weaken it. And it should not entail a reshuffling of Travkin's Democratic Party of Russia.[67]

Ultimately, Popov's preferred solutions to crisis in 1990 and in 1991 were a broad coalition of democrats and a more focused democratic party. Certain factors militated against both (as the last chapter showed). In many respects, the political prerequisites for Popov's solutions were wanting, including the political will of a sufficient number of democrats to forge a new party and cooperate. Continued commitment to a democratic movement after August 1991 and conviction that the Russian parliament was thwarting reform led Popov to threaten resignation in December.[68] He finally did resign in June 1992, announcing that he wished to devote himself entirely to the Russian Movement for Democratic Reforms, which had in January elected him its chair.[69]

Afanasyev: Self-destructive Drift and the Crisis of Power

Like Popov, Iurii Afanasyev, historian and people's deputy,[70] in December 1990 feared "the coming dictatorship," which was one step nearer because of Gorbachev's increased powers.[71] Afanasyev argued that a "coalition of conservative and reactionary forces ha[d] been gathering strength," consisting of "the party apparat, the KGB, the military-industrial complex, and the generals."[72] Gorbachev had capitulated to pressure from them. Moreover, "Gorbachev does not face reality and admit the glaring inadequacy of the present executive branch to deal with the present historical moment." One result was the "functional inability of society to move forward within the present power structure."[73] Without new administrative measures to ensure transition to "a fundamentally new economy ... we will remain stuck in our current condition of self-destructive drift."[74]

The USSR, in Afanasyev's view, was suffering "an all-encompassing crisis of power." There was "impotence in the executive," as shown "in the steady expansion of the president's powers" and in his "growing dependence on the police agencies and the army" and "on the control of force."[75] But the crisis of power was broader. It had come to include the legislative branch because the "Supreme Soviet handed over its legislative functions without a murmur to the president." This triggered a "crisis within the ruling circle," as evidenced by Shevardnadze's resignation.[76] Afanasyev saw four main contradictions in need of attention by the leadership: the "forced leveling of the republics," a transition to a market in an economy permeated by the military-industrial complex, the absence of civil society, and the state of public consciousness.[77]

The nationality problem was an old one, predating the Bolshevik Revolution. Soviet rule had subsequently "flattened out" different civilizations, "produced rivers of blood, the arbitrary division of land, and the loss of freedom. Borders were set up wherever it suited the state." "Stalinist horrors" punished and moved nations and redrew their borders. Not surprisingly, the component nationalities of the USSR "reject the idea of fraternal friendship and a unified Soviet Union: the very idea of a treaty establishing a new union has lost or is rapidly losing its attraction to them."[78] But herein lay the contradiction. The problem facing the USSR could be solved only "through cooperation among the republics, but for reasons with deep historical roots that cooperation is impossible."[79] Joint effort was vital because of the present economic division of labor, which, for example, left Kazakhstan "a source of raw materials" and Uzbekistan "hostage to its cotton monoculture." The economy could function "only in more or less coordinated rhythms."[80]

Transition to a market economy, however, was "distorted" by the enormous military-industrial complex, which swallowed up "more than half of all the machinery produced in the USSR." Afanasyev claimed that "more than 65 percent of all production is for military purposes," but "only 5 percent of military products are for long-term use."[81] The dilemma was how to transform such an economy into a market system. Centralized management and the command-administrative system had to go; but the second dangerous contradiction was that "we cannot overcome the military-industrial complex without using those centralized methods."[82] Problems were compounded by the secrecy still surrounding the size and cost of the complex.

The absence of civil society further aggravated economic transition. Here difficulties derived from the idea that "everyone or almost everyone [was] supposed to be the same."[83] People were not viewed as having different interests or as belonging to different groups. On a leash to the state, most people did not express the desire for anything new or seem to want positive changes in society. The result was "a mood in favor of equalizing" and "a willingness to live in shabby circumstances and to disregard the humiliation involved as long as a guaranteed minimum of social goods [was] made available."[84] Many people were reduced to living like cattle, and "what [was] more frightening, they [did] not ask to live any other way."[85] These characteristics demonstrated "a deep lack of civic and self-awareness," resulting in a "deformation of consciousness." A society "broken in spirit" and suffering from "social weariness" meant people "lacking in social consciousness." Criminals, for instance, had come to be seen as "normal." Intellectuals were desperate to work abroad because Soviet society did not want their creative ideas and solutions.[86]

The fourth contradiction could be found in a public consciousness that viewed a market economy according to the Stalinist logic of "I'll force you to be happy!" Until the USSR became capable of trading, even bartering, it would continue to "speak a different economic language from the rest of the modern world."[87]

These four contradictions, according to Afanasyev, were extremely difficult to resolve because of the "deepening crisis of the system and the regime."[88] The picture, however, was even more complicated because:

> The current crisis coincides with another, larger one, which began in the nine-
> teenth century—the crisis, or perhaps the exhaustion, of this Eurasian civiliza-
> tion, with its egalitarian, statist ethic and its imperial forms and values. This
> civilization is no longer workable. The autonomous elements within it of Bud-
> dhist and Byzantine Christian civilizations, elements that were capable of devel-
> oping on their own, were suppressed, and are only now getting a chance to
> strengthen themselves—a subject that deserves independent treatment.[89]

The country was facing a "long-term crisis" that had come on top of "the
collapse of Eurasia." In this context, "the possibility of authoritarianism and
its harsher form, dictatorship, remains a grave danger." Moreover, there was
"tragedy in Gorbachev's fate: the initiator of perestroika may become its de-
stroyer."[90] This final thought was hardly an original one. Sakharov had predicted it more than a year earlier, and most radicals were uttering it throughout 1990 and with greater conviction in the early months of 1991.[91]

Afanasyev's anxiety heightened in 1991, as Popov's did. In April,
Afanasyev stressed that "the authoritarian matrix is so tenacious in this
country."[92] He warned that it was not being undermined by the "peculiar
situation" in which Yeltsin, Sobchak, and Popov found themselves. The
"drama of the democratic movement," now being played out in the Russian
parliament, was one of "unpredictable outbursts" and "incoherent discussions." Obliged as leaders to take into account a range of political views,
Yeltsin and Popov had "become less radical and less decisive." And this lack
of decisiveness had disappointed erstwhile democratic supporters and
meant that the democratic movement was "in opposition to the leaders" it
had nominated. This meant danger for democrats and for their leaders,
which was not eased by the "amorphous" nature of the movement and its
lack of "a clear social base."[93] Another serious problem was that "people
who consider themselves democrats aspire to ideals not formulated on our
soil—known to us from abroad from philosophy and history. We have no
middle stratum in society that constitutes the foundation of stability for civil
society."[94]

Few commentators had referred to the importance of a middle class for
the formation of civil society. This was, indeed, an historian's analysis. In
addressing the question, Afanasyev was confronting the relevance of social
structure to polity. Popov, too, had moved in a similar direction when expressing fears of lumpen elements in society. The unspoken dilemma here
was that if a middle class really was necessary for civil society to blossom
and for democratization to be successful, then democratization would fail.

Skirting this key implication, Afanasyev went on to observe that democrats may all have rejected the idea of communism but were seriously divided about what to do in practice. In this context of divergence, he warned that a new authoritarianism was likely, advising that it was time to "keep our distance" from disappointing leaders, "not to part ways or deny them support," but "to support them more effectively."[95] How, he asked, could democrats praise Yeltsin for wrenching 50 billion rubles for Russia from the USSR's budget without first knowing how the funds would be allocated? This oversight was serious since it was not known "how resources [were] divided inside the military-industrial complex and the other areas of the national economy."[96] Above all, democrats should ask more questions of democrats and scrutinize their policies closely.

Afanasyev worried that many so-called democrats were not being democratic. He held that "democrats are supposed to criticize such actions, insisting on more radical reforms." This would constitute support for Yeltsin because support did not entail shouting, "Glory!"[97] In sum, the crisis of the democratic movement would not be resolved until democrats became democratic.

The idea that democrats lacked the skills to be democratic circulated in 1990. As the last chapter showed, in the soviets intolerance, verbosity in speeches, and the inability to compromise were some of the problems. Others expressed the view that democrats could not rise above their party backgrounds, even if they had shaken off their membership. As one lawyer remarked to me, "They have left the CPSU, but it has not left them."[98]

Afanasyev's reflections were those of a troubled democrat. Some of his concerns were also growing among reformers who wondered if historical predicament, political divisions, and social structure were once more making democracy unattainable.

Yeltsin: Coordinated Persecution and CPSU Resistance

Yeltsin approached crisis in rather different terms and saw it played out in two arenas: in his own political career and in the direction of domestic politics. Unlike Popov and Afanasyev, Yeltsin did not engage in intellectual discourse on the characteristics and consequences of crisis. Rather, his thoughts were steeped in the practical realities of day-to-day political life and were more simply put.

Yeltsin believed that his personal political crisis from 1987 onward stemmed from "coordinated persecution"[99] and that the more general political crisis was the result of the CPSU's reluctance to pursue perestroika. Yeltsin confronted directly the attempted coup of August 1991, his third crisis, and his brave and unwavering leadership did much to ensure the successful defense of the Russian parliament against troops.

In a letter to Gorbachev of 12 September 1987, Yeltsin accused Egor Ligachev of having persecuted him since the June plenum of the Central Committee of that year.[100] Later, in October 1987 at another plenum, Yeltsin delivered a speech calling for a restructuring of the work of party committees and asked to be relieved from his duties as candidate member of the Politburo. He interpreted subsequent speeches against him as a "betrayal," which was "hard to bear," especially from past friends.[101] He portrayed Gorbachev as deliberately misinterpreting his words and as being extremely cruel when, in November 1987, he instructed Yeltsin to leave his hospital bed to attend a meeting of the Moscow city committee, which then dismissed him. Gorbachev, in Yeltsin's mind, was being "inhuman and immoral."[102] Feeling the helpless victim of unjust attack, Yeltsin commented as follows:

> What is it called when a person is killed by words because, really, it was like genuine murder? After all, I could have been simply dismissed at the plenum. But no, they had to take delight in a process of betrayal when comrades who had worked side by side with me for two years without any sign of discord suddenly start to say such things that until now are hard to believe. If I had not been under such medication, of course, I would have joined the battle to refute the lies, to show the baseness of the speakers—precisely the baseness![103]

Subsequently, Yeltsin received far fewer telephone calls than usual and felt condemned to the political wilderness. He described this as a "crisis," remarking that "I had to drag and haul myself out of the crisis in which I found myself. I glanced around and there was no one. A sort of emptiness or vacuum had appeared. A human vacuum."[104]

Yeltsin saw a more general crisis in the way in which the party itself operated:

> Party organizations are at the tail end of all grand events. Here there is practically no perestroika (except in global politics). From this stems a whole chain of consequences. The result is that we wonder why perestroika has become stuck in the primary party organizations.
> Perestroika was conceived and formulated as revolutionary. But its realization, especially in the party—the same old self-serving situation, petty and bureaucratic and an outwardly loud approach.[105]

The dilemma in practice was that there was "an abundance of paperwork." There were those who, "counting every day tomatoes, tea, railway carriages," could report no substantial progress. There were "meetings about trivial questions, fault-finding objections, hunts for negative material."[106] In short, party committees retained their old inactive styles, which were contrary to the spirit of perestroika. Moreover, fear of dismissal hung over many committee members, making initiative and creative work impossible. The main result was that the party itself had put the brakes on perestroika.

To deal with this crisis, in his capacity as president of the RSFSR, on 20 July 1991, Yeltsin issued a decree on *departizatsiia* (departization). Party cells in the workplace were ordered to disband.[107] The solution to the crisis of the CPSU halting reform was to ban its party cells. In the week preceding the August coup, the main topic of conversation in the capital was how this decree would be implemented. "I wonder how it will happen," or "How will it be done?" was frequently heard.[108] *Moskovskie Novosti* in an article entitled "The First Week of Departization" wryly commented, "We have already somehow started to get accustomed to the fact that new decrees and laws just issued and passed may not be fulfilled, especially if they are distant from real life."[109]

Others praised the decree. A letter to *Kuranty* declared, "I am an ordinary communist and with both hands vote for speedy adoption of the Russian president's decree! Let's work in the factory rather than hold meetings and chat."[110] Only Polozkov's supporters, hard-line communists, the letter writer suggested, opposed the decree. And Democratic Russia welcomed it for helping conquer the "monolithic position of the CPSU." Workers could still, it noted, engage in politics out of working hours.[111] More cautious backing came from social democrats such as Oleg Rumiantsev, who wanted the decree to be ratified first by the Russian Supreme Soviet so as to gain legitimacy.[112] Viktor Aksiuchits, chair of the Russian Christian Democratic Movement, commented that "the decree is very good and vital, but it is only the first step."[113]

For loyal Leninists, Yeltsin's decree on *departizatsiia* constituted a crisis. Party cells had existed in the workplace for seven decades. The decree, coupled with the planned signing of the Union Treaty on 20 August, provoked them to act. After the coup's defeat, Yeltsin continued to curb the party's activities. On 23 August in a televised Russian parliament and alongside a humiliated Gorbachev, Yeltsin demonstrated his boosted power by calling for a suspension of the activity of the hard-line Russian Communist Party. Deputies concurred and Yeltsin immediately signed the decree, thereby overriding Gorbachev's objection that not all the party's members were involved in the coup. The suspension, Yeltsin declared, was not yet a ban and was necessary while investigations into the role of the party in the coup proceeded.[114] Yeltsin's crises of "coordinated persecution" and CPSU resistance to reform were now decisively over. Further crises, however, were just beginning for Russia.

The Democratic Union:
Gorbachev Propping Up Totalitarianism

Whereas Gorbachev, Popov, and Afanasyev talked a great deal about crisis in late 1990, members of the Democratic Union were arguing one year earlier that a crisis situation existed. The disparity in timing can be explained by very different conceptions of crisis. Gorbachev and many reformers saw totalitarianism as a system of the past that had already been partially transformed into something more democratic. The Democratic Union's documents and newspapers argued that totalitarianism persisted and that Gorbachev was propping it up.[115] This was the crisis.

The Democratic Union was not a large or influential party (as already explained in Chapters 5 and 7), but its ideas on pluralism, democracy, civil society, and crisis were more fully thought through than those of many other parties and made crucial contributions to the discourse that redefined society and polity. For this reason, they are given space here. They reflect a particular pattern of thinking that developed during processes of transition and disintegration.

According to the Democratic Union, what was taking place was, not democratization, but "the creation of more adaptable and effective forms of the monopoly of the power of the *nomenklatura*."[116] Thus, the elections of 1989 illustrated, "not a rejection of totalitarianism, but its modification."[117] The Democratic Union accused the CPSU of maintaining its monopoly hold of power by delegating no further than the top ranks of the *nomenklatura*. The CPSU was also guilty of rigging the composition of the new Supreme Soviet so that it consisted of people's deputies loyal to the CPSU. And special mechanisms guaranteed CPSU control. Cadres policy, for instance, ensured that a "party mafia" (*partomafia*) dominated the soviet executive committees, the soviets, the legal system, voters' commissions, and a host of other organizations. *Partomafia* combined with "partocracy" (*partokratiia*) ensured totalitarianism. *Partomafia* existed in central and local government and dominated the media; it also guarded CPSU monopoly control of newspapers, which meant that the unofficial press could not be sold in kiosks but only more precariously on the streets.[118] Monopoly power was thereby perpetuated, but with some liberal rhetoric to create the impression of different policies.

The myth that Gorbachev was a liberal was one that the Democratic Union set out to dispel. Why, asked one of its newspapers, did many Westerners see Gorbachev as a "liberal reformer" when nothing in his career indicated such a position? His ideas were similar to those of Iurii Andropov, Mikhail Suslov, and Andrei Gromyko. Margaret Thatcher's statement that Gorbachev was a man with whom she could do business showed a naive understanding of Soviet politics.[119] Gorbachev merely added new titles to his name, including that of an undemocratically elected president.[120] The aim of the CPSU was to create the impression that there was no alternative to Gorbachev except bloodshed and dictatorship. This was a ploy for ensuring that CPSU domination persisted.[121]

For the Democratic Union, the way out of this crisis was "liberalization of the economy, politics, and ideology." The contradictory economic policy of the CPSU, which combined direction from above with a free market, had to be rejected since it was destined to lead to "collapse." A free-market economy had to be established without totalitarian direction.[122] And an end to totalitarianism could best be brought about by the Democratic Union setting up "an alternative structure" against totalitarian ideas and against the totalitarian organizational base.[123]

One essential tactic was civil disobedience. The Democratic Union advocated demonstrations against the CPSU and refusal to cooperate with the authorities.[124] For instance, when its members were arrested, they had a policy of passive non-cooperation with the militia. They would not talk and tried to be as personally isolated from the legal process as possible, showing distance and disdain.[125] This was one aspect of building an alternative civil society. Another aspect would be the adoption of genuine free elections and the setting up of "active cells for the formation of civil society."[126] (The importance the Democratic Union accorded civil society was discussed in Chapter 6.) It was seen as an essential ingredient of normal society.[127]

For the Democratic Union, crisis could in fact be traced back to Leninism since "the plan of Lenin" had been to strangle the party, strangle Russia, and then strangle the whole of humanity.[128] A constituent assembly, now favored by the Democratic Union as one way out of the crisis, has been denied political life by Lenin in 1918. One of the Democratic Union's rallying slogans, harking back to 1917, became "All power to the Constituent Assembly."[129] The party's newspapers gave detailed accounts of how in 1917 and 1918 Lenin banned other parties as "enemies of the people" and as "bourgeois."[130]

In sum, crisis stemmed from the totalitarian nature of the system. Leninism was its origin, out of which had grown a dictatorial CPSU that dominated economy, polity, and society. Partocracy and party mafia penetrated all institutions and controlled them. Leaders of the CPSU such as Gorbachev perpetuated the system. So Gorbachev personified crisis. Communists were the enemy. Consistent with this, members of the Democratic Union in 1990 castigated the Twenty-eighth Party Congress for bringing despair and melancholy to the people. The delegates, so-called representatives of the people, did not really care what was happening in the country and were unable in the twelve days of the congress to produce one speech analyzing whether the CPSU was actually needed.[131] Likewise, when the founding congress of Russia's Communist Workers' Party took place in December 1991 in Ekaterinburg, members of the Democratic Union picketed outside to express their opposition.[132]

The Democratic Union held that the logic of totalitarianism denied a place to individuality, genuine pluralism, civil society, and humane values. Only a multi-party democracy with a separation of legislative, executive, and judicial powers could offer these. The solution to the crisis, then, necessitated a thorough destruction of present economic and political structures and a commitment to new ones. The Democratic Union's contributions to discussions of economic and political change were distinctive for their wholesale rejection of the current system. Radical answers were required; otherwise crisis would persist.

Other self-proclaimed democrats, particularly erstwhile supporters of Gorbachev such as Aleksandr Yakovlev, did not offer reflections on the nature of crisis until 1991.[133] Unlike the Democratic Union, they had previously been committed to reform within the system. Not until the end of 1990 did they begin to suspect that such reform could not proceed successfully. Their thoughts on crisis stemmed from reaction to political developments in 1990 and 1991 and were not part of a broader philosophical system of ideas, as had been the case for the Democratic Union. Nonetheless, disillusioned reformers began to reiterate some of the ideas expressed by the Democratic Union two years earlier. This did not mean that they were convinced by the Democratic Union to seek more radical solutions than they had previously advocated. But ideas espoused by the Democratic Union would have been known to them.

Miners: Partocracy, Shortages, and Price Increases

Like the Democratic Union, miners in the Kuzbass identified dominance by the CPSU as a facet of political life that had to change if crisis was to abate. In *Nasha Gazeta,* they declared, "The country is in deep crisis. The main trouble is monopolism permeating all spheres of society. The way out of the crisis is through the development of democracy and a market economy with social defense of workers and legalization of an institutionalized opposition."[134] Overlap with the ideas of the Democratic Union was high, although lacking the more philosophical trimmings.

There was a general feeling among miners in the spring of 1990 that the government had not honored the promises made after the strikes of 1989 and had therefore betrayed the miners. In Novokuznetsk at the first congress of the independent workers' movement held in May 1990, the Confederation of Labor presented a declaration of basic principles. It noted, "It is hard to come out of the crisis," but success depended on the democratic workers' movement liaising closely with peasants and the democratic intelligentsia. Above all, a "decisive 'no'" had to be said to the past, to the administrative-command system, to political lawlessness, to tyranny, to scornful attitudes toward workers, to empty shelves and low pay, to social injustice and corruption, to bad management, and to crime. The most important political task for the workers' movement was "struggle for the liquidation of the dictatorship of the CPSU and its apparat."[135]

Again, these sentiments were similar to those expressed by the Democratic Union and other democrats but did not reflect on the meaning of pluralism and civil society. Emphasis fell on the culprit of the crisis—the CPSU and its apparat. The obvious solution was their removal. Discourse was pragmatic and focused on the immediate sources of the crisis and the need to challenge them now.

A resolution adopted by the labor collective in Vorkuta in July 1990 elaborated the point.[136] The economic and political system of the Soviet state, it declared, was "not in a condition to stop the development of economic crisis." The main reason for the crisis was "the monopoly power of the CPSU" and its unwillingness, because of the privileged lives of the apparat, to promote radical change.[137] Democratization had not sufficiently changed matters because the Supreme Soviet was not in a position to check middle-level administrators in the ministries and party apparat. In sum, "the government of the USSR is not in a position to manage the country or to fulfill its functions or to carry out the resolutions of the Supreme Soviet."[138] And violent acts against progressive movements were growing. Defense of the CPSU's own power was leading to attacks on those who could adopt appropriate policies.

In response to the crisis, miners demanded radical political changes: resignation of the government; depoliticization of the KGB, MVD, army, and judiciary; the departure of communist party committees from the workplace; socialization of the property of the CPSU; a sharing of the property of official trade unions with newly formed unions; public acknowledgment by the CPSU of its mistakes and crimes; and a rotation of deputies on the Supreme Soviet. The miners declared their support for Yeltsin and argued against the view that they were instigating protests. On the contrary, Prime Minister Ryzhkov had provoked their actions, as would Prime Minister Pavlov a year later. They concluded that "the political strike is the penultimate form of organized struggle by workers for their rights. And, we hope, the last."[139] Similar views were reiterated throughout 1990 in *Nasha Gazeta*.[140]

In March 1991, striking miners demanded the resignation of Gorbachev and of his government. When ministers in April offered to double wages, miners stood firm and subsequently called for a general strike. A draft law of 16 April to ban political strikes did not deter them.[141] Only after the mines were transferred to Russia away from central control (one aspect of the process of shifting powers) did the miners vote to return to work.[142] When in August 1991 Yeltsin called for a general strike and resistance to the coup, miners immediately responded. They more than any other workers had learned how to use the strike as a political weapon.

Although rare strikes had occurred in the Brezhnev era, the weapon of strike action against the state was not wielded with confidence until 1989.[143] Thereafter strikes, particularly by miners, were viewed by the leadership as serious threats to political stability and to fuel supplies to industry and homes. Thus, how miners in the Donbass, Kuzbass, and Vorkuta interpreted the changing economic and political situation and how they reacted to it were of vital importance to politicians.

The United Labor Front: Crisis as Counter-revolution

Not all workers, however, were prepared to advocate a general strike in response to the August coup. The United Labor Front was loyal to Leninism, as it understood the term, and offered an interpretation of crisis that contrasted sharply with that of the miners. Workers' movements and organizations contributed to discourse on reform, especially after 1989, but were divided.

In its newspaper *Chto Delat'?* the United Labor Front held that "counter-revolution" in 1990 was a serious threat. A new "Soviet bourgeoisie" was active on the black market and could be found among speculating owners of cooperatives. The Soviet bourgeoisie was out "to take social revenge on 1917" and to worsen the lot of working people.[144] In sum, perestroika and democratization were undermining socialism. The United Labor Front attacked the adherents of perestroika for many of their policies. Anatolii Sobchak, for example, came under fire for making the "sensational" suggestion that several landowning families should be compensated for the property taken away from them in 1917.[145] Likewise, Popov was slandered for being a founding leader of Democratic Russia, a political group given to demagogy and "with whom the overwhelming majority of Russians have absolutely no connection."[146]

The United Labor Front believed that the way out of the crisis of counter-revolution was through the new Russian Communist Party. At a political meeting held on 18 June 1990, the United Labor Front gave its support to the party's formation. Like other Leninists, it viewed the party as based "on Leninist foundations" and as the "decisive link in the struggle for bringing the country out of the crisis."[147] *Chto Delat'?* reported that the Russian Communist Party was committed to "the rebirth of genuine Soviet power through the creation of workers' committees," thereby guaranteeing "power to the people." It pledged to fight "anti-people's economic reforms" and the sale of the country to its own capitalists and to foreign capitalists. The party wanted to see prices lowered and an increase in the standard of living for ordinary people. One of its slogans was "The solidarity of working Russia— basis of the durability of the USSR." The solution to the crisis was a strong, stable, and united state run on lines similar to those of the Soviet socialism of the past, with the Communist Party guiding the people.[148]

For the United Labor Front, crisis revolved around how to run the state. In keeping with this concern, the front page of *Chto Delat'?* published an appeal from the KGB to the general secretary of the CPSU and to the Supreme Soviet of the USSR. The appeal argued that the situation in the country was "critical," giving rise "to the question of the fate of the socialist fatherland." Although perestroika was an "objective law" that no healthy thinking Soviet citizen could dispute, the situation was such that certain forces were set to "liquidate" Soviet power, undermine socialist construction, and bring about the "disintegration of our federal state." Making use of "weapons of political demagogy, intimidation, slander, blackmail, and moral terror, they are creating a situation of social tension, of tyranny and anarchy, disorganizing the activity of organs of power and administration, infringing people's legal rights and interests." Thus, their activities coincided with those of Western special services and of foreign "anti-Soviet centers."[149]

In this context of threat to sacred socialist values, *Chto Delat'?* announced that "Soviet chekists act and will act in the interests of the people and firmly, successfully, and dependably defend the security of socialist construction, defend the rights and freedoms of every Soviet person, and defend our Soviet democracy."[150] Soviet chekists represented political salvation for the people at a time of great uncertainty. The article stressed, however, that the current generation of KGB employees had nothing in common with those who had committed crimes under Stalin.

Soviet chekists themselves argued that they were not separate from society and that they "recognize[d] their responsibility for the fate of the country." While paying lip service to "the further development of democracy and glasnost," they declared "love for the Soviet Motherland" and claimed that "for us chekists, the interests and security of the Fatherland are the meaning of all life."[151] The concepts *Otechestvo* (Fatherland) and *Rodina* (Motherland) were repeatedly used. Emphasis fell on patriotism, security, discipline, and a strong state. The KGB advocated political leadership of the people by the CPSU before the people and condemned nationalist unrest as destabilizing and the black market as unsocialist.

The United Labor Front reiterated these arguments throughout 1991. What was needed was loyalty to Leninism. All perestroika had offered since 1987 was "bourgeois counter-revolution."[152] But before 1991, the bourgeoisie's social support base had been relatively weak. Now, however, the bourgeoisie had seized the means of mass information, had secured the support of the president, and had launched onto a direct course of denationalization and privatization. These changes had led to a shift from "peaceful forms of counter-revolution to violent ones," from "bourgeois democracy to bourgeois dictatorship," resulting in "a dictatorship of the exploiting minority against the toiling majority."[153]

The crisis was that "class antagonisms have become a fact." Society was divided into exploiters and exploited, rich and poor. In this context, the United Labor Front declared that "the prevention of civil war in the country is not only necessary but also possible." To achieve this meant reviving the CPSU as the political party of the working class, ending denationalization, and making Gorbachev accountable for the disorganization of the party and the disintegration of the Union.[154]

The third congress of the United Labor Front also concluded that for Soviet power to be returned to the workers, "the bourgeois presidency and parliament" had to be "liquidated" and new elections had to be held. As for economic collapse, that could be averted only by "strict measures of a centralized and planned character." It was essential to abandon "market rubbish" and to establish a state monopoly on foreign trade. The flow of natural resources to other countries had to cease, and all retail prices had to be frozen.[155] More vitriolic attacks on Gorbachev, Yeltsin, and Travkin followed sharp price increases on 2 April.[156] The only acceptable solution to the crisis of the Soviet bourgeoisie and the Soviet "dem-fascists," according to the United Labor Front, was reinstatement of the power of the CPSU. Leninism, not fascism, had to be supported.

Leninists: Crisis and the Loss of Leninism

Crisis for Leninists, a broad group of people including those in the United Labor Front, referred to the loss of those very characteristics that the democrats and striking miners wanted to abolish—Leninism, one-party rule, respect for the October Revolution, and a planned socialist economy. For hard-line Leninists, perestroika and democratization had compromised Leninism. Those on the right wing of the CPSU, including some members of the military, leaders of industry and agriculture, and some new workers' movements, subscribed to this stance. Milder Leninists accepted the need for economic reform but still adhered to the position that "if in the economy, like fresh air, we need to move forward, then in socio-political life, in party life we need to return back to Leninism. That means a return to a Leninist manner of socialism, to a Leninist understanding of the role of the Communist Party as a political leader of the Soviet people, to a Leninist style of party work and of party leadership."[157] For both groups of Leninists, salvation had to come from a Leninist Communist Party. This was precisely what Popov, Yeltsin, Afanasyev, Travkin, striking miners, and different democratic groups were arguing against.

Discourse in political meetings attended by Leninists was often heated. When in September 1990 the CPSU convened a meeting at its agitation-propaganda headquarters in Moscow to discuss economic reform, CPSU members wearing medals shouted at the professional economists on the platform and angrily defended socialism and Leninism.[158] The start of the scheduled discussion of the Shatalin plan was delayed twenty minutes as members of the audience repeatedly cried, "We have already heard all this."[159] In the lively disorder that preceded the speakers' presentations, workers asked who would suffer from the transition to a market economy. They feared that the people would witness factory closures, unemployment, and unaffordably high prices. When the invited speakers were finally allowed to begin, they were regularly interrupted with interjections from the floor that the Shatalin plan was not socialist, was not popular, and meant a move toward an exploitative market economy. Here economic reform and what it might bring were the crisis. The stormy meeting took place in an auditorium with one of Lenin's slogans enshrined on the wall: "All propaganda and agitation must carry a genuine communist character." The floor was certainly upholding Lenin's message, while the sponsoring CPSU was trying to convince its party faithful that reform was Leninist. The CPSU was failing.[160] Pressures on the CPSU by its own membership to halt reform were strong. Discourse was belligerent, volatile, and divided.

Loyal to the values expressed on the floor of the meeting, more than thirty political groups put their signatures to "An Announcement of Socio-political Organizations and Movements of Socialist Choice" in February 1991.[161] For the Communist Party of the RSFSR, the United Labor Front, Soiuz, the Russian Writers' Union, Interfronts, Otechestvo, Women for a Socialist Future for Our Children, the Moscow club of Communists-Leninists, Edinstvo, the All-Union People's Patriotic Front, the Leningrad branch of the Russian Academy of Sciences, and others, the "socio-economic situation" was now "critical." The features of the crisis were clear and included "anarchy and chaos, a wrecked state, destitution, and blood. Political disagreements are acquiring an antagonistic character. They have reached a climax of separatism and nationalism; economic and cultural ties between republics and regions are collapsing."[162]

"Masked by slogans of national rebirth and sovereignty," "fascist forces" had come to power in separate regions of the country, the announcement continued. "Calling themselves democrats, they propagate nationalism and chauvinism, shamelessly trampling on the rights of individuals." These developments were leading to "a disintegration of the Union of Soviet Socialist Republics." In these "emergency conditions," a meeting of "socio-political organizations and movements supporting the socialist choice of our people" had taken place advocating "the consolidation of all patriotic and international forces of the country."[163] Their stated aims were to preserve the union, support socialism, uphold the constitution, oppose separatism, and "back all positive actions of higher organs of state power while at the same time publicly criticizing their inconsequentiality and indecisiveness."[164] There was no time for mistakes and tests. In the forthcoming referendum on 17 March, citizens should vote to preserve the USSR since the "fate of the motherland" was at stake.[165]

By 1991, many members of right-wing groups and movements had become appalled by developments in society, economy, and polity. *Gorbastroika,* as they disparagingly called it, had resulted in unacceptable levels of crime, immorality, a new bourgeoisie, and a lack of discipline, order, stability, and effectiveness in politics. For at least five months before the coup, Leninists had been openly advocating a state of emergency. On 2 April, at the second congress of Soiuz, its chair, Iurii Blokhin, called for an immediate state of emergency to last six months.[166] At the same time, Colonel Viktor Alksnis called for a special session of the USSR Congress of People's Deputies to oust Gorbachev.[167] The verbal attacks on Gorbachev by members of Soiuz temporarily quieted down at the end of April after Gorbachev and leaders of the republics signed a republican declaration.[168] For the right, Gorbachev needed to appear firm and in control. So actions such as his strike ban of 16 May in energy, coal, oil, chemicals, and petrochemicals were seen in a positive light.[169] But with Yeltsin's growing authority in Russia, his decree on *departizatsiia,* and the looming date of 20 August for the signing of the Union Treaty, "crisis" for the right was mounting.

Leaders of the August Coup:
Crisis and the State of Emergency

Leninists briefly welcomed the coup of August and the new messages delivered by the media. Television and radio suddenly changed from lively debate to sterile announcements and classical music. Broadcasts on 19 August and the *Pravda* published on 20 August informed citizens that Vice-President Genadii Yanaev had taken over the powers of the president because of Gorbachev's ill-health. Yanaev had proclaimed a state of emergency "with the aim of overcoming the deep and many-sided crisis; political, internationality, and civilian confrontations; chaos; and anarchy that threaten the life and safety of citizens of the Soviet Union, the sovereignty, territorial integrity, freedom, and independence of our Fatherland."[170] The state of emergency ostensibly met "the demands of a wide section of the population for the adoption of the most decisive measures for the prevention of society's slide into general national catastrophe, for the upholding of law and order."[171]

The State of Emergency would obtain for six months and would be led by a state committee for the state of emergency in the USSR (GKChP SSSR). In addition to Yanaev, the GKChP SSSR was composed of Oleg Baklanov, first deputy chair of the Defense Council; General Vladimir Kriuchkov, chair of the KGB; Valentin Pavlov, prime minister; Boris Pugo, minister of internal affairs; Vasilii Starodubtsev, chair of the Union of Peasants; Aleksandr Tiziakov, president of the Association of State Enterprises; and Marshal Dmitrii Yazov, defense minister. Decisions of the GKChP were to be "strictly" implemented by "all organs of power and management, people in posts, and citizens on the whole of Soviet territory."[172]

In its "Appeal to the Soviet People," the GKChP declared that "deadly danger" was hanging over "the motherland." Gorbachev's reforms, which had been intended to bring "dynamic development" to the country, had run into a "dead end." In place of enthusiasm were "lack of trust, apathy, and despair." Power at every level had lost credibility. Malicious destruction was spreading in all state institutions, and "the country had effectively become ungovernable."[173]

Taking advantage of political changes, "extremist groups" had emerged favoring a "liquidation of the Soviet Union and a disintegration of the state." They had cynically speculated on nationalist feelings "as a screen for the satisfaction of their own ambitions." A situation of "moral-political terror" had resulted. They now had to answer "before mothers and fathers" for deaths and for a half-million refugees. Because of them, tens of millions of Soviet people had lost the peace and joy of life that they had previously enjoyed as "a united family."[174]

The "crisis of power," in turn, had had a "catastrophic" effect on the economy. A "chaotic" drift toward the market had resulted in "a burst of egoism." In addition, "a war of laws" and "centrifugal tendencies" had contributed to the destruction of economic mechanisms. This had led to falling standards of living and to "the flourishing of speculation and the black market." Without urgent measures to stabilize the economy, there would be starvation and destitution. But only irresponsible people would seek help from abroad. The solution had to be internal.[175]

For leaders of the coup, crisis affected polity and economy. But society, too, was seriously suffering. Even "elementary personal safety" was more and more "under threat":

> Crime is rising rapidly—is organized and politicized. The country is immersed in a gulf of violence and lawlessness. Never in the history of the country has there been such a spread of propaganda on sex and violence, putting the health and life of future generations under threat. Millions of people are demanding measures against the spreading tentacles of crime and flagrant immorality.[176]

"Bitter reality" demanded action. Solving the food and housing problems would be among the first tasks of the emergency committee. The people could help by upholding labor discipline, by showing pride in their Motherland, and by being patriotic.

Emergency powers were declared to cope with social collapse, crime, lawlessness, insecurity, nationalist violence, economic disintegration, and political chaos. Decree number one of GKChP, also published on the front page of *Pravda,* gave the coup leaders sweeping powers, banned social movements and political parties, and prohibited political meetings, demonstrations, and strikes. Political pluralism effectively became illegal, and crucial prerequisites for a multi-party system were removed.[177]

As self-proclaimed president, Yanaev also informed leaders of other states and the general secretary of the United Nations that the state of emergency was "temporary," would last for a half-year, and did not indicate a denial of deep reforms. It was, in fact, necessary "to save the economy from disintegration and the country from starvation, to ward off an increase in the threat of widespread civil conflict with unpredictable consequences for the peoples of the USSR and for the entire world community." The aim was to create the conditions for guaranteeing the safety of citizens through "fast stabilization" and a "normalization of socio-economic life." Otherwise, tension, confrontation, violence, and suffering would increase.[178]

The loud message relayed to citizens and to the world was that military force was necessary if a healthy economy and polity were to be restored. The implicit message was that glasnost, democratization, and a growing pluralism of thought and action had produced a devastating crisis for economy, polity, and society combined. The order, stability, normality, and morality upheld by the CPSU had been undermined.

Polity Divided

As all the foregoing views demonstrate, discourse about solutions to the crisis were diametrically opposed and irreconcilable. Agreement between the Kuzbass miners and the United Labor Front was impossible. The former wanted an end to domination of the party apparat and more radical economic reforms toward a market economy, whereas the latter still championed Leninism and advocated vigilance against counter-revolution. The working class was split on the desirability of Leninism and leadership by the CPSU.

This split extended to broader political groupings. Leninists rallied together under the loose umbrella of "socialist choice" and proclaimed that democrats were synonymous with fascists. Leninists charged that when democrats were in power, they threatened the unity of the Union. Leaders of the August coup would have found encouragement for their actions in any of the materials published by Leninists in 1990 and 1991. In the week before the coup, Leninist papers such as *Volia, Molniia, Edinstvo,* and *Chto Delat'?*

enjoyed a high profile in the Moscow underpasses, while the democratic press was hard to spot. Potential backing for a coup did exist in society, but its leaders failed to foresee that democrats in a newly politicized society, even if in the minority, were sufficiently hostile to the past to struggle against its return and were confident enough now to resist force. Escalating crisis had provoked the coup, but alternative interpretations demanded defiance of it. Opponents of the coup were varied and divided among themselves. And many of those who took to the streets around the Russian parliament lacked formal political affiliations but were committed for various reasons to an end to the CPSU in power.

Gorbachev's interpretation of the crisis was proved seriously wanting by events. His solution of strengthening the people's belief in perestroika at a time when it had obviously failed was a non-starter. His calls for stepped-up law and order, stronger executive powers, and gradual devolution to the re-publics did not address central aspects of the crisis. Most important, he lacked viable remedies.

Popov had a better grasp of the structural need for interstate associations to address the nationalities question and for radical overhaul of the political system to make it function effectively. He also showed a pragmatic commit-ment to coalition in an attempt to push consistently for economic reform. Although it was politically easier for Popov not to sit on the fence, Gorbachev's need to steer between Leninists and reformers and to seek com-promises paralyzed his ability to direct political change. And his inability to rise above his own party background ultimately became his own political crisis.

By contrast, Yeltsin's readiness to name the CPSU as a barrier to reform, to challenge its hegemony by banning party cells in the workplace, and to ex-press his support for independence for the republics, meant that his political program was congruent with the demands emerging from a rapidly chang-ing society and polity. Yeltsin was prepared to redefine society and polity more thoroughly than Gorbachev was and in so doing offered a more legiti-mate leadership in the eyes of reformers. Afanasyev's observation that Gorbachev could not face reality and could not see the glaring inadequacy of the executive to deal with the historical moment was most apt.

NOTES

1. *Izvestiia,* 16 November 1990, p. 1; *Izvestiia,* 17 November 1990, pp. 1–3; *Bakinskii Rabochii,* 17 November 1990, p. 1; *Bakinskii Rabochii,* 20 November 1990, p. 1.

2. *Moskovskie Novosti,* no. 3, 20 January 1991, p. 1.

3. The situation was not defused until Yeltsin successfully managed to get the mines transferred to Russia's jurisdiction. For details of the growing conflict and its

resolution, see RFE/RL Research Institute, *Report on the USSR,* vol. 3, no. 17, 26 April 1991, p. 29; RFE/RL Research Institute, *Report on the USSR,* vol. 3, no. 18, 3 May 1991, p. 25; RFE/RL Research Institute, *Report on the USSR,* vol. 3, no. 20, 17 May 1991, p. 37.

4. *Volia,* no. 2, March 1991, p. 1.

5. RFE/RL Research Institute, *Report on the USSR,* vol. 3, no. 18, 3 May 1991, pp. 25–26.

6. For details, see Michael Rywkin, *Moscow's Muslim Challenge: Soviet Central Asia* (London, C. Hurst, 1982), pp. 26, 34–44.

7. Interview in Moscow, September 1990.

8. Discussion of the shadow economy can be found in F.J.M. Feldbrugge, "Government and shadow economy in the Soviet Union," *Soviet Studies,* vol. 36, no. 4, 1984, pp. 528–543; Dennis O'Hearn, "The consumer second economy: Size and effects," *Soviet Studies,* vol. 32, no. 2, 1980, pp. 218–234.

9. Amartya K. Sen, *Poverty and Famines: An Essay on Entitlement and Deprivation* (Oxford, Clarendon Press, 1981).

10. For details of the 1990 grain harvest, refer to footnote 19, Chapter 1.

11. Akademicheskaia Hotel, Moscow, September 1990.

12. Conversation in Moscow, September 1990.

13. Cited in *The Independent,* 7 December 1990, p. 21. See also Stephen Dalziel, "Gorbachev: Food by decree," BBC World Service, 11 January 1991.

14. Tat'iana Tolstaia suggested that "Russians secretly feel that the West is obligated to feed them, that this is only just and fair, the result of the magic word or threat or spell that sets the aid of enchanted powers in motion. In this way did lazy Emel, the hero of a Russian fairy tale, catch a pike. The fish begged to be released, and Emel agreed, on the condition that the fish promise to help him." *The Guardian,* 25 June 1992, p. 25.

15. *Materialy XXVIII S"ezda KPSS* (Moscow, Politizdat, 1990), p. 3.

16. Ibid., p. 5.

17. Ibid.

18. Ibid.

19. Ibid., p. 7.

20. Ibid., p. 8.

21. Ibid.

22. Ibid., p. 9.

23. The Law on Secession, passed in April 1990, had required a two-thirds majority in referendum to be adopted. In the Baltic, only Lithuania, which was 80 percent Lithuanian, could be assured of a sufficient vote in favor. The law also specified a five-year transition period to secession, which was far too slow for eager nationalists.

A draft Union Treaty was eventually released in November 1990. For details, see *Izvestiia,* 24 November 1990, pp. 1–2. For subsequent debate see "Soiuznyi dogovor: Vriad li s"ezdu udastsia naverstat' to, chto upushcheno," and "Rasstanovka sil: Tsentr politicheskoi zhizni peremeshchaetsia v respubliki," both in *Moskovskie Novosti,* no. 50, 16 December 1990, p. 9.

24. Gorbachev was firm that the treaty should be accepted. See *Materialy Plenuma Tsentral'nogo Komiteta KPSS 8–9 Oktiabria 1990 g* (Moscow, Politizdat 1990), pp. 11–12; *Pravda,* 13 December 1990, p. 1.

25. *Bakinskii Rabochii,* 20 November 1990, p. 1.

26. Ibid. The Supreme Soviet gave backing to Gorbachev's proposals with 316 votes in favor, 19 against, and 31 abstentions.

27. Ibid.

28. RFE/RL Research Institute, *Report on the USSR,* vol. 3, no. 3, 18 January 1991, p. 47.

29. *Izvestiia,* 29 December 1990, p. 8.

30. *Pravda,* 15 November 1990, p. 2.

31. See *Bakinskii Rabochii,* 9 April 1991, p. 1; *Pravda,* 24 April 1991, p. 1; *Pravda,* 26 April 1991, p. 1; *Pravda,* 30 April 1991, p. 1.

32. Discussion in Moscow, August 1991.

33. Anders Aslund, *Gorbachev's Struggle for Economic Reform,* 2d ed. (London, Pinter, 1991), p. 187.

34. Gertrude E. Schroeder, "The Soviet economy on a treadmill of perestroika: Gorbachev's first five years," in Harley D. Balzer ed., *Five Years That Shook the World* (Boulder, Westview, 1991), pp. 31–48.

35. Ibid., p. 35.

36. Aslund, *Gorbachev's Struggle for Economic Reform,* pp. 185–196.

37. *Pravda,* 24 April 1991, p. 1; *Pravda,* 30 April 1991, p. 1; RFE/RL Research Institute, *Report on the USSR,* vol. 3, no. 16, 19 May 1991, p. 29.

38. In 1959, Gavriil Popov graduated in economics from Moscow University and stayed on to teach there. In the same year, he joined the CPSU. Before perestroika, he had been arguing for the need to teach management techniques. In 1988, he was appointed editor of the journal *Voprosy Ekonomiki* (Questions of Economics). In 1989, he won a seat on the Congress of People's Deputies and there became a leader of the Inter-Regional Group. In 1990, he was elected chair of the Moscow City Soviet. Popov left the CPSU in July 1990. See Archie Brown, ed., *The Soviet Union: A Biographical Dictionary* (London, Weidenfeld and Nicolson, 1990), pp. 296–297.

39. Gavriil Popov, "Perspektivy i realii," *Ogonek,* no. 50, December 1990, pp. 6–8; continued under the same title in *Ogonek,* no. 51, December 1990, pp. 5–8.

40. Ibid., no. 50, p. 6.

41. Gavriil Popov, "'Obraztsovyi gorod' stal simbolom krizisa perestroiki," *Kuranty,* 15 November 1990, p. 5.

42. Ibid.

43. Popov, "Perspektivy i realii," no. 50, p. 6.

44. Ibid., no. 50, p. 6.

45. Popov, "'Obraztsovyi gorod' stal simbolom krizisa perestroiki."

46. Popov, "Perspektivy i realii," no. 50, p. 6.

47. Ibid.

48. Ibid., p. 6.

49. Ibid., pp. 6–7.

50. Popov, "'O braztsovyi gorod' stal simbolom krizisa perestroiki."

51. Popov, "Perspektivy i realii," no. 51, p. 7.

52. Ibid., no. 50, p. 7.

53. Ibid., no. 51, p. 5.

54. Interviews with deputies and academics, Moscow, 1990 and 1991.

55. Popov, "Perspektivy i realii," no. 50, p. 7.

56. Ibid., no. 51, p. 6.

57. Ibid., pp. 6–8.

58. Ibid., p. 8.

59. Ibid.

60. *Demokraticheskaia Rossiia,* no. 1, 1990, supplement, p. 1.

61. *Programmy Rossiiskogo Narodnogo Fronta v Podderzhky Perestroiki/RNF/K Narodnomu Bogatstvu;* see, too, the Moscow Popular Front's *50 Otvetov na 50 Voprosov.* These are both undated pamphlets that appeared before mid-1990.

62. Ibid.

63. *Izvestiia,* 2 July 1991, pp. 1–2.

64. *Argumenty i Fakty,* no. 29, July 1991, p. 1.

65. Ibid., pp. 1–2.

66. Ibid., p. 1.

67. Ibid., p. 2.

68. In December 1991, Popov threatened to resign as mayor of Moscow over differences with the Russian parliament regarding economic reform. See *Moskovskii Komsomolets,* 10 December 1991, pp. 1, 3.

69. For Popov's official reasons for resigning, see *Kuranty,* 6 June 1992, p. 1. For immediate reactions, consult *Kuranty,* 9 June 1992, p. 1; *Argumenty i Fakty,* no. 21, June 1992, p. 1.

70. Iurii Afanasyev studied history at Moscow University and later specialized in French history. In 1980, he became head of the history section of Kommunist. In 1986, he became rector of the Historical Archival Institute in Moscow. He was elected in 1989 to the Congress of People's Deputies and, like Popov, was one of the leaders of the Inter-Regional Group, which pushed for more radical reforms. He left the CPSU in April 1990. He became active in Memorial, an anti-Stalinist group that aimed to build a memorial to the victims of Stalin and repression. A modest memorial now stands opposite the KGB headquarters. See Brown, ed., *The Soviet Union,* pp. 2–3.

71. Yuri Afanasyev, "The coming dictatorship," *New York Review of Books,* vol. 38, no. 3, 31 January 1991, p. 36. Here Iurii is rendered Yuri since the source does not adhere to the Library of Congress transliteration system.

72. Ibid.

73. Ibid.

74. Ibid., p. 37.

75. Ibid., p. 39.

76. Ibid.

77. Ibid., pp. 37–39.

78. Ibid., p. 37.

79. Ibid.

80. Ibid.

81. Ibid.

82. Ibid., p. 38.

83. Ibid.

84. Ibid.

85. Ibid.

86. Ibid.

87. Ibid.

88. Ibid., p. 39.

89. Ibid.

90. Ibid.

91. Andrei Sakharov, *Mir, Progress, Prava Cheloveka* (Leningrad, Sovetskii Pisatel', 1990).

92. Iurii Afanasyev, "Demokraty v oppozitsii k demokratam?" *Moskovskie Novosti*, no. 14, 7 April 1991, p. 9.

93. Ibid.

94. Ibid.

95. Ibid.

96. Ibid.

97. Ibid.

98. Interview, Institute of State and Law, Moscow, September 1990.

99. Boris Yeltsin, *Ispoved' Na Zadannuiu Temu* (Moscow, Ogonek-Variant, 1990), p. 8.

100. Ibid.

101. Ibid.

102. Ibid., pp. 72–76.

103. Ibid., p. 78.

104. Ibid., p. 79.

105. Ibid., p. 8.

106. Ibid.

107. *Kuranty*, 25 July 1991, p. 1; *Argumenty i Fakty*, no. 29, July 1991, p. 2.

108. Conversations in Moscow, August 1991.

109. Igor' Stadnik, "Pervaia nedelia departizatsii," *Moskovskie Novosti*, no. 33, 18 August 1991, p. 7.

110. *Kuranty*, 27 July 1991, p. 1.

111. *Kuranty*, 9 August 1991, p. 1.

112. *Kuranty*, 27 July 1991, p. 2.

113. *Kuranty*, 25 July 1991, p. 1. For other reactions to the ban, see *Kuranty*, 26 July 1991, p. 1; *Kuranty*, 31 July 1991, p. 2.

114. RFE/RL Research Institute, *Report on the USSR*, vol. 3, no. 36, 6 September 1991, pp. 68–69. A decree suspending the activity of the Moscow city party was signed by Popov (p. 71). Communist activity in the army, KGB, and TASS was also banned. Supreme Soviets in the republics outlawed communist activity, too. See also RFE/RL Research Institute, *Report on the USSR*, vol. 3, no. 35, 30 August 1991, p. 53.

115. *Uchreditel'noe Sobranie*, no. 2, July 1989, p. 1. These ideas were expressed in a resolution adopted in July 1989 at the second meeting of the coordinating councils of the Democratic Union, which took place in Leningrad (a city already called St. Petersburg by the party's members). Similar ideas had been announced earlier, although less well worked out, in Demokraticheskii Soiuz, *Paket Dokumentov* (Moscow, 9 May 1988). See, too, *Svobodnoe Slovo*, 22 May 1990, p. 1; *Svobodnoe Slovo*, 21 August 1990, p. 3.

116. *Uchreditel'noe Sobranie*, no. 2, July 1989.

117. Ibid.

118. Ibid. See, too, B. Bukovskii, "Kto protivostoit Gorbachevu," *Uchreditel'noe Sobranie*, no. 3, August 1989, pp. 1–2. At the time the Democratic Union made these remarks about monopoly control over newspapers, it was indeed impossible to buy the unofficial press in kiosks. This situation changed in 1990 and 1991.

119. Ibid.

120. *Svobodnoe Slovo*, 22 May 1990, p. 1.

121. *Uchreditel'noe Sobranie*, no. 2, July 1989, p. 1.

122. Ibid.

123. Ibid.

124. Ibid. See, too, Demokraticheskii Soiuz, *Paket Dokumentov; Svobodnoe Slovo*, 8 August 1989, p. 2.

125. Information acquired in 1990 from a member of the Democratic Union who had been arrested several times.

126. *Uchreditel'noe Sobranie*, no. 2, July 1989, p. 1.

127. *Svobodnoe Slovo*, 8 August 1989, p. 2; Demokraticheskii Soiuz, *Paket Dokumentov*.

128. *Svobodnoe Slovo*, 21 August 1990, p. 3.

129. *Uchreditel'noe Sobranie*, no. 2, July 1989, p. 1.

130. *Uchreditel'noe Sobranie*, no. 3, 1989, p. 3; *Svobodnoe Slovo*, 16 April 1991, p. 5; *Svobodnoe Slovo*, 24 September 1991, p. 1.

131. *Svobodnoe Slovo*, 21 August 1990, p. 3.

132. Boris Iarkov, "Na fone parovoza," *Moskovskie Novosti*, no. 48, 1 December 1991, p. 9.

133. Aleksandr Yakovlev, "Nuzhen novyi shag," *Izvestiia*, 2 July 1991, p. 2.

134. *Nasha Gazeta*, 10 July 1990, p. 1. *Nasha Gazeta* was then the newspaper of the union of workers of the Kuzbass. Later that year, it became the paper of the workers' movement of the Kuzbass.

135. *Nasha Gazeta*, 15 May 1990, p. 2.

136. "Shakhtery protiv partokratii," *Novaia Sovetskaia Rech'*, no. 2, August 1990, p. 2. *Novaia Sovetskaia Rech'* suggested that the resolution was representative of the views of most miners.

137. Ibid.

138. Ibid.

139. Ibid.

140. *Nasha Gazeta,* 25 September 1990, p. 3; *Nasha Gazeta,* 2 October 1990, p. 1; *Nasha Gazeta,* 9 October 1990, p. 4; *Nasha Gazeta,* 30 October 1990, pp. 4–7.

141. RFE/RL Research Institute, *Report on the USSR,* vol. 3, no. 17, 26 April 1991, p. 29; See also RFE/RL Research Institute, *Report on the USSR,* vol. 3, no. 18, 3 May 1991, p. 25.

142. Miners in the Kuzbass, Rostov, and Komi regions came under RSFSR jurisdiction. On 8 May, forty-one out of fifty-three mines in the Kuzbass voted to return to work. In Vorkuta, all but two mines went back to work. Refer to RFE/RL Research Institute, *Report on the USSR,* vol. 3, no. 20, 17 May 1991, pp. 37–38. For details of a meeting between Yeltsin and the miners, consult RFE/RL Research Institute, *Report on the USSR,* vol. 3, no. 19, 10 May 1991, pp. 24–25.

143. Betty Gidwitz, "Labor unrest in the Soviet Union," *Problems of Communism,* November-December 1982, pp. 25–42.

144. *Chto Delat'?* no. 4, 1990, p. 1.

145. Ibid.

146. Ibid., p. 2.

147. Ibid., p. 1.

148. Ibid., p. 1.

149. Ibid.

150. Ibid.

151. Ibid.

152. *Chto Delat'?* no. 8, 1991, p. 1.

153. Ibid.

154. Ibid.

155. Ibid.

156. *Chto Delat'?* no. 9, 1991, p. 2.

157. V. A. Bobkov, *Vozrozhdenie Dukha Leninizma* (Moscow, Politizdat, 1989), p. 3.

158. Meeting of 29 September 1990, Agitation and Propaganda headquarters of the CPSU, Moscow, which I attended.

159. For details of the Shatalin plan, refer to footnote 21, Chapter 1.

160. Different debates took place in different rooms. One was led by representatives of the KGB, who argued that since all civilized states, such as the United States, had a secret service, there was no need for the KGB to disband. Moreover, since the CIA tapped telephones, the KGB was not going to stop doing so. This behavior was normal for a secret service.

As well as being held in a grand party building, the conference provided excellent food for lunch, quite unrepresentative of what was obtainable elsewhere. Further details of the meeting are given in Mary Buckley, "Brezhnev era takes on a rosy glow amid the economic gloom," *Glasgow Herald,* 13 November 1990, p. 13.

161. *Volia,* no. 2, March 1991, p. 1.

162. Ibid.

163. Ibid.

164. Ibid.

165. Ibid.

166. *Nezavisimaia Gazeta,* 23 April 1991, p. 1. See also RFE/RL Research Institute, *Report on the USSR,* vol. 3, no. 18, 3 May 1991, pp. 25–26.

167. RFE/RL Research Institute, *Report on the USSR,* p. 26.

168. RFE/RL Research Institute, *Report on the USSR,* vol. 3, no. 19, 10 May 1991, p. 32.

169. For a thorough analysis of the events in April and May, refer to Abraham Brumberg, "Russia after perestroika," *New York Review of Books,* vol. 38, no. 12, 27 June 1991, pp. 53–60.

170. *Pravda,* 20 August 1991, p. 1.

171. Ibid.

172. Ibid.

173. Ibid.

174. Ibid.

175. Ibid.

176. Ibid.

177. Ibid.

178. Ibid.

9

Alternative Crises

*I*N POLITICAL ARENAS, discourse about crisis was ultimately dominated by two irreconcilable sets of argument. As the last chapter showed, reformers wished for more political change and elements of a free market, while Leninists fought to uphold the hegemony of communist leadership and to maintain a state-socialist economy. Reformers and Leninists offered conflicting assessments and incompatible solutions. Although neither grouping was homogeneous or united in its perspective, each was nonetheless sharply demarcated from the other. A politically significant division existed between them.

During 1991, it became increasingly clear that the two could not co-exist harmoniously within current structures. An outcome to conflict was required that gave one political control at the expense of the other. Attempts by centrists such as Gorbachev to seek compromises between them or to accommodate each sequentially were no longer politically viable. During 1990 and 1991, tactical shifts by the president brought diminishing success, generally lowering his credibility still further. An outcome congruent with the general wishes of only one of these groupings was necessary. The direction of political change since 1988 meant that democratic demands on the state were likely to increase, especially demands for independence of the republics, and that conservative resistance to them would grow. So long as a solution was not reached (which given the constellation of political forces was unlikely), in a context of economic failure, political chaos, and social collapse, tensions were likely to build, not abate.

But although the diametrically opposed interpretations of crisis coming from radical reformers and Leninists were the most significant ones for the crisis of state power, a host of other perspectives on crisis existed. These included a range of centrist positions and those that sought much less conventional solutions, such as anarchism and monarchism. There were also groups and movements preoccupied with discrimination against nationality and gender. Still others agonized over religious vacuum and ecological crisis.

Not all groups and movements dwelt on economy or polity as the main problems, finding other issues more pressing.

Like all complex societies, the USSR enjoyed myriad arguments about the contemporary predicament. A diversity of alternative definitions of crisis came from Pamiat, patriots, monarchists, Christians, greens, feminists, and anarchists. Their political impact in 1990 and 1991 may have been minimal, but for an understanding of the breadth of assessments of reality coming from society, they merit attention. In particular, they illustrate how discourse on crisis extended beyond conventional political categories to embrace concerns peripheral to mainstream politics but of importance to the social groups and movements whose interests they articulated (even if they did not represent them in political outlets or promote their mobilization). Taken together, they are not evidence of an established civil society, but they can be seen as elements of an embryonic one, notwithstanding the unattractiveness of Pamiat and some patriotic groups. In fact, one topic hitherto missing from Soviet and post-Soviet discourse is the significance for civil society of the emergence of groups and movements independent of the state that make demands on the state, not just in competition with other groups for scarce resources but also at their expense in morally harmful ways.

Pamiat: Genocide of the Russian People

Like other political groups, Pamiat cried crisis in 1990 and had been doing so since 1987. But Pamiat's crisis, like that of other Russian patriotic groups, was substantially different from those already discussed.[1] The main crisis, according to Pamiat's Novosibirsk newspaper of the same name, was "genocide of the Russian people." In a letter addressed to the president of the USSR and to the chairs of the Supreme Soviets of the USSR and of Russia, Pamiat declared that "the critical situation" in the country was complicated by the growing strength of "mixed-nationality enemies," by "disintegration of the Union," by growing "anarchy in the economy," and by "a fall in the moral health of the people."[2] Members of Pamiat were writing to politicians because they believed that there was no way out of this critical condition without bringing the genocide of Russians to a halt.

According to Pamiat, genocide was caused by "an ideological offensive against Russians" waged "in all directions." An undermining of the education system, a discrediting of the army, and a hounding of Russians by other nationalities were taking place. And "the zionist movement is, in essence, the main culprit." Allegedly, "the multi-million Russophobic press and television do everything possible to hide from the people the process of fast zionization [*sionizatsiia*] of Russia." Zionists, along with the top echelons of the scientific and state apparat and Western monopolists, were seizing control of the shadow economy.[3] The genocide of Russians, however, was not new. Any nationality or group with aims of "world supremacy" had discriminated against Russians and annihilated them, "including Mongol conquerors, Napoleon, Hitler, and contemporary enthusiasts of world government managed by powerful finance monopoly capital."[4] In short, Russians had been victims across the centuries.

Pamiat charged that the defamation of Russians was common in the media. Russians had been accused of fascism and anti-Semitism, which was part of a "planned discrimination" that kindled discord among nationalities. "Special guilt" in perpetuating this fell to "members of the Politburo A. N. Yakovlev and V. A. Medvedev; academics S. Shatalin, L. Abalkin, and T. Zaslavskaia; publicists N. Shemelev, G. Popov, V. Korotich, E. Evtushenko, E. Yakovlev, P. Gutiontov, and so on."[5] Pamiat demanded that the guilty, past and present, be held accountable. Towns, streets, and squares named after them should be renamed. Zionist organizations should be banned and instigators of zionist congresses taken to court. A political and economic equality of Russia with other republics needed to be restored and a separate Russian media established.[6]

Pamiat characterized the official press as unpatriotic and warned that "a very alarming situation" existed. For every one patriotic journal printed in Russian, there were forty that propagated Russophobia and insulted the dignity of Russians.[7] A "zionization of the press" was occurring at home and abroad. Papers were propagating the myth that anti-Semitism was raging in Russia. In fact, there was civil war in the Caucasus, enmity between Uzbek and Kirghiz, and hatred for Russians in Georgia, the Baltic states, and elsewhere. For example, "in Kishinev, eighteen-year-old Dmitrii Miroshin was murdered simply because he spoke Russian."[8]

Pamiat urged supporters to subscribe to patriotic papers and journals such as *Literaturnaia Rossiia* (Literary Russia), *Nash Sovremennik* (Our Contemporary), and *Molodaia Gvardiia* (Young Guard).[9] Pamiat also pledged support for a letter to the government, signed by seventy-four Russian writers, that had first been printed in *Literaturnaia Rossiia* and that expressed concern that under the banner of "democratization" and a "legal state" and under the slogan of "struggle with 'fascism and racism'" destabilization and racism were occurring. *Ogonek, Sovetskaia Kul'tura* (Soviet Culture), *Komsomol'skaia Pravda, Knizhnoe Obozreniia* (Book Reviews), *Moskovskie Novosti, Izvestiia, Oktiabr'* (October), *Iunost', Znamia* (Banner), and other publications all allegedly attacked the Russian people. Pamiat argued that the writers' letter marked the beginning of Russian rebirth and should be a familiar document "to every Russian family, to every Russian person."[10]

Pamiat's newspaper printed in Moscow showed more explicit monarchist sympathies and adopted the slogan "For Faith, Czar, and Fatherland! Patriots of the world unite!" Under the heading "Pages from Bloody History," it carried an article on the "ritual murder" of the czar's family.[11] Elsewhere it printed Petr Stolypin's program for saving Russia.[12]

Pamiat's "Short Program," adopted in the spring of 1989 at a meeting in Novosibirsk, outlined the organization's goals. These included the establishment in Russia of "missing links of statehood of the Russian people" and "a rebirth of its national culture and distinctiveness." Integral to the process were "a struggle against Russophobia and barracks internationalism," "a defense of the feeling of Russian national dignity," inculcation of love for the Fatherland, constant readiness to defend it, and respect for Russian history. Pamiat claimed to defend "social justice," "humanistic moral ideals," and "constructive suggestions in the fields of culture, ecology, economics, and politics. It declared itself in favor of "cultural dialogue and exchanges with the West" but against the spread of Western "mass culture" and "the plunder of the country's natural wealth by foreign capital."[13]

More specifically about politics, Pamiat argued that "Russia must have its own communist party, which would represent Russia inside the CPSU; its own Academy of Sciences; its own Writers' Union, Union of Actors, Union of Artists, Union of Teachers, Union of Medical Workers, Union of Cinematographers, and so on. Russia must have its own central television channels and own radio broadcasting."[14] Russia had to assert itself as a republic so that its status of "colony" within the USSR could cease. The way out of this crisis was "to mobilize all patriotic forces of the Fatherland."[15] Although the activities of Pamiat quickly caught the eyes of the West, which was primarily the result of its anti-Semitic strand, its following among Russians paled alongside support for other patriotic groups

Patriots: The Secularization of Culture and Discrimination

By 1990, there were different sorts of patriots in Russia, so it would be incorrect to suggest that the ideas outlined here were shared by all.[16] According to *Otchizna* (Fatherland), there were three patriotic trends. The first was the movement of communist patriots upholding Marxism-Leninism and defending workers. The United Labor Front discussed in the previous chapter falls into this category. The second was a national movement of Russian patriots supporting socialism and its development on nationalist lines. This movement favored state ownership of industry and mixed ownership of agriculture. The third was the monarchist movement composed of various groups expressing support for absolutist monarchy, constitutional monarchy, and parliamentary monarchy. They were all "for the rebirth of Russia, for the renewal of the spirituality of the people with active participation in the Orthodox church (even the Marxist-Leninists, with tiny exceptions, understand the necessity of this)."[17] Russian patriotism was thus multifaceted.

Many patriots criticized the secularization of culture since it ran against the grain of spiritual renewal. One of the strongest attacks was published in *Zemskii Sobor* (Assembly of the Land), a literary supplement to *Veche,* the paper of the Okhta section of the Russian patriotic movement Otechestvo. In a six-page article on "The Foundations of Christian Culture," Professor I. Il'in began with an analysis of "the crisis of modern culture." He argued that "Christian humanity is living through a deep religious crisis" in which "a wide anti-christian front is trying to create an un-christian and anti-christian culture."[18] This crisis, however, was not new and dated back to the thirteenth and fifteenth centuries. But today's culture "is more isolated from christianity" and "in general is losing religious spirit, thought, and gifts." An irreligious world outlook was growing and broadening. The dilemma for politics was that "an atheistic state leads the people like the blind leading the blind into a pit." Moreover, "atheistic communism is infinitely more terrible and more dangerous than atheistic capitalism." The only "creative way out" is through embracing christian culture and cultural rebirth, spurred on by love, contemplation, and wisdom.[19]

Integral to cultural rebirth was "Christian nationalism." Il'in held that nationalist feeling did not contradict christianity but that it received from christianity "a higher thought and foundation." Moreover, before God, nationalism contemplated its people's spirit, talents, inadequacies, historical problematic, dangers, and temptations.[20] Nationalism was "a system of actions flowing from this love, from this belief, from this will, and from this contemplation."[21]

One source of anxiety for patriots was why citizens emigrated. *Veche* pointed out that estimates for 1990 indicated that between two hundred and seven hundred thousand people would leave Russia. In an article entitled "Brain Drain?" K. Eremeev suggested that qualified specialists left for the West because, "not believing in God, 'new' emigration does not believe in Russia." Their own atheism, not the lack of freedom of speech and of serious political parties, was driving them out. Therefore, "you talk of a 'brain drain'? It would not be a conscience drain! And Russia is left with its conscience, the spirit of the people is preserved, its intellectual strength is regenerated."[22] In short, Russia was losing those who were spiritually expendable.

Another concern for patriots was the political neglect of Russian issues. In an open letter to deputies of the Supreme Soviet, *Tretii Rim"* (Third Rome), newspaper of the Russian patriotic movement, declared that other republics received preferential treatment. During the First Congress of People's Deputies, "we witnessed discussions of problems in the Baltic, in the Caucasus, and in many other regions of the country. With pain and bitterness we became convinced that, in fact, only Russian problems were not discussed at the congress." Valentin Rasputin, Vasilii Belov, and others had pressed for some discussion about Russia "but had not found a response at the congress from the majority."[23] This was one more confirmation of the fact that Russia had been discriminated against for more than seventy years. Unlike other republics, Russia had lacked its own political structures, its own academy of sciences, and a host of other organizations, including its own mass media. In addition, the social infrastructure of Russia's main towns was much worse than that of towns in other republics, and "Moscow—the most important city in Russia—ranks seventieth on this indicator."[24] Russia's budget was inadequate and proportionately less than that of other republics.

Patriots believed that since 1917 Russia had suffered a "national tragedy." Russians and other peoples living in the RSFSR had been "the objects of discrimination," which had led to "considerable spiritual impoverishment, physical and moral degradation of these peoples and [had] put Russia on the verge of national catastrophe." The Russian Patriotic Movement demanded a restoration of equal rights of the peoples of Russia with other nationalities.[25] It also declared that dividing Russians into those on the left and those on the right made Russians forget that they were Russian.[26]

The patriots' ideas appealed, although not always entirely, to many Russians. Some arguments appealed to the lumpen elements that Popov feared in 1991 were becoming a force with which to reckon. The populist strands of patriotism appealed to those looking for easy solutions to fill an ideological void. In 1992, alliance between communists and patriots was a potential threat to Yeltsin.

Monarchists: The Virus of Bolshevism

Monarchists of various degrees of conviction, like patriots, criticized the previous seventy years of communism for destroying Russian culture. The main difference between monarchists and some patriots (but not all) was that they advocated Russia's salvation through monarchy and devoted considerable space in their newspapers and bulletins to Nicholas II, to his family, and to biographies of White generals. Symbols of imperial rule adorned their publications, such as the two-headed eagle on Ufa's *Sobornyia Vedomosti* (Assembly's Record), on Irkutsk's *Vedomosti* (Record), and on Moscow's *Tsar' Kolokol"*. Their titles were also written in old Russian spellings.

According to *Sobornyia Vedomosti,* "Russia [had] effectively lost its twentieth century." As a result of "cultural degradation and terrible genocide," twenty-five to thirty thousand churches and not less than fifty thousand state buildings and palaces had been destroyed. Hundreds of thousands of works of art, frescoes, and 20 million icons had been lost.[27] *Vedomosti* held that "seventy years of bloody experiments on the people plus five years of perestroika have more than clearly shown the impossibility of building a normal society on 'Leninist precepts.'" An "anti-people's dicta-torship" was responsible for the destruction of ecology, culture, and tens of millions of people. Those who were left were demoralized and alienated. "Sickle and hammer" had come to mean "death and hunger." Bolshevism was "an evil," a "virus," a "type of spiritual AIDS." Bolshevism was "a logi-cal conclusion of a spiritual Antichrist" that could not therefore be over-come without an orthodox Christian rebirth of the Russian people.[28] Ac-cording to the priest Genadii Yakovlev, "Rus is standing at an historical crossroads." What followed would either be "repentance and a return to ho-liness" or "prophecy of the Apocalypse and quick death in 'the Great Whore of Babylon' [*nad Velikoi bludnitsei*]."[29]

The fate of Russia and its salvation, as propagated in *Tsar' Kolokol",* were linked to "the return of national consciousness to orthodox monarchy."[30] It declared that "The Czar is the sun of Russia!" and that "Russia is the ruler of the universe!"[31] Reprinting a statement that marked Nicholas II's accession to the throne, the publication argued that "Czarist power is vitally necessary and generally wholesome" because only it could bring together into "one po-litical body" a countless multitude of peoples. Without the Czar there would be "encroachment on life and infringement of property, immorality, civil dis-sension, and revolt. Without czarism, chaos and death would result."[32]

Tsar' Kolokol" frequently carried pictures of Nicholas II and imparted in-formation about him. Typical adulations began, "His imperial majesty, sov-ereign emperor Nikolai Aleksandrovich—the last autocratic Russian mon-arch ... the last in a line of divine protectors of orthodox statehood."[33] Historical details about earlier czars were also given.[34] *Tsar' Kolokol"* fre-quently asked, "Is it possible to restore the monarchy to Russia?"[35] Its pages considered this a live question but "perhaps correctly solved only from an eschatological perspective" since the Antichrist had killed the czar. The issue was therefore a mystical one.[36]

An ugly thread of anti-Semitism was woven through *Tsar' Kolokol".* For example, "the villainous and ritual murder" of the czar and his family "was inspired by leaders of the world Talmud-reading yids [*zhidovstvo*] and was "a cosmic event of great mystical-ethical significance."[37] Russia had since been enslaved and plundered by alien destroyers who sometimes concealed their real identities by taking Russian names. A war was raging between "atheistic talmudism" with its "mental terror" and "orthodox monar-chism," which was "concealed in the recesses of the people's hearts."[38] Some, for instance, were blaming the murder of Aleksandr Men' in Septem-ber 1990 on members of the Russian Orthodox church. But it was appropri-ate to ask who Men' really was and what role he played in the talmudistic intrigues against the Russian Orthodox church. He was, after all, a Jew practicing as an Orthodox priest. What sort of combination was this? Atheism was not part of orthodoxy.[39] A central message of *Tsar' Kolokol"* was that "the most important task of zionism is struggle with christianity, above all with orthodoxy—the most loyal preserver of Evangelic truth."[40] Many monarchists believed that the Russian Orthodox church was superior to others and under attack from atheists, who curiously included Jews.

In sum, monarchists condemned Bolshevism as evil, linked it to zionism, and called for a return of the monarchy as champion of truth and as salvation for the Russian people. A return to czarism was not, of course, a viable political option in 1991, nor did the idea enjoy more than minority support. But in a social climate in which what had been banned or disapproved of by communists now earned positive acclaim, flirtations with czarism were in vogue for some.

Christians: The Evil of Atheism

Protestants and some Christian democrats, like patriots, criticized atheism as an evil but saw salvation, not through monarchy and anti-zionism, but through democratization. The main agendas for many Christians in the late 1980s and early 1990s were how to end atheism and the emptiness of the past and how to prompt spiritual regeneration.

Christians were heartened by the eventual passage in October 1990 of the Law on Freedom of Conscience and Belief. The official draft had appeared in the press in June 1990 after having been discussed, without speed, during the relevant bureaucracies since early 1989.[41] Its eventual adoption restored to believers many previously denied rights and was described by *Vestnik Khristianskoi Demokratii* (Christian Democratic Herald) as "the first success" in "many years of struggle of believers for their rights."[42] Whereas in 1989 the fourth seminar of independent Christian societies had met and produced a fresh edition of the *Biulleten' Khristianskoi Obshchestvennosti* (Bulletin of the Christian Community), which discussed the draft law, attention in the 1990s was able to shift to a broader agenda of spiritual revival.[43]

For the Christian Democratic Union of Russia (KhDSR), the rebirth of Russia would come about through confession and repentance. In *Vestnik Khristianskoi Demokratii*, the KhDSR argued that ideology had pushed society into "the abyss of fratricidal war," resulting in "deadly alienation" and "a mechanical unity in the collective." A "whole continent of spiritual life" was "hidden in the depths of our society." Salvation could come about only through "democratic development on the basis of Christian moral principles." The immediate goal was "to stop the exploitation of the individual by the state." The Christian Democratic Union adopted the slogan "Love, Freedom, Solidarity."[44] Formed in 1989, its members wanted to build "ethical-moral foundations" as expressed in evangelism and as "given to us by Jesus Christ."[45]

Analysis was predicated on the belief that "a lack of morality is the most grave vice from which Soviet society suffers." Leaders, like executors, were "the main objects of the people's wrath."[46] The Moscow section of the KhDSR emphasized that religious preferences did not matter, be they Orthodox, Catholic, or Protestant. It was committed to defending different religious ways of life and was "devoted to the basic values of christian civilization: freedom, support, and justice. The person for us is the goal, not the means for achieving goals."[47]

In a similar vein, the Russian Christian Democratic Party appealed to Christians, Muslims, and Mohammedans to struggle against "the atheistic education of children" and to press for religious education in schools. Its message was that "atheism is abuse, persecution, subversion, and an outcasting of God." Hitherto children had been plunged by "devils" into "satanic organizations: Octobrists, Pioneers, and Komsomol." This amounted to an "ideological enslavement of children" to the devilry and materialism of Stalin and Lenin.[48] Many christian democrats stressed that they were not striving to build a christian democratic society at large; rather, they were fighting "only for the equal participation of christians alongside other strata of the population for the creation of a legal state and productive economy."[49]

According to evangelical Christian Baptists, "moral foundations" were sorely needed. The transition away from ideology required "a social and individual consciousness based on humanism."[50] But at a time when myths were rapidly being destroyed and past secrets were being revealed, "religious consciousness" was developing slowly. It was imperative that in the move away from "stagnation" there be renewal "in the spiritual sphere." To promote this, individuals should observe "practical christianity" through charity and mercy.[51] Baptists also argued that perestroika could not be successful without a "moral foundation." The country was facing a "serious dilemma" because some businesspersons were taking advantage of perestroika and exploiting the new limits to freedom. The market might be the only guarantee of a higher standard of living, but "an understanding and adoption of ethical norms" were vital and had to "take place in parallel with the development of a more open economy."[52] In short, ethics had to become part of market relations. The key lay with the church. *Protestant* suggested that "the Church [could] propagate ethics through its teachings and inspire through example." This was vital since "the height of the pyramid depends on the size and strength of its foundations."[53]

Issues of morality heightened in 1991. *Put'* (The Way), paper of the Russian Christian Democratic Movement (RKhDD), condemned in January the acts of Soviet troops in Lithuania. The "drama" was feared to be "a prelude to a basic attack against anti-totalitarian forces."[54] The duma of the movement issued a statement that offered support "to the peoples of the Baltic in their struggle against tyranny," declaring, "Your freedom is our freedom!" and warning that the country must not be allowed to become an arena "for the forces of evil." The duma appealed to God to preserve "our peoples." These, of course, included Russians in the Baltic. The RKhDD appealed to Lithuanians to guarantee "the democratic rights of all citizens" regardless of nationality and religion and warned Russians in the Baltic states that "totalitarianism drove us to a dead end—legal, political, and economic. Playing on the crisis, created by themselves, union powers are desperately trying to make you the blind instrument to use for their ends."[55] The movement's carefully worded general message was that "the path to personal freedom lies only through respect for the freedom of others."[56]

For these diverse christians, crisis was atheism propagated by Marxist-Leninist ideology and enshrined in the satanic organizations of state socialism. Salvation could come only through God, through practical christianity, and through respect for individuals. Christian democrats attempted to bring these ideas to the political arena through political parties and through membership of christian factions in the soviets.

Greens: Ecological Catastrophe

Whereas Christians were concerned about the evil of atheism, active greens (many of whom were Christians) focused on the abuse of the environment and the planet. Most greens believed that "ecological crisis" was imminent and that the survival of humanity was at stake. Nature needed defending now, and the countryside had to be saved. The ecological situation was worsening, and action was necessary to prevent disaster.[57]

Their detailed attention to ecological issues meant that, unlike democrats, greens gave less direct consideration to political structures and economic policy, although these were discussed insofar as their results affected the environment. And although greens held common views about the seriousness of the ecological catastrophe, they often differed from one another on other political questions. Greens could be anarchists, social democrats, socialists, or liberals. Some patriots, too, showed green tendencies. Green groups formed in different areas to address local ecological problems and also some came together as a broader movement to establish a green party.

Justice cannot be done here to the variety of green issues and activities. A sentiment common to many, however, was expressed by Genadii Danilov in a local green newspaper: "The violence of people to nature is like the violence of one individual to another—destructive for everyone. We came together to oppose the barbaric treatment of nature: to defend what survives, to cure mutilation, to resuscitate waste."[58] Danilov was chair of the Serebrianka club, formed in September 1989 in Moscow's First of May district. He stressed that unless citizens incorporated green ideas into their world outlooks, "society [would] not survive." Unfortunately, changing outlooks was "a long and difficult process." At best, citizens could do everything for their local areas. Serebrianka was committed to looking after Izmailov Park.[59] Other green struggles targeted local industry. In Kuibyshev, for example, in August 1989 the ecological-political club Al'ternativa and the Movement for the Creation of a Green Party organized picketing outside a chemical weapons factory.[60]

Green newspapers aimed to enlighten the public about the gravity of ecological problems, to pass on information about particular trouble spots, and to muster support. For instance, *Zelenyi Ostrov* informed readers that Uzbekistan had the highest level of toxins in its soil. Every year it was being sprayed with six thousand tons of pesticides.[61] The dried-up Aral Sea had already sent out SOS signals. And next would come the stories of the Azov and Caspian seas because "rivers carry into them a deadly number of poisonous substances. These include industrial waste, residues of fertilizer, and simple output of 'big chemicals.'"[62] Academic V. I. Fisinin told readers that "every year in the country 3 billion tons of fertile soil either disappear or are ruined from wind erosion. In the last quarter of a century we lost around 20 million hectares of agricultural land."[63] Green discourse set out to inform citizens of individual cases of pollution and to enlist support for agitation against them.

In a similar spirit, the movement "Green peace," based in Krasnoiarsk, provided readers of its paper *Ekologicheskii Vestnik* with detailed maps of the concentration of fluorine and aluminum in Krasnoiarsk's soil. Entitled "Krasnoiarsk in Danger," commentary on the maps noted that the highest level of aluminum desirable was 0.01 percent but that in some parts of Krasnoiarsk it exceeded 10 percent. Similarly, in some areas fluoride was five to twelve times higher than recommended levels.[64] *Ekologicheskii Vestnik* also reported green developments in other republics, such as the formation of the Lithuanian Green Party in July 1989 and its general goals— "independence, ecological health, demilitarization, and a neutral Lithuania living according to the principles of free will, generally accepted values, and harmonious existence of people and nature." The paper also provided coverage of the Latvian Green Congress of January 1990, with its focus on "the defense of the surrounding countryside and the health of people."[65]

In keeping with the international spirit of the green movement, some publications translated green materials from the West. In *Tretii Put'*, for instance, the organizational committee of the Green Party translated West German materials on "the ecological crisis and the transformation of society." They blamed capitalism for much of the world's destruction and concluded that "it must be overthrown," but they also held that socialism alone was not an adequate answer to the ecological crisis. The salvation of human life hung on "fundamental changes in industry and in the structure of consumption of the majority of people in industrial countries."[66] In this way, Western ideas were disseminated.

Although greens viewed ecological issues as catastrophic, they noted that green ideas were not new. In the 1890s, a famous Russian writer had written to a friend in France, "One can still catch sterlet in the Moscow River, but no longer salmon. Nature is dying." The contemporary version of this had sadly become, "One could 'catch' only 'contaminated flora, insoluble industrial waste, synthetic cleansing agents, detergents, domestic waste, and so on.'" In Riga, polluted city reservoirs had become "one of the most serious ecological problems." The only way forward was for the "iron logic" of the past to be replaced by "green logic and green ideology."[67]

In 1991, the burst of new informal newspapers included green ones such as *Spasenie, Nabat,* and *Ekologicheskaia Gazeta.* Since 1991 also marked the fifth anniversary of the Chernobyl disaster, much of their coverage was devoted to political cover-up, radiation, its consequences, and inadequate resources. Early reporting of the tragedy was also reprinted. *Spasenie*, for instance, reminded readers what had been written about "the fire" at Chernobyl in *Pravda* in April and May 1986. The bottom of *Spasenie*'s front page carried the image of a baby floating in the air and exposed to billowing smoke from reactors. Numerous hands stretched up to reach the child but failed.[68] The picture suggested the impossibility of helping the younger generation, which had fallen victim to forces out of most people's control.

In a different vein, in March 1991, *Nabat* carried an article entitled "Mothers Were Right." Thirty-two young Komsomol members who had traveled against their mothers' wishes to Chernobyl to help feed victims now complained they had not received the payments that they had been promised: "In 1986 they paid us twice, then stopped. Now they have paid up to 25 percent. It turned out that we lost our health for no purpose when from radiation we all wheezed and lost our voices. We had blisters on our hands, our legs, too."[69] Lack of funds also prevented many laws from being implemented. It took four long years for a law protecting citizens suffering from the Chernobyl catastrophe to be passed. But without money, the law amounted to "empty paper."[70] *Nabat* also reported that "there is a Chernobyl program in Belorussia. There is a package of laws concerning Chernobyl. But the most important is missing—money—especially for science." There were just four rubles in early 1991 in the budget of the Scientific Research Institute of Radiation Medicine of the Belorussian Ministry of Health. By contrast, the Institute of Biophysics was well-funded.[71]

By the early 1990s, greens were encouraging citizens to think differently about the world and about themselves and to realize that ecological problems were pressing and paramount. Konstantin Klimenko, editor of *Ekologicheskaia Gazeta,* saw his task as follows: "'the ecology of our surroundings begins with the ecology of the soul'—that is my belief. I hope I fulfill this principle on the pages of this paper."[72] The editorial board took an active interest in the work of the committee of the Supreme Soviet of the RSFSR concerned with ecology and reported attendance at its meetings.[73] The newspaper intended to shape people's thinking about green issues, influence policy making as much as possible, and gather information from politicians about what was being done.

Greens may not have managed to push ecological issues to the top of formal political agendas, but by the early 1990s they had become persistent in promoting awareness of broader global crisis and local environmental problems. Their discourse, although often distinct from mainstream political debate, was increasingly incorporated into it. Issues such as Chernobyl made green discourse hard to ignore. And if many politicians gave ecological issues low priority, citizens affected by them increasingly did not.

Feminists: Discrimination Against Women

The arguments of feminists probably reached a smaller section of society than did the issues of green newspapers. Women's groups did not appear with anywhere near the speed characterizing the formation of popular fronts and nationalist movements. But once women's groups did emerge, they exhibited an immense diversity of goals, hopes, and strategies. What united them was the belief that women suffered ill-treatment or discrimination. That was the crisis. But how they interpreted this varied, as did their recommendations and solutions.

The Free Association of Feminist Organizations (Svobodnaia Assotsiatsiia Feministicheskikh Organizatsii), was formed in 1990 by Ol'ga Lipovskaia and Nataliia Filippova. Lipovskaia was already editing her journal *Zhenskoe Chtenie* in Leningrad and had developed an extensive network of international contacts through visits to the West.[74] SAFO's declaration stated:

> The position of women in Soviet society can be described as one shaped by discrimination. This position has been enforced by historical and cultural traditions and fortified by the adherents of a vicious political system. It is in dire need of change. While having granted women the right (more precisely, the need and responsibility) of work, our system has been unable to change the social ste-

reotypes that define relations between the sexes. As a result, a double burden has been placed on the shoulders of women. On the one hand, they must undertake difficult, often servile, unskilled labor. On the other, they must assume responsibility for childrearing and the family.[75]

Society, moreover, often blamed women for its social and demographic problems, such as juvenile delinquency, birth defects, prostitution, and divorce. "Entrenched myths" preserved rigid gender divisions, and these were maintained by "male-constructed power structures."

Laws had never established "genuine parity" of the sexes, so one pressing goal was "to work toward tangible equality for women in all spheres of human activity." The lag in humanitarian and political thought in the USSR hindered this. A second aim was to "break down the tendency to restrict women to domestic, unskilled work as well as the tradition of defining labor as 'feminine' or 'nonfeminine.'" A third was "to renovate and democratize many social institutions. In the home we must not return to 'traditional' values but rather rid ourselves of archaic stereotypes." What was needed was "a new kind of family," one "based on mutual partnership where each parent partakes equally in the raising of children, in financial support, and in the emotional climate of the family." SAFO proclaimed that these principles should result in every member of the family possessing an "equal right to human individuality." Above all, since the social image of women had been deformed, "cultural renovation" was pressing.[76]

Taking the argument further, SAFO proclaimed that "one of the reasons for the present-day crisis is that almost half of human creativity is alienated from cultural-historical progress—the voices of women." Thus, women's absence from politics was one factor behind crisis in the USSR. No political leaders, parties, movements, or groups subscribed to this view of crisis except women's groups. SAFO hoped to help women develop "feminine self-understanding" and "start a campaign that will oppose the sexual objectification of women." Lipovskaia and Filippova contended that "we need alternative programs of education whose goals would be the establishment of Western-style feminist consciousness."[77]

Not all new women's groups agreed with these conclusions. Women for a Socialist Future for Our Children (Zhenshchiny za Sotsialisticheskoe Budushchee Nashikh Detei), for example, opposed a market economy and wanted to see the CPSU retain a leading role in society.[78] For these women, Gorbachev's economic and political reforms constituted crises. They condemned *Gorbastroika,* as did other opponents of reform, as a form of "bourgeois restoration" and fascism.[79] Although they did not see themselves as feminists, they were concerned to protect women from unemployment. Lipovskaia, by contrast, supported a market economy and vigorously criticized the CPSU (she had briefly been a member of the Democratic Union).

Women nationalists in Lithuania who formed a women's group within Sajudis announced that "men in Lithuania should conduct political struggle, while women should create a beautiful home. There is no point in having an autonomous Lithuania if home life is not improved."[80] These women advocated the division of gender roles from which SAFO was trying to move away. They readily admitted that "we want women to become women and men to become men. We are not a feminist movement." Crisis for women in Sajudis amounted to Russian domination of Lithuania. This included the "monstrous information" dished out to children in kindergartens and financial and ideological control over the Lithuanian edition of *Soviet Woman*.[81]

Women nationalists in Ukraine had also formed a separate women's group within Rukh. Crisis for them, too, was Russian domination. The solution, as for women in Sajudis, was independence. A minority of the members of the Women's Community of Rukh, however, were self-proclaimed feminists, such as Solomea Pavlychko, and supported sustained attacks on discrimination against women, actions given less support by non-feminist members. Despite this division, the Ukrainian feminists managed to include an attack on patriarchal values in their statute: "The Women's Community of Rukh calls on women to reject the patriarchal values of the past, to fight for genuine equality of women and men in society, in guarding the home hearth, in bringing up children, and in political and social activities. The traditional patriarchal division of roles already brought, and will bring again, devastating results to the whole of Ukrainian society."[82] Here, patriarchy is the implicit crisis. For women like Pavlychko, unless patriarchal behavior patterns were challenged, Ukraine would continue to be an oppressive society.

Different women's groups came together in Moscow in 1990 and then again in Dubna in 1991 at the First Independent Women's Forum. Opening papers delivered in Dubna included "Woman as an Object and Subject of Social Transformations," "Women's Movement: Inside View," "Woman as an Object of Consumption," and "Women and the Market Economy." Discussions followed in sessions concerned with women's entrepreneurship in a market system, current issues of the independent women's movement, women and art, and discrimination within patriarchal culture.[83] Women were finally coming together independently of the CPSU to explore issues according to their own agenda. The Second Independent Women's Forum convened in Dubna in November 1992, continuing this trend.

Women's political parties also began to form in 1990. The United Party of Women (Edinaia Partiia Zhenshchin) defined its main task as preventing the exclusion of women from discussions about the future of their country.[84] The Christian Democratic League of Women of Moldavia had as its central goal to draw women, "regardless of nationality and belief, into activity for the spiritual rebirth and democratization of society."[85] The shared concern here was the need to involve women in politics.

By the early 1990s, then, independent women's groups and women's parties were growing in number and in size. Although not all described themselves as "feminist," those that did aimed to challenge patriarchy, traditional gender roles, and sexual stereotypes. It did not automatically follow, however, that Western feminism was a guiding model. As Ol'ga Lipovskaia remarked:

> The strong myth of Mother Russia will keep Soviet women attached to the family. This is a very serious part of Russian culture—communal activity and communal ties are very strong. ... This means that most feminist activity and the development of feminist ideas will be located in the family. There will be less emphasis than in the West on separatism and division between the sexes, much more desire to find compromises in the realm of family life.[86]

Perhaps, in part, Lipovskaia's words reflect a mistaken view of Western feminism since separatist radical feminism is just one strand of thought alongside non-separatist radical feminism, liberal feminism, and socialist feminism. But to date, self-proclaimed Russian feminists have not viewed separatism as the way out of current crises. Separatism, like individualism, jars with the collectivism of Russian culture. The feminists' starting point is an attack on sexual stereotypes.

The philosopher Ol'ga Voronina is at the forefront of Russian thinking on sexual stereotypes. She argues that modern thinking on emancipation requires "a change in traditional models of social relations between the sexes with men dominating and subordinating women in all spheres of life."[87] But a problem for women is that "equal rights" were a "gift of the state" and declared in a "traditional-patriarchal culture" in which sexual stereotypes abounded.[88] Women's strength and potential were harnessed by the workplace, home, and social life, but no one asked what these spheres gave to women. Thought was not devoted to women's personal development. Instead, the stereotype of "female predestination" (*zhenskoe prednaznachenie*) dominated.[89] Whereas mothers experienced conflicts between family responsibilities and their careers, fathers did not. The all-pervasive influence of stereotypes was such that women were rarely able fully to demonstrate their knowledge and abilities. Society's attitudes toward women and toward working women had to change if they were to develop as individuals. The "sphere of social consciousness" was most instrumental in discriminating against women: "Precisely here women are most of all valued as a different being from men, according to nature, psychology, destiny, possibilities, and abilities. There is no need to say, of course, that all female characteristics are valued much less than male."[90] Salvation would come only through a "democratization and humanization" of society leading to equal opportunities for the personal development and "self-realization of all people, regardless of social origin, age, nationality, and sex." The result would be the emancipation of women and men.[91]

One hurdle in moving toward Voronina's goal, apart from a deeply embedded patriarchal culture, was the fierce reaction against everything for which the CPSU had stood. Precisely because the emancipation of women had been a gift of the state, it was, for many, something to resist. A tenacious strand of popular culture was the desire to reclaim women's femininity. Many confusingly interpreted this to mean that emancipation should be opposed since it had denuded women of femininity.

By the end of 1991, some women who had previously opposed the idea of a women's political party, were now arguing in favor. Galina Sillaste, a sociologist, called for "an independent and confederal women's party."[92] Interviewed in *Moskvichka*, Sillaste noted that "the peculiar isolation of women in our society not only persists but is also perhaps even strengthening." She recalled that when, during the previous session of the Congress of People's Deputies, M. Rakhmanova had stood up and suggested a separate women's chamber, the men had laughed ironically. Sillaste believed that a women's party would be "new, difficult, but necessary" to champion equal rights and defend "the specific interests of women in all spheres of social life."[93] The crisis of falling percentages of female people's deputies resulting from the abandonment of fixed quotas of representation, the low percentage of women candidates, and the reluctance of voters to elect women were troubling some women politicians and commentators, even though in the past a more visible female political presence had not meant greater power for women.[94]

If the new "male democracy," as Ol'ga Lipovskaia described it, will not defend women's interests, more women may find the idea of a women's party attractive.[95] This may be particularly so throughout the 1990s as women experience higher rates of unemployment than men and continue to worry about price increases and food purchases. Although many women will, as before, doubt the efficacy of political activity and lack time for it, still others may remain skeptical about the place of a women's party in malestream political structures. In 1992, however, evidence suggested that some male politicians were finally trying to appear sensitive to women's issues, albeit not in feminist terms. Yeltsin appointed Ekaterina Lakhova to his Kremlin team of presidential counselors to address issues concerning the family, motherhood, and children.[96] And in May, the Social Democratic Party of Russia established a new organization called Women for Social Democracy.[97] The likely pattern for the future is one of growing diversity as parties form women's sections and as women who wish to be politically active but cannot find a comfortable place in these conventional arenas form alternative women-only groupings. The appeal of feminist discourse is likely to increase, rather than diminish, although it clashes with core assumptions of Russian collectivism and nationalism and seems destined to remain a minority discourse. The image of "emancipated woman" constructed by the Soviet state that is now fiercely rejected, does little to help.

Anarchists: Bonapartism of the Party-State Apparat

Like feminism, anarchism was not widely supported in society at large. Nonetheless, anarchist arguments were part of the lively political discourse of the late 1980s and early 1990s. And anarchist newspapers enjoyed a profile on Moscow's streets.

Debates within anarchist circles after 1989 revealed several views of the current crisis. According to one strain of anarcho-syndicalism, a bonapartist regime prevailed, representing "a transition stage from Marxist totalitarianism to a bourgeois-bureaucratic authoritarian 'legal state.'"[98] Another position held that civil war had begun in December 1989 in the Caucasus, thanks to the party-state apparat.[99] More pointed attacks on the mafia and the state being "two sides of one coin" came from members of the Anarcho-Communist Revolutionary Union.[100] But above all, salvation would result from a "revolution of the people." And this "social revolution" amounted to "a wrecking [*krushenie*] of obsolete social relations," which would come about through the active will of the mass of the people combined with direct action from the revolutionary avant-garde. Revolution was the "realization of freedom," as Mikhail Bakunin had understood it.[101]

Those who believed that bonapartism prevailed argued that between a "more left Supreme Soviet" and "a more right Central Committee of the CPSU" there was a president, more like an emperor, who held the title of head of state but who was also "head of the *nomenklatura* of the communist aristocracy." Gorbachev and the Supreme Soviet could together triumph over the Central Committee; similarly, Gorbachev in cooperation with the Central Committee could triumph over the Supreme Soviet. Apparently, "therefore neither the Supreme Soviet nor the Central Committee could triumph over Gorbachev." What was the way forward? According to the "Indian variant," many parties could develop, real power rest in the hands of the *nomenklatura* of the Indian congress, but the monarchical dynasty of Nehru and Gandhi is retained. According to another variant, economic crisis and social tension could undermine the people's belief in the economic underpinning of Gorbachev's "liberalism." A coup by the army and KGB would result, and new military leaders would continue down the path of economic modernization on a capitalist basis, possibly with the help of the West. But only time would tell whether Russian bonapartism could end in a "Paris Commune" or a restoration of the "Bourbons."[102]

Other anarchists emphasized that civil war had already started in the Caucasus. Moreover, "bloodshed was advantageous to those who had consciously led the people to the blind alley of civil war" because they could liquidate the democratic rights and freedom that remained in the name of dealing with a state of siege. The "party-state apparat" had provoked the war and was now shedding crocodile tears for the dead. The way forward was through "power to the people, not to the parties."[103]

Anarcho-communist revolutionaries believed that the key to changing the system was to smash the state along with "its younger brother—the mafia." They asserted that "anarchy, more precisely anarchistic communism, will finish off the mafia once and for all." Once state capital and private property were gone, there would be no mafia. Hitherto, the "fascist mafia fist" had spilled proletarian blood. Social revolution, communism, and anarchy combined could end this situation.[104]

Social revolution, anarchists stressed, "is not a 'senseless and ruthless' riot; it is not revelry of vile and base passions; it is not a breaking of ribs and skulls. No!"[105] Social revolution meant smashing obsolete social relations, thereby directly hitting the exploiters. Anarchists did not oppose freedom; on the contrary, they were its champions. Constitutional freedoms were "a paper fiction" that "gave the people no guarantees." And "political freedom is deceit if it is not backed up by economic and social freedom." Moreover, "so long as social inequality exists—nothing can be said about freedom."[106] Therefore, "the present is struggle; the future is freedom."[107]

Anarchist social revolution as a way out of crisis was not taken seriously by most politicians and voters. Nonetheless, a minority of citizens, notably young ones, subscribed to these views.[108] Since anarchist thought had enjoyed some popularity in nineteenth-century Russian society, its reemergence in reaction to another highly repressive system should not be surprising.[109]

Conclusion

An immense diversity of views about *krizis* and how to surmount it existed in the two years leading to the failed coup in 1991. Although both democrats and anarchists made an oppressive party-apparat their main target, how they interpreted its significance varied, as did visions of what should succeed it. Whether the *nomenklatura* was defined as totalitarian, authoritarian, or Bonapartist, plans for ending its domination of power differed greatly. Gavriil Popov's arguments in favor of defederalization, denationalization, and desovietization contrasted with the vaguer plans by anarchists for sweeping social revolution. Similarly, the democrats' hope for a mixed economy of state and private ownership and the anarchists' preference for self-managing utopia offered entirely different economic answers. Disagreements within the democratic movement and within anarchism heightened the diversity. And inevitably ideas, particularly those of democrats, altered, matured, and rigidified in response to changing events.

Like anarchists, monarchists lacked a power base or widespread support. The restoration of czarism was as unlikely as an anarchic social revolution in the spirit of Bakunin. But ideas of Russian rebirth did enjoy a strong resonance in Russia and continued to do so after the coup. Russian nationalism and support for the Orthodox church struck a deep, if undefined, chord within the population. Sadly, too, anti-Semitism sounded a note here, finding its loudest adherents among patriots, although it was certainly not absent from some orthodox christians in their pontifications about the need for "morality" and an end to evil. For Pamiat, a mythical "zionist threat" was the biggest crisis of all. But not all religious groups embraced anti-Semitism; some took pains instead to elaborate what moral changes were necessary to combat spiritual vacuum and irresponsibility.

Green ideas about ecological crisis spread across the political spectrum. Russian patriots bewailed the decimation of the Russian countryside and shared some green concerns. Democrats worried about pollution in general. Purer greens viewed ecological catastrophe as the main crisis facing the country and world humanity and argued for local political action on whatever ecological issue called for attention. Feminists, by contrast, although not necessarily unsympathetic to green issues, viewed discrimination against women in a patriarchal society as a serious crisis requiring campaigns to end all sexual stereotypes.

In 1990 and in 1991, *krizis* was arguably the most frequently and differently used term in political discourse. Never before in the history of the Soviet state had so many political leaders, movements, parties, and embryonic groups been convinced that crisis existed. A similar situation had obtained in 1917 before the Soviet state was forged. Then, as in 1990 and in 1991, interpretations about the past, present, and future varied, as did recommendations for how best to proceed.

In 1990, discourse about crisis was widespread and part of broader processes of economic collapse and political disintegration. In retrospect, it seems unlikely that the state would have disintegrated without such arguments being advanced. They were part of disintegration. And the political relevance of these arguments did not abruptly end once resistance to the coup proved successful. They remained part of a changing society that was likely to play a growing, if undefined, role in politics. Moreover, they were among the pressures that Yeltsin had to confront.

NOTES

1. According to *Ruskii Kur'er*, after May 1990, the Dvizhenie "Pamiat'" (Pamiat Movement) adopted the new name Ruskii Narodno-demokraticheskii Front Dvizhenie Pamiat, or the Russian People's Democratic Front Movement Pamiat. The previous leaders had been Igor' Sychev, Ivan Myshkin, and Vladimir Novikov. An earlier split had taken place in 1987 when the Dvizhenie "Pamiat'" broke away from the

Patrioticheskoe Ob"edinenie "Pamiat'" led by Dmitrii Vasil'ev. This wing then became National'no-patrioticheskii Front "Pamiat'." During 1989–1990, Sychev's group apparently evolved away from Stalinism and toward an orthodox monarchical ideology. See *Ruskii Kur'er,* May 1991, p. 2.

The preservation of churches, monuments, and culture has always been one of Pamiat's concerns. The neglect and destruction of churches are interpreted as one part of the general attack on Russian culture. For discussions of this, refer to *Pamiat* (Novosibirsk), no. 2, 20 May 1990, p. 1; *Pamiat* (Novosibirsk), no. 3, 3 June 1990, p. 2.

2. *Pamiat* (Novosibirsk), no. 4, 17 June 1990, p. 1.

3. Ibid.

4. Ibid.

5. Ibid.

6. Ibid.

7. *Pamiat* (Novosibirsk), no. 1, 6 May 1990, p. 1.

8. *Pamiat* (Novosibirsk), no. 6, 15 July 1990, p. 1.

9. *Pamiat* (Novosibirsk), no. 1, 6 May 1990, p. 1.

10. Ibid.

11. *Pamiat* (Moscow), no. 3, January 1990, p. 7.

12. Ibid., p. 4. Stolypin was Nicholas II's prime minister.

13. *Pamiat* (Novosibirsk), no. 5, 1 July 1990, p. 1.

14. Ibid. Consistent with this position, Nina Andreeva, author of the notorious letter discussed in Chapter 2, published a short article in an earlier *Pamiat* on the First Congress of the Russian Communist Party. See Nina Andreeva, "Ob initsiativno-uchreditel'nom s"ezde RKP," *Pamiat* (Novosibirsk), no. 3, 3 June 1990, p. 2.

15. Ibid. *Pamiat* (Novosibirsk), no. 5, 1 July 1990, p. 1.

16. For analysis by a Russian researcher at the Institute of History in Moscow, refer to Valerii Solovev, "Chto takoe 'russkoe delo'" (Working paper).

17. *Otchizna,* no. 5, September 1990, p. 1.

18. I. A. Il'in, "Osnovy khristianskoi kul'tury," *Zemskii Sobor,* 1 October 1990, p. 1.

19. Ibid.

20. Ibid., p. 5.

21. Ibid., p. 6.

22. K. Eremeev, "Utechka mozgov?" *Veche,* no. 5, August 1990, p. 1.

23. *Tretii Rim",* no. 1, December 1989, p. 1.

24. Ibid.

25. Ibid.

26. Ibid., p. 2.

27. *Sobornyia Vedomosti,* no. 1, p. 1. No date is printed on this. It is probably 1990.

28. *Vedomosti,* no. 2, 1990, p. 1.

29. Ibid.

30. *Tsar' Kolokol"*, no. 7, 1990, p. 4. Note here that the hard sign at the end of *kolokol* has been readopted.

31. Ibid., p. 3.

32. Ibid., pp. 2–4.

33. *Tsar' Kolokol"*, no. 2, 1990, p. 2.

34. *Tsar' Kolokol"*, no. 5, 1990, pp. 1–2.

35. *Tsar' Kolokol"*, no. 1, 1990, p. 1.

36. Ibid.

37. *Tsar' Kolokol"*, no. 7, 1990, p. 4.

38. *Tsar' Kolokol"*, no. 7, p. 5.

39. Ibid., pp. 8–10. Aleksandr Men' was an extremely popular priest. His churches were generally full wherever he was sent to work, and shortly before his death he was attracting large crowds at public lectures.

40. Ibid., p. 12.

41. John Anderson, "The council for religious affairs and the shaping of Soviet religious policy," *Soviet Studies*, vol. 43, no. 4, 1991, pp. 703–704.

42. *Vestnik Khristianskoi Demokratii*, no. 15, August 1990, p. 2. For details of the recent history of Russian Christian democracy, consult I. P. Vasil'eva, "Rossiiskie khristianskie demokraty: Politicheskie vzgliady i idealy," *Sotsial'no-politicheskie Nauki*, no. 7, 1991, pp. 108–120.

43. *Vestnik Khristianksoi Demokratii*, no. 15, August 1990, p. 2.

44. Ibid.

45. B. N. Berezovskii and N. I. Krotov, *Neformal'naia Rossiia* (Moscow, Molodaia Gvardiia, 1990), p. 237.

46. *Sobor*, no. 4, May 1990, p. 4.

47. *Sobor*, no. 1, March 1990, p. 1.

48. *Khristianskaia Politika*, no. 2, August 1990, p. 1.

49. *Sobor*, no. 4, May 1990, p. 1.

50. *Protestant*, no. 5, May 1990, p. 3.

51. *Protestant*, no. 4, April 1990, p. 4.

52. *Protestant*, no. 6, June 1990, p. 3; *Protestant*, no. 5, May 1990, p. 3.

53. *Protestant*, no. 6, June 1990, p. 3.

54. *Put'*, no. 1, January 1991, p. 3.

55. Ibid.

56. Ibid.

57. *Zelenyi Ostrov*, May 1990, p. 1.

58. Ibid.

59. Ibid.

60. *Tretii Put'* (Kuibyshev), no. 12, 1989, p. 13.

61. *Zelenyi Ostrov*, p. 1.

62. Ibid.

63. Ibid.

64. *Ekologicheskii Vestnik*, no. 4, March 1990, p. 3.

65. Ibid., p. 1.

66. *Tretii Put'*, p. 6.

67. Natal'ia Lebedeva, "Ekologiia goroda," *Potentsial*, no. 3, May 1990, p. 3. She did not name the "famous person."

68. *Spasenie*, no. 3, April 1991, p. 1.

69. *Nabat*, no. 3, March 1991, p. 1.

70. *Nabat*, no. 1, March 1991, p. 7.

71. *Nabat*, no. 3, March 1991, p. 7.

72. *Ekologicheskaia Gazeta*, no. 1, February 1991, p. 1.

73. Ibid., p. 3.

74. For further details of *Zhenskoe Chtenie*, see Mary Buckley, "Gender and reform," in Catherine Merridale and Chris Ward, eds., *Perestroika: The Historical Perspective* (Dunton Green, Edward Arnold, 1991), pp. 72–74.

75. *Declaration of the Free Association of Feminist Organizations* (1990).

76. Ibid.

77. Ibid.

78. *Rabotnitsa*, no. 1, January 1991, p. 5.

79. *Volia*, no. 2, March 1991, p. 1.

80. Buckley, "Gender and reform," pp. 70–72.

81. Ibid.

82. Solomea Pavlychko, "Between feminism and nationalism: New women's groups in the Ukraine," in Mary Buckley, ed., *Perestroika and Soviet Women* (Cambridge, Cambridge University Press, 1992), p. 94.

83. First Independent Women's Forum, Dubna, 29–31 March 1991, Program.

84. *Rabotnitsa*, no. 1, January 1991, p. 5.

85. Ibid.

86. Ol'ga Lipovskaia, "New women's organisations," in Buckley, ed., *Perestroika and Soviet Women*, p. 80.

87. Ol'ga Voronina, "Zhenskii vopros," in A. I. Prokopenko, ed., *SSSR: Demograficheskii Diagnoz* (Moscow, Progress, 1990), p. 353.

88. Ibid., p. 357.

89. Ibid., p. 361.

90. Ibid., p. 369.

91. Ibid., p. 373.

92. *Moskvichka*, no. 19, 1991, p. 2.

93. Ibid.

94. Mary Buckley, "Political reform," in Buckley, ed., *Perestroika and Soviet Women*, pp. 54–71.

95. Lipovskaia, "New women's organisations."

96. Lakhova had previously been chair of the Russian parliament's committee in the same field. Like Yeltsin, she is from Sverdlovsk.

97. RFE/RL Research Institute, *Research Report*, vol. 1, no. 21, 22 May 1992, p. 75.

98. *Volia*, no. 2, September 1989, p. 1.

99. *Volia,* no. 5, November 1990, p. 1.

100. *Chernoe Znamia,* no. 3, 1989, p. 1.

101. *Chernoe Znamia,* no. 3, 1990, p. 1.

102. *Volia,* no. 2, September 1989, pp. 1, 4.

103. *Volia,* no. 5, November 1990, p. 1.

104. *Chernoe Znamia,* no. 3, 1989, p. 1.

105. Ibid.

106. *Chernoe Znamia,* no. 3, 1990, p. 1.

107. Ibid.

108. For an analysis of anarchism, consult V. A. Barsamov, "Anarkhistskoe dvizhenie v SSSR," *Sotsial'no-politicheskie Nauki,* no. 10, 1991, pp. 84–91.

109. For discussion of anarchism in nineteenth-century Russian political thought, see Franco Venturi, *Roots of Revolution* (Chicago, University of Chicago Press, 1960); and George Lichtheim, *A Short History of Socialism* (London, Weidenfeld and Nicolson, 1970), pp. 56–64.

10

Conclusion

Perestroika is not a stroll down a worn path. It is an ascent up a mountain, often along an untrodden path.

—Mikhail S. Gorbachev, January 1987

Liquidation of Soviet structures will be completed in December so that we can start to live a qualitatively new way without the Soviet Union by January.

—Boris Yeltsin, December 1991

I don't go to the pharmacy.
I don't go to the doctor.
Now I treat my illnesses
Only with hunger.

—Anti-government rhyme, September 1992

THIS BOOK HAS ATTEMPTED to show the different ways in which discourse redefined society and polity from 1985 to 1991. Sanction to apply glasnost to social and political problems was one vital element in this process. In a context of democratization, glasnost nurtured reassessments and debates, even though its own status was often taken to be uncertain right up to 1991.

New public discourses reflected divisions in society and strains in polity; they also exacerbated both by exposing them, thereby sharpening disagreements. Ensuing disputes led to demands for a redefining of society and polity in practice. This required political action. Mobilization, conflict, violence, and revolution were among the consequences.

Although the opening of social issues paved the way for more critical assessments of political ones, the latter would not have developed automatically without sanction from Gorbachev. Nonetheless, new interpretations of social reality were facilitators. Once the reappraisal of polity began, it proceeded with rapid momentum and resulted in a crisis of power, which was exacerbated by economic collapse and nationalism. Although many aspects of the crisis gripping the disintegrating polity could not be analyzed here, the heterogeneity of views cited indicate some of its complexities. Above all, the redefining of society and polity contributed to citizens perceiving reality differently and to making previously inconceivable demands on the state. The influence of alternative ideas in this historical context of political transition and breakdown was considerable.

The End of State Socialism

Gorbachev had not anticipated that the "untrodden path" of perestroika would entail a reconceptualizing of society and polity that would break out of the parameters of state socialism. New discourses included condemnations of Lenin, scorn for the CPSU, demands for a multi-party system, and clamors from the republics for independence. Nor, on the other side of the mountain, had he expected to find Yeltsin proclaiming the imminent liquidation of Soviet structures and the birth of the Commonwealth of Independent States. When on 1 December 1991, voters in Ukraine chose independence, their referendum tolled the end of the Union.[1] When on 8 December the leaders of Russia, Ukraine, and Belarus surprised the world and other republics by signing the Treaty of Minsk, a political route emerged, even if uncharted and troubled.[2] Boris Yeltsin, Leonid Kravchuk, and Stanislau Shushkevich were committed, if only temporarily, to the new CIS. After feeling left out, the leaders of Kazakhstan, Uzbekistan, Kyrgystan, Turkmenia, Tadzhikistan, Azerbaidzhan, Armenia, and Moldova joined in. Georgia remained outside. Gorbachev opposed the plan, but stripped of power, influence, and now authority, he was finally constrained to support it. The final paradox of his leadership was that his actions, and reactions to them, resulted in the political superfluity of the USSR and his own presidency. A prior paradox had been that as Gorbachev's de jure authority to wield extensive powers increased after March 1990, his de facto power was decreasing and was being perceived by his critics as illegitimate.[3] The new commonwealth of eleven independent states was officially born on 21 December 1991, with the signing of the Alma Ata Declaration, thereafter to be ratified in the Supreme Soviets of each of the states.[4]

The Union of Soviet Socialist Republics finally disintegrated after the combined effects of glasnost, democratization, nationalism, and economic crisis had undermined the structures, mechanisms, and values of the command-administrative economy, the one-party system, democratic centralism, the "friendship of peoples," and the fictions of official histories. The immensely corrosive power of glasnost had enabled challenges and diversity

Рис. Л. ВОРОБЬЕВА.

"That's it!" On 1 December 1991, Ukrainians voted overwhelmingly for independence. The results of this referendum tolled the end of any arrangements for a Union among republics. From the end of August, after the failed coup, up to the referendum, various unsuccessful attempts had been made to draw a half-hearted Ukraine into agreements about coordinated economic reform and political decision making. Now the possibility was finally tossed away. SOURCE: *Izvestiia*, 2 December 1991, p. 1.

to appear in the media that prepared for explicit diversity and difference over political arrangements.

If we define political revolution as the overthrow of established political structures leading to fundamental change in the political process of a country and in the political ideas of the leadership, then one definitely occurred after August 1991. It would, however, have been impossible without prior political, social, and economic changes. Nor would it have been conceivable at that precise moment without the imposition of the State of Emergency, which acted as the trigger. Political revolution in the USSR was not an instant, discrete, or fleeting event. On a structural level, it required prior phases of change, without which the final rupture of the old system could not have taken place. Structures at the center were disintegrating over time, propped up by fewer key political actors, as powers were increasingly assumed by republics.

A case can be made that just as czarism had become increasingly anachronistic by the beginning of the twentieth century, so Soviet socialism ceased to "fit" the society that was emerging toward the end of the century. But lack of congruence between society and polity did not automatically lead to fundamental political change. Rather, a reform process promoted from above set in motion the necessary mechanisms for transforming the political system. Reinterpretations of reality and politicization of the people, both integral to reform, resulted in actions that ultimately made significant political differences. Society could not be squeezed into a straitjacket congruent with the ideas and practices of Leninists, as coup leaders attempted in August 1991, because democrats with diametrically opposed views were committed to alternative political visions. Although the existence of democrats was not a sufficient factor for successful resistance, it was helped by the popular legitimacy they enjoyed in the recently elected Russian parliament. Also crucial was backing from key actors in the military and Russian security service. Although many had silently supported the coup leaders, particularly rural Russians, the political activity of a minority, as in 1917, swayed the course of history.

Redefining Society and Polity

The pursuit of top-down reforms in the Soviet system could not instantly, or easily, facilitate a switch from silence on a given topic to wholehearted recognition. The well-established mechanisms and attitudes embedded in that system militated against this. Predictably, the years 1985 and 1986 were relatively silent ones in comparison with the burst of reporting that followed in 1987. The silence surrounding the accident at Chernobyl in April 1986 best illustrates the point. The world learned about the tragedy, not from the Kremlin, but from Swedes monitoring increases in radiation. But subsequently the Soviet press did mention and then discuss the disaster. Applying a "hesitant glasnost," journalists in piecemeal fashion looked at the causes and consequences of nuclear radiation. But the tale was told exceedingly slowly and incompletely.[5] In 1991, on the fifth anniversary of the tragedy, the green press and more radical journals were still imparting fresh information. Coverage of the Armenian earthquake in December 1988 was, by comparison, immediate, extensive, and more thorough.[6] The context in which it took place was markedly different, inevitably affecting how glasnost was applied. Moreover, the disaster was not due to human error as Chernobyl had been, although shoddily built housing did seriously contribute to the death toll.

It would be a mistake, however, to suggest that 1985 and 1986 were insignificantly silent years. The writings produced in them may have been much tamer than those published by the end of 1987 and much less critical than those found in *Moskovskie Novosti* in 1990 and 1991, but new topics did nonetheless receive coverage. And styles of reporting and news presentation started to change. Inevitably, 1985 saw the least open discussion. But television coverage in late 1985 of *raion* party conferences in the huge buildup to the Twenty-seventh Party Congress of February 1986 was noticeably different. Critical speeches were broadcast. More interviews with ordinary citizens about their opinions were screened. Often surprised faces, when approached, uncertainly asked, "Can I speak frankly?" with an apparent blend of fear, disbelief, and wonder. Roundtable discussions became more popular, illustrating a diversity of opinions.

At the end of 1985, Gorbachev's call for "new ways" was already making tiny inroads into the style and presentation of television programs. And although many social and political problems were yet to be uncovered, more forceful criticisms about some issues were nevertheless made, such as the poor state of housing. Thus, 1985 brought a moderate change in style to reporting, which contrasted with the greater rigidities of 1984, 1979, or 1968. Opinions different from those allowed during the Brezhnev years were shown to be acceptable on some topics. The idea was being planted that citizens should express their opinions more freely in public and that open disagreements among specialists were more acceptable than before.

New issues edged onto agendas in 1986. Prostitution, for example, was deplored, thereby undermining the old ideological line of the past that it did not exist under socialism.[7] By the end of 1987, prostitution had received as much coverage as it took the general issue of crime at least another year to accumulate. But even crime received occasional treatment in 1986, such as reporting on child kidnapping.[8] Rare articles on abortion also appeared in that year.[9] Although numerous silences persisted in 1986, many had partially broken, and although 1986 did not bring a general exposure of all previously stifled problems, patterns instigated by Gorbachev indicated that future years might. Many Soviet intellectuals in late 1985 and 1986 expressed hope for greater freedom of expression. If anything, 1986 was a year in which those who wanted change began, with constrained excitement, to wonder if it might not finally occur. The old political structures had not significantly changed, but turnover in top jobs had begun.[10] Although new faces did not guarantee new ways, and although old structures and mechanisms could not deliver more democratic procedures, the stated policy goals of the new leadership carried promise of a bundle of reforms. It seems appropriate to hypothesize that attempts from above to instigate freer debate in systems whose structures, norms, and values have not been radically changed through revolution and in which critical comments have hitherto been punished, will result in open discussions that are halting and uncertain until the fear of reprisal is significantly reduced.

The contrast between 1985 and 1987 in the coverage of new issues was immense. Drugs, crime, prostitution, and suicide were generally not mentioned in 1985. By the end of 1987, they had been addressed in several newspapers, magazines, and journals. Thus, 1986 and 1987 marked the uncovering of social problems. But their treatment, as shown in Chapters 2 and 3, was initially sensational, rather than analytic; moralistic, rather than dispassionate; and descriptive, rather than explanatory. Individual stories of tragedy were told and the dangers and vulnerabilities of life revealed. But the reasons for them were not systematically assessed. The best attempts at analysis were made in *Ogonek, Sotsiologicheskie Issledovaniia, Nedelia,* and *Moskovskie Novosti.* Yet perhaps this is what one should have expected. Many newspapers worldwide attempt, not to analyze, but to sensationalize, grip, and shock. Moreover, many of the stories told by journalists were inevitably shocking given the silences of the past. What was initially missing was the analytic reporting, commentary, and debate characteristic of a quality press, perhaps best typified by *Le Monde.* Nevertheless, there were clear exceptions. Alla Alova's discussions of AIDS or Irina Vedeneeva's reporting on drugs, although highly sensational, also included high-level discussion.[11]

Another reason for the tentative use of glasnost from 1985 to 1987 was that many citizens were uncomfortably unsure of how to apply it, anxious about what would result in approval or condemnation. Uncertainties were complicated by the fact that no one knew if these new trends would endure. If reforms were reversed, would those who had readily behaved in new ways be punished? Many commented that fear was "in the blood" or "in genetic make-up." As a haunting and insidious residue of the past, it served to restrain debate. This system-created fear, along with deeply ingrained suspicion of others, figured in reactions to glasnost, although, as one might expect, there were differential responses to the use of glasnost linked to individual personalities, political position, and facility for independent thinking.

More socially embarrassing topics, such as rape and child abuse, received relatively sparse coverage in these early years or none at all. Child abuse did not come onto public agendas until 1990. By 1991, very little sensational or factual reporting on these sexual issues had been published. Although silences persisted in discussions of all social problems, there were stark contrasts in the degree of openness about drug abuse and child abuse, as Chapter 3 showed. By the 1990s, society knew far more about crime statistics, the painful lives of drug addicts, and the fate of prostitutes than it did about the frightening experiences of gang rape or abuse by parents. Even after 1989 when soft pornography was on sale on the streets of Moscow and Leningrad, the press failed to address sexual crimes. Pornographic videos also circulated among men. Tapes passed from hand to hand. As in the old samizdat days, copies were made and the original passed on. Here old practices repeated themselves, although the moral quality of the content was much debased. The sexual double standard, public prudery about sex (alongside casual sex and hedonism in private), low levels of sex education, a dearth of female editors, and the absence of a large women's movement may have accounted for the lack of discussion of sexual violence. Even women's magazines retained their silence. This topic in 1990 and in 1991 was one for the agendas of newly emergent feminist groups only. A similar pattern had applied in Western liberal democracies.[12]

Exposure of social problems, particularly of crimes, led to the view that society was collapsing. Crime, drug addiction, prostitution, and other social problems were believed to be worsening. For many, "socialist morality" had been seriously compromised, and prospects for an orderly society looked bleak. Economic shortages were thought to contribute to rising crime statistics, and promises of more consumer goods made some citizens who could not obtain them legally seek other means. As a consequence, fear and anxiety among citizens grew, resulting in more frequent calls for law and order. The rumor spread that crime rates would continue to soar. At a time of crisis in ideology and an absence of a widely shared value system, opinion surveys indicated that the most popular figure was not Lenin, Stalin, Gorbachev, or even Sakharov: It was Jesus Christ.[13] Many citizens searched for alternative belief systems. Religion captured some—from Russian Orthodoxy to Hare Krishna. Others sought significance in flying saucers. As one woman in a Moscow suburb told me, "I saw them out of the window of my fourteenth-story flat. Other people did, too. Have you read that part of the Bible that says that another people will come to us? I believe it will be people from another planet." Others turned to faith healing. Even though superstition, omens, and mysticism have long played a role in Russian culture, moral vacuum and identity crisis enhanced their relevance.

Dismay at the system was reinforced by public debates on housing and health care. Scrutiny of poor housing and of inadequate medical care prompted shame at homelessness, overcrowding, and high rates of infant mortality and abortion. Reporters delivered the message that the state of housing and hospitals was appalling, demanding overhaul and investment. Living standards and services, long considered "achievements," were now redefined as crises.

Although early coverage of social problems had exposed the seamy aspects of socialism, it did not directly challenge the political legitimacy of the Central Committee of the CPSU. Exposure of the failures of social policy did indirectly suggest that policymakers had made bad decisions and that inadequate funds had been channeled into health care and hospitals, but these did not necessarily mean that socialism was reprehensible, merely that policymakers were working badly. In addition, sections of society as well as Leninist leaders were not yet prepared in 1985 for discussion of political reform, and deeply ingrained behavior patterns militated against it. The tentative early treatment of some social issues, such as suicide, illustrated just how hard it was to break out of past patterns.

The very nature of the Soviet political system and the largely co-terminous place in it of the CPSU, fortified by its "weapon," the KGB, very much limited the scope of debate about politics. From 1985 to 1987, discussion was muted. The most lively issues on the agenda were how to increase political accountability and how best to revitalize the CPSU.

New political concepts were cautiously welcomed. Once Gorbachev had injected legitimacy into socialist pluralism, even academics who were unquestionably committed to it used the term carefully, as though anxious not to offend or wary of the negative reactions it could provoke. The message of many supporters in 1988 was that socialist pluralism should be defended, but it should also be protected from demagogues. It should be allowed to develop, but within safe limits. It should revitalize politics, but not excessively. Initially, many used debate about socialist pluralism to attack the past and overcome past inadequacies. Socialist pluralism could move society away from socialist monopoly and could counter totalitarian tendencies. There were more discussions about what socialist pluralism could overcome than what it would signify for the future.

Only after the elections of 1989 and 1990 was pluralism decoupled from its socialist component and increasingly defended on the simple grounds that choice was needed in a normal and civilized polity. Referring more to the present and future than to the past, theorists began to link pluralism to a multi-party system. More farsighted theorists linked pluralism and parties to the development of civil society. But they were rare. In 1990, many political scientists found it hard to conceive what civil society would look like and therefore thought the use of the term premature. Not until after August 1991 did it find more fertile political soil. But even then, many viewed reflection on the term as an irrelevant luxury since political chaos and uncertain direction still reigned.

Discourse about politics took place at two levels. There were general discussions of concepts such as pluralism, democracy, and, to a much lesser extent, civil society. These had serious implications for how politics was reformed in practice and for future strategies and visions. Then there were more inductively inspired discussions about how to deal with specific problems for democracy as they arose. These were closely shaped by historical context. Issues could be raised in 1990, such as the need to redefine the relationship between administrative levels, that would not have been taken seriously in 1987, except by nationalists. Now practical problems stemming from the ways in which elected deputies behaved needed solutions. Only in this setting could conflicting interpretations of *slovobludie*, nihilism, quorum, factions, parties, sovereignty, and ungovernability be put forward. Discourse revolved around the specific problems and hurdles of "learning democracy."

Whereas incorporation of the concept of pluralism into political discourse had been halting and partial, by the end of 1990, crisis was more thoroughly explored by a broader spectrum of society because serious crisis existed, directly affected everyone, and occurred at a time when debate about politics was much more open. Discussions of crisis were also pitched at two levels. There were particular crises, the details of which could be described, such as the housing crisis, the economic crisis, or the crisis situation resulting from disputes over Nagorno-Karabakh. Then there was "the" crisis, a more general state of society, economy, and polity that was variously interpreted by groups across the political spectrum, as Chapters 8 and 9 discussed. Although a case cannot be made that a flourishing civil society existed in 1990, competing views about crisis illustrated that a rich pluralism of thought was being expressed on public agendas; an embryonic civil society was forming. Different views and nascent interests could be identified, although they were often shifting and not always coherent; but those interests generally lacked well-formed political institutions to defend them or political outlets in which they could press their case. Members of the Inter-Regional Group of people's deputies or of Democratic Russia were better placed politically than were many greens, monarchists, or feminists, who belonged to tiny and loose groups that lacked political influence or easy access to decisionmakers. Their predicament did not radically change after January 1992.

Discourse in society about the crisis included images of the Great Soviet Past and the Glorious Western Present. Although their adherents saw glory in very different systems, they shared pessimism in the disintegrating Soviet present and in whatever replaced it. In November 1990 a poll showed that just 1 percent of respondents thought that the USSR could extricate itself from the current crisis during 1991. Only 8 percent thought this could be achieved in two or three years. Fifteen percent suggested it would take five or six years, and 16 percent thought it would take to the year 2000. Twelve percent believed "never," and 16 percent found it hard to say.[14] Citing evidence from another poll one month earlier, Tat'iana Zaslavskaia pointed out how citizens persisted in being helpless and passive, believing that the state should solve their problems.[15]

Redefinition Continued

Notwithstanding revolution, new leaderships, and new policies, many of the social and political issues of the Gorbachev era remained. Priorities on formal agendas changed and new issues were formulated, but old problems of crime, drugs, medical care, pluralism, learning democracy, and crisis were ever-present and in some senses worsening. Their features may have altered, but they still needed to be addressed.

Approaches to them indicated similarities and differences with past patterns. The trend toward more empirical analysis continued. Fresh work on prostitution, for instance, produced clearer social portraits of the age groups of the women involved. Data analyzed by Iurii Karpukhin and Iurii Torbin suggested that 69 percent of hard-currency prostitutes were younger than thirty and 7 percent were underage. By contrast, 68 percent of "street" and "station" prostitutes were older than thirty. And 23 percent of hard-currency prostitutes had enjoyed some higher education.[16] Prostitution appeared to be positively correlated, not with low levels of education, but with the desire to make more money.

Commentators continued to draw more explicit linkages across social problems. When Major General Boris Voronov, head of the Crime Prevention Department of the Ministry of Internal Affairs, announced increases in crime in the first quarter of 1992, he named unemployment as the cause. Crime had risen by one-third, and juveniles were again disproportionately responsible.[17] The tendency to blame broken homes and single-parent mothers was decreasing as economic reform brought unemployment and homelessness. The consequences of economic reform were to blame.

One important difference characterized discourse in 1992. The old tendency not to blame government policies for social problems was diminishing. New economic reforms were known to be the source of social deprivation. This could not be covered up by absurd ideological assertions that results could only be positive. A new realism about the sources of hardship was evident.

This greater realism meant that discourse inevitably addressed the hardships of economic reform and its consequences. Journalists, academics, politicians, and political actors gave more attention than before to destitution. The issue was unavoidable after tenfold price increases in January and February 1992. There was open acknowledgment of growing poverty and of the prohibitiveness of the price of basic foodstuffs.

One unexpected result of uncertainty about the future in 1991 was that in early 1992 the birth rate in the capital fell by one-third. Although not a result of the 1992 price increases, women's political discourse linked the two for political effect. Anger at price increases and their impact on motherhood were reflected in a pamphlet that circulated in March 1992 in the Mossovet. Addressed to people's deputies, it noted that the price of diapers first went up from eighty kopecks to four or five rubles. This increase was bad enough. But then came a jump to seventy-three rubles, seventy-five kopecks for thin calico diapers and to ninety-nine rubles, twenty-two kopecks for flannel ones. The right to motherhood and the right of the Russian nation to exist were the new issues. The women asked for special protection for mothers and threatened an "All-Russian women's strike" of the withdrawal of sexual intercourse if all the items necessary for child care were not made freely available: cots, baths, high chairs, prams, and other items.[18] Economic reforms were thus increasing the pressure on women to abort and provoking new directions in women's politics. Even though most women were unlikely to unite on this platform, preferring to see hardships as common to women and men, their inclination to abort was seriously affected by economic hardship and by the closure in August 1992 of Russia's only two condom factories.[19]

But despite more forthright condemnations of government policies, the old criticism persisted that honesty in reporting was lacking. In May, television coverage of Victory Day was noticeably selective. Yeltsin was shown in Gorky Park among supporters willing to make sacrifices for his policies. Heckling from non-communists was not shown.[20] Likewise, the old fear about the fragility of glasnost became recast into a fresh anxiety about the durability of freedom of speech. When in July the Russian Supreme Soviet voted to take over the ownership of *Izvestiia,* claiming that its independent status was illegal, democrats feared a renewed attack on the free press.[21] Ruslan Khasbulatov's criticism that reporting in *Izvestiia* had been driving a wedge between parliament and government indicated that political considerations were not far away.[22] In addition, persistence of a huge secret service meant that instruments of interference were still in place and could be used by political leaders should they so wish. The legal state was still seriously deficient and also required elaborate changes in the judiciary, although these had begun.

So although after 1992 the redefining of society and polity occurred in a much freer atmosphere than had existed under Gorbachev, that openness could be qualified. Although the explicit values of the regime encouraged a loosening of restraints on debate, anxiety that restrictive mechanisms could be reintroduced did not entirely abate. Optimists cited the regime's willingness to open archives and to release more official information, while pessimists noted that this information was often sold to the West for financial gain. Instead, they asked about what was not being released.

In a new context of accelerated economic reform, different concepts inevitably entered discourse. As before, these were shaped by circumstances of the moment. Fear of *bunt* (revolt) was expressed and was linked to high prices and unemployment. To the already long list of crises was added the "labor crisis." In Russia, 64,000 people were officially unemployed at the beginning of 1992. In September, the figure reached 250,000 and was projected to be 2.5 million by January 1993.[23]

Whereas in 1990 citizens had frequently said, "I am in despair" (*Ia v otchaiane*), now they lamented more than before that there were no limits left (*bespredel*).[24] In daily life, Russians were overtaken by disorientation,

Рис. В. ШИЛОВА.

Sharp price increases in January and February 1992 left many citizens disoriented and impecunious. The gap between rich and poor grew. The number of people begging increased alarmingly. This cartoon suggests a novel way of asking for money on the escalator inside a metro station. SOURCE: *Moskovskaia Pravda*, 26 March 1992, p. 1.

expecting worse situations to come. Although the topic of money dominated most conversations, few could say with certainty how much they now earned, precisely when they might be paid, or how much it cost today to send a letter. The apparent absurdities of economic reform puzzled many. By the fall of 1992, more food had appeared in the shops, but people could not afford everything they needed. Was it not strange, some asked, that a liter of milk cost fourteen rubles but an excellent seat in the Moscow Conservatory was only ten rubles? Life had become *neponiatno* (incomprehensible).[25] Citizens expressed a similar lack of understanding about their entitlement in October to a *vaucher* (voucher) worth ten thousand rubles.[26] A common reaction to the government's attempt to share the state's wealth was "I do not understand what to do. Should I sell it immediately or try in December to have a share in industry? And if so, in which factory? How do I know?"[27] And of regret to many was the invasion of yet more English words. "Vouch-

СВОБОДНАЯ
ЭКОНОМИЧЕСКАЯ
ЗОНА

Рис А. БАВЫКИНА.

"Free economic zone." In 1992, the attractiveness of becoming a free economic zone caught on in different parts of Russia. This had been one feature of economic reform in the People's Republic of China. Budget deficits in Russia, however, were enormous, foreign debts were high, productivity was falling, and many citizens felt that their purses were empty in comparison with the past. SOURCE: *Izvestiia*, 8 October 1992, p. 1.

er" had arrived, along with "marketing," "check," and "coupon," all polluting the beauty of the Russian language.

For escapism the nation became locked into the Mexican soap opera "The Rich Also Cry." At work citizens chatted about dilemmas in relationships among the main characters. Whereas in 1989 the country had been mesmerized by the first television broadcasts of the Congress of People's Deputies, a little more than three years later many watched with similar fascination the visit of the show's star, Veronica Castro, to Moscow.[28] Just as Western fans had once swooned over the Beatles, Russians of all ages suddenly devoured Castro's every word. Her performances far surpassed Khazanov's jokes in popularity.

Simultaneously, Yeltsin's popularity, like Gorbachev's earlier, fell. Whereas in September 1991 Yeltsin had enjoyed the trust of 80 percent of those surveyed, by March 1992 this had fallen to 43 percent.[29] And just as

Рисунок Вадима Мисюка.

"I know and I feel where the dangerous edge is." This portrayal of Yeltsin walking on a precarious political tightrope followed a speech the day before in which he had declared, "I am not the head of government, but the head of state." Journalists commented that he was trying to distance himself from the unpopular consequences of his government's economic reforms. Also on the political agenda was the worsening conflict between Georgia and Abkhazia and the question of whether Russia was becoming involved. In 1992, the growing threat hanging over Yeltsin was that one wrong move on economics, politics, or the nationalities question could bring an avalanche of problems. In some respects, Yeltsin's predicament was similar to Gorbachev's before him. SOURCE: *Nezavisimaia Gazeta*, 7 October 1992, p. 1.

rumors had been rife under Gorbachev about civil war and military coups, these persisted. Yeltsin's insistence that a coup was unlikely did not reflect popular opinion.[30] In a poll conducted in Russia in July, 46 percent thought a coup was likely, and 58 percent said they would support it. A high 68 percent thought that authoritarian rule would bring better living standards. Sixty-five percent considered it would help reduce crime. Support for democracy and human rights was relatively low—25 percent and 15 percent, respectively.[31]

Russian support for resorting to a firm hand in troubled times continued to be strong. The ideals of democracy were not deeply embedded in the social fabric, despite much rhetoric in the West that this was the case. Moreover, the process of democratization in Russia was still frail. Even though discourse among democrats reiterated the need for a stronger party system with larger and fewer main parties, reality continued to show the opposite. Groups, parties, and movements remained numerous and generally weak. Sergei Stankevich, now state adviser for political questions, told readers of *Izvestiia* that judging the political influence of parties was a complicated task, particularly since there was a tendency to link a given party to one person. "The vast majority of people prefer to orient themselves, not on the party, but on a personality. Therefore, the parties themselves are more often distinguished by the names of leaders: they talk of Travkin's party, Rumiantsev's party, Rutskoi's party, Zhirinovskii's party."[32]

Stankevich held that it was easier to talk about the spread of different ideas than about the role of parties. In fact, parties still lacked clearly formulated ideological platforms. Like others, he argued that a "normal" multiparty system would not develop until several parties formed a "developed structure throughout the country."[33] Whereas discourse after 1988 had agonized that the electoral system and the polity were not normal, now the regret was more specifically applied to the party system.

The official list of sixteen registered parties with memberships, published in July 1992, supported Stankevich's claims (see Table 10.1). Membership could be as little as 139 or as many as 28,000.[34] And although membership statistics were unreliable, however many were claimed (a much higher 100,000 by the DPR in July 1992), in all cases the figure was insufficient to build a tentacular network across the vast Russian landmass. And new parties continued to form, contributing to the fractured picture. For example, in April a group of communists formed the United Communist Party of Russia, attempting to revive the Russian Communist Party. They hoped to halt privatization, revive the USSR Supreme Soviet, and maintain a united army.[35] In May, a committee came together to discuss the creation of the Union of All-Russian Renewal.[36] In the same month, some of Russia's leaders founded the Union for Democracy and Reform.[37]

TABLE 10.1   Registered Political Parties in Russia, July 1992

Political Party	Membership at Registration	Date of Registration
Democratic Party of Russia	28,608	14 March 1991
Social Democratic Party of the Russian Federation	5,089	14 March 1991
Republican Party of the Russian Federation	5,000+	14 March 1991
Peasant Party of Russia	2,143	12 April 1991
Party of the Russian Christian Democratic Movement	6,027	6 June 1991
People's Party of Free Russia	5,233	18 September 1991
Russian Christian Democratic Party	2,356	25 September 1991
People's Party of Russia	1,318	25 September 1991
Constitutional Democratic Party (Party of People's Freedom)	2,079	25 September 1991
Russian Bourgeois Democratic Party	1,771	4 November 1991
Russian Party of Democratic Transformation	637	19 November 1991
Socialist Workers' Party	2,500	21 November 1991
Russian Party of Free Labor	1,734	9 December 1991
Christian Democratic Union Christian Democratic Union of Russia	1,395	9 December 1991
Russian Communist Workers' Party	6,000+	9 January 1992
Conservative Party	1,399	15 January 1992
Party of Constitutional Democrats of the Russian Federation	660	15 January 1992
National Republican Party of Russia	5,037	15 January 1992
European Liberal Democratic Party	5,890	23 January 1992
Free Democratic Party of Russia	1,696	17 February 1992
Political Party "New Left"	115	20 February 1992
Republican Humanitarian Party	139	10 March 1992
Russian Social-Liberal Party	348	12 March 1992
Russian Party of Communists	2,900+	19 March 1992
Party of Economic Freedom	662	25 June 1992

Source: Adapted from *Argumenty i Fakty,* no. 24, July 1992, p. 8.

Flux in coalitions persisted in 1992. For example, in May the DPR, the People's Party of Free Russia, the Party of Renewal, and the parliamentary faction Smena formed Civic Union, a centrist coalition.[38] Civic Union advocated stabilization of the economy, integrity of the Russian Federation, and an end to social tension. Civic Union rejected the demand that the Russian parliament be abolished.[39] Then on 4 July, more than forty political groups came together to form a bloc in support of Yeltsin. They included Democratic Russia and the Russian Movement for Democratic Reforms. Their aim was to counter the perceived alliance of nationalists and communists, both of whom were resisting economic reform. Democrats also hoped to provide an alternative to Civic Union.[40] When on 9 July they signed a document proclaiming the formation of the bloc Democratic Choice, the Russian Movement for Democratic Reforms, headed by Popov, did not participate. Among the signatories were Democratic Russia, the Republican Party, and the Russian League of Businessmen. Once again, Democratic Russia and the Movement for Democratic Reforms were not working together.[41]

New Agendas

Many of the "new" social and political issues discussed in earlier chapters will remain on the political agendas of the national legislatures within the CIS or on agendas of their attentive publics throughout the 1990s and beyond. How politicians and their critics will debate them and how effectively policy implementation proceeds will be influenced by the priorities of political leaderships, financial possibilities, pressures and obstructions from society, evolving political cultures, constellations of political parties, and the nature of emergent executive, legislative, and judicial relations. The role of Western governments in rescheduling debt and in providing aid, together with the investment patterns of foreign firms, International Monetary Fund requirements, expectations of Western help, and rejections of it, will also affect perceptions of how some issues should be tackled and shape policy formulation and implementation.

Debates and policies are likely to vary across the vast landmass that was the USSR. Religion, level of economic development, and nationality are but three factors likely to influence discourse and policy preferences. And their significance may vary according to state and national composition of that state. As before, nationalism is likely to take on different characteristics with various implications.

One instructive lesson from Soviet history is that in each of its periods, the "cultural filter" of society often resisted, redefined, and distorted policies and messages delivered to it from those in power.[42] What leaders wish to "make" of economy, society, and polity can be objected to by social groups and selectively recast to suit their interests. Tensions and disputes in society filtered through cultural prisms can turn policies into something not initially intended by their instigators. Many of Moshe Lewin's generalizations about the early years of Bolshevik power can be applied to the Gorbachev era and to the Russian present. Bearing this in mind, we can conclude that it is analytically constraining to see Yeltsin's Russia only as an example of transformation from the residues of state socialism to democracy. Although it is indeed this, it is also much more. How Russian leaders wish to redefine reality, both in conceptual terms and in practice, will be shaped not just by conflicts among themselves but also by pressures from society. These include more than the interests of different groups, which are still often slow to form and represent themselves effectively. Enduring cultural patterns are especially relevant. Collective values, the tenacity of connections, institutionalized corruption, and patriarchal practices will defy, manipulate, and contradict many policies. Harvard economists attempting to give advice should heed the lessons of the past and not assume policies that should theoretically work, will do so in a Russian setting. Study of social and political discourse will reveal some of the reasons they may not. What is certain is that policymakers alone will not mold the future of Russian history; that will occur in their interaction with the social fabric.

The 1990s and beyond will see continued tensions, conflicts, and instabilities in economy, polity, and society. Discourse will be fired by them and contribute to their volatility. In turn, social divisions, economic results, and political behavior will shape the sorts of issues that come onto a multitude of political agendas and contribute to a varied discourse about those issues.

NOTES

1. *Izvestiia,* 2 December 1991, p. 1.

2. *Izvestiia,* 9 December 1991, p. 1.

3. S. I. Benn and R. S. Peters pointed out that "supreme power" can be understood either as "supreme legal authority, competence or entitlement (i.e. a *de jure* use of power)" or as "a supreme ability to induce men [*sic*] to take a desired course of action, by bringing some sort of pressure to bear upon them (a *de facto* use)." See their *Social Principles and the Democratic State* (London, George Allen and Unwin, 1958), p. 257.

For discussion of how the terms *power* and *authority* are frequently confused, consult D. D. Raphael, *Problems of Political Philosophy* (London, Macmillan, 1976), pp. 66–75. For a provocative challenge to established wisdoms, see Leslie Green, *The Authority of the State* (Oxford, Clarendon Press, 1990), pp. 59–62.

4. *Izvestiia,* 23 December 1991, p. 1. The leaders of Kazakhstan, Kyrgystan, Turkmenia, Uzbekistan, and Tadzhikistan stated in an earlier meeting in Ashkabad their intention to join the CIS. See *Izvestiia,* 13 December 1991, p. 1. In October 1992, the Azerbaidzhan parliament voted against ratification. The Moldovan Supreme Soviet had failed even to discuss it.

5. David R. Marples, *The Social Impact of the Chernobyl Disaster* (London, Macmillan, 1988).

6. *Izvestiia* gave extensive coverage of the earthquake in Armenia throughout December. See the following editions: 9 December, pp. 1, 6; 10 December, pp. 1, 6; 11 December, pp. 1, 6; 12 December, pp. 1, 6; 13 December, pp. 1–2, 6; 14 December, pp. 1–2, 6; 15 December, pp. 1–2; 16 December, pp. 1, 6; 17 December, pp. 1, 6; 18 December p. 5; 26 December, p. 1; 30 December, p. 1.

7. D. Mysiakov and P. Iakubovich, "'Dama' s podachkoi," *Komsomol'skaia Pravda,* 9 October 1986, p. 2.

8. E. Letskaia, "Ukrali rebenka," *Nedelia,* no. 14, 31 March–6 April 1986, p. 12.

9. Iu. Sergeev, "'Otvetstvennost' za nezakonnoe proizvodstvo aborta," *Meditsinskaia Gazeta,* 16 July 1986, p. 3.

10. Archie Brown, "Gorbachev and reform of the Soviet system," *Political Quarterly,* vol. 58, no. 2, April-June 1987, pp. 139–151.

11. Alla Alova, "Lushche ne dumat'?" *Ogonek,* no. 26, June 1989, p. 28; Irina Vedeneeva, "U cherty," *Ogonek,* no. 8, February 1988, pp. 19–23.

12. See, for instance, Susan Brownmiller, *Against Our Will: Men, Women and Rape* (Harmondsworth, Penguin, 1991); Beatrix Campbell, *Unofficial Secrets* (London,Virago, 1988).

13. Iurii Levada, "Chego boitsa," *Moskovskie Novosti,* no. 49, 9 December 1990, p. 9.

14. Ibid.

15. *Komsomol'skaia Pravda,* 30 October 1990, p. 2.

16. Iurii G. Karpukhin and Iurii G. Torbin, "Prostitutsiia: Zakon i real'nost'," *Sotsiologicheskie Issledovaniia,* no. 5, 1992, p. 111.

17. RFE/RL Research Institute, *Research Report,* vol. 1, no. 22, 29 May 1992, p. 69.

18. Irina Ivashenko, 20 March 1992, pamphlet.

19. *The European,* 20–23 August 1992, p. 4.

20. RFE/RL Research Institute, *Research Report,* vol. 1, no. 21, 22 May 1992, p. 75.

21. RFE/RL Research Institute, *Research Report,* vol. 1, no. 31, 31 July 1992, p. 77.

22. Ibid.

23. Iurii L. Neimer, "Ot krizisa obshchestva k krizisu truda," *Sotsiologicheskie Issledovaniia,* no. 5, 1992, pp. 23–32. Unemployment figures are according to *Rossiiskie Vesti,* 15 September 1992, p. 3. Seventy percent of the unemployed were female, and every third or fourth woman was younger than twenty-two.

24. Conversations in Moscow, September 1992.

25. Ibid.

26. *Rossiiskie Vesti,* 22 September 1992, p. 3. Vouchers must be spent by the end of 1993. Citizens can either sell them or use them to buy shares in companies to be auctioned in December 1992.

27. Conversations in Moscow, September 1992.

28. *Argumenty i Fakty,* no. 33, September 1992, p. 1; *Sobesednik,* no. 38, September 1992, p. 12.

29. *Kuranty,* 25 March 1992, p. 1.

30. RFE/RL Research Institute, *Research Report,* vol. 1, no. 29, 17 July 1992, p. 80.

31. Ibid.

32. Sergei Stankevich, "Chto takoe partiinaia zhizn' segodniia," *Izvestiia,* 20 April 1992, p. 2.

33. Ibid.

34. *Argumenty i Fakty,* no. 24, July 1992, p. 8.

35. RFE/RL Research Institute, *Research Report,* vol. 1, no. 16, 17 April 1992, p. 79.

36. RFE/RL Research Institute, *Research Report,* vol. 1, no. 21, 22 May 1992, p. 75.

37. RFE/RL Research Institute, *Research Report,* vol. 1, no. 23, 5 June 1992, p. 74.

38. Ibid.

39. RFE/RL Research Institute, *Research Report,* vol. 1, no. 27, 3 July 1992, p. 77.

40. RFE/RL Research Institute, *Research Report,* vol. 1, no. 29, 17 July 1992, p. 80.

41. RFE/RL Research Institute, *Research Report,* vol. 1, no. 30, 24 July 1992, p. 78.

42. "Cultural filter" was usefully adopted by Moshe Lewin in *Soviet Society in the Making* (London, Methuen, 1985).

About the Book and Author

How did Russian journalists, academics, and political actors approach social and political issues in the Gorbachev era and in the chaotic period that followed? What factors did they choose to stress? How did they present material that had been taboo for so long? What did they overlook—and why? These are among the central questions addressed by Mary Buckley as she introduces the diversity of ways in which Russians have redefined their society and polity since Gorbachev initiated glasnost.

The book begins by exploring how "new" issues such as crime, drugs, prostitution, AIDS, rape, child abuse, and suicide suddenly became topics for open discussion. Expanded coverage provided citizens with previously withheld, initially intoxicating information; yet in a context of failed economic reform the news also contributed to fears of deviance and social collapse. Growing media exposure of serious problems in housing and health care prompted shame at the failures—previously proclaimed as achievements—of social policy.

New interpretations of social problems paved the way for critical reevaluations of how politics worked, bringing even more pressure to bear on the system. As the process of redefinition extended to polity, it became clear that politicians and newly emerging political groups were divided in their responses to pluralism, democracy, civil society, and crisis. Buckley highlights the range of public reaction by drawing on newspapers and journals across the political spectrum as well as on interviews with people's deputies, journalists, academics, and lawyers. She looks beyond mainstream political groups to consider the views of patriots, miners, Leninist workers, Pamiat, monarchists, Christians, greens, feminists, and anarchists. Buckley's use of jokes, rumors, and myths circulating in Moscow and St. Petersburg enriches her analysis by bringing to life the emotional dimension of reform as expressed on the street, in meetings, in theater, and in film. Taken together, all this information reflects the complexities of the changing social milieu.

Many of the images and ideas that blossomed during the Gorbachev years led to social and political visions that were incongruent with the prevailing system. As these visions grew in strength in an increasingly divided society, they played a part in transforming transition into breakdown and disintegration. The Commonwealth of Independent States has inherited this diversity and the deeply rooted problems so long buried by the communist regime. In her conclusion, Buckley considers continuities and changes in approaches to social and political problems in Yeltsin's Russia.

Mary Buckley is senior lecturer in politics at the University of Edinburgh.

Index